BUSINESS AND
GENERAL
REFERENCE
BOOK SERIES
FROM IDG

Sailing For Dummies®

Quick Reference Card

Basic Maneuvers

Jibing

Wind

1. Say "Ready to jibe," to alert your crew, and then say "jibing" as you begin turning the boat away from the wind.

   1

2. Say "Boom coming across" as you pull the main over to the new side.

   2

3. Let the main out on the new jibe and trim the jib on the new leeward side.

   3

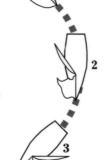

Tacking

Wind

3. Trim the new jib sheet, and keep turning until your sails are full on the new tack.

   3

2. Keep turning the boat as the sails begin to luff; release the jib sheet; the crew and skipper switch sides.

   2

1. Say "Ready to tack," to alert your crew, and then say "tacking" as you start turning the boat into the wind.

   1

Bas[ic]

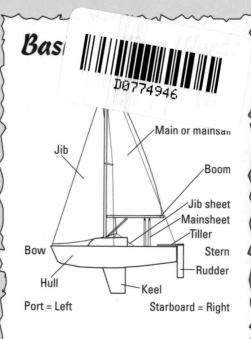

Main or mainsail

Jib

Boom

Jib sheet

Mainsheet

Tiller

Bow

Stern

Rudder

Hull

Keel

Port = Left   Starboard = Right

The Points of Sail

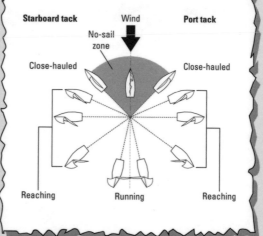

Starboard tack   Wind   Port tack

No-sail zone

Close-hauled   Close-hauled

Reaching   Running   Reaching

...For Dummies: Bestselling Book Series for Beginners

Sailing For Dummies®

Basic Rules of the Road

For all boats:

1. **Moving boats must avoid stopped boats.**

2. **Large ships have right-of-way in confined areas, such as a channel.**

   Large ships and boats towing other boats can't turn or slow down easily, so don't cross their bows.

3. **Sailboats have right-of-way over powerboats (except for under Rule #2).**

4. **All boats should maintain a proper lookout.**

5. **If you need to make a course change to avoid a collision, turn early and make a large turn so that the other boat clearly understands your intention.**

When two sailboats meet:

1. **The boat on starboard tack has right-of-way over the boat on port tack.**

2. **The leeward boat has right-of-way over the windward boat.**

3. **An overtaking boat has to keep clear.**

Safety Do's and Don'ts

✔ **Do** have a readily accessible life jacket for every person on board.

✔ **Do** have the rest of your basic safety gear, such as an anchor and paddle. (Additional gear is required on larger boats.)

✔ **Do** look at a chart of the area before leaving the dock.

✔ **Do** use navigation lights if you go sailing between sunset and sunrise.

✔ If your boat flips over (capsizes), **do** stay with the boat.

✔ **Do** know the man-overboard drill and capsize procedures for your boat.

✔ **Do** stop by your local boat store for a copy of the boating laws in your area, and make sure

that you comply with the required safety regulations.

✔ **Do** check the local marine weather forecast before you leave the dock.

✔ **Do** be aware of your boat's *draft* (how deep it is) and the depth of the water at all times.

✔ **Do** bring a hat, sunscreen, sunglasses, and water.

✔ If you're in charge, **don't** sail on boats or in weather conditions beyond your capabilities.

✔ **Don't** sail near rocks, shallow water, strong current, or a lee shore (the shore that the wind is blowing onto).

✔ **Don't** throw trash overboard.

✔ **Don't** drink alcohol while operating a sailboat.

...For Dummies: Bestselling Book Series for Beginners

Praise, Praise, Praise
For Sailing For Dummies

"... easy to read and understand and should provide a ready reference for any sailor. Beginners to big boat sailors should enjoy the 'poking fun' at the 'upscale' side of the sport. Intermediate sailors can make use of the much more advanced theoretical 'stuff.' I would grade this new book another success for IDG!"

— Allan R. Birnbaum, Chairman,
Creative Homeowner Press

"It takes someone with the depth and understanding and love for the sport like Peter Isler to bring us this book that provides both simplicity and clarity to the great sport of sailing, and that should forever banish the old saw 'sailing is too complicated for me to ever learn.' Not!"

— Micca Hutchins, Editor, *Sailing* Magazine

"Peter and JJ Isler each began teaching sailing in yacht club programs when they were still in college. Countless classes, championships, and cruises later, they reveal in this book the easy, deliberate style that has taken each of them to the top. You don't have to qualify as a dummy to benefit from this comprehensive work."

— Keith Taylor, The Sailing Forums on CompuServe

"None of us wants to encounter dummies at sea. Now along come the Islers to help keep them off our waterways. Their book provides an interesting read, easy instruction, and a handy reference work. Its users will be dummies no longer, thank goodness."

— Walter Cronkite, CBS Special Correspondent

"Peter and JJ's enthusiasm for the thrill and the fun of sailing brings this comprehensive guide to life in every chapter. Whether you're a novice or several years into this fascinating sport, the Islers' knowledge and insight will speed you along your course to sailing mastery."

— John Burnham, Editor, *Sailing World* Magazine

"... Its authors are universally respected in sailing, for both their competitive records and their ability to explain its mysteries to land lovers. I know of no one else who is simultaneously winning races . . . and explaining them . . . to the public."

— Robert Hopkins, Jr., Former U.S. Olympic Coach
and America's Cup Navigator

SAILING

FOR

DUMMIES®

SAILING FOR DUMMIES®

by JJ and Peter Isler

IDG
BOOKS
WORLDWIDE

IDG Books Worldwide, Inc.
An International Data Group Company

Foster City, CA ♦ Chicago, IL ♦ Indianapolis, IN ♦ New York, NY

Sailing For Dummies®

Published by
IDG Books Worldwide, Inc.
An International Data Group Company
919 E. Hillsdale Blvd.
Suite 400
Foster City, CA 94404
www.idgbooks.com (IDG Books Worldwide Web site)
www.dummies.com (Dummies Press Web site)

Library of Congress Catalog Card No.: 97-71816

ISBN: 0-7645-5039-X

Printed in the United States of America

10 9 8 7 6 5 4

1E/RX/QY/ZY/IN

Distributed in the United States by IDG Books Worldwide, Inc.

Distributed by Macmillan Canada for Canada; by Transworld Publishers Limited in the United Kingdom; by IDG Norge Books for Norway; by IDG Sweden Books for Sweden; by Woodslane Pty. Ltd. for Australia; by Woodslane (NZ) Ltd. for New Zealand; by Addison Wesley Longman Singapore Pte Ltd. for Singapore, Malaysia, Thailand, Indonesia and Korea; by Norma Comunicaciones S.A. for Colombia; by Intersoft for South Africa; by International Thomson Publishing for Germany, Austria and Switzerland; by Toppan Company Ltd. for Japan; by Distribuidora Cuspide for Argentina; by Livraria Cultura for Brazil; by Ediciencia S.A. for Ecuador; by Ediciones ZETA S.C.R. Ltda. for Peru; by WS Computer Publishing Corporation, Inc., for the Philippines; by Unalis Corporation for Taiwan; by Contemporanea de Ediciones for Venezuela; by Computer Book & Magazine Store for Puerto Rico; by Express Computer Distributors for the Caribbean and West Indies. Authorized Sales Agent: Anthony Rudkin Associates for the Middle East and North Africa.

For general information on IDG Books Worldwide's books in the U.S., please call our Consumer Customer Service department at 800-762-2974. For reseller information, including discounts and premium sales, please call our Reseller Customer Service department at 800-434-3422.

For information on where to purchase IDG Books Worldwide's books outside the U.S., please contact our International Sales department at 650-655-3200 or fax 650-655-3297.

For information on foreign language translations, please contact our Foreign & Subsidiary Rights department at 650-655-3021 or fax 650-655-3281.

For sales inquiries and special prices for bulk quantities, please contact our Sales department at 650-655-3200 or write to the address above.

For information on using IDG Books Worldwide's books in the classroom or for ordering examination copies, please contact our Educational Sales department at 800-434-2086 or fax 317-596-5499.

For press review copies, author interviews, or other publicity information, please contact our Public Relations department at 650-655-3000 or fax 650-655-3299.

For authorization to photocopy items for corporate, personal, or educational use, please contact Copyright Clearance Center, 222 Rosewood Drive, Danvers, MA 01923, or fax 978-750-4470.

About the Authors

JJ and Peter Isler have been sailing for most of their lives. JJ grew up around boats in San Diego, California, learning to sail in a little 7-foot dinghy called a Sabot. Peter started out loving powerboats and fishing (boys can be so strange!), but took up sailing after his family moved to Connecticut when he was thirteen years old.

The Islers are well known throughout the world of sailing as top competitors and teachers. They both have taught sailing to people of all ages and experiences. Peter played an important, early role in developing US Sailing's educational program; coached at the Olympic level; and helped found the American Sailing Association, which accredits sailing schools and certifies sailors and instructors.

Peter has twice won the America's Cup, serving as navigator aboard *Stars & Stripes* with Dennis Conner in 1987 and 1988. An accomplished small-boat sailor, Peter was Intercollegiate Sailor of the Year in 1976 while at Yale University. He was the top-ranked U.S. sailor on the professional match-racing circuit from 1989 to 1993 and remains active as a tactician and skipper at various Grand Prix events.

Peter has also been very active in the media. After 1988, he shifted his America's Cup energies to television, where he has been a featured analyst in ESPN's Emmy-award-winning Cup coverage in 1992 and 1995. He is presently Editor at Large of *Sailing World* magazine. Recently, he was awarded the prestigious Southam Award by the sailing industries' Sail America Foundation. Peter produces and hosts various television programs, including *Classics* on Speedvision Network and *Sailors Log* on Outdoor Life Network.

JJ was the tactician and starting helmsman for the *America*³ Women's America's Cup team in 1995. With crew Pamela Healy, JJ won the Bronze Medal in the Women's 470 class in the 1992 Olympics in Barcelona. She is a two-time Rolex Yachtswoman of the Year (in 1986 and 1991) and has won three World Championships and numerous national titles. JJ was the first female to compete in a number of events on the international match-racing circuit. She graduated from Yale University in 1985, where she was captain of the sailing team and a collegiate All-American.

While spending most of their time racing sailboats, the Islers continue to teach a number of clinics each year. They reside in San Diego with their daughter, Marly; their two cats; a rabbit; three sailboards; JJ's Olympic sailboat; and a lot of miscellaneous sailboat parts that Peter plans on using someday.

ABOUT IDG BOOKS WORLDWIDE

Welcome to the world of IDG Books Worldwide.

IDG Books Worldwide, Inc., is a subsidiary of International Data Group, the world's largest publisher of computer-related information and the leading global provider of information services on information technology. IDG was founded more than 25 years ago and now employs more than 8,500 people worldwide. IDG publishes more than 275 computer publications in over 75 countries (see listing below). More than 90 million people read one or more IDG publications each month.

Launched in 1990, IDG Books Worldwide is today the #1 publisher of best-selling computer books in the United States. We are proud to have received eight awards from the Computer Press Association in recognition of editorial excellence and three from *Computer Currents'* First Annual Readers' Choice Awards. Our best-selling *...For Dummies®* series has more than 50 million copies in print with translations in 38 languages. IDG Books Worldwide, through a joint venture with IDG's Hi-Tech Beijing, became the first U.S. publisher to publish a computer book in the People's Republic of China. In record time, IDG Books Worldwide has become the first choice for millions of readers around the world who want to learn how to better manage their businesses.

Our mission is simple: Every one of our books is designed to bring extra value and skill-building instructions to the reader. Our books are written by experts who understand and care about our readers. The knowledge base of our editorial staff comes from years of experience in publishing, education, and journalism — experience we use to produce books for the '90s. In short, we care about books, so we attract the best people. We devote special attention to details such as audience, interior design, use of icons, and illustrations. And because we use an efficient process of authoring, editing, and desktop publishing our books electronically, we can spend more time ensuring superior content and spend less time on the technicalities of making books.

You can count on our commitment to deliver high-quality books at competitive prices on topics you want to read about. At IDG Books Worldwide, we continue in the IDG tradition of delivering quality for more than 25 years. You'll find no better book on a subject than one from IDG Books Worldwide.

John Kilcullen
John Kilcullen
CEO
IDG Books Worldwide, Inc.

Steven Berkowitz
Steven Berkowitz
President and Publisher
IDG Books Worldwide, Inc.

Eighth Annual Computer Press Awards ≥1992

WINNER
Ninth Annual Computer Press Awards ≥1993

WINNER
Tenth Annual Computer Press Awards ≥1994

WINNER
Eleventh Annual Computer Press Awards ≥1995

Authors' Acknowledgments

First, we'd like to thank Jane Fetter, JJ's mom, who has been raising our daughter while we've been chained to our computers worrying about how to put this sport into words. This book never would have happened (at least not anywhere close to deadline) without Jane and Tom Fetter giving Marly so much time and love. And we promise, promise, promise (even cross our hearts) that before we *ever* commit to anything like this again, we will line up a baby-sitter or day care in advance. (*Author's note:* JJ made a similar promise during the 1995 America's Cup training). Peter's mother Marilyn (who frequently made the two-hour drive down from her home in Los Angeles) also helped keep Marly happy and well-cared-for during some of the busier periods of authorship.

We'd also like to thank the ...*For Dummies* folks, especially our patient and supportive editor, Rev Mengle, and our main copy editor, Christy Beck, who impressed us by being able to tell the difference between a ketch and a yawl. Hopefully, we can meet and thank you guys in person someday, and you can tell us how poor our grammar really is. Their leader, Sarah Kennedy, made us feel special, kept the project on track, and even helped with some of the editing!

Many people participated in the creation of this book, including our good friend Brad Dellenbaugh, who handled the illustrations and kept us on the straight and narrow with his technical editing and understanding of human anatomy; and Sally Samins, who shot the photos (and helped us find the ones we couldn't shoot). Jeff Johnson helped immensely with organizing (and starring in) the photo shoot, as did our neighbor, Aine McLean (a great capsize-photo model). Other people and organizations who helped smooth the way for us that we would like to recognize and thank are: Harry Munns; Pat Healy; Doug Ament at H&S Yacht Sales; Geri Conser (for that great aerial photo of JJ and Pam); Offshore Sailing School; Billy Black; Kristen Lawton, Doug Skidmore, and Matt Miller at Hobie Cat; Jason Campbell; Tom Leweck; Cam Lewis; Skip Novak; our agent, Mark Reiter; Marty Ehrlich; John Burnham; Rich Roberts; Katie Poe; JJ's dad, Tom Fetter; Dennis Conner; the San Diego Yacht Club; the American Sailing Association; the US Sailing Association; and the Hewlett-Packard Company.

People who have played a key role in Peter's education as a sailor and a teacher include Ted Jones, who bent some rules at Norwalk (Connecticut) Yacht Club so Peter could join the junior sailing program; Kendrick Wilson; Tyler Keys; Tom Whidden; Stan Honey; Steve Benjamin; Dave Perry; Lenny Shabes; Robert Hopkins; Gary Jobson; and John Rousmaniere.

JJ would like to thank her sailing instructors — Jack Wood, Mark and DeAnn Reynolds, and Dave Perry — for instilling an early and lasting love of the sport. Also, thanks to Pamela Healy, the U.S. Olympic Yachting Committee, and Bill Koch for giving her the opportunity to take her sailing to a higher level.

Finally, we would like to thank you for your interest in "our" sport. May the wind always be at your back, and if it must come from ahead, may your sails be well shaped and trimmed in tight!

Peter and JJ Isler
La Jolla, California

Publisher's Acknowledgments

We're proud of this book; please register your comments through our IDG Books Worldwide Online Registration Form located at: http://my2cents.dummies.com.

Some of the people who helped bring this book to market include the following:

Acquisitions, Development, and Editorial

Project Editor: Rev Mengle

Acquisitions Editor: Sarah Kennedy, Executive Editor

Associate Permissions Editor: Heather Heath Dismore

Copy Editors: Christine Meloy Beck, Michael Simsic

Technical Editor/Illustrator: Brad Dellenbaugh

Editorial Manager: Seta K. Frantz

Editorial Assistants: Chris H. Collins, Darren Meiss

Production

Project Coordinator: Debbie Stailey

Layout and Graphics: Cameron Booker, Elizabeth Cárdenas-Nelson, Angela F. Hunckler, Todd Klemme, Brent Savage, Kate Snell

Proofreaders: Melissa D. Buddendeck, Joel K. Draper, Robert Springer

Indexer: Steve Rath

Photo Credits

All photos by Sally Samins, except for the following: Page 29, Billy Black; Page 40 (c), Peter Isler; Page 189, Skip Novak; Page 243, Bob Grieser; Page 280, Peter Isler; Page 287, Geri Conser; Page 290, Hobie Cat Co.; Page 293, Hobie Cat Co.; Page 309, Rich Roberts; Page 334, Bob Grieser

General and Administrative

IDG Books Worldwide, Inc.: John Kilcullen, CEO; Steven Berkowitz, President and Publisher

IDG Books Technology Publishing: Brenda McLaughlin, Senior Vice President and Group Publisher

Dummies Technology Press and Dummies Editorial: Diane Graves Steele, Vice President and Associate Publisher; Mary Bednarek, Director of Acquisitions and Product Development; Kristin A. Cocks, Editorial Director

Dummies Trade Press: Kathleen A. Welton, Vice President and Publisher; Kevin Thornton, Acquisitions Manager

IDG Books Production for Dummies Press: Michael R. Britton, Vice President of Production and Creative Services; Beth Jenkins Roberts, Production Director; Cindy L. Phipps, Manager of Project Coordination, Production Proofreading, and Indexing; Kathie S. Schutte, Supervisor of Page Layout; Shelley Lea, Supervisor of Graphics and Design; Debbie J. Gates, Production Systems Specialist; Robert Springer, Supervisor of Proofreading; Debbie Stailey, Special Projects Coordinator; Tony Augsburger, Supervisor of Reprints and Bluelines

Dummies Packaging and Book Design: Robin Seaman, Creative Director; Jocelyn Kelaita, Product Packaging Coordinator; Kavish + Kavish, Cover Design

◆

The publisher would like to give special thanks to Patrick J. McGovern, without whom this book would not have been possible.

◆

Contents at a Glance

Cartoons at a Glance

By Rich Tennant

page 233

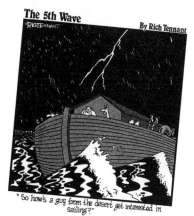

page 7

page 311

page 47

page 351

page 141

Fax: 978-546-7747 • E-mail: the5wave@tiac.net

Table of Contents

Part IV: Sailing Away for a Year and a Day — Special Situations 233

Chapter 12: Blow the Man Down: Heavy Weather Sailing 235

Introduction

. . . .

There is nothing — *absolutely nothing* — *half so much worth doing as simply messing about in boats.*

— Water Rat to Mole, Kenneth Grahame, *The Wind in the Willows*

*O*ver the course of human history, the oceans have served as highways upon which our trade and civilization has evolved. Sailing has played a crucial role in the growth and development of the world as we know it. When you get away from shore, feeling a link to those ancient mariners setting off for undiscovered lands becomes easy. When you're flying across the water, you're harnessing the same forces of nature that powered the early explorers.

Some people believe that humans are drawn to the sea because three-quarters of the planet we live upon is covered with water. Generations before you have felt the call of the wind and waves, beckoning to accept their offer of unknown possibilities — adventure and serenity. Even in today's high-tech, fast-paced world, sailing is regularly found high on pollsters' lists of desirable activities.

This allure of sailing is not a hollow charm. The farther you get into the sport, the more there is for you to experience and enjoy. Wherever you go on the water, sailing can take you away. You can let go of the pressures of everyday life as the receding shoreline gets smaller and smaller.

What is it that gives sailing such enchanting prospects? Water Rat certainly had a piece of the puzzle. Messing about in a boat — any kind of boat — is great fun. The spell that the wind casts onto the sails of a boat is bewitching to behold. Escaping the cares and stresses of everyday life, conveyed on a craft that is powered solely by the forces of nature . . . you'd be crazy to turn down that opportunity.

Well, we don't think that sailing is crazy. In fact, the sport of sailing has brought tremendous pleasure to our lives. While cruising, we've explored some of the most remote and beautiful parts of the world. While racing sailboats, we've had the chance to challenge ourselves in international competition and make friends around the globe.

Maybe the best thing about sailing is the part that your imagination can latch onto, conveying your mind to places you've never been, promising experiences yet untold. And no matter how experienced you become or how much water has passed beneath your keel, sailing still has more to offer. The sport is so vast that no one can experience all of sailing's facets in a single lifetime.

But enough generalizing. After all, you wouldn't have picked up this book if you weren't already at least intrigued by the allure of sailing.

About This Book

In this book, you can find all the information you need to go sailing. This book is a textbook, user's manual, and reference book all in one. We start with basic sailing skills and move on to cover more advanced topics, for when you widen your horizons to activities such as chartering a boat and going cruising. We even introduce you to our favorite cruising destinations. You get to practice tying knots, and we talk about what to wear on a boat. (You can skip the blue blazer, but soft-soled shoes are a must.) You find out how to sail a sailboard and a catamaran, how to tell a schooner from a yawl, and how to find the boat that's right for you. You even discover the basics of sailboat racing. We cover all you need to know to be safe on the water, and we make the whole process easy and fun!

How We Organized the Book

Unlike a novel, this book isn't designed to be read from cover to cover. Depending on your familiarity with sailing, you may want to begin by reading Chapter 1, or Chapter 5, or Chapter 15 — the choice is up to you. If we write about something important in a chapter that is covered in more depth elsewhere, we tell you where to turn. Simple? We think so.

Part I: Getting Your Feet Wet

The three chapters in this section ensure that your first experience on the water is happy and fun, even if you've never been on a sailboat before.

Chapter 1 looks at the parts that all sailboats have in common and the different types of sailboats, and explains how sailboats use the wind to move. Chapter 2 covers your options of where to go to learn to sail. And as you're preparing for that first day on the water, Chapter 3 answers that age-old question, "What should I wear?"

Part II: Getting Ready to Cast Off — Sailing Basics

This section is the meat of the book for the new sailor. In Chapter 4, you step aboard a boat and prepare the sails and gear. Chapter 5 is the big kahuna — the principles of sailing: how to get your boat from point A to point B (and back again). Chapter 6 wraps up the basics by showing you how to handle yourself and the equipment on the boat. This chapter also covers sailing away from a dock or mooring and how to launch your boat from a trailer, ramp, or beach.

In Chapter 7, we talk about safety, because you need to be prepared when you're out on the water. We show you where the safest spots are to enjoy your ride, how to rescue a man overboard, and how to get going again if your boat tips over. This chapter also covers the safety equipment you need to have on board and includes a review of your choices in life jackets.

Part III: Sailing Away — Applying the Techniques

This section is intended to be most helpful for intermediate and advanced sailors who have at least a season of sailing under their belts. Chapter 8 provides plenty of tips to sailing faster and introduces you to the subtleties of adjusting the shape of your sails. This chapter also shows you how to use a spinnaker — that colorful sail for going fast downwind.

Chapter 9 covers anchoring and advanced docking techniques — now that you have the skills to sail farther away. Chapter 10 is a great chapter for anyone interested in weather (which, by the way, includes all of us sailors). This chapter helps you know whether those dark clouds on the horizon are going to dump rain on you. And Chapter 11 covers navigation: how to read charts, plot your course, use a compass, and find your position while at sea (without having to stop at the nearest gas station for directions).

Part IV: Sailing Away for a Year and a Day — Special Situations

The first two chapters of this section are meant as reference guides. Chapter 12 shows you how to prepare for storms and what to do if you get caught in strong winds without warning. Appropriately numbered, Chapter 13 covers what to do on your unlucky day: when you run aground, break something, or have to abandon ship.

Chapter 14 returns to a more carefree topic: how to sail a sailboard — those surfboards with sails that we love and you've always wanted to try. Chapter 15 is for intermediate to advanced sailors who want to go fast on a small boat and includes how to use a trapeze and surf waves in a sailboat. This chapter also introduces you to sailing a catamaran — those fast boats with two hulls. Chapter 16 acquaints you with our favorite world of sailboat racing.

Part V: Special Considerations

Now that you're hooked on the sport, we're sure that you're daydreaming of sailing adventures. Here's the section that can help you turn those dreams into reality.

Chapter 17 introduces you to the great world of chartering (renting) sailboats and going cruising. Affordable boats are available for charter in exotic locations around the world. Chapter 18 helps you enjoy sailing with your children, because you get to go sailing more often if your family enjoys the sport, too. By Chapter 19, we're so sure that you've been bitten by the sailing bug that we introduce you to the basics of maintenance — keeping your ship in shape.

Part VI: The Part of Tens

No ...*For Dummies* book is complete without this section. Now that you love sailing as much as we do, Chapter 20 poses ten questions to help you find the right boat for you. Want to learn to sail while in paradise? Chapter 21 has a list of ten great sailing schools where you can learn to sail on vacation!

Appendixes

Appendix A covers first aid afloat — from what to have in your first aid kit to how to handle the most common medical problems at sea. Sailboats always have plenty of rope, and Appendix B reminds you how to tie those knots you practiced in Girl or Boy Scouts and tells you which one to use when. Finally, in Appendix C is a list of organizations around the world to help you find sailing schools and more information on this great sport no matter where you live.

Icons Used in This Book

You may notice icons in the margins of this book. Those icons do more than just break up the white space; they tell you something about the paragraph the icon is next to.

This symbol helps you avoid common mistakes while you're just starting out. In later chapters, this caution symbol alerts you to potential dangers. As sailors, we all need to have a healthy respect for the power of the wind and the sea.

We live in San Diego, California, but some of our favorite sailing has taken place thousands of miles away. When we mention something of special interest to the folks sailing outside the U.S., you see this symbol.

Our many years of sailing have resulted in some wonderful memories and some unusual stories. This icon indicates a story from JJ's own experiences.

Peter also has a few stories to tell, and we use this icon to point those out.

You may laugh when you find out how many strange words are part of an old salt's vocabulary. Listening to dockside conversations can be like listening to another language. Fortunately, you don't need to know the entire language to go sailing, although some "proper" yachtsmen like our nerdy friend here may be shocked to hear us say that.

Sailing has a rich history to match the sport's rich vocabulary. This icon highlights stories from the sport's lore.

We try not to be redundant in this book, so this icon points out information that we don't want you to forget.

This icon, shaped like one of the life jackets you find out about in Chapter 7, highlights advice to help keep you and your loved ones safe.

In sailing, because you're letting the wind do the work, the easy way is the right way. These tips can help you find the easy way.

Where to Go from Here

As we mentioned earlier, where you start is up to you. If you're brand-new to the world of sailing, just turn the page and start with Chapter 1. If you've been around boats before, browse through the table of contents and pick a chapter that interests you.

But do start somewhere. The faster you start, the faster we can share our love of sailing. The sport has given us both some fabulous experiences and enabled us to meet some wonderful people. Who knows? Maybe on one of our future voyages, we'll even get a chance to meet you.

Part I
Getting Your Feet Wet

"So how's a guy from the desert get interested in sailing?"

In this part . . .

Some people think that sailors are incredibly snobby rich people who hang out at the yacht club all day sipping gin and tonics, wearing blue blazers, and talking without moving their jaws (kind of like Thurston Howell III in that old television series, *Gilligan's Island*). If this intimidating vision has kept you from beginning to sail, this part is for you. We formally introduce you to a sailboat and then show you where you can take sailing lessons — from regular people and with regular people. We also dispel those blue blazer myths and answer that incredibly important question that mankind ponders every morning — what to wear?

Chapter 1

Looking at a Basic Boat

· ·

· ·

The perfection of a yacht's beauty is that nothing should be there for only beauty's sake.

— John MacGregor

*H*ave you ever listened in on the conversation of two sailors? Sailing has so many specific words that sailors can sound like they're speaking a foreign language. But don't let that turn you off. The language of sailing has an old and rich tradition, and as you become more comfortable in a sailboat, you will gradually pick up more and more of the language and become a part of that tradition yourself.

You don't want to let a lack of knowledge about terminology slow down your sailing progress, but you do want to get familiar with sailing terms, especially certain words that are more important than others. For example, if you're sailing with someone who rolls his eyes if you say the "front" of the boat instead of the "bow," then you should go sailing with someone else. On the other hand, when the skipper plans a maneuver that requires a coordinated crew effort, using and understanding the exact terms is very important so that everyone on the boat knows what's happening and what to do.

In this book, we try to avoid overdoing the sailing jargon, but even we can't get around it in the next section, "Looking at a Basic Sailboat." But don't worry. This book isn't one of those mission descriptions on *Mission: Impossible* that self-destructs after the first reading. You can always come back to this chapter and brush up on your terminology.

Terminology isn't the only thing that this chapter covers. Everyone likes to know *why* and *how* — why does a sailboat float, how do sails work, and how do I know this thing won't tip over? This chapter covers the *why* and the *how* of sailing and explains how the boat and the sails work together to keep you afloat and moving.

Looking at a Sailboat

Sailboats come in all sizes, shapes, and types, but all sailing craft, big or small, share some common features, including the five similarities outlined in the following sections.

All sailboats have a hull

The *hull* is the floating (hopefully) body of a boat, and it can be made of a wide variety of materials, including wood, fiberglass, metal, plastic — even cement! The hull can be as small as a surfboard or over 100 feet (30 m) long. Some boats, called *multihulls,* have (guess what?) multiple hulls.

All sailboats have a mast

The *mast* is the vertical pole that supports the sails. Masts are made out of a strong, lightweight material such as wood or aluminum. On bigger boats, the mast is usually supported by an array of wires called the *standing rigging.* Some boats have several masts that can support many sails. (Remember the pictures of the *Nina, Pinta,* and *Santa Maria* in your history textbook?) Sailboats can be classified by the number and position of their mast(s). At the end of this chapter, you can see many types of sailboats.

All sailboats have sails

The mast and standing rigging support the third common feature of sailboats — the *sails.* A sail is simply a big piece of fabric that catches the wind and enables you to use its force to move the boat. The *main* or *mainsail* sets along the back edge of the tallest mast. Some boats carry just the mainsail, while others have a *headsail* as well. The headsail sets in front of the mast. The most common headsail is a *jib.* Large jibs that overlap the mast are also known as *genoas.*

Many nouveau sailors are particular about the use of the word *genoa* versus the word *jib.* To be perfectly accurate, calling a genoa a "jib" is okay, but calling a small jib (one that doesn't overlap the mast) a "genoa" is wrong. Just call them all jibs to be safe.

Why do boats float?

Anything that is less dense than the fluid it sits in floats. *Density* is expressed as mass per unit volume. The density of freshwater is 62.2 pounds per cubic foot (1 gram per cubic centimeter). Saltwater is heavier at 64 pounds per cubic foot, so a heavier object can float better in saltwater than in freshwater. In saltwater, a boat floats if it is less dense than 64 pounds per cubic foot, including everything on board: mast, sails, and people. For example, if the density is 32 pounds per cubic foot, the boat floats half in and half out of the water.

The weight of a boat is called its *displacement* because the boat displaces (or pushes aside)

a volume of water equal to its weight. An object with a very light displacement, such as a surfboard, lies on top of the water like a leaf. A boat with a heavy displacement sits lower in the water, displacing more water.

Boats can be built of nonbuoyant materials, such as aluminum, steel, fiberglass, or even concrete, as long as they're designed with enough volume so that their total density is less than water. An empty aluminum can floats, but the same can sinks if you flatten it and decrease its volume. (Of course, don't try this experiment on the water — you'd be littering.)

Not all sails are created equal. High-tech racing boats have sails made out of exotic, lightweight, yet strong, materials such as Kevlar (the stuff they make bulletproof vests out of). In the 1988 America's Cup, I sailed aboard *Stars & Stripes,* a 65-foot (20-m) catamaran. Instead of "soft" sails, this boat had a "hard wing" — very similar to the wing of a 737 jet. Constructed out of carbon fiber and other very strong and light materials, this hard wing was really a mast and sail all wrapped up in one. Because of its three-dimensional wing shape, it was extremely fast — and we won the Cup! But at the end of each day of sailing, the boat had to be carefully tipped on its side (using a huge hydraulic contraption) to hide the wing from any swirl of wind behind a wall. Because you can't just lower and fold up a hard wing after a day on the water, this type of sail isn't very practical for everyday sailors.

You can use one of many types of specialty sails to make a boat go as fast as possible at different angles to the wind. The most common specialty sail is the *spinnaker* — a big, colorful, parachute-like sail used when sailing *downwind* (going with the wind). You can find more information about sails in Chapter 8.

As you can probably guess, each part of a sail has a name, too. We've identified a bunch of these terms in Figures 1-1 and 1-2.

- ✔ **Head:** The top corner of a sail
- ✔ **Tack:** The front, bottom corner of a sail
- ✔ **Clew:** The back, bottom corner of a sail
- ✔ **Foot:** The bottom edge of a sail

- **Leech:** The back edge of a sail
- **Luff:** The front edge of a sail

    Note: Like a few other words in the sailor's dictionary, this one has multiple meanings — more on that in Chapter 4.

- **Battens:** Solid slats inserted into pockets along a sail's leech to help maintain its shape

All sailboats have lots of rope

When a sailboat is *rigged* (prepared and ready to go sailing), all the ropes used to raise and adjust the sails can look like spaghetti. This pasta is all part of the boat's *running rigging.* Even the simplest sailboat, a sailboard, has several adjustment ropes, and each has its own name. Just to make things more confusing, the ropes on a sailboat are "properly" called *lines,* as in "Throw me a line." When you're starting out, though, understanding what the lines do is more important than worrying about what they're called.

Just in case you're curious, here are the names of many lines and other equipment used to control the sails. Many are identified in Figures 1-1 and 1-2.

- **Sheet:** The primary line that adjusts the sail *trim* (the angle of the sail to the wind), usually referred to with the sail it adjusts (for example, *mainsheet*)
- **Halyard:** The rope running up the mast used to pull the sails up
- **Block:** A pulley
- **Cleat:** A fitting used to tie off or secure a line so that it doesn't slip
- **Cunningham:** The control line system near the tack of a sail used to adjust luff tension
- **Outhaul:** The control line system (mounted on the boom) used for controlling the tension of the foot of the mainsail
- **Traveler:** A sail control system that can move the mainsheet attachment point on the boat from side to side
- **Boom vang:** The control line system running from the boom to the base of the mast that tensions the leech of the mainsail

Don't think that you have to memorize all these terms before stepping on a sailboat. Just look them over, put on your sunscreen, and go sailing.

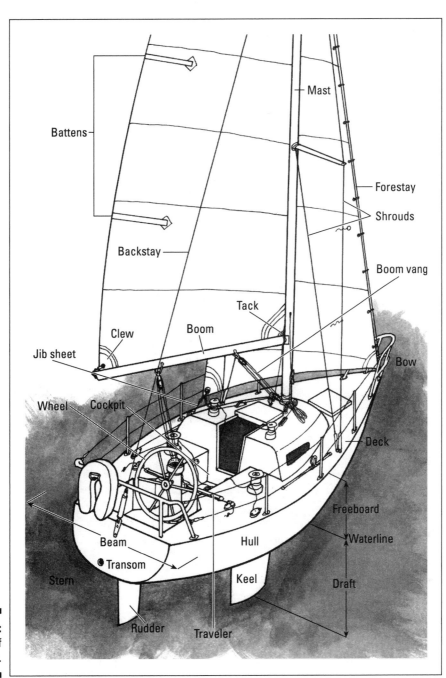

Figure 1-1:
The parts of
a keelboat.

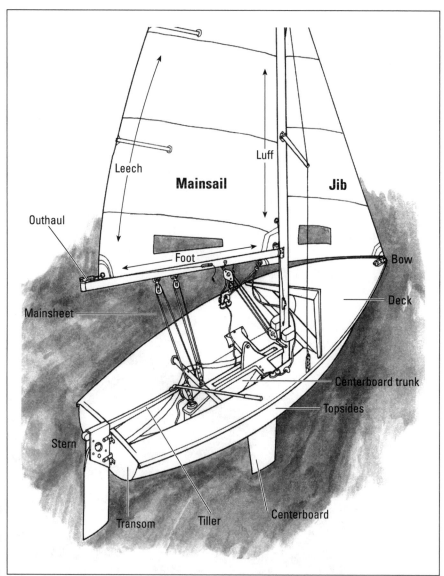

Figure 1-2:
The parts of
a dinghy.

All sailboats have underwater fins

Hanging underneath the back end of most sailboats is a moveable fin called
a *rudder*. The rudder does just what you think it does — steers the boat.
Underneath the middle of the boat is a second, larger fin. Its primary
purpose is to keep the boat from skidding sideways when the wind is
blowing over the side of the boat (see "How Sailboats Work," later in this
chapter). This fin is called a *keel* or *centerboard*. If it's fixed (not moveable)
it's a keel. If the fin is retractable, it's a centerboard.

Sailboats with keels are called *keelboats.* Figure 1-3 shows two keelboats. The one on the right is conventional. The one with three fins has a revolutionary new underbody called *canting ballast twin foil*, or CBTF. Thanks to the *ballast* (weight) in their keels (which are often made out of lead), keelboats resist the forces of the wind that make the boat tip or *heel.* The smallest keelboats are model sailboats, but keelboats that carry human passengers are usually over 20 feet (6 m) in length.

Figure 1-3: Keels and rudders come in different shapes.

PETER SAYS

Back in 1983, an Australian crew made sports history by winning the coveted America's Cup. Their win meant America's first loss in 132 years — the longest winning streak in sports. The Aussies' victory was due to a great crew, a fast boat, and a secret keel, which they managed to hide from the rest of the world until after the race. When they unveiled their boat's underbody during the celebration, the world was astonished to see wings on their keel fin. This wing technology is also being used in other areas — if you check out today's modern jet aircraft, many have winglets on the ends of their wings.

A boat with a centerboard is called a *dinghy.* The centerboard may also be called a *daggerboard* or *leeboard,* depending on its position and movement (see Figure 1-4). When retracted, a centerboard lives in a *centerboard trunk.*

Because all types of centerboards lack the weight of a keel, the sailor on a dinghy must move from side to side to balance the boat and keep it from tipping over — something that occurred automatically on a keelboat, thanks to its ballasted keel fin.

We hate to do this to you, but now that you understand the basic similarities of all sailboats, we need to introduce you to some more of that sailor's language we talk about at the beginning of this chapter. Take a closer look at the two basic types of sailboats we discuss in this book — keelboats and dinghies — in Figures 1-1 and 1-2 to see some other common parts of sailboats (most are common to both keelboats and dinghies).

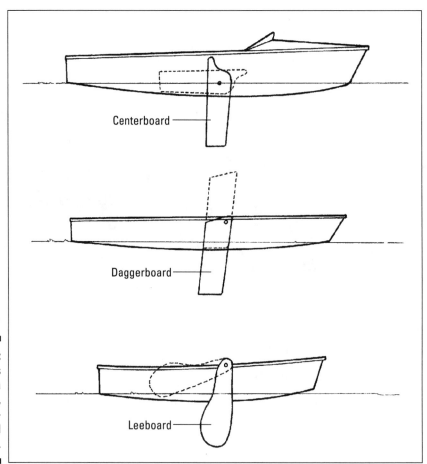

Figure 1-4:
Dinghies
featuring a
centerboard,
dagger-
board, and
leeboard.

Centerboard

Daggerboard

Leeboard

All boats are different, so we can't guarantee your boat has all (or only) these parts, but these figures and lists are a start! Keep in mind that you can always come back to these pages; you don't need to memorize these terms now.

Some more parts of keelboats and dinghies are defined in the following list:

- ✔ **Backstay:** The support wire that runs from the mast down to the stern.

- ✔ **Forestay:** The support wire that runs from the mast down to the bow. Also called the *headstay*.

- ✔ **Shrouds:** The support wires that run from the mast down to the middle of the deck on either side. Sometimes called *sidestays*.

- ✔ **Boom:** The horizontal pole that supports the bottom edge of the mainsail. The boom can swing from side to side as the boat turns, so be careful not to get in the boom's way as it swings or else . . . boom!

- ✔ **Tiller:** The lever arm that controls the position of the rudder; commonly found on smaller boats (instead of a steering wheel).

- ✔ **Wheel:** On larger boats, the steering wheel that controls the position of the rudder.

- ✔ **Bow:** The front of the boat. The direction toward the bow is *forward*.

- ✔ **Stern:** The back of the boat. The direction toward the stern (the opposite of forward) is *aft*.

- ✔ **Cockpit:** The area where the crew sits to operate the boat.

- ✔ **Deck:** The top of the hull.

- ✔ **Hull:** The floating part or body of the boat.

- ✔ **Topsides:** The outer sides of the hull.

- ✔ **Transom:** The outer sides of the stern.

- ✔ **Beam:** The width of the boat at any point. The *maximum beam* is the widest point.

- ✔ **Waterline:** The water level on the hull.

- ✔ **Draft or Draught:** The distance from the water's surface to the deepest point on the boat. The draft can also be referred to by the verb *draw,* as in, "Our boat draws seven feet."

- ✔ **Freeboard:** The distance between the deck of the boat and the water.

How Sailboats Work

Although you don't really have to know how a sailboat works to enjoy sailing, finding out how it works can be fascinating. Modern America's Cup teams spend millions of dollars trying to quantify what makes a sailboat move — and move fast (or at least faster than the competition). Boat movement is a highly complex problem dealing with fluids of vastly different densities (air and water), and your boat operates on the confused interface between those two fluids. Figuring out the best wing shape for flying at Mach 2 at 60,000 feet is much easier than figuring out the best hull and sail shape for a racing sailboat because, with aircraft, you only need to consider the interaction with air.

To understand the physical principles involved, take a look at the basic forces that propel a sailboat: the motion of air over sails, and water over a centerboard or keel. When a sailboat is sailing with the wind behind it, what's going on is pretty obvious: The sails act like a parachute out in front of the boat as the boat moves with the wind. But the dynamics get more interesting when a crew wants the sailboat to sail at an angle to the wind.

First, look at how a simple *airfoil* (wing) generates lift. Put your hand out the window of a moving car with your palm facing forward, and it simply gets pushed backward. But when you slowly rotate your hand into the wind, tipping your palm downward, you can feel your hand begin to lift up. This *lift* is due to the motion of the air that passes above and below your hand. As you begin to twist your hand, the air traveling over the top of your hand speeds up relative to the air streaming under the bottom, as shown in Figure 1-5. Fast-moving fluids create low pressure, so by twisting your hand, you generate a low pressure area over the top of your hand. This difference in pressure (caused by your hand "wing" with a slight *angle of attack* to the airflow, or slightly turned into the wind) results in an upward force that lifts your hand, as well as a slight sideways force pushing your hand downwind. Understanding these two forces is crucial to understanding lift and why a sailboat moves forward. The same basic principle of wings works for birds, planes, and sailboats.

Figure 1-5:
Hands out a car window at different angles to the wind feel different forces.

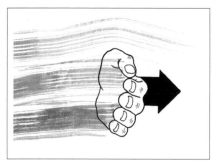 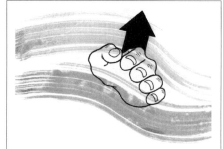

Here's what happens when a boat sails upwind. First, look at the sail. When you pull in the mainsheet and fill the sail with wind, the sail creates a wing shape. That wing has an angle of attack to the wind flow. Just like your hand out the car window (or any airfoil at an angle of attack to the flow), the air over the back side of the sail goes faster than the air on the front side. The resulting difference in pressure creates lift — a force pushing the boat sideways and forward.

If the airflow over the sail was the only force involved, sailboats would slip sideways as well as forward. A sailboat, however, has wings above and below the water. When a sailboat begins to move through the water, the underwater wing (centerboard or keel) also creates a force that, when combined with the sail force, moves a sailboat forward. Here's how: Like any other wing, the water passing over the back side of the centerboard or keel goes faster than the water passing over the front side. The resulting difference in water pressure created by this flow of water pulls the boat forward and sideways — but in the opposite sideways direction of the sail force. The opposing sideways forces cancel each other out, as shown in Figure 1-6, and the forward forces remain.

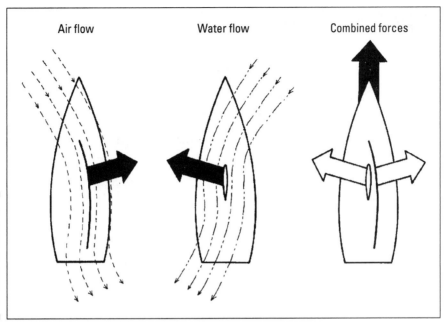

Air flow   Water flow   Combined forces

Figure 1-6:
Flow over
sail and
keel and the
resulting
forward
force.

Together, the forces of the wind on the sails and the water on the center-board or keel enable the boat to sail a close angle to the wind. You can't sail straight into the wind, though, because the sails would flap like a flag, and you wouldn't generate any forces on the sails. Most modern sailboats can sail within 45 degrees (or closer) to the wind direction, a remarkable feat when you consider the fact that the sailing ships in which the likes of Magellan explored the world were so inefficient that they could barely sail within 90 degrees to the wind.

This description is, necessarily, somewhat simplified. You see, even today, over 200 years after a guy named Bernoulli discovered the differences in pressure generated by fluid flowing at different speeds, scientists are still fine-tuning the theory of the physics involved in making a sailboat sail upwind.

The fact that the physics involved are so complex can make sailing even more fun, because you, the sailor, can be a test pilot, fiddling with the various adjustments of sail shape and the boat's angle to the wind to squeeze even more performance out of your craft . . . or you can just go sailing.

As you pursue the sport of sailing, you will always have more to discover. If you stick with it (which is pretty easy to do, considering how much fun sailing is), you will find, as we do, that decades later, you still have much more to master and enjoy about this incredible sport.

Types of Boats

Sailboats come in an infinite number of shapes and sizes. That's the beauty of sailing — you can't help but find a boat that's just right for you. You can get a good idea about how fast a boat is just by how it looks. Just like you can tell that a big Cadillac or Mercedes-Benz is going to be pretty comfortable inside but not very fuel efficient, you can tell that a big, heavy, wide boat is a good cruiser but isn't going to break any speed records on the water. Here's a look at the many different types of boats.

Sailboards

A *sailboard* is basically a surfboard with a sail. Even sailboards come in many different sizes and shapes, depending on their intended use and the skill level of the rider.

Sailboarding (also called *windsurfing*) is easy to pick up — as long as you're willing to spend a few hours mastering the basic skills (and falling in the water over and over while trying). Windsurfing is a great way to enjoy the sport with equipment that you can throw on the roof of your car. For pure-fun recreational sailing (as opposed to racing), we love sailboarding more than any other aspect of our sport. For those of you who doubt the aerobic benefits of the sport of sailing, try windsurfing for an afternoon. We promise that every muscle in your body will be tired afterward. For more on sailboarding, see Chapter 14.

Multihulls

Earlier in this chapter, we define a *multihull* as a boat with multiple hulls. A boat with two hulls is called a *catamaran;* three hulls, a *trimaran.* Multihulls can be thrilling to sail — with a little wind, one hull lifts out of the water, and you feel like you're flying across the water. You can find out more about sailing a cat in Chapter 15.

Bigger multihulls are great cruising boats. Because of their width, they're very stable. Multihulls are fast, too, because they're very light and don't have heavy keels or as much surface area underwater as *monohulls* (boats with one hull) of the same size. Huge, 60-foot (18-m) multihulls compete in races across oceans. Some of these competitions are for solo competitors, and some are for full crews. (For more on the crazy world of offshore racing, see Chapter 16.) But most of the world's sailing and racing takes place in the most common type of boat, the monohull.

It's a ship; no, it's a yacht; no, it's just a boat!

A ship is defined by Webster's Dictionary as a "large seagoing vessel" or "a sailing vessel having a bowsprit and usually three masts...." A boat is a "small vessel propelled by oars or paddles or by sail or power." A "yacht" is defined as "any of various relatively small sailing or mechanically driven ships that characteristically have a sharp prow and graceful lines and are ordinarily used for pleasure cruising or racing." In the U.S., a yacht is the snobby cousin of the boat, but in New Zealand and much of the current and former British Empire, the word *yacht* has no snob connotations and can be used safely, without giving away anything about yourself, in place of *boat* or *sailboat.*

In this book, we refer to *boats* or *sailboats,* and we then differentiate between bigger sailboats with keels (keelboats) and smaller sailboats with centerboards (dinghies). Check out Chapter 2 for our thoughts on which boats are best for beginners.

Monohulls

Monohulls can be classified as keelboats or dinghies, as we say earlier in this chapter. Boats can also be characterized by their *rigs* — the type and number of masts they have and the types and number of sails they carry.

Boats with one mast

Two types of sailboats have one mast:

- **Sloops:** The most common type of single-masted monohull is the sloop. Sloops have either a *masthead rig* or a *fractional rig.* Telling the difference is easy — just look at the point where the forestay attaches to the mast. If the forestay attaches at the top of the mast, the rig is a masthead rig, and the mainsail and jib are hoisted equally high. On a fractional rig sloop, the forestay stops about three-quarters of the way up the mast, and the mainsail is taller (and often larger) than the jib.

  Some sloops are called *cutters* because their mast is positioned very far back (about halfway) from the bow.
- **Catboats:** The catboat doesn't have a jib, only a mainsail.

You can see examples of sloops, cutters, and catboats in Figure 1-7.

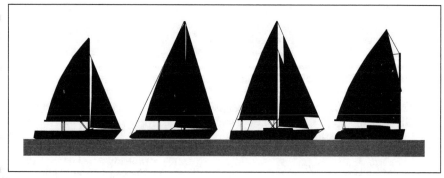

Figure 1-7:
One-masted sailboats: A fractional rig sloop, a masthead rig sloop, a cutter, and a catboat.

Boats with two masts

Very few modern boats are built with two masts, but being able to identify these older types of boats is great fun. The most common types are

- ✔ **Ketches:** A *ketch* has two masts, with the front one being taller. The smaller mast is called the *mizzen*. To be a ketch, the mizzen mast must be in front of the *rudder post* (the attachment point for the rudder).

- ✔ **Yawls:** The yawl rig is very similar to the ketch rig and is usually seen only on older boats. The only difference between a yawl and a ketch is that on a yawl, the mizzen mast is aft (behind) of the rudder post.

- ✔ **Schooners:** The schooner is a very traditional rig with two or more masts. The front mast *(foremast)* must be shorter than the main mast. If the sails are rigged in the old fashioned, *square rigger* manner (with rectangular sails set on booms crossing the mast like a T), then you get into another family of rig names, which we will kindly not list here.

You can see examples of two-masted boats in Figure 1-8.

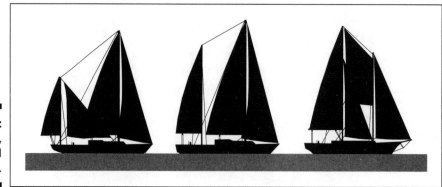

Figure 1-8:
A yawl, ketch, and schooner.

The difference between a ketch and a yawl seems hard to remember — and pretty insignificant. You are correct about the latter, but I have a trick that can keep you from ever confusing ketches and yawls again. K comes before Y in the alphabet, and a ketch's mizzen mast comes before yawl's! Easy, huh? Of course, how do you know where the rudder post is without swimming under the boat? I never have figured that one out.

Mainsail types

Just so that no one feels left out, we want to run through the different mainsail types:

- **Marconi rig:** This is the most common rig, where the mainsail is a triangle shape with one boom. This rig became popular in the 1920s. It was called a Marconi rig because with its supporting wires (standing rigging) and tall height (compared to the *gaff rig*), it resembled the radio towers built for Guglielmo Marconi's invention. This rig is so prevalent now that no one refers to it by a special name.

- **Gaff rig:** The Marconi rig replaced the gaff rig that you still see on older, more traditional boats. A gaff rig has a four-sided mainsail attached to two booms, one at the bottom of the mainsail at the normal place and a shorter one at the top called the *gaff.*

- **Lateen rig:** A lateen rig is an ancient mainsail arrangement that can be found on the popular Sunfish dinghy. With this rig, the bottom boom crosses the mast and attaches to another spar called the *lateen,* which both pivot around the mast. A lateen mainsail has three sides.

- **Wishbone rig:** The wishbone rig is common on sailboards and some small sailboats. The two-piece boom is shaped like a wishbone.

See Figure 1-9 for examples of these mainsail types.

Figure 1-9:
The Marconi, gaff, lateen, and wishbone rigs.

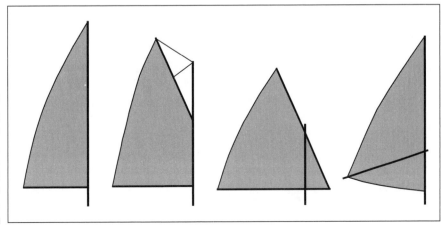

For the love of boats

Sailboats come in an amazing variety, and huge improvements have been made in comfort and speed since man first used the power of the wind to cross the seas. In Mesopotamia over 5,000 years ago, the first papyrus-reed boats were used for travel to various trading ports. These ancient boats were heavy and slow, probably rarely reaching 4 knots of speed. The latest speed sailing records are over ten times that speed on trimaran hydrofoils with hard wing sails similar to aircraft, including the Australian tri-foiler *Yellow Pages Endeavor*. (*Hydrofoils* have plates or fins, attached by struts, for lifting the hull out of the water at high speeds.)

When Magellan set sail in 1519 with five heavily laden ships bound from Europe to the eastern tip of Brazil, the journey took two months. In 1994, the catamaran *ENZA* skippered by Peter Blake and Robin Knox-Johnson circumnavigated the globe in 74 days, 22 hours and 17 minutes. With the constant developments in boat design and technology, expect to see the latest records broken quickly. The great thing about sailing is that after you master the basics, the same principles apply on all sailboats.

Chapter 2

Where Should You Go to Learn?

There be three things which are too wonderful for me,
Yea, four which I know not:
The way of an eagle in the air;
The way of a serpent upon a rock;
The way of a ship in the midst of the sea;
And the way of a man with a maid.

— *Old Testament,* Proverbs 30:18,19

Suppose that you don't know how to sail but want to learn. (A pretty good guess, because you're reading this book, right?) Sailing is a very accessible sport if you know where to look. Believe it or not, plenty of people would love to introduce you to the joys of sailing. Depending on where you live, how old you are, and who you know, you may have any number of options. This chapter answers some key questions such as where you can go to get started in sailing and what type of boat you should start on. We help you choose a sailing school and look at all your options for finding out about this great sport.

Where Can You Go to Learn?

Here's a look at the different ways you can learn to sail:

- ✔ **You can learn from friends.** Peter was introduced to sailing in his teens by some friends. If you have friends with a sailboat, your first taste of the sport may be aboard their boat, too. Someday, hopefully, you will share the joys of sailing with your friends. But unless your friends are certified sailing instructors with plenty of free time to dedicate to your education, you should just enjoy the ride and plan on getting your first formal training from a true professional.

- ✔ **You can learn by reading books and magazines.** Many books have been written on all aspects of sailing — from learning to sail to adventures at sea and everything in between. At the end of this chapter, we suggest some of our favorites. Like many sports, sailing is part mental and part physical. You can study its theories from an article, a book, or in a classroom, but some things can be discovered only with the wind in your face and your hand on the tiller or ropes.

- ✔ **You can learn on your own.** Purchasing (or borrowing) a boat and teaching yourself to sail is entirely possible. After all, it isn't nuclear physics. However, we don't recommend learning on your own (in fact, we totally discourage it) because, at best, you teach yourself bad habits, and it takes a long time. Teaching yourself may even be downright dangerous. When we leave the shore behind, we sailors are in the hands of Mother Nature — and she can be a harsh taskmaster on occasion. We devote an entire chapter of this book to safety afloat (Chapter 7) and provide safety tips throughout all the other chapters, too. You can practice on your own, but learn from a professional first.

- ✔ **You can learn in a formal class from a professional instructor.** Have an idea of where we're headed yet? We feel very strongly that, despite all the options, you should get your education from a pro. See "Choosing a Sailing School," later in this chapter.

What Type of Boat Should You Learn On?

Not only can you choose where and how to learn, but you may have a choice of what kind of boat to start on. We both learned how to sail on dinghies, and so did Dennis Conner, Ted Turner, and most other "famous" racing sailors. But then again, we learned as kids, and dinghies are nearly universally used in junior sailing programs. To refresh your memory from Chapter 1: Dinghies are smaller boats (usually under 20 feet or 6 m long) with a retractable centerboard. You may also recall that dinghies can tip over. Keelboats are usually bigger with fixed keels that provide extra stability.

Bottom line: Consider the pluses and minuses of dinghies and keelboats outlined in this section, and then go take lessons from the best instructor you can find!

Dinghies

Many sailing schools and junior programs instruct beginners in small (10 to 14 feet or 3 to 4 m long) one-person boats; others use larger two- or three-person dinghies. Ideally the boat has a relatively stable hull shape (not too tippy) and a conservative amount of sail area, as shown in Figure 2-1. No need to be breaking any speed records on your first sail!

Figure 2-1: The 420 is an internationally popular two-person training dinghy.

Pros

These are the advantages to using a dinghy for your training:

- ✔ **They are responsive.** Due to the boat's light weight, changes in helm, weight position, and sail trim give instantaneous feedback. You can really "feel" the boat sail.

- ✔ **The helmsman trims a sail.** On most dinghies (especially the single-person variety), the helmsman must do more than just steer, providing a more complete understanding of how things work.

✔ **They are inexpensive.** Therefore, they're favored by many programs that have limited budgets.

✔ **Smaller size makes them less intimidating.** Would you rather take your driver's ed. class in an economy-size compact or a minivan?

Cons

Learning to sail on a dinghy does have the following disadvantages:

✔ **They can capsize.** You can argue that the possibility of capsizing is a "pro," especially because we think that everyone who sails a dinghy needs to know how to right a capsized boat. (We cover that subject in Chapter 7.) Finding out how to right a flipped boat, however, is not a first priority if you start on a keelboat.

✔ **They are wet.** Being wet can be uncomfortable. Typically, you sit lower to the water in a dinghy than on a keelboat. But hey, if water hurt, sailors wouldn't go sailing (at least not as often). Check out Chapter 3 for some clothing ideas to protect yourself from the inevitable dampness of sailing.

✔ **The instructor doesn't ride with you.** Having the instructor with you is an option, but some small dinghies get pretty cramped with two people on board. Often, the instructor follows you in a motorboat, shouting advice as needed.

Keelboats

Most commercial sailing schools that cater primarily to adults use small (20- to 28-foot or 6- to 9-m) keelboats as their introductory training vessel, as shown in Figure 2-2. The *sloop rig* (see Chapter 1) is the most common. Ideally, the boat has a large, open cockpit area capable of holding a class of one to four students plus an instructor. Again, a boat that doesn't have a cloud of sail area is easier for the neophyte crew to handle.

Pros

Advantages to starting off on a keelboat include

✔ **The instructor is on board.** Getting instant feedback is nice. Plus, learning with other students on board can be fun.

✔ **You won't capsize.** Removing the constant distraction of a possible capsize enables students to concentrate on learning to sail.

✔ **A keelboat is more comfortable to sail.** On a dinghy, you must pay constant attention to where you're sitting in order to keep the boat from tipping over too far. One of the things you should be learning on any boat is where to sit (see Chapter 4). On a keelboat, however, you

Figure 2-2:
The Colgate
26 is
the first
keelboat
designed
specifically
for sailing
schools.

don't affect performance very much if you're a little slow to react or are out of position by a foot or two. Plus, as we've said before, keelboats are drier — although you don't get any guarantees that a big wave won't come right over the side and land on your lap!

✔ **It can use an engine.** If the wind dies or if there is no wind in the harbor, you can start up the engine and make your way to the good sailing water more quickly.

Cons

Here are the disadvantages to starting your sailing career on a keelboat:

✔ **The boat is a "duller instrument."** Keelboats are heavier and less responsive to the subtle changes in sail trim and heading that are immediately apparent on dinghies. This fact can make "feeling" the boat, which is such an important part of learning to sail, more difficult.

✔ **Everything pulls harder.** The heavier the boat, the bigger the sails and the more load on all the control ropes. So the boat may be rigged with devices like winches to provide mechanical advantage.

✔ **The boat may steer with a wheel.** Steering wheels are normally used on larger (over 40 feet or 12 meters long) keelboats, and some smaller ones have them, too. But tillers provide a much better feel of the boat and the water flowing past, so you probably have more fun learning on a boat with a tiller.

Keep It Easy the First Time

Here are the ideal conditions for learning to sail, in order of priority:

- ✔ Light to medium winds (6 to 12 knots) that are very steady in direction.

- ✔ Smooth water in an area that is protected from surf, swells, and wind-blown waves.

- ✔ An uncrowded, open area with minimal obstructions and room to sail in any direction. Not having to contend with other boats when you're learning can enable you to focus on the task at hand.

- ✔ Warm air and water — over 70 degrees F (21 degrees C) each is nice; in the 80s F (upper 20s to low 30s C) — sheer paradise!

Of course, if you live in Stockholm, you may have to wait a long time for the air and water to get that warm. The key features are the first three. If the wind is constantly shifting or so light that the sails don't fill, getting in the groove and feeling what's happening can be difficult. In contrast, too much wind is a bad thing for beginners. The waves throw the boat around, the sails flap so loudly that you can't hear your instructor, and everything happens way too fast. In short, you have a very difficult time understanding what is happening and why.

Choosing a Sailing School

Now that we've strongly recommended that you start your sailing career with some lessons, we want you to consider a few things before you choose a sailing school. Children and teens may have some options, such as summer camps and junior programs at clubs, that aren't available for adults. So we first look at choosing the best school for kids and then look at what's best for adults.

Children and teens

Many areas have specific programs for kids. They're most commonly located at a yacht or sailing club, camp, or through some community program and are conducted during school vacation in the summer months. Don't be put off by the fact that you're not a member of the club, student at the university, or whatever. Most private yacht club junior programs welcome nonmembers (thankfully, or Peter would still be playing baseball today). You should check out the registration process in the winter months to make sure that the class doesn't fill up before your child is on the list.

If you find more than one potential program in your area, ask your child to help make the decision. Nine times out of ten, the best class is with his or her friends. I kept sailing mainly because all my friends sailed. If it's fun, your child is more likely to stick with it!

Here are some questions to ask when checking out a youth sailing program:

- ✔ **Schedule:** Some programs run for two months, others in biweekly increments. Advanced groups may meet in the afternoon and beginners in the morning. Make sure that you know the number of hours your child will be sailing per day. What about lunch? Hungry kids don't learn very much.

- ✔ **Type of boats:** Find out what type of boat beginners sail. Do you need to own a boat or does the club provide one? In some programs, if you don't own the boat, you have to crew. Crewing is fine for intermediate sailing, but beginners need to learn to steer the boat, too.

- ✔ **Grouped by age or ability:** Most programs are divided by age groups, which can create a small problem if your child is starting a few years late like Peter did. Ask the organizers how they will solve this question.

- ✔ **Curriculum:** Some programs (especially yacht clubs) may stress racing (which we love) over recreational sailing. This approach is okay, but having a balance is nice, and it's best if the fun factor is high.

- ✔ **Instructors:** What is the ratio of instructors to students? What certification do the instructors have? Often instructors are college students; find out how many have previous teaching experience. It's always a good sign if an instructor is rehired for the next season.

- ✔ **Safety:** Has the program had any problems in the past? What sort of special equipment, safety procedures, and insurance does it have? What are the age and swimming requirements?

- ✔ **Equipment:** What equipment does your child need? Are life jackets provided, or must you provide your own?

Adults

If your community has sailboats and sailors, you probably have a community sailing program or a commercial sailing school or two to choose from. Yacht clubs, universities, and some charter/boat rental companies may also offer instruction. Of course, you can always look in the Yellow Pages under "Schools" or "Sailing." However, we tried that in San Diego and came up with zilch. We finally found a list under "Boating Instruction." You can ask a sailor or someone at a marine business for recommendations, and a boat show can be a good source of information, too.

Fortunately, you have another way. In the U.S., two organizations oversee national educational programs that certify instructors and provide commercial schools with curriculum and standards. You can contact each of them to receive a list of accredited schools.

The American Sailing Association: Founded in 1983 (Peter was one of the founders and remains on the Board of Directors), the ASA initially licensed the Canadian Yachting Association's acclaimed educational program for use in the U.S. Since then, this educational system has evolved and become highly regarded in the field of sailing education. The ASA instructor certification program is the backbone of the system. Over 150 commercial sailing schools are affiliated with the ASA and offer student certification to the multilevel ASA program that begins with Basic Keelboat Sailing. Although the ASA system began with keelboats, an increasing number of small-boat and community-oriented programs are using the ASA small-boat and boardsailing program, which was modeled after some of the most successful programs in Europe.

American Sailing Association
13922 Marquesas Way
Marina del Rey, CA 90292
310-822-7171 or 800-877-7774, ext. 1512 (for a list of ASA-affiliated schools)
Web site: http://www.american-sailing.com
e-mail: ouch9@cinenet.net
usenet: alt.sailing.asa

US Sailing Association: US Sailing is the national governing body for the sport of sailing. Its primary role for over a century has been to oversee the racing side of the sport, including the U.S. Olympic Sailing Team, which JJ was on in 1992. US Sailing is the U.S. representative to the International Sailing Federation, the organization that produces the racing rules and represents the sport of sailing (yachting) in the International Olympic Committee. US Sailing has long been involved in yacht club junior sailing programs, due to its focus on racing. Recently, US Sailing developed a certification system similar to the ASA's; its Keelboat Certification system starts beginners with the Basic Keelboat standard. US Sailing also has an instructor certification program.

US Sailing Association
P.O. Box 1260
Portsmouth, RI 02871
401-683-0800
Web site: www.ussailing.org

Learn to sail at summer camp

The American Camping Association (800-428-2267) publishes a guide to camps that categorizes them by activities. The list costs about $17, but you can also find that information for free on the Internet at the association's Web site (http://www.aca-camps.org), which includes a "search" feature to help you find the camps with sailing (or even modern dance, if there are any).

Outside the U.S.

Some countries have a national authority like ASA or US Sailing that promotes a standardized educational system. You can contact the International Sailing Federation in England (see Appendix C) for a list of countries with national learn-to-sail programs. That organization should be able to provide you with a list of accredited schools. Otherwise, you can always ask for recommendations from local sailors or marine businesses.

The following section can help you interview a school to see whether it's right for you.

Interviewing a potential school

Here are some points of information that you want to find out from a sailing school during your selection process:

- **Curriculum:** Does the introductory learn-to-sail course offer certification to a national standard? Don't settle for an answer like, "Our program is better than ASA or US Sailing certification," unless you have some inside info on the program. Just because a school doesn't offer certification doesn't mean that its course is deficient; the course may be great, but if it doesn't comply with some standard other than its own, how would you know? Also ask how long the class is. The typical learn-to-sail course at a commercial sailing school takes place over four days, often two weekends, and combines classroom and on-the-water training.

- **Instructors:** Are the instructors certified? If only some of them are, make sure that your instructor is certified.

- **Boats:** What kind? Dinghy or keelboat? Wheel or tiller? Engine?

- **Class size:** How many students will be on the boat? Can you take private lessons? Having other students on the boat with you has advantages and disadvantages. In order to get enough time at each position, you probably don't want more than four students (including yourself) on the average 25-foot (8-m) keelboat.

Free sailboat rides

Another source of sailing school information in the U.S. is the National Sailing Industry Association. Its "Discover Sailing" program mails a list of sailing schools to people who call its hot line number: 800-535-SAIL. A cool feature of the Discover Sailing program is the promise of free, 30-minute sailboat rides to all newcomers to the sport. When you call the 800 number, you're directed to a nearby sailing business (it may not be a school) that will give you a free sailboat ride. Make no mistake — this is definitely not a substitute for a lesson from a certified school and instructor, but it's a great way to get a taste of the sport.

- ✔ **Bad weather/makeup days:** How much wind is too much for the entry-level course? What is the school's policy for making up blown-out days?

- ✔ **Safety:** Ask about the school's safety record and any special safety procedures. Does it have any swimming requirements?

- ✔ **Equipment:** What do you need to bring? Most schools provide life jackets but not foul-weather gear.

- ✔ **Post-class sailing:** Does the school have a boat(s) available for graduates of the basic sailing course to take out to build sailing experience? If so, are there any special policies regarding its use?

- ✔ **Higher education:** Does the school have further classes that you can take after you have some experience?

Your sailing instructor

Desirable features for a beginning sailing instructor include

- ✔ **Certification:** With certification, you know your instructor has made an effort to measure his skills and knowledge against a national standard.

- ✔ **A good teacher:** No matter how good a sailor the instructor is, communication and teaching skills matter most.

- ✔ **Patience:** Instructors need this quality in spades the 50th time someone asks them to explain something.

- ✔ **A sense of humor:** After all, it's sailing, not something serious like tax preparation. The more fun the students have, the better they learn.

- ✔ **Ability to anticipate potential problems:** This quality has everything to do with experience. When the boat is all the way downwind in a narrow passage with rocks on each side, it's too late.

- ✔ **Communication skills:** The ability to make complex things perfectly understandable — sort of like the ...*For Dummies* series of books!

Sailing instruction for women

Some great T-shirts are available for sailing couples. Hers says, "Don't yell at me, I'm doing the best I can," and his shirt says, "I'm not yelling." If these slogans describe your sailing relationship, you may want to look into sailing instruction specifically for women. You can find many programs around the U.S. One program run by Womanship (based in Annapolis, Maryland) has specific classes for women, including "Sail Yourself Safely Home," a two-day clinic designed to help a less-experienced spouse feel confident of her ability to get back to shore in case of an accident to the experienced spouse.

Other Boating Courses

Because you're in the learning mood, you may also consider taking classroom courses. Although you may not find classes that specifically teach sailing, you can probably find generic boating courses that cover subjects like safety, seamanship, basic rules of the road, navigation, knots, and weather. Some of these courses are oriented for powerboaters (we sailors call them *stinkpotters* behind their backs), but most of the classroom subjects pertain equally well to sailing.

In the U.S., contact the U.S. Coast Guard's Boating Safety Hotline at 800-368-5647 or the Power Squadron at 888-828-3380 for further information on classes.

Learning on Vacation

Why not take sailing lessons during your vacation to an exotic (and warm) waterfront location? Such vacations are a great way to find the time in your busy schedule to get out on the water and figure out which way the wind is blowing. You can use the same sources we have mentioned in this chapter to find sailing schools at your vacation destination, or check out Chapter 21.

Thousands and thousands of more-experienced sailors take sailing vacations by *chartering* (renting) boats. We cover that sort of ultimate vacation in Chapter 17. Many sailboat charter companies offer a more advanced course designed to introduce an experienced sailor to the joys of *bareboat* chartering (chartering a boat "bare" means with no skipper or crew), but don't expect them to offer a beginning, learn-to-sail course. Call first.

Practicing

After you graduate from your first course in sailing, practice all those newfound skills and build your experience level. Although many schools offer classes in "higher education," don't rush it. You should spend a season or more just building your skills before you embark on the next level of education. Your new skills and knowledge fade quickly if you don't keep practicing.

We may discourage learning to sail from friends, but after you learn the basic skills in a class, having friends who are sailors is great. Sailboat owners are often happy to find eager crew. You don't have to be a lifelong friend; just let it be known around the docks that you're willing to help with sailing duties and make a few sandwiches. Crewing for someone more experienced is a great way to build your own knowledge.

You can also take advantage of the opportunity to try out other types of boats. If you learned in a keelboat, find someone to take you out on a dinghy, or vice versa. Sailing different boats can be a great way to expand your horizons, because each boat is different in the way it's rigged and handled.

Unless you live on a body of water where you just absolutely have to have your own boat, you probably should rent or borrow boats (if you have generous friends) for the next phase of your education in the sport. That way, you can try out different kinds of boats and avoid sinking all your funds into a boat that may not be right for you. We discuss the considerations involved in picking out your first boat in Chapter 20.

Many commercial sailing schools also have sailing clubs or charter/rental operations, and they love to get repeat business from their recent graduates. Renting is a great way to get sailing time without the joys (and hassles) of owning a boat. You may even want to hire an instructor for an afternoon just to refine those basic skills that you're practicing.

If you're not one of its students, a boat rental company may want to see proof of your experience level before it lends you one of its boats, which is one reason why you want to take your course at a facility that offers national certification. The rental company may also require you to be "checked out" on a particular boat by one of its staff before renting to you, no matter how experienced you say you are.

Just because you've taken one course in sailing doesn't mean that you're ready for an around-the-world cruise. Avoid sailing in wind and sea conditions beyond your ability. These experiences come with time, and now is the time for gaining confidence in mild conditions.

Higher Education

After you've spent a season or so refining your basic sailing skills, you're ready to take the next step in your education. If you're interested in cruising and recreational sailing aboard keelboats, then you should head to the next levels of certification, such as those offered by the ASA or US Sailing. For example, the ASA's progression of standards is as follows:

- ✔ Basic Keelboat Sailing
- ✔ Basic Coastal Cruising
- ✔ Bareboat Chartering
- ✔ Coastal Navigation
- ✔ Advanced Coastal Cruising
- ✔ Celestial Navigation
- ✔ Offshore Passage Making

How far you go within the structure of an educational system depends on what kind of sailing you want to do and what other opportunities you have for gaining experience and practical education. After you've taken three or so levels of education over a couple of years, you may be comfortable enough to stop there. Others may enjoy the challenge of moving up the certification system.

If you're more interested in racing, then you have to find a boat on which you can race. Spread the word that you're an eager and willing crew. We know of no better way to learn to race than to get out there and do it. For more on the world of racing sailboats, read Chapter 16. During the off-season, you may consider taking one of the sailboat-racing classroom courses offered in your area. Two popular national racing seminar series are North U. and Performance Racing Seminars. We have taught in both of them; who knows, maybe we will see you there!

Sailing Magazines and Books

Because sailing is part mental and part physical, you can expedite your schooling by reading. (Hey, you already know that — you have this book in your hand.) We both accelerated our sailing education when we were young by reading everything we could on the subject. A number of great sailing magazines offer a combination of instruction, entertainment, and feature stories for the sailor. Our favorite is *Sailing World* because it focuses on the racing aspect of the sport (and Peter is the Editor at Large). Some other great national magazines in the U.S. are *Cruising World, Sail, Yachting,* and *Sailing.*

Countless regional publications are aimed at the sailor. The coolest one, without question, is the San Francisco Bay area's *LATITUDE 38*. You may be able to find these publications for free at your local marine store.

This is a list of some of our favorite sailing books. (For our favorite children's books, see Chapter 18.)

- ✔ Nathanial Bowditch, *The American Practical Navigator*
- ✔ Erskine Childers, *Riddle of the Sands*
- ✔ Paul Elvström, *Expert Dinghy and Keelboat Racing*
- ✔ Ernest K. Gann, *Song of the Sirens*
- ✔ Alfred Lansing, *Endurance*
- ✔ C. A. Marchaj, *Sail Performance*
- ✔ Patrick O'Brian, *Master and Commander* (then read the series)
- ✔ Dave Perry, *Winning in One-Designs*
- ✔ John Rousmaniere, *The Annapolis Book of Seamanship*
- ✔ Joshua Slocum, *Sailing Alone Around the World*

Chapter 3

What to Wear

Be valiant, but not too venturous. Let thy attire be comely, but not too costly.

— John Lyly

*F*ace up to the fact that you're going to get wet on a sailboat. Maybe just a bit of innocuous spray will come aboard, but at some point, you're likely to be confronted with a big wave that wants nothing more than to jump down your collar and soak you and all your clothes. If that water is 90-degree F (32-degree C) Gulf Stream soup on a hot day, a douse is welcome. But on a blustery, cool day, you want to stay as dry as possible — and staying dry means wearing some sort of waterproof outerwear.

We recommend that you go sailing several times and find out what aspect of sailing is your favorite before you spend your money on special sailing gear. Make sure that your purchase really fits your sailing needs. You may find that the boat you love is a sailboard, so a wet suit is your big clothing purchase (see the left photo in Figure 3-1). Or you may decide to go dinghy sailing and wear the gear shown at center in Figure 3-1. Or you may find that your greatest love is coastal and offshore keelboat sailing, and you want to invest in foul-weather gear for wet days (see the right photo in Figure 3-1).

Figure 3-1:
From left, JJ in windsurfer gear; dressed for dinghy sailing; and Peter in foul-weather gear rounding Cape Horn.

Do you need to rush out and buy all sorts of new gear to go sailing? You probably already own clothing that can work just fine for your first few sails. After you identify the type of boat and sailing you prefer, you can begin shopping for a nice set of foul-weather gear, a wet suit, or whatever special sailing gear is most appropriate. In this respect, sailing is like skiing: Although a wide range of sports-specific clothing is available, you don't need to be in any rush to spend large amounts of money as long as you can find clothing in your current wardrobe that works.

When to break out the blue blazer

If someone with a roman numeral in his name asks you to go sailing with several hundred of his closest friends on his yacht, chances are good that the boat is a powerboat, not a sailboat, and you should wear a blue blazer. Other than that, you're rarely expected to wear the traditional blue blazer on the water. The only times we've ever worn blazers and cocktail party attire on the water were for a wedding, a boat christening, or some other really formal party. One top international sailor we know doesn't even own a blue blazer. But before you head off to lunch at the New York Yacht Club (which, by the way, is in midtown Manhattan, not on the water), throw on a coat and tie.

Even at formal parties on large yachts, wearing soft-soled shoes is still best. Women should avoid hard-soled shoes as well, especially spike heels. If you're invited to go sailing on a fancy yacht, especially an antique wooden boat, be forewarned that you may be asked to take off your shoes to prevent damage to the wooden decks. So make sure that your toenails (and your date's — always more embarrassing) have been trimmed in the last year and that your socks are presentable.

Your clothing needs depend on three factors: the weather, the water temperature, and what size boat you're going out on. Weather and water temperature considerations are fairly obvious: If you head out to sail on lovely (and chilly) Lake Ontario in the early springtime, you definitely need to bring more layers than your friend who decides to go to Key West for a learn-to-sail summer vacation.

But the size of the boat plays a role in deciding what to wear and bring, too. Aboard a small boat with a centerboard (dinghies and catamarans), you're very close to the waves — and when it's windy, plenty of spray comes aboard. Plus, you always have the chance of capsizing and taking an unexpected swim, so you want to be dressed to stay warm even if you get wet. On a larger boat, you sit higher off the water — with the benefit being a drier ride. Also, bigger sailboats (keelboats) resist capsizing, so your clothing needs are different.

When I started racing, I didn't have any special sailing clothing and couldn't afford to buy any. Sure, I got soaking wet and cold a few times, but at least I was out there having fun. Hey, a little water never hurt anyone, especially when a hot shower and a change of clothes are waiting back on shore!

Staying Warm + Dry = Having Fun

Planning what to wear for a day on the water is similar to preparing for a long hike. For both, you need to consider whether you will still be comfortable if you get damp or wet.

In this section, we assume that you're not going sailing right after the first thaw, and we take a look at what clothing you can bring for a typical daysail in light or moderate winds in the summer months.

Layering

When getting dressed to go sailing, keep in mind that the temperature on the water varies much more than it does on shore. One minute the wind is light, and you're basking in the sun with your shirt off; the next minute the wind comes up across that cool water, and you want your jacket in a hurry.

Bring clothes that can be worn in layers so that you can vary your attire depending on your comfort needs. Layering is an efficient way to stay toasty when the air is cold because the air trapped between the layers warms up and acts as extra insulation. When the temperature rises, you can strip off layers until you reach your comfort zone.

On top

The best way to keep warm on the water is to stay dry. That advice may sound pretty basic, but staying dry while on the water requires a little forethought — especially about the top layer. We recommend that your outside layer be a windbreaker-style jacket.

No matter where I go sailing, the first item that gets packed into the sea bag is a windbreaker (with a lining if the weather's cool). In all but the wettest conditions (or the tropics!), this jacket is my outside layer when sailing.

You probably already have such a jacket in your closet. Most any nylon-shell jacket works just fine for 95 percent of your sailing requirements. A windbreaker that's a little oversized is nice, so that you can wear a sweater or a couple of layers underneath. Good pockets to keep your hands warm (and store stuff) are nice features, too.

Some incredible synthetic materials that are "breathable" have been developed for the active-wear market. These fabrics are truly waterproof to water coming in from the outside, but they allow water vapor to escape from the inside, minimizing that clammy feeling you get from most waterproof clothing. You may want to invest in a jacket made of one of these new materials eventually, but keep your gear simple for your first few outings.

When You're Going to Get Wet

If you're sailing a dinghy in summertime conditions, you will have more fun when you aren't too concerned about staying dry. Here are some clothing tips for dinghy sailing:

- ✔ Bring a towel and a change of clothes and leave them on shore. Nothing's worse than having to drive home in wet, salty underwear.

- ✔ Leave the gear bag on shore. You probably have only enough room on board a dinghy for a bottle of water, a tube of sunscreen, and a jacket (which may get soaking wet, too).

- ✔ Leave your car keys and wallet in a safe place on shore, too.

- ✔ Unless your hobby is being a finalist in wet T-shirt contests, wear a bathing suit underneath your clothes.

- ✔ Cotton is great for keeping you cool on hot days, but it doesn't retain heat when it's soaking wet. Wool does a much better job of retaining heat while wet, but modern polyester fleece materials such as Polypropylene, Capilene, and Polartec are the best underlayers when conditions are really wet and chilly because they wick water away from the innermost layer so that your skin stays drier.

✔ Because you're always sitting down on a dinghy, the tread on your shoes is less important. Wet suit booties may be the most comfortable.

✔ Reapply sunscreen often if you're getting wet.

✔ Don't forget to wear a life jacket!

Foul-Weather Gear

Whether on a dinghy or a keelboat, if you decide that you really don't want to get wet (even in nice weather), here's what to look for in a pair of *foulies* — foul-weather gear:

✔ **Style:** Separate chest-height overalls and a jacket are the most versatile and warmest styles. (Remember the importance of layers?) Plus, the jacket can be a stylish addition to your shoreside attire. One-piece suits are popular with small-boat (dinghy and catamaran) sailors because they are less bulky and easier to move around in. *Dry suits* feature elastic cuffs at the neck and wrists.

✔ **Material:** Suit your style, but don't get too fancy. Many manufacturers offer several different lines of foul-weather gear. Lighter weight is for active, small-boat racers in temperate conditions, and heavy, "bullet-proof" gear is for cold-weather offshore sailing. If you're in doubt, go for the medium-weight gear.

✔ **Room to move:** Make sure that you still have a full range of motion, even with your warmest layers on underneath. Bigger is better.

✔ **Construction:** Water can leak at the seams, so make sure that the seams are sealed by tape on the inside. Look for extra fabric on the seat and knees — these areas can wear out from the rough surfaces on a boat.

✔ **Hood:** A built-in hood that can be folded away under the collar is invaluable when it starts to rain.

✔ **Pockets:** Make sure that the overalls as well as the jacket have pockets — bigger and more are better.

✔ **Color:** Choose bright colors so that you stand out in a crowd — and especially so that you can be seen if you fall overboard. Avoid white or blue outerwear because you may be hard to find in the water.

On Your Feet

Sailing barefoot may seem like a good way to get in touch with nature, but running around without shoes is an open invitation for a stubbed toe — or worse. On any bigger boat where you're going to walk on a wet, slippery deck, nonslip shoes are required equipment. Pick shoes that are non-marking, like the shoes you wear on a tennis or basketball court. You probably own a pair of sneakers or soft-soled athletic shoes that are fine for your first season of sailing.

For years, I wore sneakers aboard big race boats because they were so much more comfortable than leather boating shoes and because they provided plenty of grip on a slippery foredeck. A few years ago, the shoe companies came out with athletic shoes with a true, nonslip sole made for boating. Now I wear those shoes until the weather's so wet that I have to break out the *sea boots* (very high waterproof boots).

Some shoe treads work great on boats (we find that soft rubber soles with plenty of grooves to grip the deck are best). If you find yourself slipping around the deck in your regular shoes, you may want to buy a pair of special sailing shoes.

Bringing the Right Gear

Ten (actually more than ten, but who's counting?) items to have in your gear bag include the following:

✔ **Life jacket:** Even if you can swim the English Channel in your sleep, always make sure that you have a life jacket aboard before going sailing. If you're sailing with friends or taking sailing lessons, life jackets are probably provided, but always ask to be sure. If you get bitten by the sailing bug (its bite is a real doozie!), you should purchase your own life jacket — especially if you plan to sail aboard small boats (dinghies and catamarans). See Chapter 7 for everything you need to know about life jackets. Although life jackets used to be bulky and uncomfortable, nowadays you can find U.S. Coast Guard-approved life jackets that are comfortable and not confining. On a wet, windy day, a life jacket can be a welcome additional layer of clothing!

✔ **Jacket or foul-weather gear and/or a bathing suit:** Now you have both weather extremes covered.

✔ **Nonslip, rubber-soled shoes:** Don't go offshore without them.

✔ **Sun stuff — sunglasses, hat, and sunscreen:** The glare of sunlight (even on a lightly overcast day) reflecting off the water and sails makes these items essential. Make sure that you have a string or some sort of retainer for your **sunglasses** and your hat. We have proven beyond a doubt that sunglasses sink.

When we're going to be on the water all day, we put sunscreen on first thing in the morning, when we brush our teeth, because sunscreen is most effective when it has time to soak in. (One word of caution: Be careful not to confuse your sunscreen with your toothpaste.) Then we reapply sunscreen before going out on the water, and we try to remember to add another layer a couple more times during the day. Don't forget to put sunscreen on the back of your neck, on your ears, and on the backs of your hands, and be sure to use a product with an SPF (Sun Protection Factor) of 15 or higher.

When I sail in the tropics, I wear a long-sleeved shirt (an old button-down) and lightweight, long pants every few days, just to give my skin a rest from the sun.

✔ **Gloves:** Sailing gloves are a good investment, unless your other hobby is rock climbing and your hands are well calloused. Head to your local marine store for a good pair. Open-fingered gloves are best so that you can still use your fingertips for tying knots and opening the lunch box.

✔ **Hairband:** Keep long hair in a ponytail or a braid. Loose hair can get caught in the lines and blocks and then pulled out in big chunks. (That's painful even to think about — ouch!)

✔ **Water:** Drinking plenty of water is crucial on hot days to prevent dehydration, so throw an extra bottle in your bag. Avoid alcohol when you plan on operating the boat, just as you do when operating a car.

✔ **Snacks:** Having an extra apple or orange (skip the fruit that can get squashed), a granola bar, or an energy bar can make you pretty popular if an intended short sail turns into a three-hour tour.

✔ **Sailor's choice:** We're divided on this one. JJ wants a cellular phone (such a Californian), but Peter would bring a knife ("a sailor's best friend"). Your choice may be seasickness pills.

What to leave on shore

Leave the jewelry at home — you don't want to lose your grandma's pearls overboard. Take off your rings, too, because you have to grip ropes with your hands, and rings can pinch your fingers (or worse!). Any item of clothing or equipment (such as a camera) that water can ruin should stay on shore. (If you must bring it, at least put it in a zip-top bag.) We say it again — sailing is a wet sport, and even the biggest boats can get wet down below.

Stowing your gear

If the boat is big enough to have a cabin down below, go ahead and put your gear bag down there, preferably off to the side on a bunk or in a cubbyhole so that people don't step on it. Keep your bag off the floor where water can collect. Carry your extra clothes in a small duffel bag or backpack that can close securely. Ideally, this bag is waterproof — or at least water-resistant. Leave your nice leather bag or suitcase at home, and bring only what you need — bringing too much stuff on someone else's boat is considered uncool.

If you're sailing a dinghy, few (or no) storage places are truly dry. All your gear (and yourself) can get wet, so bring the minimum amount of stuff and try to find a good place to stash it — maybe you can find a mesh bag somewhere, or you can tie down your jacket out of the way somewhere.

Our final piece of advice for the eternal question of "What should I wear?" is to ask the people with whom you're going sailing. They have the best idea of what gear works well on their boat.

Part II

Getting Ready to Cast Off — Sailing Basics

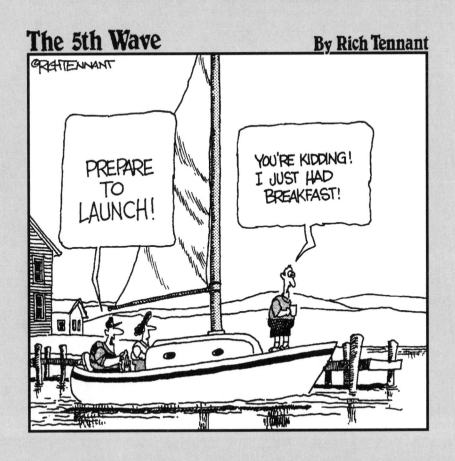

In this part . . .

Say that you're standing at the edge of a lake, ready to go for a swim. Are you the type who gets a running start and dives in? Or do you go to the edge and dip your toe before slowly wading in? If you're the first type, you probably opened the book right to this part — and that's okay. This is the part of the book that is the most helpful for beginners, the one that introduces the basics of sailing. It also covers how to prepare your boat for sailing and how to launch your boat. Of course, we hope that you're so hooked on this sport that you continue reading (and even go back to what you missed in Part I).

Chapter 4

Before You Leave the Dock

And biased by full sails, meridians reel
Thy purpose — still one shore beyond desire!
The sea's green crying towers a-sway, Beyond.

— Hart Crane

Climbing aboard a sailboat can be trickier than you think, especially on a small boat. Because you want to maintain your cool image with the crew, pay close attention to this part. When you're safely aboard (and hopefully still dry), you need to prepare the boat for sailing by attaching all the parts and pulling up the sails. After you complete this process of *rigging* the boat and *hoisting* the sails, you're probably ready to sail away from the dock. However, in some places, such as marinas with many boats around, you may have to motor your boat out into open water before hoisting the sails and having fun.

Most first-time sailors have a sailing instructor or experienced friend put the mast up and *launch the boat* (get it in the water). In this chapter, we assume that your boat is already launched and tied to a dock or *mooring* (a permanently anchored buoy). If you have to put up the mast or launch the boat, see Chapter 6.

In this chapter, we primarily focus on the rigging systems common to a small (20- to 25-foot or 6- to 8-m) keelboat, an approach that provides an excellent general introduction to the different components involved in the rigging process, no matter what boat you sail. However, every boat is different, and your boat may have some steps to rigging that are peculiar to its type. That's why we recommend that you rig the boat with an instructor or someone who knows your boat.

Climbing Aboard

How you climb aboard depends upon the boat type. This section has tips for boarding all kinds of boats. We start with the tippier boats — dinghies — and then cover how to climb on a bigger keelboat.

Climbing aboard a dinghy

Dinghies, as we explain in Chapter 1, are smaller boats (usually under 20 feet or 6 m long) that carry no *ballast* (weight) in their moveable centerboard. You may also recall that dinghies can tip over. Because this is a "learn to sail" book rather than a "learn to swim" book, make sure that your first step into a dinghy is as near to its *centerline* (an imaginary line that runs down the center of the boat from end to end) as possible, near the midpoint from *bow* to *stern* (front to back). Now you know why we suggest in Chapter 3 that you carry your gear in a bag — so that you can easily hand it to someone on board or throw it into the *cockpit* (the inside of the boat, where the crew sits). You need both hands free for climbing onto the boat.

If the dinghy has wire rigging *(shrouds)* connecting the mast (near or at its top) to the right and left sides of the boat for support, you may want to hold one for balance and to keep the boat near you as you step on board. You may also want to consider starting from a sitting or crouching position on the dock. In any case, keep your weight as low and close to the centerline as possible, as shown in Figure 4-1.

Figure 4-1:
JJ shows how to stay dry while climbing into a dinghy.

Coming up with any funny stories about falling in the water while at the dock is tough, because even if we've fallen in while climbing aboard, we'd never write about it — it's too embarrassing.

Putting the *centerboard, daggerboard,* or *leeboard* (the retractable fin underneath a dinghy) down all the way increases the boat's stability, which makes moving around the boat much easier. Therefore, putting down the fin is the first thing you should do after you climb aboard.

The boat becomes much more stable when it's moving and the pressure of the wind is in the sails, but until you're sailing, keep your weight as low and near the centerline as possible as you rig the boat.

Climbing onto a keelboat

Although keelboats have more stability, due to their ballasted keel fin, keelboats can be tricky to board, too. The bigger the boat, the higher the *freeboard,* or the distance between the boat's deck and the water. Bigger (over 25 feet or 8 m) keelboats usually have *lifelines,* a wire perimeter around the deck supported by metal poles called *stanchions.* Lifelines help the crew stay on board, but they can be tricky to climb over when boarding.

Smaller keelboats often don't have lifelines, so you can use the same techniques to climb aboard as outlined for dinghies. However, boarding a larger keelboat with lifelines from a dock near water level requires different methods. Maybe some stairs lead from the dock up to an open gate in the lifelines, making you feel like you're boarding the *Queen Mary.* Or, on some boats, an open *transom* (back end) makes boarding a breeze. But if you must navigate up and over lifelines, try to grab a shroud with one hand and then step up on deck and swing one leg over the lifelines, sort of like mounting a horse, as shown in Figure 4-2.

Don't grab the lifeline or stanchion for support if you can reach a shroud; they may not be strong enough to support your weight.

If you're not so athletically inclined, and the lifelines don't have a gate or the transom doesn't have an opening to facilitate your entrance, you can always crawl through the lifelines. Your ego can survive having to crawl on board better than being left at the dock.

Figure 4-2:
Peter climbs over the lifelines on a keelboat.

Rigging the Boat

You *rig,* or prepare the boat for sailing, by attaching all the necessary parts, including the sails. The best way to find out how to rig a boat is to watch someone else rig it and then try to rig it yourself next time.

Until you're more experienced, always check with your instructor or a knowledgeable sailor to make sure that you rigged everything properly before hoisting the sails.

Even when Peter and I go sailing on a new boat, we always end up asking the owner at least a couple of questions about rigging the boat — questions such as which line gets rigged where. (Of course, I'm better about asking questions than Peter — just like in our car, he never asks for directions, no matter how lost we are.)

Preparing the sails

As we discuss the process of rigging sails, keep in mind that many variations are possible. For example, on some boats you store the mainsail (folded, or *furled*) on the boom, under a cover to protect it from the sun. In that case, take the cover off and skip to the section about attaching the halyard.

Preparing the mainsail

The first sail to prepare is the mainsail. You may need to take the sail out of its bag and lay it on the deck lengthwise, still in its folded state, with the leading edge toward the front.

Inserting the battens

Start by checking to see whether the mainsail has *battens* that you need to insert. Battens are wood or fiberglass slats that insert into *batten pockets* on the sail's back edge, or *leech,* as shown in Figure 4-3. Battens help the sail project its designed airfoil shape and protect it from excessive flapping.

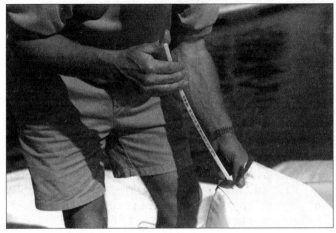

Figure 4-3:
Insert battens into the pockets along the sail's leech.

If one end of the batten is more flexible, insert that end first.

Make sure the battens are secure, so that they don't slide out of their pockets when the sails *luff* (flap). Sailmakers use many different systems to keep the battens in place. We often add strong tape or a few stitches of sailmaker's thread over the pocket openings to ensure that the battens don't fly out on a windy day.

Sliding in the foot

If the *foot,* or bottom edge, of your sail has a rope (sometimes covered by fabric) sewn onto it, then you need to slide the foot of the sail into the track or groove on the top of the boom. Start at the *clew* (the sail's lower back corner) and slide the sail all the way down the boom from front to back, as shown in Figure 4-4. This process usually takes two people — one to feed the rope into the track and the other to hold the sail and help slide it along. Instead of a foot rope, some mainsails have many small plastic or metal slides attached along the foot that you insert into the groove on the boom, similar to the foot rope.

Figure 4-4:
Sliding the mainsail foot rope into the track on the boom.

Mainsails designed without a rope along the bottom edge are called *loose-footed* sails. For these sails, you can skip the preceding section and go straight to the sections on attaching the tack and clew.

Attaching the tack

The *tack* (bottom front corner) of the mainsail usually attaches to a fitting at the front of the boom or to the *gooseneck* (the fitting that attaches the boom to the mast), as shown in Figure 4-5. Preparing the mainsail is starting to sound like ". . . your hip bone attaches to your thigh bone . . .," but keep with us; it all makes sense when it's put together.

Figure 4-5:
Attach the mainsail tack to the fitting near the front of the boom.

All three corners of the sail have a grommet or a strap loop to enable you to attach them to the proper control lines or fittings. A *grommet* is a plastic or metal ring built into a sail. Quite commonly, a *shackle* (a closed metal hook) is used to connect one or more of the corners to the appropriate fitting. (See Appendix B to find out how to tie a *bowline,* the best knot to use when tying a line to a sail.)

Attaching the clew

Next, attach (usually with a shackle) the clew to the outhaul at the end of the boom. The *outhaul* is the control line system, found at the back of the boom, that tensions the mainsail's foot.

Some smaller dinghies (usually under 16 feet or 5 m) should be launched with the mainsail already hoisted and luffing (flapping). With these boats, attaching the clew is the last thing you do before leaving the dock. But on most boats, attaching the bottom corners of the mainsail (the tack and the clew) before you hoist is easiest. After you attach the clew to the outhaul, pull the outhaul rope snug and secure it.

Attaching the halyard

To hoist the sail to the top of the mast, you use a halyard. A *halyard* is a rope or wire, attached to the top corner *(head)* of the sail, that's rigged to let you raise the sail to the top of the mast from cockpit level.

Before attaching the halyard, pull it taut and look up, following the line all the way to the top of the mast. Unwind any wraps or tangles before attaching the halyard to the sail.

The halyard gets attached to the head of the sail by a shackle or a rope knot, preferably a bowline. You can read all about knots in Appendix B.

Always make sure that the halyard is securely attached. Use pliers to tighten a shackle with a screw pin or make sure your bowline is secure.

One of the most embarrassing moments in sailing is when a crew hoists a sail sideways. Don't laugh, because all of us have done it by mixing up the sail's corners when rigging. You can often tell which corner is which by the position of the *bolt ropes* (for example, only the tack of the mainsail can have a bolt rope on either edge) or the angle of the corner (the head usually has the smallest angle), or you can write the corner's name on the sail.

Prefeeding the luff of the main

No, the *luff* (the front edge of the sail) is not a hungry animal. To *feed the luff* means to slide the top end of the luff into the groove in the back edge of the mast just above the boom — just like we explain with the foot of the sail. On some boats, you feed the first foot or two of the top of the sail into the mast before hoisting; on others, you leave the halyard off, keep the head of the sail down on deck or tied up on the boom, and wait until it's time to hoist.

Preparing the jib

If your boat has a jib, here is how to prepare to hoist this forwardmost sail. (A *genoa* is a large jib. For simplicity, we always use the term *jib*.)

1. **Take the jib out of its bag and set it down on the foredeck lengthwise, with the front edge toward the bow.**

   Jibs are attached at the three corners (fortunately, they share the names *head, tack,* and *clew* with the mainsail) plus along the front edge *(luff)*.

2. **Attach the tack to the shackle or fitting near the bow.**

3. **Prepare the luff for hoisting.**

   The system for attaching the jib to the *forestay* (a support wire from the mast running down to the bow, also called *headstay*) can vary. Some sails attach with snaps or clips *(hanks)* located at intervals along the luff of the sail. Others have a *luff tape,* similar to the foot and luff ropes in a mainsail, which slides into a special, grooved channel built into, or attached onto, the forestay. With this system, the tape must be fed as the sail is being hoisted. On a jib with hanks, you clip them onto the forestay (starting at the bottom and working upward) without hoisting the sail, as shown in Figure 4-6.

Figure 4-6: This jib is ready to hoist, with the snaps attached to the forestay.

4. **Attach the halyard to the top of the jib.**

   As with the main halyard, pull the jib halyard taut and look up to ensure that it isn't twisted.

5. **Attach the jib sheets, ensuring that they're fed through the proper *blocks* (pulleys) and cleats on each side of the boat.**

   Many different jib sheet systems are available. The sheets (there are two, one for each side) may be attached to the sail with a bowline (there's that knot again!) or a shackle and are then run back to the cockpit, where they're controlled by the crew. Jib sheets must be rigged through a specific path that may include passing through several pulleys. Figure 4-7 shows the jib sheet system on a typical dinghy.

6. **Secure the jib so it doesn't blow into the water before hoisting.**

Figure 4-7:
Jib sheet
system on a
420-class
dinghy.

Checklist before hoisting the sails

Before you hoist the sails, make sure that everything is ready for you to leave the dock. When you hoist the sails, they begin to flap in the wind — which, although safe, is not very seamanlike, because the flapping puts extra wear on the sails. Therefore, you want to get sailing as quickly as possible after hoisting the sails. Here's a checklist you can use to make sure that you're ready to go:

✔ **The boat is in a good position to depart and is pointing "into" the wind.** Trying to raise the mainsail before pointing the bow of the boat toward the wind is a common mistake of new sailors. If the boat isn't pointed into the wind, raising the mainsail may be impossible, because the wind fills the sail when it's partway up, putting too much load on the halyard. After you determine where the wind is coming from (see Chapter 5), think about where you can put your boat so that it points into the wind. A boat secured at the bow naturally points into the wind (unless affected by strong current).

✔ **The control lines — especially the main and jib sheets — are properly rigged and have plenty of slack.**

✔ **Everybody is on board.**

✔ **Life jackets and safety gear are handy.** Chapter 7 covers safety.

✔ **Loose gear is stowed.**

✔ **Main and jib are properly rigged and ready to hoist.**

✔ **The rudder (and centerboard if your boat has one) is down and secured.** Secure the rudder so that it stays with the boat if you capsize. Most dinghy rudders have a spring clip or tie-down line to keep it from sliding out if the boat flips. For dinghies with daggerboards, use a restraining line (shock cord works well) that lets you adjust the daggerboard up and down but keeps it attached to the boat in case of a capsize.

✔ **You have proper clothing and sunscreen on.**

Before hoisting, make sure enough open water is around so that you can sail away easily. Nothing's more embarrassing than casting off from the dock only to smash right into an adjacent boat. With that warning in mind, you may want to walk your boat to a less-crowded location before hoisting.

Raising the Sails

Now you're ready to raise the sails. The general rule is to hoist the mainsail first, although which sail goes up first often isn't a big deal. However, you may decide to get under way with just the mainsail, saving the excitement and extra responsibility involved with using the jib for later.

Hoisting the mainsail

As we say earlier in this chapter, you must feed the mainsail luff (usually a covered rope or slides) into the mast for hoisting. Unless you're vigilant, the luff invariably gets pinched and stuck as you hoist. On a dinghy, you may have to feed the luff in yourself as you hoist. On a bigger keelboat, assign one person to stand next to the mast to feed the luff into the groove, as shown in Figure 4-8. Someone else (and, if need be, a third person) can then slowly and steadily pull up the halyard.

You just have to be different, don't you?

Your boat may be rigged differently, but most boats share at least several of the steps in this chapter. Some boats have the jib permanently rigged on a roller furler, so the jib is kept rolled up around the forestay even at the dock, as shown in the figure. To unfurl the jib, all you have to do is pull on one line!

Some boats (including sailboards) don't even have a main halyard. The mainsail on these boats has a sleeve running along the luff that slides onto the mast like a glove slides onto a finger. Then the mast and sail are set into the boat together. Chapter 6 covers putting a mast up, and Chapter 14 covers rigging sailboards.

Here are some definite exceptions to the "hoist the mainsail first" rule:

✔ If the dock is oriented in such a way that you can't point the boat into the wind, you may want to hoist the jib first and then sail downwind to an area where you can point the bow toward the wind and raise the mainsail. This maneuver is tricky, though, so don't try it without an instructor or experienced sailor on board.

✔ Some dinghies must have the jib hoisted first because the tension of the jib halyard keeps the mast secure in the boat.

Jib on a roller furler

Figure 4-8:
Feeding the mainsail luff into the groove in the mast during hoisting.

Hoisting the mainsail with a winch

Boats over 25 feet (8 m) long may have a winch to help pull up the halyards. A *winch* is a revolving drum that increases the sailor's ability to pull on a rope. See Chapter 6 on how to use a winch.

To raise the main halyard by using a winch, start by putting a couple wraps of the halyard line in a clockwise direction around the winch drum. You want just enough wraps to enable you to hold the line without it slipping. As the load increases (when the sail is partway up), you need to add a wrap or two.

Even with a winch, the easiest way to hoist a sail on a bigger boat is by *jumping* (pulling on) the halyard at the mast. Have a crew member (the jumper) stand at the mast where the halyard exits (presumably above the jumper's head — otherwise jumping doesn't work). Now he has great mechanical advantage to pull downward on the halyard. As he pulls, another person in the cockpit takes up the slack in the halyard by pulling the halyard that's wrapped around the winch. When the sail nears the top, the load may increase so much that jumping is inefficient. Then you must *grind* (turn) the winch handle (a metal arm placed in the top of the drum) until the sail is up to the top.

Mistakes to watch out for

A common problem when hoisting a mainsail is getting the luff tape jammed, which makes the halyard impossible to pull. If the luff tape jams, stop pulling the halyard and ease it until the person feeding the sail at the mast can clear the jam and prepare the sail to slide up cleanly again. If you're hoisting the halyard, watch the area where the sail is feeding into the mast so that you know when a problem is about to happen.

Make sure that the *mainsheet* (the sail adjustment rope attached to the boom) has plenty of slack in it and isn't cleated. Otherwise, the sail fills when it's halfway up, a real drag for the person doing the hoisting. Free the *cunningham* and *boom vang* to facilitate hoisting. (See Chapter 8 to discover how these control lines affect sail shape.)

Other common problems when hoisting sails happen when you forget (or try to skip) any of these steps or make a mistake in rigging the sails. An embarrassing mistake is pulling the halyard up before it gets attached to the head of the sail. On small dinghies, you can tip the boat over at the dock to retrieve the errant halyard, but on big boats, you have to climb or hoist someone up the mast to retrieve the lost halyard. (For more on doing the high-wire act up in the rigging, see Chapter 19.)

How high is high enough?

How high should you pull the sail? All the way! The amount of tension needed for optimum sail shape varies (see Chapter 8), but in general, pull the sail up until the sailcloth is taut and just barely begins to show vertical lines of tension when luffing. The windier it is, the more tension you want. The visual aid is the tension in the luff, not the position of the sail up top, as shown in Figure 4-9. In the photo on the right, the mainsail is too low — note all the wrinkles along the luff and the gap at the bottom of the mast. In the left photo, the mainsail halyard tension is too tight — note the vertical strain marks just behind the mast.

Cleating off the halyard

After you have the mainsail hoisted properly, fix it there by securing the halyard in a *cleat* (a fitting to firmly hold ropes under load).

Cleating your own horn

On dinghies and smaller keelboats, a common cleat for halyards is the *horn cleat* or *t-cleat*. These are simple fittings with no moving parts to break or malfunction. To secure a line around one of these cleats, put one complete wrap of rope around the base. This wrap provides friction to keep the line from slipping when cleating or uncleating. Then make a figure-eight and finish by twisting it to create a *hitch* on the final turn so that the end is underneath (see Figure 4-10).

Figure 4-9:
Mainsail luff tension: too tight (left) and too loose (right).

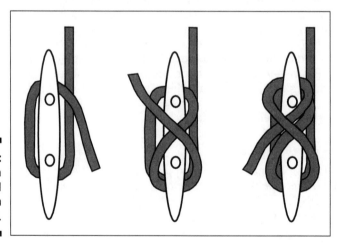

Figure 4-10:
Securing a line around a horn cleat.

Jammin' with your halyards

Another common cleating device for halyards (especially on larger boats, where the loads on ropes are higher) is a *jammer* or *rope clutch* — a mechanical fitting with a lever arm that "squishes" a rope so tight that it can't slip, even under intense load. Most jammers enable you to pull the line in when it's closed, but you can't ease it out. Keep the jammer open as you hoist the mainsail so that you can quickly ease the halyard if the sail gets pinched at the feeding point. When the sail is up and the luff is properly tensioned, you simply pull the jammer's lever down to cleat the halyard in position.

Be very careful when opening a jammer that has a rope under load. First, take tension on the rope behind the jammer on a winch so that the rope doesn't burn your hands when it rapidly eases out (see Figure 4-11).

Jammers

Figure 4-11: Jammers in action — "jammin'."

Hoisting the jib

Hoisting the jib is similar in many ways to hoisting the main. On small boats, you can hoist the jib while still tied to the dock pointed into the wind. Make sure the jib sheets are fully slackened so that the sail can luff freely (and doesn't fill) while being hoisted. You can also hoist your jib while sailing — just make sure the jib sheets are free to run so the sail doesn't fill.

Hoist a genoa while running (see Chapter 5 for the points of sail), because if you hoist it while pointing into the wind, it flaps against the mast as you hoist. By hoisting a genoa while heading downwind, as shown in Figure 4-12, it is protected from the force of the wind by the mainsail. This system works equally well even if you have only a smaller jib.

Any time you sail downwind, be careful not to jibe by mistake (find out more about jibing in Chapter 5).

If your jib has a luff rope or tape, a crew member may need to stand on the bow to feed the luff tape into the groove of the headstay. If your jib has

Figure 4-12:
Hoisting the jib while under way and pointing downwind.

hanks (metal clips) or snaps, then you don't need anyone on the bow, because those clips are attached during the rigging process.

Cleaning up your halyards

Before you let go of the dock or mooring and sail away, you need to clean up all that spaghetti of rope you create while rigging. Some sailboats have a daunting number of sail control ropes, and ropes left to their own devices have an amazing capability to knot themselves. Certain ropes, such as the halyards, can be put away so that they don't tangle with the ropes you need to *trim* (pull in) the sails.

Sometimes it's a luffing matter

One of the most common words in sailing is *luff*. The problem for a beginning sailor is that this word has multiple meanings. The forward edge of a sail is called the *luff*. That's the noun. The verb *to luff* defines the flapping motion of sailcloth when a sail is undertrimmed (or not trimmed at all). *Luffing* is also an adjective, as in "A sailboat with luffing sails can't generate any power." Got it?

Never tie off a coiled halyard in a way that you can't immediately release it to run freely; you never know when you'll want to lower a sail quickly in an emergency.

You may feed the halyard into a storage bag or coil it (see Chapter 6 for more about coiling lines) in a convenient out-of-the-way area, depending on the boat. To use a bag, start at the very end and neatly feed the halyard into the bag so that it can come out just the way you put it in — with no tangles!

If you don't have a bag for the halyard, coil it, starting a foot or two from its cleat. When you finish coiling, put your hand through the coil and pull part of the line closest to the cleat through the coil, twist it a few times, and loop it over the cleat, as shown in Figure 4-13, so that you can easily undo the coil.

Figure 4-13:
Storing a
coiled
halyard
for easy
release.

Sitting at the Dock on the Bay

After you hoist the sails, but before you leave the dock, is the time to figure out where to sit and how you're going to drive this boat. While you're sitting in the boat tied to the dock, the sails luff in the wind. This flapping is noisy, the boom is swinging back and forth just above your head, and you don't have a clue what to do next. Don't panic. Just sit low enough that the boom doesn't hit you as it swings through its arc, and take a deep breath. You need to feel comfortable with luffing because you find yourself in this position quite often when you're beginning to sail.

A *luffing* sail flaps because the wind is blowing straight along its surface from front to back — just like a flag, a luffing sail shows you the wind direction. When you *trim in* a sail (by pulling on the mainsheet rope — or the jib sheet rope, as the case may be) to make it stop luffing, you're forcing it to lie at an angle to the wind and therefore "fill" with wind. (But if you're in the no-sail zone, your sails luff even if you trim them in.)

When your sails are fully luffing, they don't have any power, so the boat slows down and ultimately coasts to a stop. Luffing sails, then, are your brakes. You apply this "sea brake" by simply letting the sheet out.

Steering the Boat

All sailboats have a *rudder,* an underwater movable fin that turns the boat. This rudder is attached to either a long stick *(tiller)* or a wheel that you use to steer. In this section, we explain the differences between these two steering systems. We also cover where to sit when you drive — on a sailboat, the driver's seat isn't always obvious.

Tiller or wheel?

Most sailboats over 30 feet (9 m) long are steered with a wheel, just like a car. Through a mechanical linkage, the wheel controls the position of your rudder. When moving forward, turn the wheel left and the boat goes to the left — and vice versa. You may think that we're stating the obvious, but you see why when you compare turning the wheel to the other way of steering a sailboat — with a tiller.

Most smaller sailboats are steered by a tiller. Using a tiller for the first time takes a bit of getting used to, because the boat turns opposite the direction you move the tiller. If you move the tiller to the left, the boat turns right; move the tiller right, and the boat goes left, as shown in Figure 4-14.

For pure sailing pleasure, I prefer a tiller on any boat up to, say, 40 feet (12 m). Although a wheel takes up less space, it compromises the "feel" of the boat. Because of all the associated machinery and connections, wheel steering has much more internal friction. With a tiller, you're directly connected to the rudder, feeling the water as it flows below the boat, and for me, that sensitivity is preferable.

"Take the helm, Mr. Sulu"

Although you can refer to the person steering a boat as the "driver," you also hear terms like *skipper* and *helmsman* (or *helmswoman*). *Helm* is another of these sailing terms with multiple meanings. The helm is the rudder or tiller — the steering device. It's also the role of the helmsman on the boat. Helm is also a technical word (explained in Chapter 8) for describing the balance of your boat's rudder when sailing.

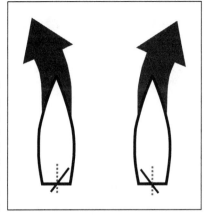

Figure 4-14: Move the tiller to one side to turn the boat the opposite way.

Where to sit when you drive

One of the easiest ways to spot nonsailors is to see where they sit on a boat. If you're driving, you not only want to be able to steer well, but you also want to look good. The following tips can help:

✔ **When steering a dinghy, keep in mind the effect your weight has on the balance of the boat.** Not only should you sit down, but your weight is most likely needed on the *windward* side (the side the wind blows on) to counteract the *heeling* (tipping) forces of the sails. (In Chapters 8 and 15, we discuss techniques for limiting heel.)

✔ **Sit just forward of the end of the tiller so that you can freely move it from side to side.** Most dinghies and small keelboats have a *tiller extension* or *hiking stick* attached to the end of the tiller that enables you to sit farther out to the side of the boat while steering. Using this extension all the time enables you to sit comfortably while steering — and look cool. Hold the tiller extension in your aft hand so that your forward hand is free to adjust the mainsheet, as shown in Figure 4-15.

Figure 4-15:
The skipper of a dinghy holds the tiller extension in one hand and the mainsheet in the other.

✔ **On keelboats with a wheel, stand or sit behind or to either side of the wheel.** On keelboats with a tiller, sit on either side, wherever you have the most visibility and feel most comfortable — although keeping your weight on the high side to counteract heeling is important on a smaller keelboat.

✔ **If your boat has a blind spot because of a cabin top or the sails, move around occasionally to peek into the blind spot.** Periodically asking a crew member to look for obstructions never hurts either.

Seating the crew

On most boats, the crew sits forward of the skipper. They often are responsible for trimming the jib and moving their weight outboard *(hiking)* to keep the boat from heeling. In most conditions, they can sit on the windward side. But if the wind is very light or if the boat's sailing downwind, they may need to sit on the side opposite the skipper to help balance the boat.

On larger boats with several crew members, divide up the jobs so that everyone can feel useful. The skipper usually steers (although nothing says you can't trade around and share the joys of being at the helm). In Chapter 8, you find out about other sail-handling jobs for the crew. As the boats get bigger, your individual weight makes less of a difference in counteracting the heeling forces, but you will still find staying on the windward side most comfortable, whether operating the boat or just hanging out.

Chapter 5

Let's Go Sailing

I find the great thing in this world is not so much where we stand, as in what direction we are moving: To reach the port of heaven, we must sail sometimes with the wind and sometimes against it — but we must sail, and not drift, nor lie at anchor.

— Oliver Wendell Holmes

Understanding the important relationship between the wind and your boat and getting yourself, your boat, and your crew ready all lead up to the best part — going sailing! If you have time to read only one chapter of this book before heading out on the water, this is the one. This chapter covers the basics of sailing. Hoist your sails (refer to Chapter 4 if you need help) and get out on the water!

Finding the Wind's Direction

The world of sailing revolves around the wind. Your boat can't go anywhere without wind (unless you fire up the engine, which, at this point, would be cheating).

A word about safety

Whether you're an old salt or a beginning sailor, being aware of safety considerations is integral to enjoying the sport. In Chapter 7, we review various safety issues in detail. But let us point out that no sailor should go out in conditions that exceed his or her ability. If you're a beginner, your first sail should be in light to moderate wind conditions in protected waters. Furthermore, as we point out in Chapter 2, the best and safest way to start sailing is to take instruction from an experienced and qualified individual. As you grow in experience, you can expand your limits.

Assessing the wind's direction is of utmost importance to a sailor. The direction of the wind is his North Star, the center of his sailboat's universe. Where he goes, how he trims his sails, whether the ride is wet or dry, fast or slow — all these depend on the wind and its direction.

Your ability to accurately sense changes in the wind speed and direction is the single most valuable skill you can bring aboard a sailboat. Increasing your sensitivity and awareness of the wind is the first step in becoming a sailor.

Feeling the wind

The best way to track the wind is simply to feel it. Your body, especially your face, can feel the exact direction of the wind if you just let it. Here's how:

Close your eyes and turn your face until you think that the wind is blowing straight at you. Rotate your head back and forth slightly until you sense that the wind is blowing equally hard across each side of your face and the "sound" of the wind is the same in each ear.

Practice "feeling" the wind whenever you can.

Using other clues to find the wind

Besides feeling the wind, you can look around and see clues to the wind's direction. A flag or wind vane on top of a mast can show the wind direction, and so can a flapping sail, which waves in the wind like a flag. On your own boat, short pieces of yarn or cassette tape tied to the *shrouds,* the wire rigging supporting the mast, can provide that crucial information. Also, look for anchored boats, which point at the wind (except in strong currents).

Another way to see the wind direction is to look at the ripples on the water. Watch the movement of a darker patch of water caused by a puff of wind. Seagulls stand facing into the wind, and, supposedly, cows always point their behinds into the wind — but unless you're sailing next to a field of cows, this bit of trivia is probably useless.

After you gain more experience, you will also be able to assess the wind speed by looking at the water. For example, whitecaps generally begin to form on waves at 12 knots of wind speed. (See Chapter 10 for more information on wind speed.)

If you find yourself getting overwhelmed by which rope to pull and what that piece of equipment is called — *relax,* and just feel the wind on your face. A sailor's world revolves around the wind, and you are becoming a sailor.

The Points of Sail

Figure 5-1 is the big kahuna of sailing, the *points of sail diagram.* As you become a sailor, you can get away with forgetting which side is starboard or which corner of the sail is the tack, but you can't sail without understanding the information in this diagram.

The points of sail diagram looks like the face of a clock, with the wind blowing from 12 o'clock. At the top of the clock face, from about 10:30 to 1:30, is the sector called the *no-sail zone.* It gets its name from the fact that it's physically impossible to sail a boat in this zone. The *no-sail zone* can be called whatever you like — you can call it the *can't-sail zone* or the *anti-sail zone* or, if the sun is setting and strange things are happening, the *Twilight Zone.* Everywhere else around the clock face is fair game for sailboats — you can point your boat anywhere in this *sail zone* and, with the sails trimmed properly, you move forward. The sail zone is further divided into three basic *points of sail:*

- ✔ **Close-hauled:** Also called *beating, sailing upwind,* or *sailing to windward.* It's the closest course to the wind that you can effectively sail, so close-hauled is right at 10:30 and 1:30.

- ✔ **Running:** The course you're steering when the wind is dead behind. Exactly 6 o'clock on the clock face if you're a stickler — from 5:30 to 6:30 if you're like us!

- ✔ **Reaching:** Anywhere between close-hauled and running.

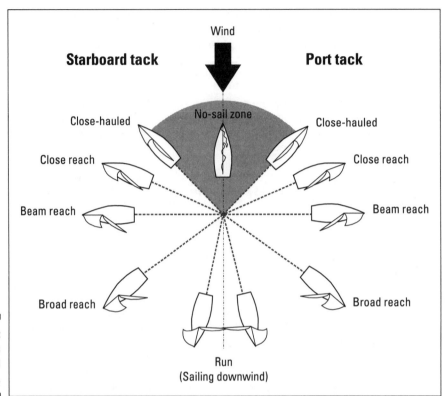

Figure 5-1:
The points
of sail
diagram.

More about that darn no-sail zone

The no-sail zone is about 90 degrees wide — about 45 degrees on either side of the wind direction, or from 10:30 to 1:30, if you like the clock. In this zone, a sailboat can't generate power from its sails and coasts to a stop. The problem is that your sails *luff* (flap) even when you pull them in all the way, and there's simply no way to get enough power to move forward.

As you enter this zone from the sail zone, the front edges *(luff)* of your sails start luffing a little bit (it looks like the front of the sail is "bubbling"), and you start to slow down. If you turn to the very middle of the no-sail zone, your sails flap like flags, and your boat quickly coasts to a stop. In fact, if you stay in the no-sail zone too long, your boat gets blown backward by the wind, and that's called being *in irons*. Getting in irons happens to every first-time sailor. Find out all about getting out of irons in the "Ironing out those irons" section, later in this chapter.

But the beauty of sailing is that you have a way around this apparently forbidden territory. To get to a destination directly *upwind* in the no-sail zone, you can take a zigzag route (see Figure 5-2), sort of like going up a very steep mountain. This technique involves sailing close-hauled and periodically *tacking* (a maneuver where you turn the boat from 1:30 to 10:30 or vice versa). With this knowledge, you can literally sail wherever you want! The wonders of tacking are explained later in this chapter.

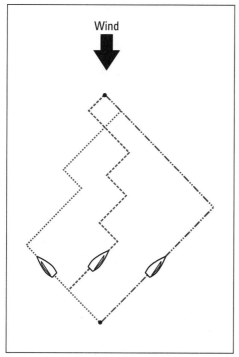

Wind

Figure 5-2:
To get your boat directly upwind, you must take a zigzag route to avoid the no-sail zone.

You must be very clear on one point: No boat can sail a course directly into (toward) the wind. If you try to do so, the sails start luffing, no matter how tight you try to trim them — like they do when the bow is pointed into the wind at the dock. The boat glides to a stop and eventually blows backward, like any object floating on the water.

Sailing in the zone

Sailing in any direction in the sail zone is as easy as *trimming* the sail (by pulling in on the control rope — the *sheet*) and off you go. Or you can just *cleat* the sail (tie off the control rope so that the sail stays in one place) and turn the boat away from the wind until the sail fills. (For more about how to pull in sails, see Chapter 6.) The points of sail diagram shows boats sailing at all different angles to the wind in the sail zone.

Why is the no-sail zone 90 degrees?

The size of the no-sail zone is slightly different for each boat. Some racing boats with very efficient sails and keels can sail as close as 35 degrees to the wind. For them, the no-sail zone is around 70 degrees wide (the angle from close-hauled on one side of the zone to close-hauled on the other). The size of the no-sail zone is also affected by the wind strength. In very light air, all boats go slower, and the "foils" (the keel, rudder, and sails) are less efficient, so you sail a wider angle to the wind in light air than you do in stronger winds.

To sail fast, trim the sails to the proper angle to the wind. As you can see in Figure 5-1, the sails are trimmed differently for the various points of sail. The sails are pulled in tight when a boat is sailing close-hauled and let out all the way when on a run. When you're reaching, the in-between point of sail, the sails are trimmed in-between. Makes sense, huh?

Reaching for the gusto

Reaching is a catchall phrase for all points of sail between close-hauled and running. Because it spans such a large range of wind angles, reaching is the easiest place to start sailing. Reaching is also the fastest point of sail and is, therefore, the most fun.

For your first time on a reach, steer the boat so that the wind is coming roughly 90 degrees across the boat and trim your sails in until they just stop flapping. Try steering the boat to the right and left a little bit, to get the feel of how it responds to the tiller or wheel.

If you're reaching on a heading 90 degrees to the wind direction, you're on a *beam reach*. A reach at any heading between 90 degrees and close-hauled is called a *close reach*. If you're reaching at a wider angle to the wind (an angle greater than 90 degrees), you're on a *broad reach*. The expression *broad-reaching through life* applies to happy-go-lucky people who never have to worry about getting upwind.

On a reach, the sails are pulled in just to the point where they're no longer luffing, as shown in Figure 5-3. Although they still look full if you trim them farther, you give up valuable power when you overtrim the sails.

An important rule for sail trim is *when in doubt, ease it out!* Check the trim of your sails by *easing* (letting out) their respective sheets slightly. If they begin to luff, you were set perfectly, so pull your sails back in to where they were. If they stay full, you were overtrimmed. Check the trim in this manner periodically.

Figure 5-3:
Reaching
sail trim:
Pull your
sails in just
until they
stop luffing.

Sailing on the edge: close-hauled

The key to sailing upwind is steering a course just on the edge of the no-sail zone, as physically close to the wind as possible — at about 10:30 or 1:30 on the clock face, depending on which side you're sailing on. Because the wind is never perfectly steady, continuous attention and subtle steering adjustments are required to stay right on the edge. When sailing close-hauled, your sails are trimmed in very tight, as shown in Figure 5-4. When they begin to luff, you can't trim them in any more, so you must turn (with the rudder) away from the wind just a tiny bit until the sails stop luffing.

When your sails are full, try to turn the boat a little bit toward the wind to see whether you can sail closer to the wind without luffing the sails. See, it really is like sailing on the edge!

Sailing upwind is a modern feat. Columbus sailed across the ocean blue by letting the sails on his square-rigger act like a parachute and push the boat along on a broad-reaching or running course. But your boat can sail upwind by efficiently harnessing the lift generated by the sail and the keel or centerboard. Therefore, you can sail much closer to the wind than Columbus ever could. For more on how this lift stuff works, see Chapter 1.

Figure 5-4:
Sailing close-hauled with sails trimmed in tight.

Running with the wind

Sailing with the wind behind you (going the same direction as the wind is blowing) is called *running* (or sailing *downwind*). Sailing with the wind at your back is great — the boat doesn't heel, and, because your forward motion reduces the wind blowing across the deck and no spray comes on board, you're warmer. Naturally, you'd like to sail on a run all the time. But unless you're going on a one-way trip, you must, at some point, pay the price by sailing back upwind.

On a run, you need to let the sails all the way out — 90 degrees to the wind. The sails act like a big barn door rather than an airfoil, so you can't find the proper trim by overeasing the sail until it luffs. The wind is simply pushing the boat along.

You've probably seen pictures of sailboats with big, colorful, balloonlike sails. These specialty downwind sails are called *spinnakers,* and they help you go even faster by catching more wind. You find out how to sail with a spinnaker in Chapter 8.

If your boat has a jib, you may find that it doesn't want to fill when you're on a run because it's in the direct wind shadow of the mainsail. You can, however, get some extra horsepower by *winging* the jib to get it out of that shadow. Simply pull the weather side jib sheet around until the sail fills on the side of the mast opposite the mainsail. Then cleat the jib sheet so that the sail is set approximately 90 degrees to the wind, as shown in Figure 5-5. Running is the only time when your mainsail and jib can set on opposite sides.

Figure 5-5:
Winging the jib can give you some extra speed when running.

Basic Sailing Terms

You need to be familiar with some basic sailing terminology before getting into sailing maneuvers. The following section covers *port* and *starboard, windward* and *leeward,* and *heading up* and *bearing away.*

Port and starboard tack

Port is left and *starboard* is right (when you're standing on a boat facing the bow). The easiest way to keep these new terms straight is to remember that both *left* and *port* are shorter than *right* and *starboard:* They both have four letters. These nautical words for left and right are optional much of the time, because their land-based cousins are equally clear, but using them is important when you're describing which *tack* a boat is on.

When sailing, a boat is always either on *port tack* or *starboard tack.* Like almost everything else pertaining to sailing, the determining factor is the wind. When you're sailing with the wind coming over the left side of your boat first, you're on port tack. When the wind is coming over the boat's right side first, you're on starboard tack. Whether you're close-hauled, reaching, or running doesn't matter; the determining factor is which side of the boat the wind is hitting first.

Windward and leeward

The left side of your boat is always the port side, but which is the *windward* and which is the *leeward* side changes based on the angle of the wind to your boat. You need to know which way the wind is coming from. The wind always hits the windward side of the boat first. The leeward side, then, is the other side of the boat. You can remember *leeward* because the word comes from *in the lee,* which means "out of the wind." The wind pushes your sails onto the leeward side. If your sails are in the center, then they're luffing and you're *in irons.* (See "Ironing out those irons," later in this chapter.)

Except when you're winging out the jib on a run, you always set your sails on the leeward side. If you get confused about which side is windward and which is leeward, simply let the jib or mainsail luff so that the sail flaps like a flag. Whichever side the sail is flapping toward is the leeward side, as shown in Figure 5-6.

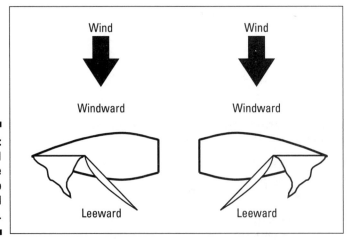

Figure 5-6:
The wind pushes the sails onto the leeward side.

Heading up and bearing away

The two phrases *heading up* and *bearing away* help you when you're steering the boat. Their definitions are also relative to the wind direction. When you make a turn toward the wind, you're *heading up*. When you're steering with a tiller (and sitting in the proper position — on the windward side, facing the sails, as we say in Chapter 4), you push the tiller away from you to head up.

The term *bearing away* is more common than *heading down* or *bearing off,* but they all mean a turn of the boat away from the wind direction. You pull the tiller toward you to bear away — assuming that you're sitting in the proper position. If you were to sail in a complete circle, you would, by definition, be bearing away half the time and heading up half the time. Figure 5-7 shows both heading up and bearing away.

Figure 5-7: Push the tiller away from you to head up; pull it toward you to bear away.

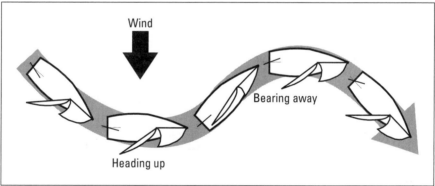

Basic Sailing Maneuvers

Now we want to introduce the basic maneuvers of *tacking* (changing tacks by turning the boat from one side of the no-sail zone to the other) and *jibing* (changing tacks by turning the boat away from the wind until the wind blows on the opposite side). Imagine that you're sailing along on a nice beam reach, but a huge rock looms in front of your bow. You can avoid this obstruction by either tacking or jibing.

We also cover the two most common mistakes when tacking and jibing: getting *in irons* (getting stuck pointing into the wind) and sailing *by the lee* (sailing on a run with the boom on the wrong side of the boat), which is a precursor to the dreaded accidental jibe.

A tack, to tack, on a tack, tic-tack-toe

The word *tack* has as many meanings in sailing as the word *luff*. The *tack* of the sail is its bottom front corner. The noun *tack* also refers to the boat's heading in relation to the wind (that is, on *starboard* or *port tack*). *Tacking* is the act of changing tacks by turning through the wind, entering the no-sail zone from one side and exiting the other.

Tacking: turning toward the wind

Earlier in this chapter, we point out that you can use a zigzag route to reach an upwind destination. First, you sail on a close-hauled course on one tack (either starboard or port), and then you *tack* (turn the boat through the no-sail zone) and sail a close-hauled course on the other tack. This maneuver of turning the boat through the dreaded no-sail zone, or "through the wind," is called *tacking,* and it results in your changing tacks (from starboard to port or vice versa).

To get to a point upwind, you can either tack once (assuming that the harbor is wide enough) or you can tack many times. Refer to Figure 5-2 to see examples.

Here are the steps to tacking:

1. **Prepare your crew by calling out "Ready to tack!"**

   Make sure that your crew is ready and in their positions.

2. **Call out "Tacking!" and begin turning the boat toward the wind (heading up), as in the top photo in Figure 5-8.**

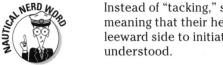

   Instead of "tacking," some sailors use the term *helm's alee* or *hard alee,* meaning that their helm (the rudder) has been put hard over to the leeward side to initiate the turn. Any hail will do, as long as it's understood.

   As you begin to turn, the sail begins to luff wildly. This step is when most beginners have problems, because if you stop turning at this point, you get stuck in the no-sail zone.

   Don't forget to duck your head as the boom swings across.

3. **Release the old jib sheet and trim the new one as the boat rotates through the no-sail zone.**

   Your crew can omit this step if you don't have a jib.

A

B

C

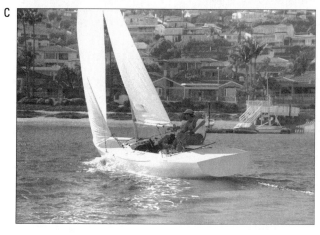

Figure 5-8:
The steps to
tacking.

4. Switch sides (see the middle photo of Figure 5-8).

You (and your crew if necessary) switch sides in order to retain visibility and to get your weight to the new windward side. There is no right time to switch sides, but you may find moving across easiest as the boat turns through the no-sail zone — especially on a dinghy where your weight is needed as ballast when the sails fill on the new close-hauled course.

5. Keep turning the boat until you exit the no-sail zone.

Slow down your turn as the sails begin to fill on the new side. When you're safely out of the no-sail zone, begin steering straight.

6. Check the trim of the sails on the new tack (see the bottom photo of Figure 5-8).

The wind is now blowing across the "other" side of the boat. Congratulations! You have successfully changed tacks. As you settle in on a close-hauled course and confirm the proper trim of your sails, you may want to cleat the sheets if they're pulling so hard that holding them is uncomfortable.

When tacking, turning all the way through the no-sail zone is important. As the boat turns and the sails flap, your boat is losing momentum. Dally too long in this zone, and you risk losing headway and getting stuck *in irons,* because the rudder works to turn the boat only when the boat is moving. So make sure that you keep turning until the boat is turned far enough on the other tack that you can trim the sails in without any luffing and start accelerating. The entire process should take about five seconds on a small keelboat.

Ironing out those irons

The most common mistake beginners make when trying to tack is to get the boat stuck dead in the water with no maneuverability. Just like on a car, the steering wheel or tiller has no effect if your boat isn't moving. Being stuck *head-to-wind* in the no-sail zone is called being "in irons." (There must be some interesting reason, going back to the days of the square riggers, why this situation is called "in irons," but that's a story for another day.) You get in irons when you don't turn the boat all the way through the no-sail zone during a tack or when you try to sail too close to the wind. (Sailing too close to the no-sail zone is called *pinching;* we cover pinching in Chapter 8.)

To get out of irons and moving again on a boat without a jib, follow these steps:

1. Uncleat or release the mainsheet.

2. **Push the tiller (or turn the wheel) to one side.**

   Keep the helm hard over until the boat backs away to a close-reaching position. Basically, you're doing the sailing equivalent of a three-point turn. To speed up the process, you can push on the boom to help the boat go backward faster.

3. **Trim the sails and steer straight (don't pinch!).**

   You're off!

Sounds easy, right? But beginning sailors tend to steer back and forth as they go backward, remaining stuck in irons. Just leave the helm hard over to one side or the other.

If your boat has a jib, you can use an easier method of escaping from the clutches of the no-sail zone.

1. **Pull the jib sheet taut on one side.**

   Either side works equally well. The sail *backs* (fills backward) and pushes the bow in the direction opposite the side the jib is trimmed on.

2. **Keep your mainsheet loose so that the main doesn't fill until the boat rotates around and is pointed on a reaching course.**

   Keep the tiller (or wheel) hard over on the side opposite the jib.

3. **Release the jib sheet and trim it in on the "proper" side as the boat accelerates.**

I can remember the first time I ever soloed a sailboat, when I was about 13 years old. I was halfway out into the harbor when it happened — I got caught in irons. Back then, I had no idea what was going on, except for the obvious fact that the boat wasn't moving at all. My sailing instructor came up to me in a motorboat and said, "Ya know you're doing something wrong," which was, of course, patently obvious. Only later did I realize that I had been caught in irons. You can't avoid getting caught in irons as a beginning sailor, so be prepared for when it happens!

Jibing: turning away from the wind

The other method of changing tacks (changing your direction so that the wind is blowing over the other side of the boat) is to turn away from the wind and *jibe*. Tacking is easier and safer than jibing, especially in strong winds. But jibing is an important maneuver, especially when you're running to a downwind destination in light or moderate wind and you just need to change your heading slightly.

In some sailing books, *jibing* is spelled *gybing,* the British style. We stick with *jibing* (*ji* pronounced as in *giant*).

Because the downwind side of the points of sail diagram doesn't have a no-sail zone, jibing should be easier than tacking, and, in some ways, jibing *is* easier, because you need to change course by only a few degrees, rather than the 90 degrees required when tacking. However, jibing is inherently more dangerous than tacking because of the force with which the boom swings across the cockpit. Keep in mind that, by definition, you're on a run when you jibe, so the sails are eased all the way out. Therefore, that boom has a long way to travel across the boat.

Here are the steps to jibing, as shown in Figure 5-9:

1. **Make sure that you're sailing nearly dead downwind on a run.**

   You can also start on a reach, but doing so requires a bigger turn, which is harder.

2. **Prepare your crew for the jibe by calling out "Ready to jibe!"**

   Make sure that your crew is in position. Reminding them to duck never hurts.

3. **Call out "Jibing!" and start turning the boat away from the wind (bearing away).**

   The traditional term is "Jibe-ho."

   Don't turn too fast — there's no need for speed because there's no equivalent to being stuck in irons on this side of the points of sail diagram.

4. **As you pass through *dead downwind,* pull the mainsheet so that the boom comes in and then gently ease the sheet out on the new side.**

   As you turn and the wind shifts from one side of the boat to the other, the wind wants to push the mainsail to the other side with tremendous force. If you don't pull the boom across in a controlled manner during a jibe, at some point it will come flying across, taking with it everything in its path — so a jibe is an especially good time to keep your head low.

5. **Stop turning and steer straight as you trim the sails on the new jibe.**

6. **Helmsman and crew change sides.**

   Like in a tacking maneuver, this step can be performed whenever you're most comfortable. On a dinghy, where your weight helps provide ballast, you want to switch sides as the boom flies across overhead or immediately afterward. Then, you're done!

A

B

C

D

Figure 5-9:
The steps to
jibing.

Given the force with which the boom can swing across, you need to make sure that your crew is ready for the maneuver. On bigger boats with several crew members, having a person other than the skipper pull in the mainsheet is safer because of the amount of line to pull in and then release after the boom crosses the boat. (Make sure that crew members keep their feet out of all that mainsheet line.) When everyone is ready, start the maneuver by saying "Jibing" and turn the boat. Feel free to add "Boom coming across" or "Duck" if you see that someone is in danger of getting hit by the boom.

Unlike a tack, where you have to keep turning the boat so that you don't get stuck head-to-wind, you may not need to turn the boat at all to jibe if you're already heading straight downwind. Just pull (or have your crew pull) the main to the other side.

In strong winds, pulling the boom to the other side of the boat in a jibe can be a tough job. In these conditions, you may choose to change tacks without jibing. Instead, just turn toward the wind, tack around, and then head down to your new course.

Equipment is easily broken when jibing in strong winds because of the sudden load on the mainsail after it swings across. On the big America's Cup-class boats, we always tacked instead of jibing before the race whenever it was windy to minimize the risk of breaking our expensive carbon-fiber battens.

Avoiding jibing by mistake

An accidental jibe (when the wind pushes the boom across unexpectedly) can be dangerous because the boom comes flying across with tremendous force and can cause severe injury to any body parts in its path.

Jibing by mistake occurs when you sail *by the lee* — sailing on a run with the wind coming across the same side of the boat as the boom is on (see Figure 5-10). Sailing by the lee only occurs when the wind is coming from behind, so you should be vigilant to it anytime you're broad reaching or running. The accident usually occurs when the helmsman loses concentration and inadvertently turns the boat away from the wind too far. Sailing by the lee can also occur if the wind shifts direction when you're steering straight.

Sailing by the lee can be very dangerous, especially in stronger winds, because if the wind pushes on the "back" side of the mainsail, it forces the boom across the deck very suddenly. You can usually sail 5 or 10 degrees by the lee (compared to dead downwind) without having the boom fly across. But, depending on the setting of your mainsail, as you sail farther and farther away from dead downwind on the "wrong" heading, at some point that wind is going to send your mainsail and boom whizzing across via special delivery.

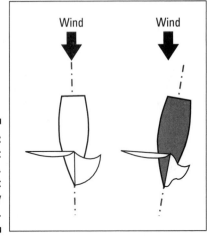

Figure 5-10:
Left:
Running.
Right:
Sailing by
the lee.

You can prevent sailing by the lee by watching your sails and the wind direction. Some boats have an arrowlike wind indicator at the top of the mast that can help. Also watch the battens; if they're trying to flip over, you're in a trouble zone.

Another good indicator that you're close to this trouble zone is when your jib collapses because it's totally blocked by the main. Keep asking yourself, "Where is the wind coming from now?" If the wind is coming dead behind you, head up a little onto a broad reach (on the proper tack) to avoid the embarrassment and potential danger of an accidental jibe.

If the boom does start to come over unexpectedly, be sure to yell "Duck" as loud as you can to warn your crew to DUCK!

One of the great collegiate sailing coaches was longtime Tufts University sailing coach Joe Duplin. Joe was a world-renowned racer, famous for his creativity on the race course and his New England accent but not for his patience with teaching beginning sailing to inexperienced pupils. Joe would sum up all the information in the last two chapters in two sentences. Pointing to the tiller, he would say, "This is the steering wheel; pull it this way to turn right and this way to turn left." Then, grabbing the mainsheet rope, Joe would finish the lesson by saying, "This is the accelerator; to speed up, pull it in; to slow down, let it out!"

What to say to your crew

As you can probably guess, sailors have many terms for the person who steers the boat — *skipper, captain,* and *helmsman* are three. The one name you don't want to be called is "Captain Bligh" — as in Captain Bligh from *Mutiny on the Bounty.*

An interesting psychological phenomenon can happen when a seemingly normal person gets behind the wheel or tiller of a sailboat — he or she can turn into a power-hungry maniac, screaming orders and treating everyone on board like scum. If you don't want a mutiny on board your boat, make sure that you treat your crew the way you'd want to be treated.

"Tacking!" and "jibing!" are important commands, but the "Ready to tack/jibe!" command is equally important. Your crew needs some time (30 seconds or so) to get in position before you start the turn. If it's windy, you may have to yell (nicely) to get them to hear you.

Planning your maneuvers in advance to give your crew time to get ready is a skipper's responsibility. For safety sake, the skipper should always look to make sure that everyone is prepared and in a safe spot *before* turning the boat. If someone gets hit by the boom, most often the skipper is at fault.

Chapter 6

Basic Seamanship and Launching Your Boat

* *

In This Chapter

▶ Pulling in lines

▶ Using winches and cleats

▶ Sailing away and returning to docks and moorings

▶ Leaving a boat secure

▶ Launching a boat

▶ Putting up a mast

* *

It was with a happy heart that the good Odysseus spread his sail to catch the wind and used his seamanship to keep his boat straight with the steering-oar.

— Homer

*W*ebster's Dictionary defines seamanship as "the art or skill of handling, working, and navigating a ship." This definition is purposefully vague regarding what size boat or what kind of wind and sea conditions — the presumption is that to be a good seaman, you must be able to handle your boat in all conditions. To be a responsible sailor, you must also have a healthy respect for the power of the wind and sea.

In this chapter, we cover some basic seamanship skills. For example, you find out how to pull in a sail safely so that a sudden gust of wind doesn't overpower you and pull the rope from your hands. We also discuss how to leave and return to the dock or mooring and cover the variety of ways to get your boat from land to sea.

Pulling In Lines

Some lines on sailboats are lightly loaded, and adjusting them is easy. But others carry tremendous load, especially in strong winds. Trying to pull these lines can result in strained muscles or burned hands. Consider the forces on a line before uncleating it and trying to hold it. "Plucking" the line like a guitar string gives you an indication of the load on it. If the line feels like a steel rod and makes a note like a high G, then don't try to pull it.

To help use all your strength, make sure that you're in the correct position to pull. You may need to sit down across from the line with your feet pushing against some solid object. Fully extend your arms and grab the line with both hands for maximum pulling power, as shown in Figure 6-1.

Figure 6-1:
Aine
McLean
demonstrates
good body
position for
maximum
pulling
power.

If you can't pull the line even when you're in the correct position, don't give up. Sailors of all ages and sizes can operate any boat because various combinations of pulleys and winches provide the mechanical advantage to enable a wimp to do the work of a hulk.

Using blocks

Mainsheets and most of the other lines on a sailboat run through *blocks* (pulleys). Some blocks just change the direction that the line travels, but when several blocks are used in combination — block-and-tackle systems — they make the line easier to pull. The amount of extra lifting power, called *purchase,* depends on the number of pulleys used and the arrangement. Without delving into the mechanics involved, a *four-part* mainsheet system (also referred to as a *4:1* system) requires only one-fourth the effort to pull in the sail as compared to a single rope hanging from the boom (a 1:1 system). The disadvantage is that you have to pull in four times as much line to bring in the sail.

A *cascading* arrangement multiplies the benefits, so a 2:1 system used with a 4:1 system provides an 8:1 mechanical advantage, as shown in Figure 6-2. We talk about the care and selection of blocks in Chapter 19. No matter what style, purchase systems all have the same purpose: to optimize the mechanical advantage so that the average person can pull the line and sail the boat easily.

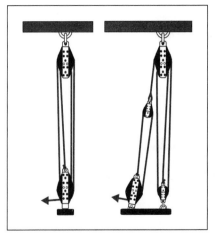

Figure 6-2:
A 4:1 purchase system (left) can be made into an 8:1 cascading system by adding a 2:1 system (right).

Regardless of the block-and-tackle system you use, you need to keep the line from slipping when you have the sail trimmed where you want it. To prevent slipping, you have two options: Hold on to it, or cleat it.

Ratchet blocks

Some blocks *ratchet,* which means that they turn freely when you pull the line but don't turn at all in the other direction. This extra friction makes the line easier to hold. Ratchet blocks are common on the mainsheets and jib sheets of smaller keelboats and dinghies. They usually have a button or lever to turn the ratchet-action off and let the block turn freely in both directions, which is useful in light wind. The extra holding power of a ratchet block makes hanging onto the mainsheet on a windy day much easier.

Cleats

Face it — most sailboats have more control lines than you have hands. Although certain creative sailors have been known to use their mouths to hold a rope or two (not recommended by the American Dental Association), most control lines have some sort of cleat to hold them.

Horn cleats and jammers (see the section on hoisting sails in Chapter 4) are very secure cleats and are best for lines such as halyards that you don't adjust often. Two other types of cleats, Clamcleats and cam cleats (shown in Figure 6-3), are easy to uncleat, which makes them well suited for mainsheets, jib sheets, and other lines that you need to adjust regularly.

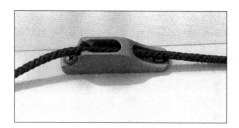

Figure 6-3: Clamcleat (top) and cam cleat (bottom).

A *Clamcleat* has grooves that make it look like the two sides of a clam shell. These grooves help hold a line that's under load. A *cam cleat* has two moveable, notched jaws that use spring action to open and to grasp the line. To uncleat the line, you pull up and toward yourself (sometimes forcefully) to lift it out of the jaws. The best thing about these two cleats is that they're easy to use.

If your boat uses cam cleats or Clamcleats, make sure that the line is all the way down in the jaws, so that it stays securely cleated.

Using winches

Remember the old Charlton Heston movies in which sweaty, ragged sailors pulled in ropes, grunting "Heave, ho," like an ancient tug of war, while a barbaric foreman cracked a whip? Nowadays, you can use a *winch* to pull in that line (and leave your whip at home). Winches, another way to provide mechanical advantage to adjust ropes under load, are used mainly on bigger boats, where loads on lines can get really heavy.

Winches use a system of gears inside a round cylinder called a *drum* to give you the necessary pulling power. Always wrap the line clockwise around the drum, using more wraps as the load on the line increases. Put as many wraps around the drum as you need — the wraps provide the friction so that you can hold a heavily loaded line in your hand.

You turn the drum with a removable metal handle called a *winch handle.* This process is called *grinding* (and the folks who do it on big racing boats are called *grinders*).

Grinding

While one person grinds, the other person pulls in (or *tails*) the line that feeds off the drum. One person can do both jobs, but doing so is less efficient. Some winches are *self-tailing,* meaning that they have notches that grip the line and hold it in place so that one person can grind without needing anyone to pull the rope. However, grinding is often a two-person process, as shown in Figure 6-4.

Figure 6-4:
Jeff
Johnson
grinding a
winch with
Peter
tailing.

Here are some tips to grinding and tailing properly:

✔ **Choose the right speed.** Many winches have two or more speeds or gears. You change gears by changing the direction you turn the handle, so you can shift speeds if the grinding gets harder.

✔ **Grind in a full circle, using two hands if necessary.** If you can't complete a circle, turn as far as you can and then ratchet the winch handle back to your starting point.

You're stronger pulling than pushing.

✔ **If you feel the rope slipping, then either you aren't pulling hard enough or you need to add a wrap on the drum.** For light loads, only one or two wraps are usually needed; for heavier loads, four wraps are usually enough. Ideally, you add just enough wraps just before the line gets loaded up, because too many wraps may cause a tangle called an *override.* In the next section, we discuss adding a wrap to a loaded winch and avoiding overrides.

✔ **Stand in a comfortable position over the winch.** You can grind a winch sitting beside it (and some winches are placed where standing over them is impractical), but you won't be able to grind as hard.

✔ **When you're not grinding the winch, remove the handle and place it in its holder.** These expensive items have never passed the float test, and having the handle already removed is safer if you must quickly release the rope on the winch.

Adjusting lines safely on a loaded winch

A line under tremendous load can be dangerous to ease or trim. Think first. The last thing you want is to burn your hands as a rope goes whizzing through them. Remove any rings from your fingers, because rings can get caught on a line. Be especially careful with winches when you're wearing gloves. Make sure that your gloves are snug-fitting, because extra fabric can get caught and pinched by the line spooling onto the winch drum.

When you need to add a wrap to a loaded winch, carefully hold the line with both hands. Maintain tension on the line as you take both hands all the way around the winch, turning your hands to keep your fingers from getting caught, as shown in Figure 6-5.

Figure 6-5:
Keep pulling on the line as you use both hands to add a wrap on a highly loaded winch.

To *ease* (let out) a line slowly and safely, hold onto the line with your right hand and put your left hand on the wraps on the winch. Slowly "milk" the line out counterclockwise, a couple of inches at a time, keeping some pressure on the line.

To take all the wraps off a winch quickly (common in a tacking maneuver on bigger boats that use winches for their jib sheets), pull up on the line with a slight rotating motion. Before you take off the wraps, make sure that the long tail of the jib sheet is free to run, not tangled around your foot (or a body part of your crew!).

When releasing a jib sheet on a winch during a tacking maneuver, wait until the load has just eased on the sheet before removing all the wraps on the winch drum. Watch for the jib to begin luffing up front as an indication that the helmsman has begun turning the boat. If you cast all the wraps off the winch drum too early, you risk burning your hands as the highly loaded rope runs out. Wait too late, and the jib fills backward.

At some point, probably when you're already having a bad day, you're going to get an *override* — a misfed line that effectively creates a knot around the winch, shown in Figure 6-6. Overrides can be caused by improper winch placement or by having too many wraps when you pull in a slack line.

Figure 6-6:
An override.

In light air, you may be able to untangle the mess by pulling the rope's end up and around the winch the "wrong" way (counterclockwise). In stronger winds, taking the load off the rope going to the winch and then untangling the mess is usually best.

Making work easy through teamwork

This may be the most valuable sailing tip in this book: You can make pulling in the lines easier through clever driving.

For example, grinding in the jib sheet on a big cruising boat in strong winds can be a real chore. But if the skipper simply heads up slightly toward the wind, the sail begins to luff, and the load decreases. You may even be able to pull in the sheet by hand. Another way to substantially decrease the load on most of the sail control ropes is to turn the boat downwind on a broad reach or run. (Careful — no accidental jibes, please!)

Next time you're faced with a really difficult physical task on a sailboat, ask yourself whether the job can be done more easily by steering the boat at a certain angle. Usually, the answer is yes.

To take the load off the override, rig another line to do the same job. Or you can tie another line to the tangled line (forward of the tangle) with a rolling hitch (see Appendix B) and then tighten the new line so that you have slack in the tangled part. The final option, when danger is imminent or none of the other methods work, is to cut the infringing rope with a knife. Be sure to cut the line near its end (near the clew of the jib on a jib sheet, for example) so that it's still usable (and only a little bit shorter).

Being an Able Seaman

As Murphy's Law suggests, the line that you absolutely have to let out *now* is in a huge knotted mess with every other line, including your shoelaces. A good sailor takes the time and effort to clean up the mess and make the ropes as neat as possible. Keeping lines neat is important from a safety standpoint, too, because being able to let out the mainsheet quickly when a big puff hits can keep you from swimming.

In Chapter 4, we tell you how to put a halyard away so that it's tangle-free when you need to lower the sail. Any line not in use should be coiled so that you can store it. See Chapter 19 on properly storing your lines.

To coil, start at one end and make loops of equal size (usually about 3 feet, or 1 m, in diameter) until you get near the other end. When you have about 5 feet ($1^1/_2$ m) left, make three or four tight loops around the "throat" at one end of the coil and then put the end through the coils, as shown on the left in Figure 6-7, or take the doubled end through the top of the coil and back over the top for an even more secure coil. These ways of finishing off a coil are more secure than the one we describe in Chapter 4.

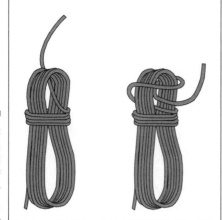

Figure 6-7:
Ropes
coiled and
finished off
securely for
storage.

Someday, you will need to throw a line accurately and far. The key is to start with a well-coiled line. Put a few coils (up to about 15 feet or $4^1/_2$ m) in your throwing hand and hold your other hand (with the rest of the coils) open and pointed at the target so any extra coils can feed out as needed. Then throw (underhand) the coils, aiming slightly above the target. You can see Peter throwing a line in Figure 6-8.

Figure 6-8:
Throwing
a line.

Now that you know some of the tricks of working with lines, you can find out how to get away from and get back to the dock.

Leaving the Mooring or Dock

Untying and getting under way from a dock or *mooring* (a permanently anchored buoy) is called *casting off.* Getting under way can be tricky because you're usually in a confined area with many other boats (not to mention the shore) nearby and because the rudder doesn't provide much control while you're getting the boat going. We strongly encourage you to get some lessons before sailing, but if you don't, try to have an instructor or a knowledgeable friend along on your first few sails to help you get away from the dock or mooring.

Using the iron headsail (the engine)

If your boat has an engine, you can motor away and put the sails up after you're in open water. But knowing how to sail away from a dock or mooring (and back again) under sail is a good idea, in case your engine decides not to cooperate some day.

The biggest concern when using the engine (besides polluting the environment) is keeping lines from getting tangled in the propeller. We discuss that problem and other mishaps in Chapter 13. Make sure that no loose lines are dangling off the side of the boat, and always let go of the *mooring line* (the line permanently attached to a mooring buoy) on the windward side so that you don't run over it as the boat sideslips while building speed.

Leaving the mooring under sail

Leaving a mooring is usually easier than leaving a dock because the boat is already in relatively open water. But getting the boat turned to an angle out of the no-sail zone is trickier. (We're assuming that your boat is tied by the bow and is pointed into the wind.) Here are the steps to sailing away from a mooring buoy, as shown in Figure 6-9.

1. **Before casting off a dock or mooring, plan your best escape route.**

   Look for a course that enables you to sail away on a reach, which gets you up to speed quickly. Make sure the whole crew knows the plan.

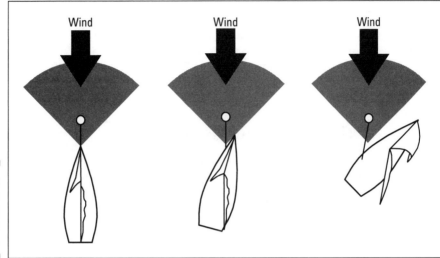

Figure 6-9:
Getting the
boat sailing
from a
mooring.

2. **The forward crew unties the mooring line but continues to hold it.**

   On bigger boats and in strong winds or current, one person won't have the strength to win the tug of war on the mooring line. In this case, keep one full wrap of the line around the base of the horn cleat on the bow (if available) to add friction and to make it possible to hold on yet be ready to cast off quickly.

3. **With the main luffing, back the jib.**

   Trim the jib on the side opposite the direction that you intend to sail so that the jib *backwinds* (fills with wind backward) and pushes the bow away from the no-sail zone. Make sure that the mainsheet has plenty of slack so that the main can fully luff and won't fill. See Chapter 5 on getting your boat out of irons — it's the same technique.

4. **Walk the mooring line back along the windward side to shoot the boat forward.**

   Have the crew holding the mooring line uncleat it and move toward the stern — on the windward side, so that the line doesn't get caught under the boat. As your crew moves back, your bow is pushed forward, especially on smaller boats, helping you gain speed and control. On bigger boats, holding the bow line is too difficult after it's uncleated, so just give it a good heave away from the boat when the skipper gives the command.

5. **The crew lets go of the mooring and trims in the sails.**

   Off you go!

How do you know which side to back the jib on? Say you want to leave the mooring on starboard tack. When you're sailing on starboard tack, the jib gets trimmed on the leeward (port) side. So to get the boat to *fall off* (exit the no-sail zone into the sail zone) on starboard tack, trim the jib all the way on the starboard side so that it fills with wind on its "back" side and pushes the bow toward a starboard tack course.

Leaving the dock under sail

As you can see in Figure 6-10, the key to easy arrival and departure from docks is to always tie up on the dock's *leeward* side. If you try to leave the windward side of the dock under sail, the boat slips sideways as it gains speed and drags along the dock — not good form! Plus, being tied to the leeward side of the dock is better because the wind pushes the boat away from the dock, minimizing the chance of scratching the hull against the dock.

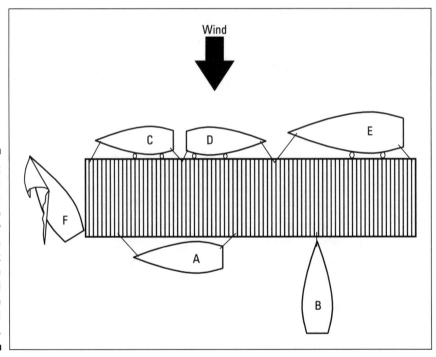

Figure 6-10: Boats A and B are the easiest to sail away from the dock because they're tied on the leeward side.

If you want to depart under sail and your boat isn't tied up on the dock's leeward side, move it. Boats under 25 feet (8 m) long can usually be moved to a better location by pulling them with the dock lines or by holding onto a *shroud* (one of the wires supporting the mast) and pulling. On a bigger boat, you can use the engine and put the sails up in open water. If the dock is crowded, the best spot (at least temporarily) may be tied up head-to-wind off the corner of the dock.

Just like when you leave a mooring, you don't want to let go of the dock until you have the boat turning so that you will be safely out of the no-sail zone. If you have room at a dock, you can begin to turn the boat by pulling in on the bow line and walking the boat along to generate forward motion so that the rudder is effective.

If you have plenty of space, you may be able to gain speed (and thus *steerageway* — the speed needed to steer) by having your crew give a push as they jump on board or by sailing close enough to a nearby boat or dock to push off and get some extra speed.

After you're safely away from the dock, remove any *fenders* (the rubber cushions tied to the side of the boat to keep it from hitting the dock) and store them down below out of the way. Also untie any dock lines, coil them up, and store them out of the way, too.

Getting Back to the Dock or Mooring

Leaving this subject without discussing how to get back to the dock or mooring would be like teaching you to ski and sending you down the mountain without telling you how to stop. In skiing, you can always stop by running into a tree or a big snowbank. This technique works in sailing, too — you can always run the boat aground or into the dock — but considering how expensive insurance is, we want to give you cheaper and less painful alternatives.

The key to docking or mooring is slowing down at a controlled rate before you get there. You slow down by luffing the sails and letting the boat glide to a stop. The trick is knowing when to start luffing so that you keep enough steerageway to reach the dock without having so much speed that the phrase *ramming speed* becomes applicable.

When in doubt, err on the slow side. If you find that you aren't going to reach your destination, you can always accelerate by retrimming your sails. There is a catch: If you slow down so much that the boat no longer steers and if your boat is pointed in the dreaded no-sail zone, you're out of luck and in irons, as we describe in Chapter 5. Getting in irons is a big problem when you're in a confined area, so please, don't go too fast or too slow!

What if you're approaching too fast and can't kill enough speed? The best solution is to turn the boat around and try the approach again. (Nothing like a practice run to help you judge when to begin luffing your sails on the second try!) In fact, a wise sailor on a new boat always does some practice runs out in the open, next to a buoy or some other floating object, to help judge how the boat maneuvers as it decelerates.

Here are some other tricks that you can use to slow the boat:

- ✔ **On smaller boats, you can kill speed by *backing the main*.** Backing the main is like having a huge air brake. To back the main, push the boom toward the wind (the sail fills backward). Don't try this technique unless you're strong enough to control the boom and you know to let it go (and duck) if the boom begins winning the pushing contest.

- ✔ **You can kill speed with the rudder.** If you think you're coming in too fast, make some big S-turns so that the boat has more distance to slow down. Make sure that your crew is ready for this maneuver and is holding on.

Coming back to the mooring

Always make a plan before you attempt to make a landing on any object. In the case of a return to a mooring buoy, make sure that the whole crew knows which mooring you plan to pick up. Designate one person to grab the mooring buoy or its line, depending on the buoy's configuration. That may require a *boat hook,* a pole with a hook on the end, to help extend his or her reach. Other crew should be ready to luff the sails on your command.

1. **Approach the buoy on a close reach and steer at an imaginary point two to three boatlengths directly downwind from the buoy.**

   Adjust this offset distance based upon the coasting/stopping characteristics of your boat. Lighter dinghies slow down very quickly. On heavier boats, the extra momentum makes slowing down harder.

2. **Depending on the wind strength and your boat speed (and other factors, such as current, discussed in Chapter 12), use your best judgment to decide when to luff the sails to begin to kill speed.**

3. **When you're almost directly downwind of the buoy, and if your rate of deceleration appears to be correct, turn in a smooth arc toward the wind and coast up to the mooring pointed directly toward the wind.**

   If you're going too fast, abort the approach and make another try. If you're going too slow, retrim the sails. If you can't see the buoy, have a crew member point at it for you. As the bow reaches the buoy, the boat (ideally) comes to a dead stop.

4. Have the crew attach the boat to the mooring buoy.

Use a strong line and securely attach it to both the buoy and the boat (a cleat or some other strong object on the bow). Make sure that the skipper is informed when the boat is secure.

5. Now you can lower the sails to stop their incessant flapping!

On a boat with main and jib, dropping the jib (and maybe even clearing it away from the foredeck) before making the approach is usually best. Doing so gives the crew more room to work up forward, reduces your sail power, and gives you more visibility. The downside is that without a jib, you have less control and ability to get out of irons, so be very careful to keep steerageway.

Coming back to the dock

Docking under sail is often trickier than sailing up to a mooring because the dock is usually in a more confined space. However, the same basic rules apply:

- ✔ **Approach the leeward side of the dock.**
- ✔ **Approaching slower is better.**
- ✔ **Don't go too slow; if you stop, you lose steerageway.**
- ✔ **Plan your approach so that your crew knows what to expect.**

An ideal situation is a dock with the wind blowing almost parallel along it. Like with the mooring buoy, plan your approach so that the boat has room to coast into position as it decelerates (see Figure 6-11). When the boat is close enough (and going slow enough), have a crew member step from the middle of the boat onto the dock so that you can begin securing the dock line(s). Never yell for someone to jump; let the person who's going to get off judge when the boat is close enough to make his move. In this type of approach, in which the sails are still up, the first line to be secured is the bow line. After the boat is tied up, begin lowering sails and further securing the boat as required.

If you must tie up to the windward side of a dock, sail into a position directly upwind of the dock, lower your sails, and let the wind gently push you down to the dock.

When a boat is approaching a dock, never put any part of your body between the boat and the dock. Repairing a little fiberglass is easier than repairing your body.

Figure 6-11:
Approach the dock with enough room that you can turn up and coast to a stop.

Docking under power

Slower is better when docking — including when docking under power. Having an engine doesn't make the boat as maneuverable as your car. In fact, at low speeds, the rotation of the propeller makes the boat pull, or turn easier, to one side. In open water, practice slowing the boat to see how much this propeller torque turns the boat and in what direction, especially in reverse gear. As with docking under sail, the momentum of the boat, the wind pushing the hull, and other factors such as current also affect your maneuverability. When you've discovered the maneuvering characteristics of your boat under power, the principles of docking remain the same as those outlined in the preceding section.

Always drop the sails (and get those lines out of the water) before docking a sailboat under power! Approach slowly; never rely on reverse to slow the boat down.

Tying Up a Boat: Leaving It Secure

When your sailing day is done and it's time to return to the rigors of your shoreside life, you want to make sure that your boat is happy until you next get an opportunity to visit it. Any boat is happy to hang temporarily from a single bow line, but for more permanent storage, you need several lines.

This section discusses how to tie up your boat securely and safely to a dock. The following principles apply to all boats, but they're most useful when you're securing a larger keelboat alongside a dock:

- ✔ Always check for *chafed* (damaged) parts of the line.

- ✔ Always use *fenders* (rubber cushions) between the boat and the dock or pilings.

- ✔ Always use spring lines — they're Peter's favorite dock lines.

- ✔ Docking line must be amply strong and thick — at least $^3/_8$ of an inch (1 cm) for a 20-foot (6-m) boat. Nylon line works well.

- ✔ Don't pull the stern and bow lines too tight. Ideally, the boat lies just off the dock so that it doesn't rub.

- ✔ Tie bow and stern lines at about a 45-degree angle away from the boat to hold it secure.

Spring lines

Spring lines are incredibly effective. Tied from the middle of the boat, they prevent the boat from surging forward or backward and keep it securely positioned so that the few fenders in the middle of the boat are always in the right place. Figure 6-12 shows a boat tied up by 1) bow line, 2) forward spring line, 3) aft spring line, and 4) the stern line. In very rough conditions, you can add additional spring lines and double up all the lines.

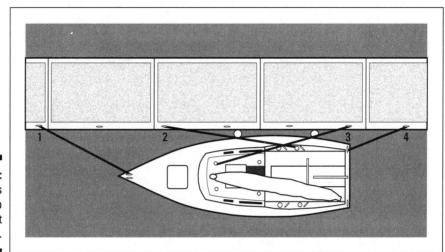

Figure 6-12: Spring lines help keep this boat secure.

Make sure that dock lines are secured at both ends. See Chapter 4 for information on tying off a line on a cleat; if you have to tie off to a piling, use a bowline or clove hitch, as shown in Appendix B.

Watch out for that tide!

As you discover in Chapter 10, most large bodies of water have *tidal flow,* thanks to the moon. When tying up your boat, use some common sense. If your boat is going to float up and down on the tide, avoid tying it to something that doesn't float, such as a piling. If you tie your boat incorrectly to a piling or fixed dock at high tide, you may come back to find your boat suspended out of the water at low tide.

If you must leave your boat tied up to a fixed piling or dock in tidal waters, add more angle (and, therefore, more length) to all your dock lines by tying them farther along the dock. Turn to Chapter 9 for more tips on other docking scenarios.

Getting Your Boat into the Water

As we mention in Chapter 4, when you first begin to sail, you probably don't have to worry about launching the boat — the school or the boat's owner more than likely has taken care of that. At some point, however, you may find yourself ready to sail but with a boat that is high and dry. This section goes over how to launch both keelboats and dinghies in the situations you're mostly likely to find yourself in.

Launching a trailerable sailboat

Getting your boat into the water can be an involved process — one that sometimes even includes putting up the mast. Many small keelboats (under 25 feet or 8 m long) and dinghies are *drysailed* — that is, they're stored on dry land. Storing a boat on dry land means less maintenance (no barnacles or weeds to scrape off the bottom) and no docking fees. Storing your boat on a trailer makes sailing in many different places quite easy. Keep in mind that objects wider than 8$\frac{1}{2}$ feet may require extra permits to trailer on highways. For this reason, most trailerable keelboats are smaller than 30 feet (9 m).

Two common methods of launching a keelboat or large dinghy are by using a *hoist* (crane) or with a trailer off a ramp.

Whether you're launching from a trailer or a dolly, or carrying a smaller boat by hand, you must be aware of any power lines after you put up the mast on land. Fortunately, most yacht clubs, launching areas, and marinas have removed overhead power lines, but we want you to be vigilant.

Most boats stored on trailers have drain plugs. Leaving this plug out keeps rainwater from collecting in it. But more than a few sailing trips have been ruined by neglecting to put the plug back in before launching, so be sure to check the plug — and note that some boats have several plugs!

Using a hoist or crane

Launching a boat by using a hoist or crane is easy — as long as you have someone to help, the proper lifting bridle, and a boat that weighs less than the maximum allowable weight for the crane. Here are the general steps to using a hoist to launch your boat:

1. **Move the boat so that it's underneath the crane.**

   Many cranes have an arc painted on the ground to help guide you in placing your boat. Place the boat so the crane pulls the boat straight up and off the trailer. On boats with a *backstay* (a wire extending from the top of the mast to the back of the boat), you may have to swing the crane's arm over the boat as it's wheeled into place (see Figure 6-13).

2. **Attach the *lifting bridle* — the wire or rope sling arrangement that balances and lifts the boat.**

   Check the lifting bridle (or other lifting device) and attachment points for wear.

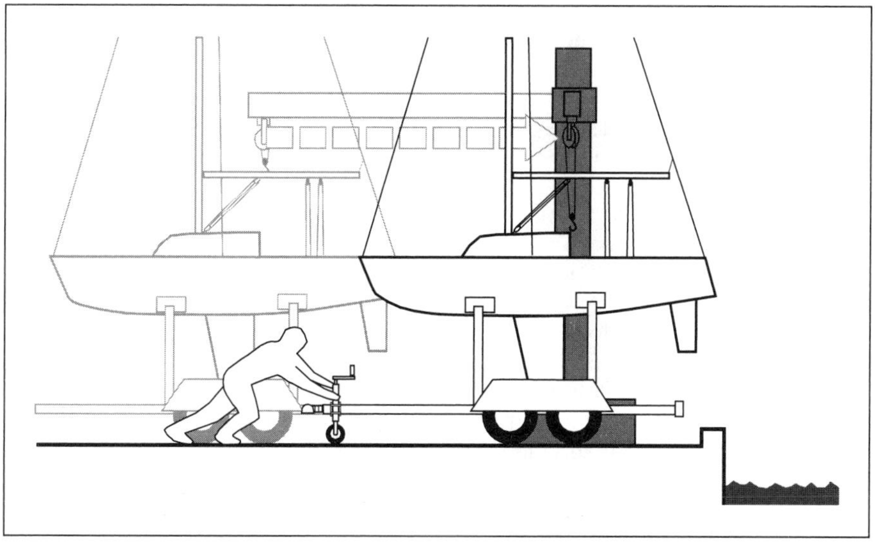

Figure 6-13:
As the trailer is pushed under the crane, swing the crane's arm past the backstay.

3. **Attach the bow and stern lines so that the boat can be rotated into position as it is lowered into the water.**

   Never let anyone stand or walk underneath a boat on a hoist.

4. **Have one person operate the hoist and one hold the lines.**

5. **Begin lifting, making sure that the mast and shrouds are clear of the crane's arm.**

   Try to keep the boat perpendicular to the arm as you swing the boat out over the water and begin lowering.

   Don't try to put your boat in alone; make sure that you have a buddy.

6. **When the boat is in the water, one person can unhook the lifting bridle while the other secures the bow line.**

You still have a few chores to finish up:

   ✔ **Before rigging, move the boat and trailer away so that others can use the crane.**

   ✔ **Swing the arm back over shoreside.**

Because the greasy chain or cable from the hoist can mess up your sails (and your hands and anything else), always rig the sails after the boat is in the water and the crane is long gone.

Launching from a trailer off a ramp

Our two main rules for successfully launching off a ramp are

   ✔ **Accept that you're going to get your feet wet.**

   ✔ **Plan ahead.** Stop, get out of your car, and check out the ramp before you back the trailer down. Look at its angle, check for a big drop-off at the end, and plan where you want to position your trailer. Then look at the dock space. When the boat is launched, where are you going to tie up so that you can hoist the sails? How are you going to get to that dock?

When you have a good plan in mind, get in your car and go for it. Backing up a car and trailer is sort of like patting your head and rubbing your stomach at the same time — it can be difficult. Trailers are very well-behaved beasts when going forward, but going backward is another story. The most common malady, jackknifing the trailer, is caused by oversteering. If your boat and trailer are light enough for one person to handle, you may want to disconnect the trailer and carefully walk the trailer into the water. But be careful — ramps can be steep and slippery.

Here are the general steps to launch your boat from a trailer on a ramp by using a car:

1. **Put the mast up.**

   See the section "Putting up a mast," later in this chapter.

2. **Position your car and trailer parallel to the ramp.**

   Going backward is much easier when you don't have to turn.

3. **Remove all the various lines and straps used to secure the boat, except for the bow line.**

4. **Go slowly down the ramp and correct any tendency to jackknife by turning the back of your car in the same direction the back of the trailer is turning.**

5. **Back up until the boat is just floating off the trailer, before the wheels (or at least the brakes and wheel bearings) of your car touch the water.**

6. **Make sure that your parking brake is set and then get out of your car to disconnect the boat from the trailer.**

   Saltwater is highly corrosive (as you know from when salt is put on the roads after a snowstorm), and even in freshwater, cars can't swim, so don't put your car in the water.

   If the bottom of the ramp has slimy algae, be careful! This stuff is as slippery as ice.

7. **When the boat is afloat, unhook or untie the bow from the trailer.**

   This is the part where you're going to get your feet (and maybe your legs) wet. If a dock is nearby, you may be able to take the bow line, walk around to the dock, and pull the boat to you while staying dry, but don't count on it.

   If no dock is available, you may want to consider rigging the sails (but not hoisting them) before you launch, because you probably have to climb in the boat from the water, similar to when launching from a beach, which is described later in this chapter.

8. **After your boat is launched and you've tied it to the dock, go back and move your car and trailer.**

Launching without a trailer

Dinghies are commonly drysailed, and because most are lighter than keelboats, you can often launch one off a dock or ramp or even off a beach without the need of a hoist or a trailer.

Small dinghies can be transported on roof racks on top of your car. To get the boat down without damaging it, find several friends and follow these steps, shown in Figure 6-14.

Figure 6-14:
Get plenty
of help
when lifting
a boat.

1. **Find a *dolly* (lightweight trailer for movement by hand) or padding to put the boat on.**

2. **Find enough people so that lifting the boat is easy.**

3. **Slide/lift the boat off the roof and lower it down, carefully setting the edge of the boat (at its widest point) on the padding.**

   Always make sure to set your boat on padding to protect the hull.

4. **With most of the weight supported on that edge, flip the boat over in the air so that it's right-side-up.**

5. **Lift and set the boat on the dolly or padded area for rigging.**

   Now, depending on how you're going to launch, you can prepare the boat to go sailing. (See Chapter 4 for more about rigging.)

Sliding a dinghy off a dock

Even without a dolly, lightweight dinghies can be launched off the dock — you just need the lifting skills of some friends to get the boat into position at the edge of the dock.

When you have the boat set at the side of dock, get all the gear ready to sail (see Chapter 4) if you haven't already. Lift the boat on each side and slide it into the water (see Figure 6-15). If the dock doesn't have padding at the edge, add some padding to cushion the hull as you slide it in. Then grab the bow line and tie the boat to the dock to further rig it and hoist sails.

Figure 6-15:
Lift on either side of the boat and slide it in.

Any time you must lift a boat, always ask for plenty of help. Bend your legs and keep your back vertical to avoid injury.

If the wind is very light or is blowing from the dock toward the water, you may consider hoisting the sails before you launch, but you usually hoist the sails afterward. Just remember to put the centerboard down when you first get in the boat, or else the boat is very tippy.

Starting from the beach

Launching off a beach is tricky unless the wind and wave conditions are really mild. Ideally, there are no waves, but you do have an *offshore* (wind blowing from shore to water) or *sideshore* (wind blowing parallel to the shore) breeze, so that sailing straight off the beach on a reach is easy.

You need to do a few things before putting the boat in the water:

✔ **Consider hoisting one or both sails while the boat is still on the beach, because hoisting them is difficult after the boat is launched.** Doing this makes carrying the boat into the water harder, however.

✔ **If your boat has a *kick-up* rudder (one that rotates up and out of the water), then rig it in the "kicked-up" position before launching.**

✔ **Rig the boat and store all your gear on board.**

Boats can be rigged in any number of ways, so don't be afraid to ask your instructor or the owner for assistance if you're not sure about any of these points. See Chapter 4 for how to rig a typical boat.

Now you're ready to launch the boat off the beach:

1. **Grab as many people as you can and carry the boat into the water.**

   You can't avoid getting wet here! Keep the bow pointed toward the wind if the sails are hoisted.

2. **When the boat is floating in knee- to waist-deep water, have someone hold the bow while at least one crew member climbs into the boat to prepare it for sailing.**

   The boat is incredibly tippy at this point because you can't put your centerboard down very far until you're in deeper water.

3. **Hoist the sails and lower the rudder (if it's the kick-up variety) at least partway (if the water is very shallow) while someone maintains hold on the boat at the bow.**

4. **Have the last person push the boat off on a reaching course and climb into the boat.**

   You're sailing!

When you're the someone holding onto the boat in the water, keep these safety tips in mind:

- ✔ **Consider wearing shoes — sharp objects may be underwater.**

- ✔ **If the waves are big, try to keep the boat pointed perpendicular to the waves, just like a surfboard going out through the surf.** That way, the waves have less chance of grabbing your boat and throwing it — and you — back on the beach. This task may be difficult if the sails are up.

- ✔ **In waves, never stand between the boat and shore.** Always stand on the seaward side of the boat (although doing so may be difficult if the sails are hoisted).

Unless you're sailing in a place where there are no substantial waves (including the powerboat variety), never leave the boat halfway in the water with the bow pulled up on the beach. Crashing waves can hurt the boat, or it may float away.

Returning to the beach

Coming back to the beach can be even more difficult than launching. Again, you can't avoid getting wet. Here are the basic steps to bringing a sailboat onto the beach:

1. **Luff your sails and kill your speed a long way out and approach the beach slowly, with the sails fully eased.**

2. **If the water is shallow, pull up your rudder and centerboard partway before the approach.**

3. **When you're close to shore, turn the boat head-to-wind and stop.**

4. **Have your crew jump overboard (you should be close enough to shore that they can stand on the bottom) and hold the boat's bow while you drop sails, fully pull up the centerboard, and remove or kick up the rudder.**

5. **Jump in the water and get the dolly or additional people to help carry the boat onto the beach.**

   Dragging the boat on the sand scratches the bottom.

Putting up a mast

Some boats are stored with the mast up. Other boats (usually dinghies) require the crew to *step,* or put up, the mast before every sail. A number of different techniques can be used to step a mast, depending on the boat's equipment. Some masts on bigger dinghies and keelboats are so heavy that they require a crane (or some other special lifting device) to help. If this is your first time stepping the mast, make sure that you have experienced help. On smaller boats (up to about 14 feet or 4 m in length), one person can usually lift the mast up and into position in the boat, but having help never hurts.

We say it again: If you're putting a mast up on land, first take a good look around for overhead power lines.

To get the mast from horizontal to vertical, follow these steps:

1. **Have someone push the tip of the mast upward while the base is secure against your foot or other object.**

2. **When the mast is vertical, lift it into position.**

   You may find that handing the vertical mast to someone sitting in the boat is easier.

   If you get uncomfortable, be sure to ask for help; few sounds are louder than a mast falling over into the parking lot!

3. **When the mast is set into its mast step, you can begin to attach all the standing rigging (*shrouds*, *forestay,* and *backstay).***

   Often, attaching the standing rigging is a two-person job, to make sure that the mast remains vertical during the process (see Figure 6-16).

Figure 6-16:
One person holds the mast while the second person secures the shrouds and forestay.

4. **As you attach the standing rigging, carefully inspect all the fittings that support the mast and make sure that they are secure.**

   Tighten any shackles with pliers and make sure that the fittings are secure. (Check out Chapter 19 on shackles and other rigging gear.)

Some small dinghies have free-standing masts without any standing rigging. On these boats, you may need to slide the sleeve on the luff (front edge of the sail) over the mast before putting it up, as shown in Figure 6-17.

Figure 6-17:
Putting on a Laser sail by sliding the sleeve over the mast.

Chapter 7

Safety: One Hand for the Boat, One Hand for Yourself

There isn't no call to go talking of pushing and pulling. Boats are quite tricky enough for those that sit still without looking further for the cause of trouble.

— J.R.R. Tolkien

*N*ever underestimate the power of Mother Nature! When you sail on the water, you're her guest, and even on the most relaxing of sailing days, you need to be respectful of her capacity for pure brute strength.

Safety on the water comes in many forms and at many levels. On a hot summer day, reapplying sunscreen and remembering to drink enough water may be your primary concerns. If you're out in the open ocean being tossed about by waves that make your boat seem like a toy, however, you're going to push your skills of seamanship to their limits, and the concept of safety is going to take on a very real meaning.

Although we always stress that you should *never* go sailing on a boat or in conditions that exceed your experience and comfort level, you should expect the unexpected any time you head out on the water. Like they say in the Boy Scouts — be prepared. Making sure that you have the requisite skills and equipment to handle whatever happens on your sailboat is the only safe way to approach a day on the water. Having fun when you sail is easy. Being prepared is what this chapter is all about.

Staying on Board

PETER SAYS

If you sail long enough, you're probably going to fall overboard sometime. (We both have!) Not many people know this (including the millions who were watching on TV), but the day we won the 1987 America's Cup, I fell overboard.

A few minutes after we crossed the finish line, our support boat brought aboard about 25 team members and a few coolers of champagne, which made the deck of the *Stars & Stripes* pretty darn crowded. I was up on the bow celebrating and decided to return to my "spot" in the back of the boat and chat with some folks there. Rather than walk on a sea of people gathered on the windward side, I decided to take the express route, down the leeward side. I was making my way aft, holding a rope on the boom for support, when a big wave hit the boat. That made me put more weight on the rope, and *pop* — it came uncleated. The next thing I knew, I was being dragged through the Indian Ocean at 9 knots, holding on to the end of that rope for dear life.

I survived — with only a mild razzing from my teammates, who watched me flail in the water. But I tell you what — the following safety tips for holding on and danger areas to avoid are definitely important. Some of these tips are more applicable for larger keelboats, but no matter what kind of boat you sail, they will come in handy.

Hold on

Rule Number One is *hold on.* The old saying "one hand for the boat, one hand for yourself" is just as true today as in the days of square riggers. You're responsible for your own safety first, and you never know when a wave, a gust of wind, or an unexpected grounding is going to take away your footing.

Here is a basic rule that will hopefully scare you into holding on for (shall we say) dear life. The U.S. Coast Guard calls it the 50-50-50 rule — if you're in 50-degree F (10-degree C) water for 50 minutes, you have a 50 percent chance of survival. You lose body heat quickly in cool water, and as the body cools, its functions shut down. The medical term for loss of body heat is *hypothermia,* and it can occur even in 70-degree F (21-degree C) water. See Appendix A for tips on treating hypothermia.

Here are some tips to help you stay on board:

- ✔ **Be ready for anything.** A boat can get tossed about in any direction, or it can come to an abrupt stop if it runs aground.

- ✔ **Different areas of a boat are safer than others, but sitting down in the cockpit is usually the safest place on deck.**

- ✔ **If you must stand, bend your knees for better balance.** This lowers your center of gravity and lets your legs be shock absorbers.

- ✔ **Many boats have grab rails along the cabin top, and you can hold onto the lifeline with your other hand as you walk forward.**

    Note: Lifelines need regular inspection for rust and wear. Relying on a lifeline can be risky. If the water's really rough, use a solid object inboard of the rail for support.

- ✔ **Never hold on to *running rigging* (lines used to trim sails), whether it's in use or not.** That's the rule Peter broke on *Stars & Stripes*.

- ✔ **Sitting down with your feet braced is the best position to work when out of the cockpit (that is, on the foredeck).** If the water's too rough to walk around, you can crawl or even slide on your bottom to move around safely. And if it's that rough, you definitely should be wearing a safety harness, as we discuss later in this chapter.

- ✔ **Wearing nonskid shoes helps provide traction.** Even with the best shoes, however, decks can be as slippery as ice.

Be aware of danger areas

As you move around the boat, be aware of the danger areas. They include

- ✔ **Anywhere in the plane of the boom when it swings across in a jibe or tack (see Figure 7-1).** This warning includes all the associated rigging, including the boom vang and the mainsheet.

- ✔ **Anywhere outside of the cockpit where you walk or stand.**

- ✔ **At the bow and the stern.** If you must go to these places, hold on tight, because the motion of the boat is accentuated at the ends.

- ✔ **In the path of the jib and jib sheets during a tacking maneuver.** This path runs from the foredeck all the way back on either side to where the jib sheets go through pulleys heading for the cockpit. During a tack (or jibe), when the headsail flaps in the wind, the sailcloth and those ropes are like whips.

- ✔ **In the "slingshot target zone" of pulleys under high load.** If the block were to break loose, it would go flying.

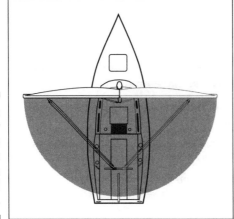

Figure 7-1:
Stay clear
of the
possible
path of the
boom and
its rigging.

✔ **On the leeward side of the boat.** The *leeward,* or downwind, side is especially dangerous if the boat is *heeling* (leaning from the wind); that side is closer to the water, and gravity is pushing you that way.

✔ **Shiny areas, such as varnished wood or plastic hatch covers.** Those areas are probably as slippery as they look. Most bigger boats have a *nonskid* (textured) surface on deck to help keep you vertical, but look where you step. Sails on deck are also very slippery.

Yes, you figured it out — the safest place in most boats is the cockpit (as long as you stay low and watch out for the darn boom). The deck can be dangerous during maneuvers or in rough seas at any time.

Make sure that anyone in these areas is aware of the potential danger and, if the situation warrants, tell them to move and explain the reason why. If you're the helmsman of a boat, make sure that everyone is in a safe position before maneuvering.

A golden rule of sailing is that the captain or skipper is responsible for the safety of his crew. Unlike the Navy, where orders from a superior are unbreakable, the identity of the person in charge isn't always crystal clear while recreational sailing. Everyone on board is expected to look out for his or her own comfort and safety and to communicate any concerns or questions to the skipper and other people on board. Bottom line: No matter what role you have on the boat, you can't leave your common sense on shore.

Staying Safe with Life Jackets

Wearing a life jacket increases your chances for survival in the water — that's why they're called *life* jackets. About 80 percent of boating-related deaths are from drowning. The USCG requires USCG-approved life jackets (called *personal flotation devices* or PFDs) on board all boats. How many and what type depends on the size of your boat and the number of people on board.

For boats under 16 feet (5 m) long, USCG regulations require one wearable life jacket for each person on board — even on canoes and kayaks. For boats over 16 feet long, you must have one life jacket for each person *plus* one throwable flotation device, which must be immediately accessible. These life jackets must be USCG approved, in good and serviceable condition, of appropriate size for the intended user, and readily accessible.

Many states have additional regulations. You can get information about the federal and state requirements at your local marine store or by calling the USCG at 800-368-5647.

If you're sailing outside the U.S., check with the local authorities to be certain that you're abiding by their laws; you can be assured, however, that the USCG regulations are highly respected standards in the international boating community.

Types of life jackets

Life jackets vary by how they're used, and which one you need depends on where you're sailing. Some types are more suitable for rough ocean sailing, while some are more comfortable (and, therefore, more likely to be worn) for daysailing in warm, protected water.

- ✔ **Type I:** The Type I life jacket, also called an *off-shore life jacket,* provides the most buoyancy. It floats the wearer face-up even when he or she is unconscious. The Type I life jacket — one of three types shown in Figure 7-2 — is quite bulky. But if you're going to be in the water for any length of time, this is the one you want.

- ✔ **Type II:** The Type II, or *near-shore buoyancy vest,* is designed for use in calmer, inland waters, and it provides less buoyancy than a Type I. It's also the most uncomfortable life jacket to wear. The jacket in the safety icons in this book resembles a typical Type II life jacket.

- ✔ **Type III:** Also shown in Figure 7-2, this *flotation aid* is for use in protected waters where a quick rescue is probable. It provides as much buoyancy as the Type II, but this buoyancy is distributed for ease of movement rather than to help you float head up. It can be comfortably worn all day, but it doesn't provide sufficient buoyancy in big seas. We both own this type of life jacket for dinghy sailing.

Figure 7-2:
Types I, III, and IV flotation devices.

✔ **Type IV:** Also shown in Figure 7-2, the Type IV is called a *throwable device* because it's meant to be thrown to a person in the water, who can hold onto it until rescued. On a boat over 16 feet long, a Type IV PFD must be on deck and immediately accessible to throw. Usually, you keep the Type IV near the helm so that the driver can quickly throw it.

✔ **Type V:** The Type V is called a *special-use device* or a *hybrid inflatable life jacket.* Each Type V is intended for a specific activity (such as sailboarding) and must be worn all the time. Inflatable life jackets have been very popular in Europe for some time. They're quite expensive, but they're nice because they're so easy to wear. Many of our keelboat-sailing friends wear these inflatable jackets.

In the United States, all types of PFDs must be identified as "USCG approved" by an official label.

Safety tips for using life jackets

Here are more tips to help you use life jackets properly:

✔ **Always wear a life jacket on a dinghy because it can capsize.**

✔ **As with all safety equipment, make sure that everyone knows where the life jackets are stored before you leave the dock.**

✔ **Children, nonswimmers, and anyone requiring extra assistance should always wear a life jacket.**

✔ **Don't alter a life jacket if it doesn't fit.** Get one that fits.

✔ **Don't use your life jacket as a *fender* (a pad between your boat and the dock).** Life jackets lose their buoyancy when compressed.

✔ **If your life jacket is waterlogged, throw it away.**

✔ **Make sure that the life jacket fits, especially for children.** Don't put an adult's jacket on a small child — it may slip off in the water.

Children and life jackets

Life jackets don't guarantee your children's safety around the water — you still must watch them vigilantly and know where they are at all times. Insist that your children wear the life jacket all the time. Also, making sure that the life jacket fits properly and that the child feels comfortable wearing it is very important. For more on sailing with children, see Chapter 18.

Safety harnesses

A safety harness works like an extra hand to help keep you on board as you move around the deck on bigger keelboats. Wearing a safety harness leaves your hands free for handling sheets, lines, and so on.

Never use a safety harness on a dinghy, which can capsize. Safety harnesses are only for keelboats.

Pick a safety harness that fits snugly and is the proper size (they're often rated by body weight). The harness attaches to a tether that clips onto any solid object, including *jack lines.* Jack lines are ropes, webbing, or cables that run along the deck on either side of the cabin the length of the boat, specifically for use with safety harnesses (see Figure 7-3). Never attach a harness to a lifeline; they put you closer to the edge of the boat and can break. Rig a jack line so that you can clip your safety harness onto it before you leave the cockpit and never have to unclip it as you move around on deck.

Here are some recommended times to wear a harness:

✔ **Any time a man-overboard rescue would be difficult**

✔ **When on deck alone**

✔ **When sailing at night — especially if you leave the cockpit**

✔ **When sailing in rough conditions**

Figure 7-3:
By clipping your safety harness onto a jack line, you can have both hands free to work anywhere on deck.

Harness tether

Jack line

Rescuing a "Man Overboard"

Obviously, both men and women can fall overboard, but *man overboard* is the hail that most people remember from the old movies, and it's still the standard hail when someone goes over the rail.

We know that all this talk about falling overboard must sound melodramatic, but going for an unexpected swim is probably the biggest danger facing the sailor. You and your crew need to be prepared to deal with such a situation *before* it happens. Waiting until someone is actually in the water is too late.

Avoiding this situation by staying on board is the best advice. Wearing a life jacket can help you if you fall overboard, but the key to your survival is how the rest of the crew on the boat responds.

Successfully retrieving someone from the water involves four key steps. The following sections discuss each step of a man-overboard drill in detail.

Each of these steps requires practice so that the crew works together to complete them automatically in an emergency. You and your crew can practice by retrieving a hat. If you get sunburned in the time it takes you to get your hat back, you probably need more practice (and more sunscreen). Another good way to brush up on your safety skills is to watch a safety video. You can find good videos and books on safety at sea at your local marine store. We recommend *Cruising World* magazine's "Safety at Sea" video series.

Step 1: Keep the swimmer in sight

If you see someone fall overboard, yell to alert the rest of the crew to the emergency, but don't take your eyes off that person. You're now the designated spotter. If, for some reason, you can't perform that job (say, you're driving), make sure that someone else is spotting before you take your eyes off the swimmer. If you lose sight of the person, finding him again in the shadows and reflections of the waves can be very difficult. While you're watching, try to reassure the swimmer by shouting encouragement like, "We're stopping the boat; don't try to swim to us — we'll be right there."

Many bigger boats carry *GPS* (Global Positioning System) *navigation units.* If someone is near the GPS when a person falls overboard (many boats have a waterproof unit right on deck), he should immediately punch the button that saves the present location. Many GPS units have a special *man-overboard button,* which you can push to save the location of the swimmer. The GPS then shifts modes to help you navigate your way back to the victim. (For more information on using a GPS, see Chapter 11.)

Step 2: Throw the swimmer the life ring

Quickly getting the life ring or other Type IV flotation aid to the swimmer so that he can easily stay afloat is crucial. If you have gone swimming fully clothed, you know how hard treading water can be, and doing so is even harder in big waves. Often, these life rings have a flag that makes it easier to keep the swimmer in sight. Survival Technologies' "Man Overboard Module" (MOM) has an inflatable life ring, flag, light, and sea anchor all contained in a small package that easily mounts on the lifelines.

Aim your throw slightly upwind of the swimmer so that the float drifts to him. Also, you can probably throw the life ring farther by throwing underhand.

If you're the only person on deck, you must throw the swimmer the life ring while you keep him in sight — another reason why the life ring needs to be within easy reach.

Step 3: Stop the boat

Stop the boat immediately to minimize the distance to the swimmer. Some sailing books and schools teach a man-overboard procedure called the *figure-eight method* (shown in Figure 7-4), where the boat sails away from the swimmer on a *reach* and then tacks and reaches back to perform the rescue. The best angle to return to the swimmer is a close reach (with the wind forward of 90 degrees). Although this system gives the crew time to calm down and line up for a good approach angle (close reach) back to the swimmer, this system has two shortcomings — the distance you have to sail away and the difficulty for inexperienced crews to judge the proper angle of return.

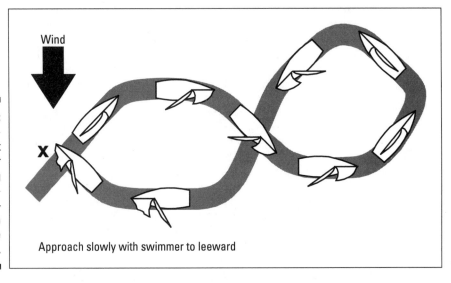

Figure 7-4: The figure-eight method for retrieving a man overboard — approach on a close reach.

Wind

X

Approach slowly with swimmer to leeward

A newer rescue technique, based on tests done by The Sailing Foundation of Seattle and the U.S. Naval Academy, is called the *Quick-Stop method,* shown in Figure 7-5.

If you have only a main and jib set, here's the procedure for a Quick-Stop rescue:

1. **Throw the life ring and keep the swimmer in sight.**

2. **Immediately tack the boat, leaving the jib sheet cleated so that it backs (fills on the back side).**

3. **The backed jib pulls the boat around onto the new tack.**

   See Chapter 5 to brush up on basic sailing skills.

4. **Drop the jib halyard and ease the main out to slow the boat.**

5. **Approach the swimmer slowly, using the mainsail to control your speed.**

You can also use the boat's engine, if you have one, to get back to the swimmer more quickly. Just make sure that you've pulled all lines out of the water before starting the motor, because getting a line wrapped

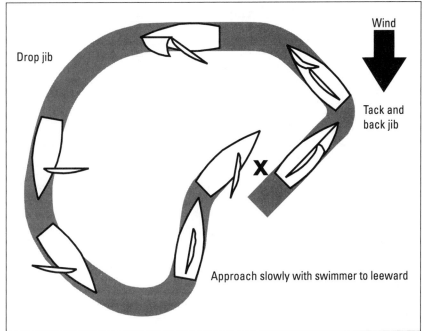

Wind

Drop jib

Tack and
back jib

X

Approach slowly with swimmer to leeward

Figure 7-5:
The Quick-
Stop
method for
rescuing
a man
overboard.

around your propeller kills the engine. When you get close enough to the swimmer to pull him back on board, put the engine in neutral so as not to endanger him with the propeller.

6. Pull the swimmer aboard.

The Quick-Stop method could be called *Man Overboard For Dummies.* It's an effective technique even for inexperienced crews because you just leave the jib cleated and the main luffing. The biggest advantage of the Quick-Stop is that it keeps the boat closer to the person in the water so that you can keep him in sight more easily — and (hopefully) rescue him more quickly.

When the spinnaker is set, the Quick-Stop method may seem a bit extreme, but it's still considered the best way to go. The helmsman simply spins the boat toward the wind immediately, backing the spinnaker, and then dropping it to the deck — the sooner after the splash the better. The spinnaker luffs against the rigging. The crew then has to wrestle the sail down on deck and get all the ropes out of the water, but at least you're near the victim.

These man-overboard routines are designed for larger keelboats. If you're sailing on a dinghy or small keelboat and drop someone overboard, the general principles still apply. You may not have a life ring to throw to the victim, so getting back to him quickly is crucial.

Step 4: Get the swimmer back on board

In many cases, the swimmer is able to climb aboard under his own steam, more embarrassed than anything else. Sometimes, though, getting the swimmer back on board can be the most difficult part of a rescue, especially if he is injured. You don't want the swimmer to get overly tired trying to swim back to the boat, so always plan on coming to him. Approach the swimmer so that he is to leeward of the boat. This way, if you're a little too cautious (which is better than being a little too daring) and end up too far to windward (upwind), the boat simply blows down to the swimmer. Plus, tossing the swimmer a line is easier when you're throwing downwind.

When the swimmer is within range, throw him a rope (preferably with yet another flotation aid attached). After you get him alongside, you probably need a group effort to heft him aboard, grabbing him under the armpits for the big pull. Of course, if you suspect that this lifting motion may aggravate an injury, you may have to get creative to make the retrieval as easy as possible on the swimmer.

 Man-overboard equipment is constantly being tried and evaluated. One of the best items is the *Lifesling* (a trademarked name for a floating horseshoe-like collar with a polypropylene "tow" line attached). By driving in a circle around the swimmer, towing the Lifesling, you make it easy for him to grab hold of the Lifesling (similar to a fallen water skier grabbing the ski rope). The swimmer can put the collar under his arms to facilitate lifting him aboard. If you don't have a Lifesling, you can improvise by tying a large bowline in a loop and throwing that line in the water. The swimmer puts the loop under his armpits, and you can winch him up.

If the swimmer is unconscious or is having trouble staying afloat, you may have to send someone into the water to help with the rescue. But don't double your trouble. Before anyone else jumps in the water, make sure that the second person has adequate flotation and, if practical, a line securing him to the boat.

 One good reason to practice man-overboard drills and discuss them with your crew is to decide in advance the best place to get back on board your boat. Don't use the back end *(transom)* of the boat in any kind of rough seas — as the boat bobs in the waves, the transom slams into the water and can seriously injure a swimmer.

Staying Calm If You Fall Overboard

If you fall off a boat, your first reaction may be anger at yourself for being so stupid. But we've talked to many people who've gone swimming, and their emotions run the gamut. One of the first things to do is get a grip on yourself so that you maximize your opportunity to facilitate the rescue and, if necessary, survive. We have a friend whose boat sank off the Carolina coast nearly 100 miles offshore. He survived nearly 24 hours afloat, but other crew members didn't. He credits his good fortune to his attitude and mental state. In case you go overboard, even for a few minutes, here are some survival tips.

Conserve energy

The biggest mistake that people make when they fall overboard is exhausting themselves by trying to swim back to the boat. Unless you can *easily* reach a nearby boat, person, or floating object (like a Type IV life ring), try to conserve energy rather than expend it. Swimming toward the wind and waves is very difficult. Also, swimming lowers your body temperature, which can speed the onset of hypothermia.

Maximize buoyancy

Your first priority, if a floating object is nearby (hopefully the Type IV life ring thrown by your crew), is to swim to it and hold on. Some boating reference books say that your clothing won't affect your buoyancy in the water, and clothing certainly helps keep you warm. But we've seen T-shirts sink in the water, and certain clothing (especially footwear) severely restricts your ability to swim or tread water. So you may want to kick off your shoes and excess clothing. Discard any heavy objects — with the exception of a knife, in case you need to cut away lines, and a flashlight, for signaling rescuers. A swimming lifesaving course (check with your local YMCA or Red Cross) can provide excellent information on staying afloat.

Here's a really neat trick: You can trap air in your jacket or foul-weather pants to help you float. By sealing all but one opening of a waterproof piece of clothing and then holding the one opening wide to catch air, you can turn this gear into a (leaky) balloon that can help provide support.

The first time I ever sailed at night on the ocean was a thrilling but also somewhat scary experience. Because I was worried about falling overboard, I put a waterproof pocket-sized strobe light in my pocket. That way, if I did go overboard, my team would have a better chance of finding me. Even today, I never sail at night without at least a flashlight in my pocket.

Conserve body heat

Because hypothermia is a very real threat, even in moderately cool water, conserving body heat is important. Here are some tips for staying warm:

✔ **Get as much of your body out of the water as possible.** At the least, keep your head out of the water.

✔ **If you're in the water with other people, huddle together to keep warm.** Huddling also helps keep everyone thinking positively.

✔ **Keep your body in a compact shape.** As you can see in Figure 7-6, a very compacted shape is the fetal position, also called the "Heat Escape Lessening Position" (HELP). With a life jacket on, you can usually stay in the HELP position with your head out of the water. If this position brings your head under water, try keeping your arms and legs together to conserve as much warmth as you can.

✔ **Tighten your life jacket.** A snug fit helps keep you warm.

Figure 7-6:
Huddling with others or the HELP position helps you conserve energy and body heat.

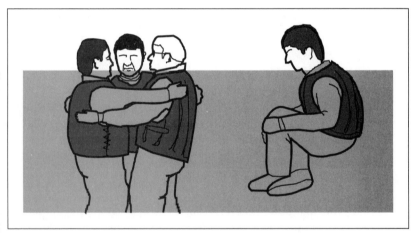

Recovering from a Capsize

One safety concern on a dinghy is *capsizing,* or having the boat flip over. Capsizing can be a nuisance, but don't fear it — it can also be fun. Dealing with a capsize should be part of every sailor's introductory dinghy-sailing lesson. Given proper preparation and practice, you can easily handle a capsize.

When the boat flips upside down, all the loose gear in the boat floats away (or sinks), so always make sure that everything is well stowed or tied into the boat.

Centerboard boats fall into two categories, with respect to capsizing: those that the crew can right by themselves *(self-righting),* and those that *swamp,* or fill up with water, and require outside assistance to get upright again. The difference is in the design of the boat and whether it has sealed flotation tanks. All modern dinghies are designed to be self-righting. Avoid sailing in a boat that swamps when no rescue powerboat is available.

The anatomy of a capsize

A boat can capsize while sailing by tipping over to leeward or to windward. A leeward capsize is common in strong or puffy winds where the boat simply heels too much and blows over, as shown in Figure 7-7. A windward capsize can occur in strong winds when you're sailing downwind. The boat just starts rolling back and forth until, finally — *crash!* The *death roll.* It sounds ominous, but you're just going to get wet. Check out Chapters 12 and 15 for ways to keep your mast and sails out of the drink on those fun, wild-and-windy days.

Make sure that the rudder and centerboard are secured so that they won't come out if the boat turns upside down. Always drain all flotation tanks and the hull before sailing, and make sure that drain holes are plugged.

Righting the boat

When sailing a dinghy, the question isn't *if* you're going to capsize but *when.* After you capsize, the sooner you start righting the boat, the quicker and easier the recovery. If you dally, the boat keeps rolling until the mast is straight down. This position is called *turning turtle,* because the hull of the boat looks like a turtle shell. Righting a boat that has turtled is much harder than righting one that's on its side, so the minute you capsize, you need to quickly hustle through the following steps (which are shown in Figure 7-8):

1. **Ensure that your crew is safe and happy (well, relatively).**

2. **Get weight on the centerboard as quickly as possible, either by climbing over the high side or swimming around.**

   Don't delay, or you may risk making the boat turn turtle.

3. **Make sure that all sheets are uncleated and loose.**

   If you don't loosen the sheets, the sails fill as you right the boat, and you will probably capsize again. You can lean over the hull to watch and talk to the crew while performing this step.

4. **Pull on the *rail* (edge) of the boat and pump your weight to get the mast to come out of the water.**

   By holding onto the hiking straps in the cockpit, your crew can get scooped into the boat as it comes upright. Having their weight in the boat as it comes up also helps prevent capsizing again immediately (a very common occurrence, especially if the mast is to windward).

5. **When you're upright, help each other on board while the sails luff.**

Figure 7-7:
Capsizing to
leeward
(top) and to
windward
(bottom) —
the death
roll.

Always get all your crew on board the boat as soon as you're upright. Just let the sails luff; you can worry about getting going again after everyone is safe.

Figure 7-8:
Getting your
boat
upright.

Sometimes, especially in wavy conditions, righting the boat is difficult because the waves keep trying to turtle the boat. One very effective technique of righting the boat under these conditions is to have the crew hold onto the bow. The boat naturally drifts with the wind until the bow is pointed directly upwind. With this technique, the crew keeps holding onto the bow until the boat is upright.

If you can't pull the boat upright by yourself, get the crew to provide more righting force by climbing up and leaning out together, as shown in Figure 7-9.

Rescuing a swamped boat

Boats that swamp are much more time-consuming to get sailing again, and doing so requires outside assistance. So never sail a boat that swamps without other boats around, and always make sure that you have a good bucket or two aboard in case you flip. Tie in these *bailers* so that you don't lose them when the boat rolls.

If you capsize in a swamper, you must first uncleat the sails and bring the boat upright by pulling on the centerboard. Then climb into the boat over the transom, so that the boat doesn't capsize again, and start bailing like mad. If you're fast and you keep the boat upright, you can slowly gain on the flood waters and get the boat dry. But be forewarned: A boat half-filled with water is very unstable and can flip again easily.

Figure 7-9:
Both crew pulling the turtled boat upright.

A much easier way to bail out the water is a quick tow from a motorboat. A motorboat with a well-secured tow rope can slowly pull the boat so that the water flows out over the transom. Keep your weight low and in the transom. Soon the water level is down to a level that you can bail out with your bucket.

If you capsize and can't right the boat or find yourself in the water with your boat swamped, *stay with the boat.* The boat is like a huge life ring, and you're much safer with the boat than without it. Try to get out of the water by sitting on the overturned hull and wait for help. If you're in the water tangled in lines, stay calm and untangle yourself.

Bringing the Right Stuff

The following items are USCG-required safety equipment for sailboats. If you're on a sailboat with an inboard engine, there are more safety requirements. At most marine stores or any USCG station, you can pick up a copy of the *Federal Requirements and Safety Tips for Recreational Boats* pamphlet. Get a copy of the boating laws of your state from the appropriate agency listed in your phone book. The USCG's Boating Safety Hotline (800-368-5647) can provide all sorts of boating safety information, including courses in your area.

Sound signals

The USCG requires a vessel under 12 meters (about 39 feet) in length to carry a whistle or horn. Loud signals help in reduced-visibility weather such as fog. Larger boats must have a sound signal audible to at least $1/2$ mile (800 m) and carry a bell.

Fire extinguishers

The USCG requires that all boats with motors carry fire extinguishers (except boats under 26 feet/8 m long with outboard engines, as long as that boat doesn't have permanently installed fuel tanks or spaces where fumes can collect, and isn't carrying passengers for hire). Table 7-1 can help you sort out the USCG regulations regarding fire extinguishers.

Table 7-1	Fire Extinguisher Requirements	
Boat Length	*Without Fixed Extinguishing System*	*With Fixed Extinguishing System*
Under 26 ft (8 m)	1 B-I	None
26–40 ft (8–12 m)	2 B-I or 1 B-II	1 B-I
40–65 ft (12–20 m)	3 B-I or both one B-II and one B-I	2 B-I or 1 B-II

Fire extinguishers for marine use must have labels certifying that they are USCG approved and/or are listed with the Underwriters Laboratories (UL) with a UL rating of 5-B:C or higher. (The UL rating of 5-B:C is equal to a B-I, which is the USCG's classification. A UL rating of 10-B:C equals a B-II.) B-IIs are larger versions of B-Is. The *B* refers to the type of fire; *B* is for flammable and combustible liquids. You may also want to carry a Type C extinguisher for combating electrical fires. The three approved types of fire extinguishers are Dry Chemical, Carbon Dioxide, and Halon. Each type has characteristics that make it more appropriate for fighting a different type of fire. With all fire extinguishers, having the right type for each fire, keeping them in good working order, and storing them in a convenient spot is imperative. For more information on dealing with a fire on your boat, see Chapter 13.

Visual distress signals

The USCG requires that all vessels (with the following exceptions) carry approved visual distress signals. Recreational boats under 16 feet (5 m) long and rowboats and open sailboats less than 26 feet (8 m) in length without an engine, operating solely during the daylight hours, need not carry these signals. A variety of signals are considered acceptable, including Pyrotechnic Devices (flares; several approved types are available) and Non-Pyrotechnic Devices (a large orange and black flag and electric flashlight are approved). A variety of combinations of these devices are considered acceptable but are too lengthy to list here. Take care when handling flares; they can cause a fire or injury. The flashlight can also be used at night to signal distress by using the international Morse code "SOS" distress signal (••• — — — •••).

Navigation lights

All boats are required to have navigation lights (also called *running lights*) at night (including dusk and dawn) and whenever visibility is reduced (such as in fog, heavy rain, or haze). See Figure 7-10 for the different configurations of approved lights for sailboats under 20 meters (65 feet). Sailboats under 7 meters (22 feet) in length may carry only a flashlight or lighted lantern to shine on your sail (and at the oncoming boat), but carrying navigation lights like those required on bigger boats is better. You can purchase a modified flashlight with a red and green light that attaches by a suction cup for temporary use.

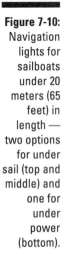

Figure 7-10: Navigation lights for sailboats under 20 meters (65 feet) in length — two options for under sail (top and middle) and one for under power (bottom).

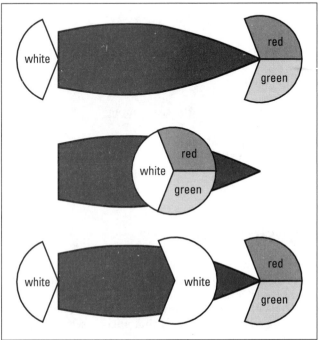

Checklist for boating safety equipment

USCG (or your state or national authority) safety regulations are a good start, but we want you to be even better prepared, so we created the following list of boating safety equipment for a typical big keelboat around 30 to 50 feet (9 to 15 m) in length, sailing in coastal waters (not across the ocean, but along it). Starred (*) items are recommended for a smaller keelboat or dinghy used for daysailing, if you have room to store them safely:

All USCG-required equipment for that boat*
Anchor and anchor rode (chain and line)*
Spare anchor
Extra line (for heaving, mooring, and anchoring)*
Radar reflector
Lifelines (wire railing around the perimeter of the deck supported by
    metal poles)
Fenders

Life jackets* (just in case you forgot they're USCG-required equipment)

VHF radio

Flashlight and spare batteries

First aid kit and manual (see Appendix A)

Safety harnesses

Drinking water and food*

Sunscreen*

For an engine: fuel and spare parts

Tool kit*

Whistle or horn*

Knife*

Chart and compass*

Boat hook

Lifesling or other man-overboard equipment

Binoculars

Spare parts for the boat

Sunglasses, hats, extra clothing*

Adequate bilge pump*

Paddle*

Offshore safety gear

If you're planning an extended trip or some significant offshore sailing, beef up your safety equipment. An important addition to your equipment is a life raft. Make sure that it's rated for the number of people you have on board and has been recently inspected. If not, or if you're unsure, check with your local marine store to find a company that specializes in inspecting and "refreshing" your life raft.

Another valuable piece of offshore equipment is the EPIRB (Emergency Position-Indicating Radio Beacon). These incredible devices are sold at marine stores and are directly responsible for saving hundreds of sailors' lives. When activated in an emergency, this device emits a distress signal on a frequency that is monitored by satellites and airplanes — which makes finding you much easier for rescuers! Check with your marine store to see whether you need to register your EPIRB.

A complete list of suggested offshore safety gear and equipment can be found in the Offshore Racing Council Special Regulations, available from US Sailing. Though much of the equipment is required for offshore racing, this publication is also an excellent checklist for cruising.

PETER SAYS

The military alphabet for use on the marine radio

When I was a kid, I memorized the military alphabet — and I'm glad I did. Knowing it is a constant source of pleasure in the most unexpected circumstances, even today!

A: Alpha	**H:** Hotel	**O:** Oscar	**U:** Uniform
B: Bravo	**I:** India	**P:** Papa	**V:** Victor
C: Charlie	**J:** Juliet	**Q:** Quebec	**W:** Whiskey
D: Delta	**K:** Kilo	**R:** Romeo	**X:** X-ray
E: Echo	**L:** Lima	**S:** Sierra	**Y:** Yankee
F: Foxtrot	**M:** Mike	**T:** Tango	**Z:** Zulu
G: Golf	**N:** November		

Using the VHF Radio

You probably want to go sailing to get away from phone calls, faxes, and e-mail, but in an emergency, a communication link can be vital. For coastal sailing, a cellular phone may be your best communication device — if it has the range to connect you to shore — but the most common form of communication on the water is through VHF radios.

VHF (Very High Frequency) radios are simply two-way radios. With a VHF radio, you can get in touch with the USCG, talk to friends on other boats, listen to marine weather reports, and even talk to marinas and yacht clubs to inquire about slip space for your boat. The radio's range depends on the power of the unit and the height of the antenna. A hand-held model has a range of a few miles; a 25-watt VHF radio attached to a masthead antenna on a 40-foot (12 m) mast has a range of roughly 10 to 12 miles (16 to 19 km). Put a hand-held radio in a waterproof bag to keep it dry, and, for extended sails, make sure that you have a supply of charged batteries.

You don't need to register a marine VHF used on a recreational boat in U.S. waters, but a U.S. boat traveling elsewhere must register the radio with the FCC (800-322-1117 or 717-337-1212).

When you use your radio, knowing which channel is appropriate to use is important. The primary calling channel is 16. Use Channel 16 to initiate a conversation, but quickly switch to another channel, because 16 is also used for emergencies, as described in the sidebar "In case of emergency: using Channel 16." Check the VHF radios on both ends to find out which channels are usable. Common ones are 9, 68, 69, 71, 72, and 78.

Two people can't talk on two radios at exactly the same time. After you finish talking, say "Over," and release the "talk" (or *transmit*) button to open the channel so that you can hear a response.

Here are the common types of radio communications:

- **Radio check:** Once or twice a year, check your radio by tuning to Channel 16 and calling "Any vessel, any vessel, this is the yacht Babbalubba, calling for a radio check, over." Don't waste the USCG's time with a radio check request.

- **Ship to ship:** If you don't have a plan to monitor a working channel such as 69, you can first call the other boat on Channel 16 and then switch to another channel as soon as you make contact.

- **Ship to marine telephone operator:** Yes, you can get connected to a real telephone by calling the marine operators on Channels 24 through 28 and 84 through 87. They instruct you to switch channels after you make contact. You can call collect or charge your call to your home phone number, but, obviously, we don't recommend giving your credit card number over the radio.

- **Ship to USCG — EMERGENCY:** The Emergency Channel for contacting the USCG is Channel 16. See the sidebar "In case of emergency: using Channel 16" for the proper procedure during an emergency.

- **Weather information:** In the U.S., a marine weather forecast and warnings are transmitted on special VHF weather channels. Check the radio's instruction book to find out how to tune to those channels, or look for a button that says *Wx*.

For more information, you may want to purchase the *Marine Radio Users Handbook,* published by the Radio Technical Commission for Maritime Services (RTCM), at 202-639-4006.

If you're sailing farther offshore, the new standard is a satellite communication device called "INMARSAT C." With this device and a personal computer, you can send and receive data (like your e-mail) from literally anywhere on the planet. The old standby (and still a wise investment for any offshore sailor) is a Single Side Band (SSB) radio. When properly installed and with a well-tuned antenna, you can communicate for thousands of miles. The worldwide distress frequency for SSB is 2182 kHz; use 1670 kHz to contact the USCG.

In case of emergency: using Channel 16

If you need to make an emergency call on Channel 16, follow these steps:

1. **If your radio has an alarm signal, press it for 30 seconds.**

2. **Say "Mayday" three times and give the name of your boat and your VHF call sign (if you have one) three times.**

3. **Give your location, either by the distance from an object on the chart (for example, "two miles east of buoy 3") or by latitude and longitude.**

4. **Explain your situation as briefly as possible, such as "Swamped and taking on water, in need of tow or rescue."**

5. **Describe the boat's type, color, and any distinguishing features — "30-foot dark red ketch with main and jib hoisted."**

6. **Tell how many people are on board.**

7. **Repeat the boat's name and call sign.**

8. **Keep repeating "Mayday" and all the preceding information on Channel 16 until someone responds.**

Two people can't talk at once on a VHF radio, so finish your transmission by saying "Over," let go of talk button, and listen for a response.

If you hear a mayday distress call, figure out whether you're close enough to help by writing down the information and computing your relative distance. If you can help, speak on the radio directly to the boat in distress and give your estimated arrival time. If you can't help, stay off the radio.

If you need help but the situation isn't an emergency — for example, you require medical assistance but not emergency evacuation — start your message by saying "Pan-Pan" (pronounced "Pahn-Pahn") three times, and then continue with the information described in the preceding steps.

Rules of the Road

In this section, we look at what you need to know to avoid collisions with other boats. Probably, your biggest concern is staying out of the way of commercial vessels: barges, tugboats, and big ships.

Here are some basic concepts to help you when your course takes you near large commercial vessels:

✔ **Be very careful around tugboats and barges.** Sometimes the towing cable (which can be several hundred yards long) between a tug and a barge submerges, creating the false appearance of a safe passageway.

✔ **Large ships and tugboats pushing barges can have a "blind spot" that extends for hundreds of feet in front of them.**

✔ **Large ships are difficult to maneuver and can't turn at all when stopped.** Avoid them — don't make them avoid you.

- ✔ **Large ships can block your wind from a long way away.** This interference can slow you down and make avoiding them difficult.

- ✔ **Large ships must stay in the channel to avoid running aground.** In these confined waters, the channel is marked by aids to navigation — usually buoys. You may need to consult a chart to find the channel. (For more information on reading a chart, see Chapter 11.)

- ✔ **The speed of large ships and tugs is very deceptive, and stopping can take them over a mile.**

- ✔ **The turbulence in the wake of a large ship can throw your boat around or worse.**

- ✔ **Understand the whistle blasts.** Five or more short blasts is the "danger" signal. Get out of the way, now!

The following rules are the basic rules when any two boats meet:

- ✔ **Moving boats must avoid stopped boats.**

- ✔ **Sailboats have right-of-way over powerboats, except for fishing vessels and large commercial vessels with restricted maneuverability (that means all big ships, especially in channels).**

And here are the basic rules when any two *sailboats* meet.

- ✔ **An overtaking boat must keep clear.**

- ✔ **The boat on starboard tack has right-of-way over port tack.**

- ✔ **When on the same tack and overlapped, the leeward boat has right-of-way over the windward boat.**

Part III
Sailing Away — Applying the Techniques

The 5th Wave — By Rich Tennant

In this part . . .

Are you hooked on sailing yet? We hope so, and the first chapter of this part gets you focused on speed — sailing fast. The final three chapters prepare you for sailing away by covering anchoring, weather, and navigating. Even powerboaters can enjoy these chapters — although anchoring next to a big *stinkpot* (powerboat) is a drag because its generator runs all night to power the air conditioner, freezer, and so on. If you want to borrow ice cubes or blow-dry your hair, however, stinkpotters can be good friends indeed.

Chapter 8

The Need for Speed: Sailing Fast

. . . .

In This Chapter

▶ Using telltales

▶ Sailing fast upwind

▶ Understanding apparent wind

▶ Adjusting the sail shape

▶ Controlling the power in your sails

▶ Sailing fast downwind

▶ Using spinnakers

. . . .

> *I wish to have no connection with any ship that does not sail fast; for I intend to go in harm's way.*
>
> — John Paul Jones

*S*ailing fast — a powerboater may think that this catchphrase is an oxymoron. But we've gone sailing with a few professional car drivers, and they've been surprised at how fast sailboats can go. Especially on a boat that's low to the water and gets plenty of spray over the deck, you always feel like you're going faster than you really are. This chapter helps you sail faster by fine-tuning the skills that you develop in your first few sails — your sense and feel of the wind and your boat's angle to the wind.

This chapter also covers how to optimize the shape of your sails. If your sails are the engines of your boat, then the *running rigging* — the lines you use to adjust the sail shape — is your throttle. Because the wind and seas are rarely perfectly steady, the optimum shape of your sail changes according to the weather conditions, just as the wing of a Concorde jet is different in shape from the wing of a B-52 bomber because of their different speed and lift requirements. To optimize your boat speed downwind, you need a *spinnaker,* a parachute-like sail, and we discuss the tricks of keeping this finicky sail doing its job. We also cover some tips on how to steer the boat faster and where to put your crew for optimum speed.

Sailing Fast

The first step to sailing fast on any point of sail is to make sure that your sails are *trimmed* (pulled in) just enough — at the perfect angle to the wind flow. After you get your sails trimmed perfectly at the beginning of the day, you can just *cleat* them (tie them off) and ignore them, right? Wrong. The angle of the sails to the wind can easily change in any of three ways:

- **The wind shifts.** A change in the wind direction can be caused by a number of reasons; check out Chapter 10 for more on wind shifts. Another reason for a change in the wind direction is discussed in the upcoming section "Understanding Apparent Wind."
- **You retrim (let out or pull in) the sails.**
- **You turn the boat.** Every course change requires a change in sail trim.

When the angle of the sails to the wind is wrong, the boat slows down or may even stop. So how can you tell when you have a problem with sail trim before you come to a stop? Looking up at the sails is your best and fastest indication of improper trim. Sails can either be perfectly trimmed, under-trimmed, or overtrimmed. An undertrimmed sail — one that isn't pulled in enough — is pretty obvious: The sail luffs (except on a run, which we cover later in the section "Sailing Fast Downwind"), which means that it's spilling air and thus losing power. An overtrimmed sail — one that's pulled in too much — is a more devious animal; it also slows you down, but it's harder to see because it still appears full. If you could see the air molecules as they travel over the sail, however, you would see that the airflow is *stalled* (turbulent, not smooth) on an overtrimmed sail, as shown in Figure 8-1. As you know from any air disaster movie, a plane that has stalled can't fly because the wings can't generate *lift* — and you know from Chapter 1 that lift is what makes a sailboat move.

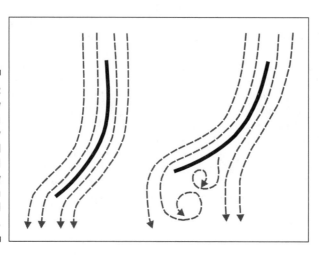

Figure 8-1:
Wind flow over a properly trimmed sail (left) and stalled flow over an overtrimmed sail (right).

How do you know whether your sail is stalled? "When in doubt, let it out" is the main rule. Ease the sheet out until the sail just starts to luff and then trim it back in an inch.

The second way is to use *telltales* as a kind of "early warning system." Telltales are little strands of yarn or cassette tape that are attached (usually with tape) to the sail. Telltales are more sensitive to changes in the flow than the sail is, so they luff sooner than the sailcloth does. You can see telltales in action in Figure 8-2.

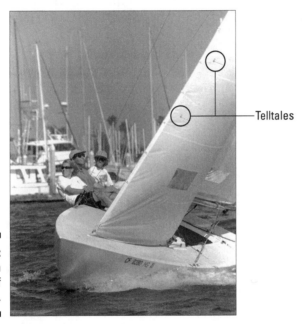

Telltales

Figure 8-2: Telltales on the luff of a jib.

Telltales placed on either side of the forward-most sail (the jib, if you have one) about a foot (30 cm) back from the *luff* (front) of the sail give an excellent indication of whether the sail is under- or overtrimmed. If the sails are perfectly trimmed for your course, both telltales (on either side) flow straight back. If you're sailing close-hauled with the sails trimmed tight and the telltales are streaming this way, you're "in the groove." If you turn toward the wind, the sail becomes undertrimmed and the inside, or *windward,* telltale starts to rise and flutter as the flow gets disturbed on the front side of the sail. Because the sail is already trimmed tight, this flutter is the helmsman's cue to turn away from the wind *(bear away).* If you turn too far away from the wind, the air flow starts to get disturbed on the back *(lee-ward)* side of the sail as the sail gets overtrimmed, so the leeward telltale starts to flutter and then droop. You can either ease the sheet out enough to get both telltales flowing again or, to stay close-hauled, the helmsman can head up until both telltales flow.

To stay in the groove when sailing close-hauled, you don't really have to keep the telltales flowing perfectly all the time. In fact, a little rise by the inside telltale occasionally is okay, especially in stronger winds. That little movement just means that you're sailing a very fine line, and you don't want to sail any closer to the wind.

When I'm racing on the pro match-racing circuit, with tens of thousands of dollars at stake over the course of a weekend, I don't want any excuse to lose. At the beginning of the regatta, when the organizers hand out our sails, one of the first things I do is put on my "steering" telltales. I use mohair yarn (it works well in damp, misty conditions) in special colors (I like green on one side and red on the other) for these telltales, and I apply them in just the right position — to the centimeter.

On boats with only a mainsail, telltales on the luff are less accurate because of the turbulence caused by the mast. Therefore, keep looking for an occasional, slight "bubble" in the front of the mainsail, indicating that the sail is just on the verge of luffing, instead of relying on telltales. However, a telltale placed on the leech of the mainsail (by the top batten is best) gives you a quick indication when the mainsail is overtrimmed (stalled) because the telltale no longer flows straight back.

Tips for Sailing Fast Upwind

To steer faster upwind, try some of the following tips:

- ✔ **Avoid stalling out:** *Pinching* the boat (sailing too close to the wind) is obvious because the sails start to luff and lose power, and you slow down. But the real reason that pinching is so slow is what is happening underwater. As you slow down, the keel (or centerboard) begins to stall, just like an airplane wing can stall at low speeds and lose its lift. When your keel stalls, the boat starts to slip sideways. The best way to get the keel working again is to ease the sails slightly, bear off 3–5 degrees wider of a close-hauled course, and get the water flow going fast again.

- ✔ **Be aware of wind shifts:** If your sail starts to luff and you're still pointed in the same direction, then the wind has shifted so that it's coming from farther ahead (a *header*). Conversely, if your telltales indicate that the wind is coming from farther behind, that shift is a *lift*. In either case, you have to alter course to get back in the groove. Headers and lifts are illustrated in Figure 8-3. For more on understanding wind shifts, see Chapter 10.

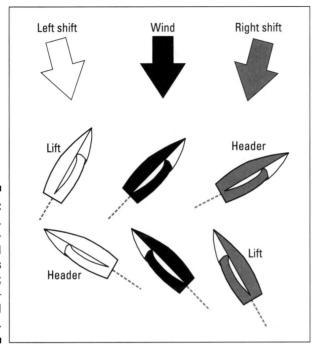

Figure 8-3:
Wind shifts.
A header —
the wind
shifts
forward;
a lift —
the wind
shifts aft.

✔ **Feel the boat:** When the boat is in the groove, the wind hits your face at a certain angle, the mainsheet tugs with a set force, the rudder pulls on your steering hand just so, and the boat heels a certain amount. By feeling and maintaining all these sensory inputs, you're in the zone! Try it with your eyes closed.

✔ **Find the groove:** Sailing fast upwind is like a balancing act; it's a game of trade-offs. You can sail the boat at a lower angle to the wind *(footing)* and go faster, or sail the boat at a closer angle to the wind *(pinching)* and go more slowly but more directly to your destination. But both those courses are slower to that upwind destination than the intermediate course, the 3- to 5-degrees-wide *groove,* shown in Figure 8-4, which provides the best compromise of speed through the water versus angle to the wind.

✔ **Fine-tune your sailing skills on a dinghy:** Because dinghies are much more responsive than keelboats, you develop your "feel" more quickly sailing a dinghy. Chapter 15 covers all sorts of sailing techniques that especially apply to dinghies.

✔ **Look around:** Try to get in the habit of looking at the telltales, then look at the point on shore you're using to keep sailing straight, then look at the water for approaching wind and waves, then look around for boats (from all directions), then back to the telltales, and on and on. Spend maybe 10 to 20 seconds looking at each station.

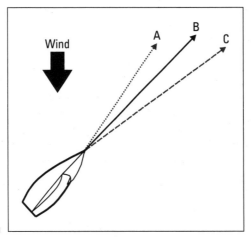

Figure 8-4:
Three upwind tracks: the pincher (A), in the groove (B), and the footer (C).

✔ **Minimize heel:** In Chapter 1, we describe how a sailboat can sail toward the wind — because the water flowing over the centerboard (or keel) creates "lift" like a wing. As the boat heels over, the centerboard tilts with it, so less lift is generated. The sails also tilt, becoming less efficient. Bottom line: Too much heel is very slow, so try and limit it any way you can. One way is by moving your weight as far outboard as possible, a process called *hiking* (described in Chapter 15). Later in this chapter, under "Controlling the power," we discuss how to limit heel if shifting your weight isn't enough.

When the wind builds so much (about 12 knots and above on most boats) that hiking can't stop the boat from heeling somewhat, you must limit the heel to the boat's maximum angle. Here are the maximum efficient heel angles for different boats:

✔ **One- and two-person dinghies:** 0 to 5 degrees heel — essentially upright.

✔ **Larger, heavier dinghies:** 0 to 10 degrees.

✔ **Scows (Flat-bottomed dinghies with two rudders):** About 20 degrees — to the point where the leeward rudder is straight down.

✔ **Catamarans:** Just enough that the windward hull "kisses" the water.

✔ **Keelboats:** 10 to 25 degrees — so that the ballast in the keel fin can get some leverage to prevent further heeling.

PETER SAYS

Buddy Melges, the "Wizard of Zenda, Wisconsin," is one of my all-time heroes in sailing. He's won the America's Cup (*America³* in 1992) and an Olympic Gold Medal (Soling class, 1972), but, more important, he is a great person who loves to share his knowledge. One time I asked him how he keeps a boat in the groove going upwind in a breeze. He said that he just watches the horizon up ahead of the boat and keeps it at a constant angle to the bow and luff of the jib.

Weather helm

When most boats are close-hauled or close reaching, they exhibit a tendency to turn toward the wind. This characteristic is called *weather helm*. It's like driving a car that has its front tire out of balance — the tiller or wheel "pulls" to one side. If you were to release the helm, the boat would turn up until it was pointed directly into the wind — dead-center in the no-sail zone. As the wind changes in velocity, the amount of weather helm changes, forcing you to alter the helm slightly to keep going straight. Although disconcerting at first, a little weather helm is natural and is simply an aspect of sailing that you have to get used to.

Understanding Apparent Wind

All the talk about the importance of a sailor's knowing the wind direction in Chapter 5 has, hopefully, sunk in deep. Furthermore, our discussion of the "perfect" sail trim in this chapter hopefully stresses the importance of being aware of the wind direction. Now we're going to throw you a curveball and see whether you can hit it.

The wind that you and your sail feel is not the same wind that's blowing over the water, making waves, giving free rides to seagulls, and causing the flag to flap on shore. The wind felt on board your boat is the *apparent wind*. The wind felt by the flag on shore is the *true wind*.

To illustrate the difference, imagine jumping on a bicycle and pedaling down the road. If it's a calm day, you feel wind in your face — the faster you pedal, the more wind, right? Well, if it's a windy day, the wind you feel in your face — your apparent wind — is the combination of the *wind of motion*, which is the wind blowing directly into your face that you create by pedaling fast, and the *true wind*, which is the wind blowing over the road.

The same thing happens aboard a sailboat: As you move forward, you create a wind of motion that, when added to the true wind blowing over the water, results in the wind you feel — the sailboat's apparent wind, as shown in Figure 8-5.

On a very fast boat, such as a catamaran or an ice boat, this capability to "make your own wind" can have some really amazing results. Check out Chapters 15 and 16 for more information on making wind on those fast boats. For mortal monohull sailors, the difference between the apparent wind and the true wind is more subtle. Here are the key features of apparent wind:

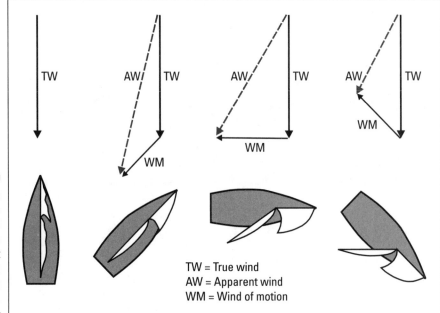

Figure 8-5:
The true
wind
and the
apparent
wind felt on
a moving
boat.

TW = True wind
AW = Apparent wind
WM = Wind of motion

✔ Except when sailing on a *run* (with the wind coming directly behind the boat), the apparent wind is always shifted farther forward (relative to the boat's bow) than the true wind.

✔ The faster you go, the more effect your wind of motion has on the apparent wind's direction and velocity.

✔ Unless you're sailing a super-fast boat like a catamaran, the apparent wind is always lighter (less velocity) when you're sailing away from the true wind than when you're sailing toward it. That's why sailing downwind feels warmer than sailing upwind.

The only thing you care about in sailing fast is the apparent wind. So don't get all confused, despite this new piece of information; the sailor's universe still revolves around the wind that he feels, and that's the apparent wind. Just know that every time we discuss the wind that is hitting your sails, we mean the apparent wind. The difference between apparent wind and true wind explains the subtle changes in wind velocity that affect sail shape, as you can read about in the next section.

Shaping Your Sails

Until this point in this book, we have only discussed the most important aspect of sail trim — the angle of the sail to the wind. That's all you need to know to make your boat go. But if you want to eke out another 10 percent of power from your sails, then you must delve into the subject of sail shape a little deeper. Come on in, the water's fine!

You discover in Chapter 1 that your sail is really a wing, generating lift as the wind flows past it. A horizontal cross section of that sea-going wing is shown in Figure 8-6.

Figure 8-6:
A cross section of a sail flipped on its side and dissected.

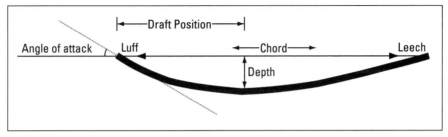

Here are the definitions of the sail features that are illustrated in Figure 8-6:

✔ **Angle of attack:** This is simply a technical term for the concept you already know as the "angle of the sail to the wind." Angle of attack is measured as the angle of the wind to the sail's chord.

✔ **Chord:** The straight line between the leading edge (luff) and the trailing edge (leech).

✔ **Depth:** The fullness of a sail, expressed as a percentage of the depth at the sail's deepest point to the length of the chord.

✔ **Draft position:** The position of the sail's deepest point, expressed as a percentage of the distance the point is back from the luff to the length of the chord.

✔ **Twist:** The amount the angle of attack changes as you look up the sail, from bottom to top, as shown in Figure 8-7.

No one except a sailmaker is concerned with the absolute quantities of depth, draft position, and twist. From a practical standpoint, sailors are mostly interested in the relative quantities — making a given sail deeper or flatter, or more or less twisted.

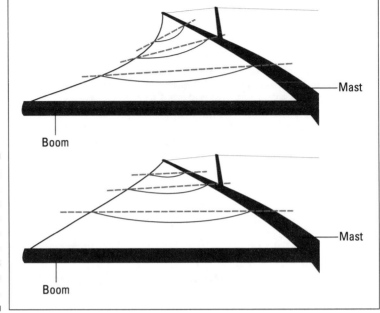

Figure 8-7:
The sail on top has excessive twist; the sail on the bottom has very little twist.

Pull That Line; No, THAT Line

Now for the practical aspects of varying sail shape while sailing. In case we haven't made our point clear enough yet, here it is again: By far and away, the most important aspect of sail trim is the angle of attack, which is controlled by that sail's sheet. Pull the sail in until it just stops luffing, and when in doubt, let it out!

Of secondary importance are a variety of fine-tuning controls. Your first goal is to get these controls in the ballpark, which gets your sail to 98 percent efficiency. From there, you can experiment with small adjustments to see whether you can get more performance out of your boat. All the basic mainsail controls are described in the following sections.

Mainsheet

The mainsheet is the biggie — the most adjusted piece of running rigging on the boat — because it controls the sail's angle of attack. When sailing upwind, the mainsheet also controls the twist. Read more about twist in the section about controlling power later in this chapter.

Halyard and cunningham (that clever pig)

The halyard is primary and the cunningham secondary in controlling the tension in the luff of the sail. Some boats don't even have a cunningham (also called the *downhaul*), a control rope that pulls the luff downward at or near the tack. In Chapter 4, we show you the two visibly obvious extremes of luff tension. Proper luff tension depends on the design and shape of the sail, your point of sail, and the wind velocity. To eke out that last inch of speed, you need to tighten your halyard and/or cunningham upwind and loosen them downwind. Increased luff tension usually moves the draft position forward and decreases the depth of (flattens) the sail slightly.

You may think that a smooth sail is fastest. However, my experience indicates that most sails in most conditions like to have the luff tension set so that just few loose wrinkles show along the lower luff. We call these *speed wrinkles*. But beware of stress lines parallel to the mast — these lines show that your halyard or cunningham is too tight.

Outhaul

The *outhaul* controls depth in the bottom of the mainsail. Again, getting the outhaul tension in the ballpark is important, and you can do so by using the same visual cues as you use to determine luff tension (except that the stress or looseness is apparent along the foot of the sail). If you can't get the outhaul perfectly set, err on the tight side, especially if the wind is moderate or strong, so start by setting the outhaul so that you can see some strain. Increased foot tension flattens the bottom section of the mainsail.

Boom vang

Most boats have a *boom vang* (also called simply a *vang*) system to control the twist of the mainsail when sailing downwind. Usually the vang is a system of pulleys connecting the boom to the mast to hold the boom down. The vang takes over primary twist control from the mainsheet when the sail is eased out on a reach or a run.

A great starting point is to set the vang when you're sailing close-hauled. With the mainsail perfectly trimmed, pull the slack out of the vang rope and cleat it. Then, as you *bear away* (turn downwind) and ease the mainsheet, the vang takes up tension. The tighter the vang, the less the twist on reaches and runs. A good rule is to put enough boom vang on so that the top batten is parallel to the boom.

Traveler

A secondary control for changing the mainsail's angle of attack is the *traveler,* but not all boats have a traveler. It moves the lower mainsheet attachment point (on the boat) from side to side, thereby changing the angle of attack without changing the sail's twist. When sailing to windward in light air after the mainsheet is trimmed for the right amount of twist, pull the traveler to windward, so that the boom is on centerline, for maximum upwind power. In heavy air, you can reduce power by dropping the traveler to leeward.

Backstay

The *backstay* is the support wire between the top of the mast and the back of the boat. Some smaller boats don't have a backstay, and some bigger boats don't have convenient means to control the backstay tension. But if your boat has a backstay control that's easy to use, you'll love the backstay, because it gives you more control over mainsail shape than any other control line except the mainsheet. As you tension the backstay, the mast bends. This bend dramatically decreases the depth of the mainsail.

Powering Up Your Sails

One great way to picture what variations in sail shape do is to think in terms of power. More power makes you go faster in a race car (until you have to go around the curve), but in a sailboat, it's not quite that simple; you have something else to consider. When a wing shape generates the all-important lift, it also generates drag. Therefore, designers of airplane wings and sailors trying to optimize their sail shape are looking for the same thing — optimizing the ratio of lift to drag. That ratio varies, depending on many variables, including the depth of the wing (sail), draft position, angle of attack, twist, and the speed of the air flowing past. Every wind speed has an optimum wing shape that maximizes the lift-to-drag ratio. (That's why some fighter jets have wings that change shape and angle, depending on how fast the plane is flying.)

In general, in light and medium winds, you need full sails for maximum power; at higher wind speeds, you flatten your sails because you need less power (and because full shapes have a great deal of drag when it's windy).

Figure 8-8 illustrates how a given sail shape changes in performance as the wind speed increases. In light winds, a fuller sail shape (say, 18 percent depth, 40 percent draft position) has a high lift-to-drag ratio, meaning plenty of power, but as wind speed increases, this shape becomes very "draggy" and slow. A better shape for strong winds is a flatter sail (12 percent depth, 45 percent draft position).

Figure 8-8:
A fuller sail shape (top) gives you more power.

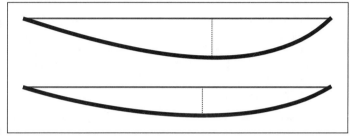

Controlling the power

We can use this concept of power to describe the effect of variations in sail shape. We start with the most important variations, moving down to the least important:

- **Angle of attack:** Power increases with increased angle — to the point where the sail stalls (when in doubt, let it out). At a 0-degree angle of attack, the sail is in line with the wind and is fully luffing — no power. As you trim the sail in, you increase the angle of attack.

- **Twist:** If the top of the sail has a 0-degree angle of attack to the wind and the bottom of the sail is perfectly trimmed to the wind, then the sail has a very *twisty* shape. Power increases with less twist — to a point (see the "Why twist at all?" sidebar). You can power up the sail by decreasing twist so that both the top and the bottom of the sail are perfectly trimmed.

- **Depth:** Power increases with depth — at least until the winds get stronger, when a deep shape has quite a bit of drag.

- **Draft position:** Draft position primarily affects the sail's capability to accelerate. Draft farther forward (about 40 percent or so) is a great accelerating shape — good for light or moderate air and waves that are constantly slowing the boat down. Draft farther aft (50 percent or more) is a better shape for straight-line speed in constant conditions.

Why twist at all?

You may think that zero twist has the most power, but that's rarely the case because of a phenomenon related to friction. At and near the water's surface, the true wind is significantly slowed by friction as it rubs against the water and waves. Moving up toward the top of the mast, the true wind speed increases. This vertical variation in true wind speed causes a situation of great interest to sailors — the apparent wind felt at the bottom of the sails is farther forward (more from the bow) than the apparent wind felt at the top of the sails. The fact that the wind shifts in direction up and down your sails (as long as you're moving and creating apparent wind) explains why zero twist is usually slow — because some level of the sail is overtrimmed and stalled. In most conditions, to get your sail at the optimum angle of attack at every level from top to bottom (for maximum power), you want to set the sails with a moderate amount of twist.

Reducing the power

On windy days, when you're sailing with the wind at or ahead of the beam (beam or close reaching and close-hauled), the boat wants to heel way over, indicating that it's overpowered. In this situation, you don't want full power from the sails. When the boat has reached its maximum heel angle (for optimum sailing speed) and the crew weight is outboard as far as possible (see Chapter 15 for more good stuff about hiking out and trapezing), then you must reduce the power in your sails. Here are four ways to do so:

✔ **Ease the sheets:** The quickest, fastest, and best way to "depower" your sails is by easing the sheet and decreasing the angle of attack. Slowly ease the mainsheet (or the traveler, if it's easier to handle, but keep the jib in unless it's really windy) and feel the heel decrease. Stop easing when the heel is at the optimum maximum angle, as discussed earlier in this chapter. It's okay if your sail luffs a little bit — you don't want to use that extra power.

✔ **Pinch:** Slowly turning the boat toward the wind also decreases the angle of attack. The danger here is that you slow down and stall out your centerboard or keel, so pinching is usually most effective when done subtly and combined with easing the mainsheet.

✔ **Add twist:** Keep in mind that adding twist is really just decreasing the angle of attack up high. Add twist by easing the mainsheet and jib sheet slightly. You can also move the jib lead back an inch or three to add twist in the jib, as described in the next section.

✔ **Make the sails as flat as possible:** Bend the mast (tighten the backstay), tighten the luff tension, and tighten the outhaul.

Trimming the jib

Some of the controls we cover in the preceding section apply to the mainsail only. But because your jib is the first sail to "see" the wind when you're sailing close-hauled, take a closer look at some of its controls.

Say it with us one more time: The sheet is the most important control because it affects the angle of attack of the sail. Get the sheet right, and you're doing better than most sailors on the water today! Simply ease out the sheet until the sail begins to luff and then slowly pull it in until the luffing just stops. When in doubt . . . (you know) . . . ease it out!

Luff tension on the jib is usually controlled by the halyard, just like on the mainsail, and the same rules apply. However, the jib doesn't have an outhaul to adjust foot tension or a boom vang to control twist. All that work is done by the jib sheet, with a little help from the *jib leads.* The jib leads, or *jib cars,* are the first fittings (usually a pulley or fairlead) through which each jib sheet (one on each side) passes as it comes from the sail on its way to the cockpit. (In Chapter 4, we describe the rigging process of the jib and the jib sheet, if you're feeling a bit confused at this point.)

Jib leads are typically adjustable fore and aft and affect the jib's twist. Move a lead too far forward and, as you trim the sheet, it pulls down on the jib leech too much, acting more like a boom vang and less like an outhaul. Move a lead too far aft and, as you trim the sheet, it pulls out on the foot excessively but doesn't pull down on the leech enough. The correct setting is in between these extremes, as shown in Figure 8-9.

Figure 8-9:
From left:
Jib sheet
lead too far
forward, too
far aft, and
just right.

Choosing the right jib

Some boats, mostly larger keelboats, have several jibs in varying sizes and strengths. In general, you want to use the biggest sail in light winds and the smallest sail in strong winds (for reduced power). Given two sails of equal size, the sail made out of the heavier cloth is better in stronger winds. Some boats have a sail selection chart that can help the crew determine which sail to use. The upwind sail selection chart in Table 8-1 is for a well-equipped 45-foot (14-m) racing boat. Figure 8-10 shows the profiles of all these sails.

Table 8-1	Sample Sail Selection Chart	
Wind Speed (Knots)	*Sail Name*	*Sail Size (% of Foretriangle)*
0-4	Light #1	152%
4-12	Medium #1	150%
9-18	Heavy #1	148%
16-23	#2	130%
20-28	#3	100%
25-35	#4	85%
over 35	Storm Jib	45%

Figure 8-10: Outlines of the different sails referred to in the sail selection chart.

Roller furlers

Some boats (mostly cruising keelboats) have a single jib that's rigged semi-permanently to the forestay with a *roller furling* system, as described in Chapter 4. This convenient system lets you roll up the sail on itself like a vertical window shade. When fully unrolled, the sail is at its maximum size. By totally releasing the sheets and pulling on a light line that is wrapped around a drum at the base of the forestay, the sail can be rolled up all the way or just partway — an instant sail change to a smaller sail! The shape of a partially-rolled jib is likely to be compromised somewhat (don't forget to move the jib lead forward), but for short-handed sailing on larger keelboats (over 30 feet or 9 m), roller furlers are much preferred over multiple headsails for ease of use.

Sailing Fast Downwind

Most of the principles of steering and trimming sails while sailing upwind apply equally well when the wind starts coming from more behind the boat. Usually, on these broader points of sail — "sailing downwind" (beam reaching and lower) — you need to increase the sails' power because the boat is heeling less. In times like these, you may want a *spinnaker* (large, lightweight, balloonlike sail used when sailing on reaches and runs) in your sail arsenal, but if you don't have one, or if your crew is on a coffee break and refuses to put up the spinnaker, here are some tips for getting the most out of your boat and sails:

- ✔ **Ease the luff tension (halyard and/or the cunningham) to make the sails as full and powerful as possible.**

- ✔ **Ease the outhaul to deepen the lower section of the mainsail.**

- ✔ **If the jib is still being trimmed on the leeward side, move the lead forward and outboard (about 1 foot on a 30-foot or 30 cm on a 9-m boat).**

- ✔ **On a dinghy, pull up the centerboard halfway to reduce drag.**

- ✔ **Make sure the mainsail (and the jib, if it's set) is sheeted properly, right on the verge of luffing.** If the wind is coming from too far behind you (broad reaching or running), then you may need to *wing out* the jib to get it to fill, as described in Chapter 5.

- ✔ **Minimize your steering to maximize momentum.**

- ✔ **Move the crew weight to make sure that your boat is level fore and aft.** For more information on the important aspects of fore and aft weight position, check out Chapter 15.

- ✔ **Set the boom vang to limit mainsail twist.**

When it won't luff

If the wind is within 10 degrees or so of being dead behind the boat (sailing on a run), the mainsail can't be eased to the point of luffing. In this case, as described in Chapter 5, the main is acting like a big barn door, not an airfoil, so you just set its angle of attack about perpendicular to the wind (that is, ease it out until the boom hits the shrouds).

Setting a spinnaker

Now for the fun sail — the spinnaker. Setting a spinnaker when going on a reach or downwind (with the wind on or behind the beam) can be like lighting up the turbochargers on a jet aircraft. Sailing with a spinnaker is fast, but because it's attached only at the corners, you can easily get into a love-hate relationship with this potentially unruly sail. Fortunately, you have this book, so get ready to love this big, fat, colorful, nylon balloon. The most common spinnaker is symmetrical, as shown in Figure 8-11.

Figure 8-11: Spinnakers in action.

Gathering your spinnaker equipment

To set a spinnaker, you need certain equipment, as shown in Figure 8-12:

- ✔ **Spinnaker pole:** A lightweight pole that attaches to the mast and supports the tack of the spinnaker when set.

- ✔ **Topping lift (also called the *pole lift* or *topper*):** Halyardlike control rope running from the mast, used to lift the outboard tip of the spinnaker pole into position.

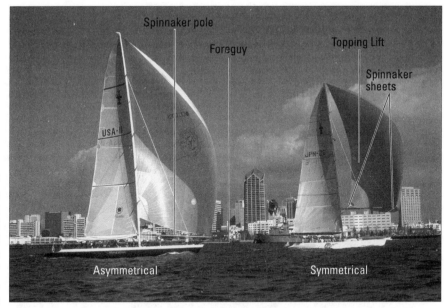

Figure 8-12:
Symmetrical
and
asymmetrical
spinnakers
and their
equipment.

- **Foreguy or downhaul:** Rope coming from the foredeck area, used to keep the outboard tip of the spinnaker pole from lifting too high.

- **Spinnaker halyard:** Rope used to hoist the spinnaker.

- **Spinnaker sheets:** Control ropes on either side of the boat used to adjust the sail's angle of attack. When the spinnaker is flying, these sheets change their names — the sheet on the windward side that goes through the fitting at the end of the spinnaker pole is called the *guy* or *afterguy.* The sheet on the leeward side is still the *sheet.* Of course, when you jibe, they swap names, because now the wind is blowing on the opposite side of the boat.

Preparing to hoist

Because spinnakers are made of ultralightweight cloth, they're most easily stored stuffed into a sail bag, or *spinnaker turtle.* Like its close cousin the parachute, a spinnaker must be meticulously prepared so that it deploys correctly. Nothing is more frustrating than expecting to see a big, powerful sail fill with air and, instead, seeing a twisted mass of nylon.

You can choose from several methods of packing the *chute* (sailor's slang for spinnaker), but they all have one thing in common: When the sail is stuffed back into its bag, all three corners are clearly separated, ready for attaching to their respective sheets and halyard, with no twists in the body of the sail.

Some racing crews on boats over 35 feet (11 m) go one step further and compress the body of the spinnaker with yarn or rubber bands so that it can be fully hoisted before it fills. This extra effort is nice but not necessary in all but the windiest conditions, as long as you use the *cruising hoist,* described later in this chapter.

Packing the chute is easiest on a nice big lawn, where you can stretch the sail out, run the leeches so there are no twists (as shown in Figure 8-13), and stuff it in the bag carefully, starting on its centerline and working toward the head and the two clews (until a chute is flying, it's said to have two clews and two leeches). The three corners of the sail (the head and clews) should be on top.

Figure 8-13:
Packing the chute the easy way, spread out on a lawn.

Sometimes a nice big lawn isn't available for packing — such as while you're afloat — but, fortunately, you can pack the chute within the confines of the boat's interior, with some creativity. Try tucking the head of the sail under a bunk cushion, and make sure the chute doesn't twist!

If you're in a rush, the chute still stands a very good chance of setting cleanly if you run one of the leeches (sliding your hands from one edge to the other and making sure there aren't any twists) and then don't twist the two corners attached to that edge when stuffing the sail into the bag. Your odds get even better when you run both leeches.

The ultimate embarrassment isn't setting your spinnaker with a twist — everyone has made that mistake innumerable times. It's setting your spinnaker sideways, with a clew at the masthead. You can't run and hide when that happens — everyone on the water sees you! And be assured that you will hear about it when you return to shore. The next section can help you avoid this ignominy.

Hooking up the spinnaker

In preparation for the set, the three corners of the spinnaker need to be attached to the three control ropes — the halyard and the two sheets. You may think that hooking up the ropes to the corners is a simple task, but, for some reason, this chore is the source of many problems. Here are some tips to make this job easier:

- ✔ **All three ropes should come up the same path to the sail.** If the sheets come in under the jib, then the halyard should, too.

- ✔ **Attach the halyard and sheets securely and to the correct corner!** Writing "head" on the head of the sail and so on really helps.

- ✔ **Make sure that your sheets and halyards are led properly — without any knots around stanchions, spreaders, and other paraphernalia in their paths.**

Hoisting: the "cruising set"

Being deliberate with each stage of setting the spinnaker pays off. Nothing is worse than a spinnaker filling when it's halfway hoisted, because then the halyard has tons of load as you haul it to the top. Here are the steps to a conservative spinnaker-setting procedure that Peter calls a *cruising set*. The beauty of this set is that the sail doesn't fill until you're ready for it.

1. **Make sure that the spinnaker is attached to the sheets and halyard properly and that the bag is secured to the boat.**

2. **Connect the inboard end of the spinnaker pole to the mast, attach the topping lift and foreguy to the outboard end, and then raise the pole.**

   The correct height depends on your boat and the wind conditions. Make sure that the guy is running through the outboard end of the pole.

3. **Turn the boat onto a very broad reach or run (be careful not to jibe accidentally).**

   This action reduces the apparent wind and lets you hoist the spinnaker behind the mainsail — protected from the force of the wind.

4. **Make sure the crew is ready and call for the sail to be hoisted.**

5. **As the sail is being hoisted, pull the guy until the clew of the spinnaker touches the pole.**

   If you're using winches, make sure that you have enough wraps on the winch drum to take the load when the sail fills. For more about winch use, see Chapter 6.

6. **When the halyard is fully hoisted and cleated, set the guy to its proper position, drop the jib, turn the boat onto the desired course, and trim the sheet as required.**

Trimming the spinnaker

Trimming a spinnaker is similar to trimming any other sail. Get the angle of attack right, and you're off and running. Unfortunately, the spinnaker doesn't luff gently when it's undertrimmed; it collapses and flaps in a loud manner that makes you feel like something is very wrong. Your spinnaker will inevitably collapse, because it's a relatively finicky sail that requires constant — and we mean constant — attention.

The key to trimming the spinnaker is working through a basic cycle — again and again. First, set the guy, then the sheet, then the pole height, and then the guy again. Here are the rules of spinnaker trim.

1. **Set the guy so that the pole is about 90 degrees to the apparent wind (less for tight reaches with the wind near the beam).**

2. **Trim the sheet so that the luff of the sail has a small curl in it.**

   If you trim just a little bit more, the curl disappears, and the sail looks completely full. If you ease just a little bit more, the curl gets larger and ultimately causes the sail to collapse.

3. **Set the outboard end of the pole height so that the tack of the spinnaker is level with the clew.**

4. **Set the height of the inboard end of the spinnaker pole, if it's adjustable, so that the pole is horizontal.**

Like every other sail, the control rope that gets the most work is the spinnaker sheet. The trimmer must tend it constantly to keep the chute full, occasionally checking the pole angle (guy trim) and pole height (topping lift setting).

The spinnaker can collapse in two ways:

- ✔ **Downwind collapse:** In this case, the sail falls into itself, usually caving in on top and ultimately hanging like a limp mass. The cure for a downwind collapse is to turn the boat up toward the wind until the sail fills and/or bring the pole aft (trim the guy) and ease the sheet.

✔ **Upwind collapse:** When the wind comes too far forward for the trim of the chute (too little angle of attack), the spinnaker collapses into the shaking mass described at the beginning of this section. The cure is to turn the boat away from the wind until the sail fills and/or trim the sheet.

Jibing the spinnaker

Any maneuver with a spinnaker can be a trial, but, thanks to the cruising set (and the *cruising takedown,* outlined in the following section), the most difficult maneuver is, without question, the jibe. You know you've jibed successfully when a) the sail fills cleanly on the new jibe with the pole set properly; b) the sail stays full during the entire jibe; c) nothing (and no one) falls in the water; and d) the crew member on the bow comes back into the cockpit with a big smile on his face. A spinnaker jibe is shown in Figure 8-14.

Here are the steps to a successful jibe:

1. **Make sure the crew is ready and in position.**

2. **Turn the boat down to a very broad reach (so that the turn during the jibe isn't very sharp) and retrim the chute accordingly.**

3. **Announce the turn into the jibe by saying "Jibe-ho," "Jibing," "Here we go," or anything else that makes sense.**

4. **Trim the guy back and ease the sheet so that the spinnaker is still trimmed perfectly.**

   Because the boat's angle to the wind is changing, this step is crucial throughout the maneuver. In a good jibe, you must continue to rotate the spinnaker so that it stays full.

5. **Turn the boat into the jibe while shifting the pole from the old windward side to the new windward side.**

   This step is often the hardest part of the jibe because it requires fancy footwork on the foredeck and coordination on the part of the foredeck team, trimmers, and helmsman to facilitate the switch. Stop the turn when you're on a very broad reach on a new jibe.

6. **When everybody is ready, the helmsman can turn up to a sharper reach (requiring further trimming of the spinnaker), if desired.**

Make sure that you rotate the spinnaker. One of the most common errors in spinnaker jibes is not rotating the spinnaker around as the boat is turned through the jibe. The result is a tangled-up mess, with the spinnaker often blowing between the forestay and the mast. Practice jibing the spinnaker without the pole to get the feel of rotating the sail with the sheets. In light air, pull the mainsheet in tight (overtrimmed) or even drop it completely to facilitate this drill.

A

B

C

D

Figure 8-14:
The steps
to a
successful
spinnaker
jibe.

Whether you have a spinnaker up or not, a jibe can be a pretty wild maneu-ver in windy conditions. The force of the mainsail swinging across and filling with a BANG on the new side can generate a major turning force that can lead to a capsize on a dinghy and a *broach* (rapid, out-of-control turn up toward the wind) in a keelboat. In windy weather (over 12 to 15 knots), the helmsman can perform an *S-jibe* to counteract the momentum caused at the moment the mainsail fills after a jibe.

Switching the pole: Dip pole versus end for end

Depending on the type of boat, you can use one of two methods for shifting the pole. The *end-for-end* jibe is common on dinghies and smaller keelboats. During the jibe, the two pole ends are disconnected and reattached so that the old inboard end is attached to the new guy, and the pole is pushed out so that the old outboard end can be attached to the mast.

The *dip-pole* jibe is common on keelboats over 40 feet (12 m). During the jibe, the pole's outboard end is disconnected from the old guy, lowered so that it can swing through the foretriangle behind the forestay, and then connected to the new guy and raised up into position on the new windward side.

Start on a very broad reach to minimize the turn. When the crew is ready, bear away (gently) to jibe while you (or another crew) haul in on the mainsheet. At the split second in the turn when the boom catches wind and begins to move across the boat, reverse the helm about 15 degrees, steering the boat back toward the old jibe. This "S-turn" counteracts the momentum of the boom and keeps the boat from turning too far when the mainsail fills on the new jibe. A second later, just after the mainsail fills with a bang on the new jibe, you can reverse the helm again and steer straight (or wherever you need to steer in order to be on a very broad reach on new jibe).

Taking the spinnaker down

When the party's over, it's time to go back upwind. The takedown is the easiest of the three spinnaker maneuvers, as long as you plan it early enough that the helmsman can keep the boat pointing downwind — hiding the lowered spinnaker behind the mainsail until everything is cleaned up and ready to go upwind. Here are the steps to a *cruising takedown:*

1. **Turn the boat onto a very broad reach and hoist the jib (optional).**

2. **Collapse the spinnaker by easing the guy forward and pulling in the sheet.**

   When the sail collapses and is docile, protected from the wind behind the mainsail, you're ready for the next step.

3. **Grab the sheet and begin pulling the sail on board.**

4. **Ease the halyard in concert with the sail being pulled in so that the sail doesn't fall into the water (drops too fast) or require a struggle from the takedown team (drops too slow).**

5. **Stuff the spinnaker into the forward hatch (if you have one) or into the back hatch or spinnaker bag.**

6. **Lower the pole and secure it and the spinnaker sheets.**

When Peter raced on *Stars & Stripes* in the America's Cup, they had four different varieties of takedowns. Dinghies and smaller keelboats often take the spinnaker down on the windward side in races. You can also find several other types of racing spinnaker sets. But those methods all require tons of practice, whereas the good ol' cruising set and takedown work on any boat and are the easiest way to get that colorful sail up and down.

Asymmetrical kites

Asymmetrical spinnakers have a luff longer than the leech and are designed to be flown like a big jib (refer to Figure 8-12). They're popular cruising sails because of their ease of use. For that same reason, they're growing in popularity on high-performance racing boats, too.

An asymmetrical spinnaker doesn't have a guy; it simply has a tack line that holds that corner of the sail down to the bow, a spinnaker pole, or a built-in bow pole called a *sprit.* At the clew are two sheets, one for the left side and one for the right, just like a jib. Sets and takedowns are still a handful (unless you use the cruising method), but jibes are as easy as pie because you don't have a pole that you have to shift (except on the very few boats that fly these sails from traditional spinnaker poles), and the sail is meant to collapse as it jibes, blowing around the front of the boat.

Chapter 9

Anchoring and Advanced Docking

. . . .

In This Chapter

▶ Picking the right anchor and rode

▶ Taking care of the ground tackle

▶ Dropping anchor — and picking it back up

▶ Anchoring under sail

▶ Troubleshooting anchoring problems

▶ Being safe and tactful at anchor

▶ Advanced docking techniques

. . . .

Anchors aweigh, my boys,
Anchors aweigh!
Farewell to college joys,
We sail at break of day.

— Alfred Hart Miles

Although nowadays many quiet little coves that used to be perfect for a peaceful night at anchor are filled with mooring buoys and marinas, knowing how to anchor is important for those times when you run out of wind or want to try to find a special spot that's all your own. Before reading this chapter, you may want to refer to Chapter 6, which covers the basics of tying up (securing your boat) to a dock or mooring (a permanently anchored buoy). Anchoring your boat is more involved than tying it to a mooring because you're responsible for lowering the anchor and making sure that it's secure. This chapter covers many different methods for leaving your boat secure on the water — whether at anchor or in a difficult docking situation.

Types of Anchors

How do you keep a floating object anchored? One way is to find a really heavy rock, tie a rope to it, and throw it overboard. But what happens when you want to leave that spot and go someplace else? Hauling that enormous rock on board may be impossible. Another problem with the rock method is wind or current. A strong wind pushes very hard on your boat, which, in turn, pulls very hard on your rock — so hard that it may simply slide or roll across the bottom. Fortunately, you have a better way — thanks to the invention of properly designed anchors.

Most anchors share the following characteristics, as shown in Figure 9-1:

- ✔ **They sink!** (An anchor wouldn't work very well if it floated, would it?)
- ✔ **They have holding power, thanks to one or more prongs or points called *flukes*.** These flukes act like the blade of a shovel to dig into the bottom. Because the flukes help grip the bottom, the anchor can weigh less, making it easier to bring on board.
- ✔ **They have a long arm, or *shank*, providing mechanical advantage to help the flukes dig in.**
- ✔ **They have some sort of feature to help keep the flukes dug in when the boat pulls from a different direction.**
- ✔ **Despite their holding power, they can be "unstuck" relatively easily.**

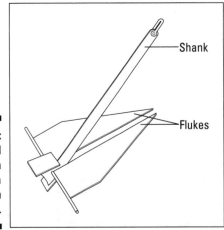

Figure 9-1:
Flukes and shank on a Danforth, a common anchor.

Several different types of anchors are commonly used by sailboats. Various anchors perform differently, depending on such factors as the type of bottom (sand, mud, grass, or rock). Each type of anchor has its own strengths and weaknesses, so choosing the correct anchor for your boat may involve some compromises.

Danforth anchor

A common sailing anchor, the *Danforth* anchor (shown in Figure 9-1), is named for the company that invented it. It's also called the *lightweight anchor;* because the large flukes bury so well, the anchor can be lighter. The Danforth needs a soft sand or mud bottom (two of the most desirable bottom types for anchoring, due to their holding potential) to grip properly. This anchor is especially popular on dinghies and small keelboats because of its light weight and low profile on board. This anchor is not perfect, however; the sharp points on its flukes can be troublesome in storage. Some larger keelboats (over 30 feet or 9 m) may carry an undersized Danforth as a "lunch hook" for easy temporary anchoring in calm conditions as well as a heavier, primary anchor.

Plow anchor

The plow anchor looks like the farm implement — hence the name. It's also called by the trade name "CQR." The plow is secure on most bottoms and is arguably the best all-around anchor for larger sailboats (over 30 feet or 9 m). Although heavier than a Danforth with the equivalent holding power, the plow can get the job done in most conditions. As Figure 9-2 shows, the plow is often kept secured up forward on a roller with the fluke hanging over the bow. You would never see this sight on a racing boat — too much weight up forward!

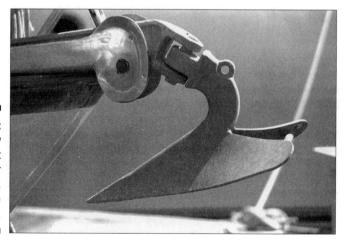

Figure 9-2:
A plow anchor set in its roller on the bow, ready to go to work.

Other types of anchors

The preceding sections describe the most common sailing anchors, but you may run across the following types, as well (see Figure 9-3):

- ✔ The *fisherman* anchor (also called the *yachtsman's* or *Admiralty* anchor) is the heaviest and bulkiest of the modern anchors. This feature alone makes the fisherman anchor less practical for sailboats.

- ✔ The *Bruce* anchor was introduced on North Sea oil rigs (those things must really pull in a storm!) and is one solid piece.

- ✔ The *grapnel* anchor has multiple sharp flukes, like fish hooks. It works well in weeds or grass but isn't normally considered a primary anchor for a sailboat.

- ✔ The *mushroom* anchor looks like its namesake. It's very heavy and can be extremely difficult to dislodge from a muddy bottom — all excellent features for its chief use as a permanent anchor for a mooring.

Figure 9-3:
The fisherman, Bruce, grapnel, and mushroom anchors.

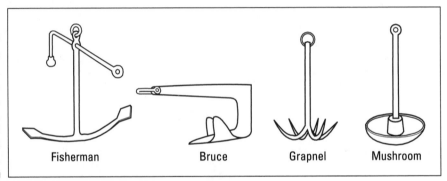

Fisherman   Bruce   Grapnel   Mushroom

Choosing the right anchor

The description of individual anchors and their characteristics should give you an idea of what kind of anchor (or anchors) you want. Table 9-1 gives you a quick rundown on what weight that anchor should be, based on the boat's size. As you can see, the fisherman anchor is really too heavy to be considered for most sailboats.

Table 9-1	Anchor Weight		
Boat Length	**Danforth**	**Plow**	**Fisherman**
20 ft (6 m)	5 lb (2 kg)	15 lb (6 kg)	25 lb (9 kg)
30 ft (9 m)	12 lb (5 kg)	20 lb (8 kg)	35 lb (13 kg)
40 ft (12 m)	20 lb (8 kg)	35 lb (13 kg)	55 lb (21 kg)
50 ft (15 m)	35 lb (13 kg)	45 lb (17 kg)	75 lb (28 kg)
60 ft (18 m)	60 lb (22 kg)	60 lb (22 kg)	100 lb (37 kg)

Adapted from Earl Hinz, *The Complete Book of Anchoring and Mooring* (Centreville, Maryland: Cornell Maritime Press, 1986).

This table is a rough guide to anchor size. If your boat is especially *beamy* (wide) or heavy, use a heavier anchor.

The Whole Anchor Package

Ground tackle is the term for the entire package — the anchor plus the *anchor rode* (the line and chain that attach the anchor to the boat). The anchor rode must be strong and elastic enough to absorb the shocks of the boat jerking in waves and wind without breaking or dislodging the anchor and must orient the force pulling on the anchor to be as nearly parallel to the bottom (horizontal) as possible.

Don't use just any rope for your anchor line. Here are a few characteristics of a good anchor rope:

- ✔ **Long enough for anchoring properly**
- ✔ **Resistant to chafe**
- ✔ **Stretchy enough to absorb the surging load without yanking the anchor out**
- ✔ **Strong enough to hold your boat in expected conditions**

Nylon rope is recommended for anchor lines because it provides the best balance of performance in these key areas.

An anchor rode should be a combination of rope and chain. Attach the chain end to the anchor. The chain sinks, so the pulling force on the anchor comes from that all-important horizontal direction, parallel to the bottom. In addition, chain doesn't chafe and allows the anchor rope to rise above any sharp objects on the bottom.

Securing the anchor and rode

The chain is usually connected to the anchor line with an *eye splice* (a permanent loop that is woven into the end of the rope) and a *shackle* (a U-shaped metal fitting) instead of simply tying a knot. Knots can come untied — and need we point out that the last thing you want is to have your anchor line come untied?

Another anchor rode worry is chafe, and with an eye splice you can use a *thimble* (teardrop-shaped metal fitting that fits tightly inside an eye splice) to cut down on chafing. (To find out about eye splices, see Chapter 19.) If you must use a knot, tie a round turn and a couple of half hitches or a fisherman's bend. (See Appendix B for the lowdown on these knots.) Regardless of the knot, you may want to further secure the bitter end from untying by *seizing* it — using a needle and thread to sew it.

With two strong shackles, you can attach the chain to the anchor line and to the anchor. Use a pair of vice grips or pliers to really tighten the shackles and then *mouse* them — run a few loops of galvanized wire or small line through a hole in the shackle pin to keep it from loosening. Grease the shackle threads so that they don't freeze up. A galvanized steel (which doesn't rust) or bronze shackle is best.

The general rule is to have chain that weighs as much as your anchor. For example, a 30-foot boat with a 12-pound Danforth anchor needs roughly 16 feet of chain attached to the anchor. Table 9-2 shows the recommended diameter of rope, diameter of chain, and length of chain to use for different sizes of boats.

Table 9-2	Anchor Rode Specifications		
Boat Length	**Nylon Rope Diameter**	**Chain Diameter**	**Chain Length**
20 ft (6 m)	$3/8$ in (1 cm)	$1/4$ in (6 mm)	6–33 ft (2–10 m)
30 ft (9 m)	$7/16$ in (11 mm)	$1/4$ in (6 mm)	16–46 ft (5–14 m)
40 ft (12 m)	$1/2$ in (13 mm)	$5/16$ in (8 mm)	18–48 ft (6–15 m)
50 ft (15 m)	$5/8$ in (16 mm)	$3/8$ in (1 cm)	21–46 ft (7–14 m)
60 ft (18 m)	$3/4$ in (19 mm)	$7/16$ in (11 mm)	27–44 ft (9–13 m)

Note: The two numbers in the right-hand column indicate the range in chain length for use with the lightest (Danforth) and the heaviest (fisherman's) anchor.

Adapted from Earl Hinz, *The Complete Book of Anchoring and Mooring* (Centreville, Maryland: Cornell Maritime Press, 1986).

Resist the temptation to go up in anchor rope diameter. You get better strength, but you get less stretch, which is important in keeping the anchor hooked in rough, surging conditions. Plus, anchor lines take up enough space on board already without increasing their diameter unnecessarily.

Anchoring with all chain

Some bigger cruising boats have all-chain anchor rodes. Obviously, these rodes are much heavier, but chain is also stronger and more durable than nylon rope. A total chain anchor rode enables you to use less *scope* (see the next section) for given conditions. Although chain doesn't stretch, it can provide some shock absorption if the rode has enough scope that it arcs down to the anchor. A pulse of wind or wave on the boat simply pulls some of this arc out of the rode, absorbing some of the energy. Boats with chain rodes usually have an electric anchor windlass — forcing the crew to handle the chain rode is cruel and unusual punishment!

Figuring scope

In the cartoons, Popeye simply drops the anchor over the side until it hits bottom and then cleats it off. That's in the cartoons. In the real world, you need to let out much more rope than the depth of the water.

The length of the anchor rode does *depend* upon the depth of the water where you're anchoring but doesn't *equal* it. You determine the maximum depth of the water you're anchoring in (at high tide), but then you multiply that number by another number to give you the length of line you need. This effect of *scope,* or the ratio between the amount of anchor rode you let out and the water's depth, is an important concept to understand when anchoring. The more scope (that is, the more rope you let out), the more the pull on the anchor is from that much-desired horizontal direction, which means better holding power, as shown in Figure 9-4.

Too little scope is dangerous — the pull on the anchor is more vertical, and your boat can easily dislodge the anchor at high tide or on the top of a big wave. You don't have to worry about too much scope, as long as you have plenty of room for the boat to swing if the wind or current shifts direction. But too much scope is a problem in a tight anchorage because your boat may swing into other boats or into very shallow water where you could hit bottom, if Mother Nature changes her direction.

The basic rule is to use *5:1 scope* (five times the depth of the water at high tide) for average conditions. For example, if the anchorage is 20 feet deep at high tide, then you let out 100 feet of anchor rode (roughly 10 feet of chain and 90 feet of nylon anchor line).

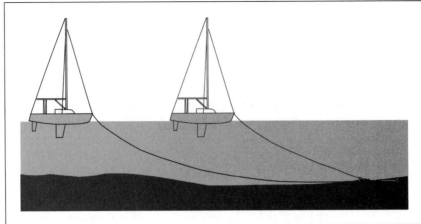

Figure 9-4:
More scope
means
better
holding
power.

So that you can easily tell how many feet or meters of line you have let out, you can sew or insert small fabric markers into your anchor line at set intervals. Never tie permanent knots in a line for this purpose because knots weaken the line.

If the conditions are very mild and you plan on stopping for only a short break on board, you can probably get away with laying out 3:1 scope. Less scope means less work hauling in that soggy wet rope when you want to get under way. If the conditions are more severe or if you will be leaving the boat, then increase the scope up to 7:1 or even more. Just like in sail trim, a good rule is, "When in doubt, let it out!"

Maintaining the anchor and rode

Because your anchor and rode spend most of the time stored in some dark compartment, inspecting this vital equipment from time to time is important. Check your chain for rusty or weakened links and examine the anchor line for chafe or wear.

The most common place for chafe on an anchor line is where the line has to turn a corner to come on board your boat. A good way to minimize wear is to build a makeshift chafe guard by slicing a short piece of garden hose and wrapping it around the anchor line where it turns the corner over the *bow chock*. If you're at anchor in rough conditions for longer than a day, periodically pull up (hard) or let out (easy) several feet of anchor line to prevent chafe in one spot.

Dropping Anchor

Dropping anchor involves more than just tying the anchor to some line and throwing it overboard. Anchoring involves such skills as picking a good spot by avoiding underwater hazards; knowing the water's depth, how much the tide will rise and fall, and the contour and type of bottom (that is, rocks or sand); and knowing what the weather is going to do. After reading this section, you'll be able to anchor like an old salt.

Picking a good place to anchor

To know where to anchor, you need to familiarize yourself with a chart of the area. (See Chapter 11 for how to read a nautical chart.) From the chart, you can determine the water depth and the type of bottom to find a suitable anchorage. On a trip, you can buy a local "cruising guide," which points out special considerations about various spots.

For comfort, you want to find an anchorage protected from the prevailing wind and wave direction. For safety, you need to find

- ✔ **A suitable bottom for securing your anchor**
- ✔ **Enough depth to avoid the danger of grounding but not so much depth that retrieving the anchor is a chore**
- ✔ **Sufficient room for your boat to swing in all directions**
- ✔ **A quiet location out of any channel**
- ✔ **A location protected from waves and strong winds**

Finding the lee

Very few anchorages are protected in all wind directions, so your first step is to note the current wind direction and review the marine weather forecast available on the VHF radio. (See Chapter 10 for more information about weather and VHF marine forecasts.) A good, protected anchorage is in the *lee* of the wind — that is, the adjacent land blocks the force of the wind and waves. If the forecast is for strong, easterly breezes, for example, you want to anchor just to the west of the protecting land mass.

Alongside a *lee shore* (shore facing the oncoming wind and waves) is the most dangerous place for an anchored boat. If the anchor slips at all, you may find yourself getting washed up onto the beach . . . or worse. Anchoring along a lee shore is like standing in the middle of the road — you may be safe for a while, but your odds aren't so good. The tricky part is that with a 180-degree wind shift, your nice, protected anchorage can become the dreaded lee shore. Check out Chapter 12 for more on the dangers of the lee shore.

Checking out the bottom

As we discuss earlier, each anchor has its "favorite" bottom types. Presuming that you're relying on one of the lighter types (rather than a fisherman's anchor), you can never go wrong by dropping the hook in some medium-soft mud. Avoid a rocky bottom, because the flukes of the anchor have nothing to dig into there. The chart often indicates bottom type.

Keeping an eye on depth

Because charts indicate the water depth at *mean low water* (low tide), seeing spots that are deep enough for your boat is easy. In waves, allow a few more feet of clearance when the boat is down in the trough. Better yet, avoid anchoring in waves; the idea of anchoring is to relax and get a break from the open water conditions.

Avoiding underwater hazards

Study the chart carefully so that you can avoid underwater hazards such as rocks, cables, and shipwrecks — these items should be well marked on the chart. No anchor works well in rocks, so you definitely want to avoid them. Nothing is worse than getting your anchor so stuck on an object that you have to go swimming or even cut it away.

Fortunately for us humans, the world is becoming more ecologically aware. For example, in the Virgin Islands (where you can enjoy some of the nicest cruising in the world, as we point out in Chapter 17), the local authorities now place mooring buoys at popular anchorages. Because tying up to a mooring is infinitely easier than dropping the hook, life is now much easier for those of us above the water's surface. But the reason for the moorings is to protect the creatures underwater. Dropping an anchor onto a coral reef causes irreparable damage to this priceless feature of our tropical oceans. Don't do it. If you must anchor near coral reefs, put on your mask and snorkel and help navigate the anchor and chain to a safe area on the bottom.

Staying away from crowds

Avoid crowded anchorages, where you're restricted in the amount of scope you can let out. In a squall, one of these neighboring boats may drag its anchor — possibly into your boat! A boat at anchor swings with the winds and current, so make sure that your boat is free to swing in a circle around the anchor (see Figure 9-5).

If you must choose a spot in a crowded anchorage, check out your potential new neighbors. A large powerboat may run a noisy generator all night. Netting on the lifelines and Mickey Mouse swim floats signify the delights of small children on board.

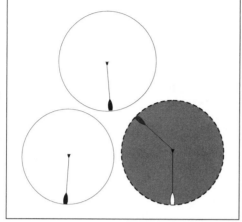

Figure 9-5:
Allow room
for your
boat to
swing
around the
anchor.

Looking out for the current

Use the chart or tide books to ascertain the local currents. Avoid anchoring in places with strong current. For more on currents, see Chapter 10.

Spending enough time choosing the best anchorage *before* you drop anchor is much easier than having to pull up that anchor and move.

Getting ready to anchor

After you study the harbor carefully and find the perfect spot to anchor, you want to put that anchor in securely on your first try. Anchoring can be stressful, and knowing that all the folks on nearby anchored boats are watching your every move doesn't help.

The key to anchoring is waiting to drop the anchor until the boat is dead in the water and just beginning to drift backward — similar to picking up a mooring (covered in Chapter 6). Keep in mind that the easiest way to go backward on a sailboat is under power. Anchoring under power also has the advantage of letting you clear the *foredeck* (area on deck in front of the mast) of sails before you get started so the crew has space to prepare the anchor without stepping on or dirtying the sails. (We show you how to anchor under sail in a few more pages.)

The most common anchoring mishaps are caused by not preparing the anchor rode to run out smoothly. Murphy's Law is definitely in force during anchoring. The knots and tangles that a long piece of rope can get itself into are amazing. While the skipper is finding the ideal anchorage, one or two crew can prepare the ground tackle.

When the skipper has selected a spot, make sure that the crew up forward know the depth, so that they can prepare enough anchor rode.

Take the time to lay out *(flake)* enough line so that it can run out smoothly until the anchor can touch the bottom, and neatly coil the remainder (with the part closest to the anchor on top) so that it's ready to run. If your boat has a *chain locker* (small compartment in the bow that holds the anchor rode "preflaked"), then you need to pull out and arrange only enough line for the anchor to hit bottom. The rest of the rope in the chain locker pays out cleanly as the boat is backed away from the anchor.

If you bring the anchor on deck, make sure that you lead the anchor line through the bow chock, under the *bow pulpit* (the metal frame surrounding the bow to which the forward ends of the lifelines attach).

Before anchoring, make a final inspection of the anchor line for chafe, check that the shackles are tight, and make sure that the bitter end of the anchor rode is tied securely to the boat.

Follow these steps to drop the anchor:

1. **Approach the spot from several boatlengths to leeward and then turn the boat head-to-wind.**

2. **Slow the boat down and stop right over your desired anchor spot.**

   This spot isn't where the boat will sit; it's where the anchor goes. The boat will lie downwind (or *down current*) of this spot. As the wind or current shifts, your boat swings around this spot (hopefully without dislodging the anchor) in a 360-degree circle.

3. **Give the signal.**

   The key to anchoring is waiting to drop the anchor until the boat is starting to go backward. Because the best judge of this matter is the skipper, the crew on the bow waits to drop the anchor until they see a hand signal (pointing down quickly works) or hear a hail such as, "Drop the anchor, mateys."

   Hails can be difficult to hear in a strong wind.

4. **Drop the hook.**

   Hook is sailor slang for anchor. See the next section for how to drop the anchor.

Dropping the hook

The safest way to lower the anchor over the side is hand over hand, although that method may be difficult at first because you may have to heave the anchor away from the boat to clear the topsides. Try not to let the chain touch the hull as it runs out. When the anchor and chain are safely in the water, let the anchor line slide out through the bow chock.

Keep your body (especially your feet and fingers) away from and out of the loops of anchor line as it pays out.

You can tell when the anchor has touched bottom — either the rope stops paying out so fast, or you feel the weight of the anchor disappear as it settles in. The foredeck crew's job isn't over when the anchor hits pay dirt; you need to let out plenty of scope (see the section "Figuring scope," earlier in this chapter). When enough line has gone out, the foredeck crew cleats off the anchor line and gives the signal to the helmsman that they're ready to set the anchor.

Digging in for awhile

You can ensure that your anchor is set and holding in a couple of ways:

> ✔ **By touching the anchor rode with your hand, you can sometimes feel the anchor bounce over the bottom, similar to taking someone's pulse.** When the anchor digs in, the bouncing stops, but the line stretches and contracts as the boat surges in waves.

> ✔ **With the boat in reverse, you may be able to see the bow dip when the flukes of the anchor take a grip on the bottom.**

If you feel jerking motions, the anchor is dragging along the bottom. If your anchor keeps dragging, you can try any of the following techniques to get the anchor to set:

> ✔ **Let out more scope.** The anchor is probably skipping along the bottom, and with more scope, the anchor can dig in.

> ✔ **A quick tug on the anchor line may get the anchor to set.**

> ✔ **Rev the engine in reverse to try to set the anchor.**

If you keep dragging, you may have to pick up your anchor and try again.

When your senses tell you that the anchor is holding, try to confirm that by watching landmarks or a range. By sighting through two objects, you can establish a line sight and watch your position to ensure that you're not dragging, as shown in Figure 9-6.

Figure 9-6:
Sighting
through a
buoy
(complete
with sea
lions) and a
large tree.

To be doubly sure that your anchor is holding, try the following:

- ✔ **Assess the expected conditions, type of anchor and rode, and antici-pated length of stay and then calculate your desired scope (as outlined in Table 9-2) and readjust the anchor line accordingly.**

- ✔ **If a convenient range is not available, take a few compass bearings on some distinctive landmarks or buoys (especially in the direction perpendicular to your anchor line) for reference.** For more informa-tion about taking bearings, see Chapter 11.

- ✔ **Share the range with your crew so they can double-check that you're securely anchored.**

- ✔ **Write down these safety bearings so that, when your insomnia kicks in at two in the morning, you can reassure yourself that your boat is okay.** However, your range and bearings change if the boat swings with wind or current shifts.

The Rules of the Road require an anchored boat to display a black ball up in the mast during daytime and a 360-degree fixed (not flashing) white light at night.

Retrieving Your Anchor

The key to picking up the anchor is teamwork between the crew and skipper. After assigning positions, including the key role of the crew on the foredeck, follow these steps:

1. **Slowly motor directly toward the anchor.**

   The helmsman probably needs the crew (who is performing Step 2) to occasionally point left or right to help keep on track.

2. **At the same time, the crew pulls the slack out of the anchor line.**

   Slack in the line is created when you move up on the anchor. This task requires almost no physical effort, because you're simply pulling in limp line.

3. **When the boat is directly over the anchor, the crew signals for the helmsman to stop.**

4. **Shift into neutral while the crew securely cleats the anchor line.**

5. **When the line is cleated, the crew signals that the helmsman can start slowly going forward again until the anchor comes free.**

   Because the anchor line is pulling up and forward (the opposite direction it was dug in) on the anchor, the flukes usually lift out of the muddy bottom easily.

   Don't blow out your back — let the boat's engine do the tough work of getting the anchor free of the bottom.

   You can tell when the anchor is free because the bow bounces up slightly and the anchor line has less pressure on it.

6. **When the anchor is free, put the engine back into neutral and begin the hardest part of the exercise — raising the anchor to the deck.**

   If you're lucky enough to have an electric *windlass* (winch-type mechanism on the foredeck used to pull in the anchor rope and chain), you may not even break a sweat in the final stage of the process as the anchor is lifted off the bottom and back to the boat; otherwise, get ready to pull and pull and pull some more.

   Regardless of the equipment on board, let the engine do all the work until the anchor has broken free from the ground. Take extra care to keep from dragging the chain (and anchor) along the hull.

7. **Before you bring your trusty anchor back on board, take a look at it as it clears the water and clean it if necessary.**

   Chances are that the anchor has some remnants of its temporary home still attached to it. Mud or sand may come off with repeated dunkings. If not, grab the old standbys — a bucket and a brush — to clean the sticky stuff off the anchor and chain before storing them.

8. Put the anchor away.

If your anchor gets stored on a bow roller, make sure that it's safely lashed in place before setting sail.

Anchoring under Sail

Anchoring under power is much easier than anchoring under sail — the sails are out of the way, the boat's easier to control, and the entire crew can concentrate on the task at hand. But if you don't have an engine or if you want to try something new, anchoring under sail is certainly possible.

Believe it or not, you want to anchor at certain times during sailboat races — such as when the current is pushing you backward faster than you can sail forward.

We recommend dropping, folding, and stowing the jib before approaching the drop spot, so that the anchor team has room to do its work.

The key to anchoring under sail is boat control — slowing the boat to a stop at your desired anchor drop spot and then *backing* the mainsail (pushing the boom out so that the main fills) to go backward until enough scope is out to get the anchor to set. At first, put the tiller in the center. After you start sailing backward, you can turn the stern to the left (to port) by turning the tiller to the right (to starboard), and vice versa. Be careful not to over-steer — a little rudder movement goes a long way. Practice going backward out in the open until you get it right. After you master sailing backward, the steps to dropping the anchor are the same as in the preceding section.

All boats are less maneuverable at low speeds — and sailboats can be tricky to get going again. So the toughest part of anchoring under sail is that, for a moment, you intentionally stop the boat, and you lose steerageway until you pick up speed in reverse. This loss of maneuverability is why we recommend practicing first in open water. Leave your mainsail up (and luffing) until you're sure that you're safely anchored, so that you can escape under sail if you have any problems.

If you do lose steerageway and are stopped dead, pointing straight into the wind, you're simply *in irons*. The technique for getting out of irons is described in Chapter 5 — put the tiller to one side until the bow is on a tack, and then you can trim your sail and get going again.

Special Considerations about Anchoring

As illustrated in the preceding sections, anchoring shouldn't be taken lightly; you need to consider many factors before anchoring properly. Whether you plan to leave your anchored boat for a picnic on the beach, go for a quick snorkeling trip, or just want some peace of mind so that you can fall asleep down below while at anchor, read this section to avoid common anchoring problems, review anchoring safety tips, and be aware of basic anchoring etiquette.

Anchoring problems

Here's our "what-if" section. We take the most common anchor problems and provide you with a solution.

✔ **You lose your anchor:** If you don't have a spare, you'd better head for a dock. This possibility is why carefully checking your ground tackle — every chain link and every shackle — before using it is so important.

✔ **You start swinging too close to another boat:** Some boats "sail" around quite a bit under anchor, powered by the force of the wind on the mast and hull. You can't do much to prevent this movement. But if you're swinging too close to another boat, either due to this "sailing" or a shift in the wind, someone has to move. Conventional etiquette says the boat that anchored last has to move, but if no one is aboard the other boat, then you just pulled the short straw.

✔ **You think your anchor starts dragging several hours after you anchored:** Keep in mind that your boat swings around the anchor depending on changes in the direction of the wind and current. The compass bearings that you took to double-check that you were securely anchored aren't valid when your boat has switched direction in the current. Before going to sleep, make sure that you have a strong mental picture of the anchorage and your boat's position — you can even mark your position on the chart or with your *GPS* (satellite navigation device; see Chapter 11). Some GPS units have an "anchor watch" alarm that rings if the boat moves out of a set area.

The added load from wind and waves in a storm may cause the anchor to drag. If you know that more wind is coming, consider seeking better shelter. If you decide to stay, let out plenty of additional scope (in rough conditions, as much as 10:1 scope may be needed). If you have a second anchor, you may want to set it (see the section "Doubling up: two anchors," later in this chapter) if you get caught in really nasty weather.

✓ **You can't pull up your anchor:** First, make sure that you start directly over the anchor with all the slack pulled out and the anchor line securely cleated. If the wind has shifted and your boat swung during your stay, you may not be motoring in the right direction to get the flukes to pull out. Try other directions, slowly increasing the engine power to apply more force.

If you're having a problem getting the anchor on deck after you've gotten it off the bottom, you may need to take the anchor line to a winch and grind the line up. Make sure that the anchor line has a good lead through the bow chock and back to the winch, without chafing on anything, and stop grinding before the chain starts rubbing on the side of the hull. Raising and lowering an anchor (especially the heavier plow or fisherman's models) can take heaps of strength, so make sure that you're using the strongest people on the boat for the job.

Anchoring safety tips

Here are some tips for anchoring safely:

✓ **Allow enough room for your boat to swing freely while at anchor.**

✓ **Always make sure that your anchor is attached to the boat before you lower it into the water.**

✓ **Anchor in a protected spot, out of the channel and in deep-enough water.**

✓ **Avoid anchoring near other boats.**

✓ **Bring a spare anchor line on board in case your primary anchor line has some chafe.**

✓ **Check that the anchor is definitely secure before leaving the boat.**

✓ **Dive down with a mask and inspect the anchor, chain, and rope if you're at all concerned.**

✓ **If you plan on many sailing excursions, bring a spare anchor and rode on board.**

✓ **In rough weather, pull in or let out several feet of anchor rode every few hours to minimize chafe on the line in one spot.**

✓ **Make sure that the anchor line is free to run (and not around your foot).**

✓ **Make sure that you use sufficient scope for the conditions.**

✓ **Never anchor on a lee shore.**

✓ **Slowly lower the anchor into the water — don't do the old "heave-ho."**

✓ **When in doubt, let it out — at least in regards to scope.**

Anchoring etiquette

When other boats are around, try to observe the following guidelines:

- **Don't overdo the amount of scope:** The more scope, the larger the arc your boat swings through — possibly getting into the space of other boats on shorter arcs if the wind or current shifts.

- **Don't stare:** Being anchored close to another boat is sort of like camping out in a stranger's living room — respect his privacy.

- **First in has rights:** When the wind shifts at 3 a.m. and your boat swings dangerously close to someone else, whoever arrived last has to pull up anchor and move.

- **Keep it clean:** No one likes to swim in someone else's garbage can.

- **Keep it quiet:** Sound carries very well across the water. No battery charging or loud music during normal sleeping hours.

- **Tie off your halyards:** This rule is a corollary to the rule about keeping quiet. In strong winds, rope halyards can beat a very loud tune on an aluminum mast. Tie them off away from the mast.

Advanced Docking and Anchoring

This section covers the more advanced methods you may need to leave your boat secure. Sometimes, you may need to get creative and use two anchors. Or you may find that you need to secure your boat to pilings or a sea wall (a common method in Europe).

Doubling up: two anchors

Mooring the boat with two anchors can help decrease dragging and swinging. The most common example is setting two anchors in front of the boat so that when they dig in, the anchor lines create an angle of about 45 degrees (see Figure 9-7). This method is good for really rough weather coming from a fixed direction, because each anchor takes about half the load of the boat's pull. A side benefit is that you can use less scope for the same holding power (but keep in mind that the more scope, the better for rough conditions). The benefit of two anchors disappears, however, in a big wind shift.

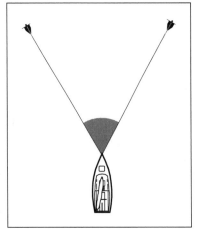

Figure 9-7:
For increased security from dragging, two anchors are better than one.

Setting double anchors is kind of tricky. You can set them from one boat, but another way, arguably easier, is to set the first anchor normally and then send a crew of volunteers in the rowing dinghy out with an anchor and rode to set the second one. Make sure that the tail of the second anchor rode is attached to the anchored boat first!

Docking Mediterranean style, or "stern-to"

Guess where this system is popular? Docking in the Mediterranean style enables you to tie up with your *stern* (back end) close to or touching the shore, man-made bulkhead, or dock — when the water is deep enough. "Stern-to" is the way the mega-yachts tie up in Saint-Tropez! Of course, many places on the Med have mooring buoys to facilitate your docking. If no moorings are available and you must use the anchor, simply pick your spot on the shore and then drop the hook the appropriate distance straight out from shore. Then back the boat in slowly, as you would in open water, until you get close to the shore or dock. Secure two stern lines (one from each corner of the back end) to the dock and adjust the tension of the anchor so that you don't hit the dock but are (hopefully) close enough to easily step on shore.

When I was with a television documentary team cruising around Cape Horn and the Beagle Channel, we used a variation of this system. Of course, no man-made docks or dredged-out harbors were around, but often the water was fairly deep right up close to shore. To get nestled in as cozy as possible and out of the icy blasts of the *williwaws* (sudden gusts of cold air from the mountains), we dropped an anchor well offshore and then took the inflatable dinghy into shore with two lines attached to the back of the boat on big spools. When we got to shore, we found the two strongest nearby trees and attached the stern lines to them (see Figure 9-8). This trick certainly was easier than setting out two more anchors!

Figure 9-8: Skip Novak's charter boat *Pelagic* nestled into a cozy anchorage near Cape Horn.

Hanging the boat between pilings

In many parts of the world, you won't have a nice, protected dock to tie alongside. Often, the sailor's best friends are *pilings* (large wooden poles driven solidly into the bottom). Your array of dock lines depends upon the position and orientation of the pilings, and you have to be creative as you plan your strategy to keep the boat from getting banged up no matter which direction the wind or current flows.

One of the most common dock arrangements is a short dock on one side and pilings on the other side. Tie the dock lines from each corner (as well as spring lines) so the boat hangs in the slot without banging into the dock or pilings.

No pilings? No problem!

If no pilings are available to hold you off a rough dock, then you may have to use a fender board to keep the boat from getting scratched up. Extra-long dock lines keep the fender board lined up properly as the tide rises and falls.

If you fear that the wind is going to blow really hard, pushing the side of your boat directly into the dock, consider alternative locations to park. If no other locations are available, you can ease the force of the boat on the dock (and your mind) by sending your rowing dinghy out with an anchor directly *abeam* (perpendicular to the centerline of the boat). Give the anchor plenty of scope, and then slowly pull it in on a winch until it grips. Lead the anchor so that it pulls the middle of the boat away from the dock with just enough tension to take the pressure off your fenders and fender boards (see Figure 9-9).

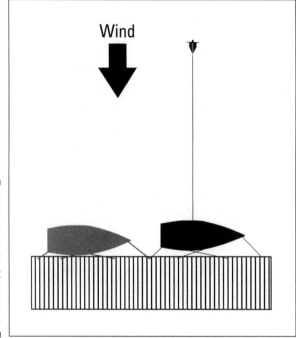

Figure 9-9:
Use an anchor to ease the pressure of the boat blowing onto the dock.

Chapter 10

All about Weather: Red Sky at Night

When it is evening, ye say, It will be fair weather: for the sky is red.

— Matthew 16:2

Weather is important in many sports — you can't play baseball in the rain, and tennis courts are abandoned when snow is on the ground. But sailing, more than any other sport, depends on weather for its very existence. Without the wind, you may as well be sitting on a raft. Fortunately, in most parts of the world, enough wind is available to sail much of the time. In this chapter, we talk about the "playing field" — the wind and the water — for our sport. We discuss how to estimate the present wind and water conditions and how to predict what is going to happen. Knowing what the weather will do next makes your sail *safer* (so you don't go out when it's too windy), *faster* (so you put up the right sails), and *more fun* (so you get the best wind for your needs).

Figuring Out How Windy It Is

Sailors around the world (whether they use the metric system or not) measure the wind speed in units called *knots* — nautical miles per hour. A nautical mile is equal to one minute of *latitude* — the horizontal lines on a chart or globe. (We talk more about latitude in Chapter 11.) A nautical mile is 6,076 feet or 1,852 km, 15 percent longer than a statute (regular) mile, so 10 knots of wind equals wind that's blowing at 11.5 miles per hour. Or, if you're used to the metric system, 10 knots equals 5.14 meters per second or 18.52 kilometers per hour.

Most sailors ignore the difference between nautical miles and statute miles and just consider knots to be equal to miles per hour. If you live in a metric-system country, meters per second times two is close to the speed in knots.

Sailors speak in terms of the *true wind* (the wind that a boat feels while sitting still) speed and direction. If your boat has an instrument system that includes a wind measurement device at the top of the mast, that system provides the apparent wind speed and direction. But unless you shelled out the big bucks for the deluxe system (which calculates true wind speed), you have to convert apparent wind to true wind by hand. (For more about the difference between the two, check out Chapter 8.)

Fortunately, you have another way to judge wind speed — by looking at the water. The chart in Table 10-1 was developed by Admiral Sir Francis Beaufort of the British Navy in 1805. He must have been a very observant guy (or bored stiff on long sea voyages), and sailors benefit from his perceptions still today. He defined wind speed in terms of a single number — the *Beaufort Force* — which is the first column in Table 10-1. In some parts of the world, marine forecasts are still reported in these units, although using knots or meters/second is more common. The cool thing about the Beaufort Scale is the remarks about the water's surface, shown in the "Water Surface Conditions" column.

Table 10-1		Beaufort Scale		
Force	*Wind Speed (Knots)*	*Description*	*Water Surface Conditions*	*Dummies Fun Meter*
0	0	Calm	Smooth, like a mirror.	Good time for a nap.
1	1-3	Light air	Small ripples.	Time for lunch.
2	4-6	Light breeze	Short, small wavelets with no crests.	All right! Now the boat's moving!

Force	Wind Speed (Knots)	Description	Water Surface Conditions	Dummies Fun Meter
3	7-10	Gentle breeze	Larger wavelets with crests.	Hey, this is really fun; great for beginners.
4	11-16	Moderate breeze	Longer, small waves, some with white caps (foamy crests).	Faster is better; time to think about putting on a jacket.
5	17-21	Fresh breeze	Moderate waves with many whitecaps.	Beginners should head for shelter; experienced sailors dream of wind like this.
6	22-27	Strong breeze	Large waves, extensive white-caps, some spray.	Great fun, but this is hard work.
7	28-33	Near gale	Heaps of waves, with some breakers whose foam is blown downwind in streaks.	Only for skilled sailors on well-prepared boats. Staying dry is impossible; your lunch is all wet.
8	34-40	Gale	Moderately high waves with edges of crests breaking into *spindrift* (heavy spray). Foam is blown downwind in well-defined streaks.	Time to head for home, no matter who you are.
9	41-47	Strong gale	High waves with dense foam streaks and some crests rolling over. Spray reduces visibility.	
10	48-55	Storm	Very high waves with long, over-hanging crests. The sea looks white; waves tumble with force; greatly reduced visibility.	

(continued)

Table 10-1 *(continued)*

Force	Wind Speed (Knots)	Description	Water Surface Conditions	Dummies Fun Meter
11	56-63	Violent storm	Exceptionally high waves that may obscure medium-size ships. All wave edges are blown into froth, and the sea is covered with patches of foam.	
12	64-71	Hurricane	The air is filled with foam and spray, and the sea is completely white.	I want my blankee!

This relationship between what the surface of the water looks like and the wind speed really works. Guessing the wind speed every time you go out on the water is fun — and good practice, too.

One of the tips that always seems to come in handy is the one for Force 4. At around 12 knots, a few whitecaps are definitely apparent on the surface.

Of course, these descriptions of the water's surface only apply in areas where the wavelets and waves have a long enough distance to build up. For winds up to about 20 knots, that means at least a half mile of open water in the direction the wind is coming from. The water can be glassy smooth right next to a beach, yet the wind can be blowing 25 knots from an *offshore* (from the land toward the water) direction. Places with this unique orientation to the wind are ideal for setting high-speed sailing records, because waves usually slow boats down.

Determining the Wind's Direction

Knowing the wind direction is crucial for any sailor. For the many ways to find the wind direction, see Chapter 5. Wind direction is defined in terms of magnetic degrees, using the 360-degree compass. If the wind is forecast to be *westerly,* the wind is expected to come from the west. If you turn toward the western horizon, a westerly wind blows straight upon your face. You can look at your compass to determine that direction is 270 degrees. (Find more about using a compass in Chapter 11.) By paying attention to the wind speed and direction, you become more aware of the overall weather picture — especially when you combine that information with the weather forecast.

Getting the Scoop

Sailors get their weather information from a variety of sources, and none is more accurate than their own observation of present conditions. But because the weather is bound to change while you're sailing, being concerned with what's coming next pays off. Here are some ways to obtain the *local marine weather forecast* before you set sail:

- ✔ **The Internet:** The Internet has a vast supply of weather information; everything from satellite photographs to the local marine forecast can be found — if you know where to look. If you're Internet literate, you can do a search by using *marine weather forecast*. Good places to start surfing are at the National Weather Service's home page (`http://www.nws.noaa.gov`) and Coastwatch (`http://www.cwatchwc.ucsd.edu/cwatch.html`). Some online services, such as CompuServe and AOL, also provide local forecasts.

- ✔ **VHF radio and telephone:** Throughout the U.S., the National Weather Service distributes a marine weather forecast on special VHF channels reserved for these broadcasts. These channels are normally identified by *Wx*. The forecasts are updated every few hours and run continuously. In extreme weather, the information may be broadcast live or updated more often. Valuable information includes expected wind speeds and directions, warnings regarding fog or large waves, and weather observations from various stations around the region. Check the front section of your phone directory for telephone access to a forecast.

   Outside the U.S., check with a local marine business to determine what radio frequencies, if any, provide a marine weather forecast.

- ✔ **News media:** Newspapers, television, and AM and FM radio stations all have some sort of weather information. Many report a marine forecast for the local waters and show the weather map.

The marine weather forecast is the butt of as many jokes among sailors as the TV weather forecast is around the water cooler at the office. But every little bit of information helps, and as you gain more experience in a given area, you develop what sailors call *local knowledge* — the ability to look at the clouds and present conditions to forecast the weather.

If you're on an extended offshore voyage, then you're out of range of TVs, newspapers, and (most likely) VHF signals. However, you also have these three sources of weather information:

- ✔ **INMARSAT C:** These satellite communication devices enable users to receive data (for example, e-mail) from a number of sources, as described in Chapter 7, anywhere you can sail on this planet!

Visual warnings

Some marinas display small-craft warning flags (in nighttime hours, they may use lights). These flags, shown in the figure, are based upon the marine weather forecast and indicate expected wind strength.

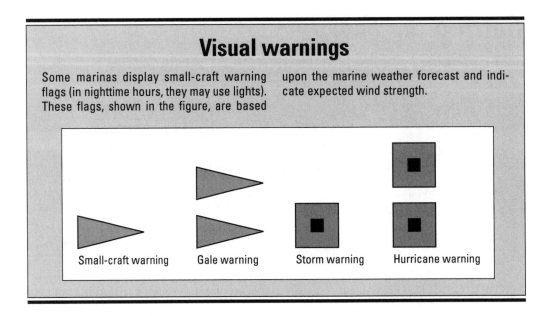

Small-craft warning   Gale warning   Storm warning   Hurricane warning

✔ **Pilot charts:** These neat charts show wind information, averaged over long periods of time; and are very helpful when planning a long voyage.

✔ **Single Side Band (SSB) radio:** The U.S. National Weather Service and other organizations distribute weather information via the SSB. Some of the broadcasts are by voice, others by Morse code, and others via data transmission to a fax machine. A popular item for offshore sailors is a stand-alone *weather fax* receiver that prints out weather maps and satellite pictures.

Whither the Weather

Although you can use all this weather information at face value, you get more value out of it if you understand some basic principles of why the wind blows. Many variables affect the weather on both a global and very local basis, making the science of meteorology quite complex. But the primary forces that shape weather are *temperature differences* and *air pressure differences*. First, we look at the big picture of the weather over the planet and then at the small picture that is important for your day on the water.

The big picture: temperature and pressure differences

If the Earth were a constant temperature throughout, you would see very few changes in the weather. But because the sun's rays strike the equator at a more perpendicular angle than at the poles, a temperature differential results. On a global scale, this surface temperature differential (hotter near the equator, colder near the poles), combined with the *Coriolis force* (which we discuss in the sidebar "The Coriolis force"), creates bands or belts of weather ringing the globe. Near the equator are the *doldrums* — an area of light, shifty, and unpredictable weather. The *tropics* enjoy relatively steady easterly winds (northeast in the northern hemisphere, southeast in the southern hemisphere), dubbed the *trade winds*. The midlatitudes on both sides of the equator are home to the *westerlies* (winds from the west), interspersed by waves of low-pressure areas circling the globe.

Another factor in creating weather is pressure differences. Wind is simply air in motion, trying to get to a position of equilibrium by moving from an area of high pressure to one of low pressure. On a *surface weather map* (as opposed to the maps of the upper atmosphere that pilots often use), pressure is depicted by lines called *isobars* that connect points of equal air pressure. Think of a weather map like a topographic map, with the areas of high pressure being mountains and the places with low pressure being the valleys. Wind flows around high- and low-pressure areas, moving downhill at a small angle to the isobars, spiraling clockwise (in the northern hemisphere) out of a high-pressure area and counterclockwise into a low-pressure area, as shown in Figure 10-1. In the southern hemisphere, the direction of rotation is opposite.

The closer together the isobar lines, the steeper the mountain or valley, and the faster the wind blows. Looking at the weather map of a hurricane is cool; incredibly tight isobars ring this immensely "deep" low-pressure area.

The Coriolis force

The fact that the wind doesn't simply roll straight down that high-pressure "mountain" can be disconcerting — and the reason why it doesn't is the *Coriolis force*. Because the Earth is a huge spinning ball, things on a very large scale (like air heading away from a high-pressure area) that are trying to move in a straight line get pulled into a curve.

No, the Coriolis force isn't why Greg Maddux's curve ball frustrates batters, and it isn't even the reason why water spins down a toilet or sink drain (although your science teacher may have used that as an example). On the massive, planetary scale that weather features such as high- and low-pressure areas operate on, the Coriolis force comes into play, explaining why wind spirals along the isobar lines.

Figure 10-1:
Isobars on
a weather
map
indicate air
pressure
and help
predict
wind
strength
and
direction
(see
arrows).

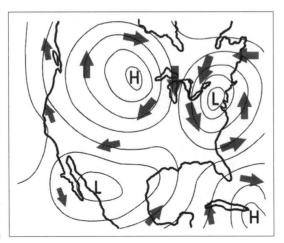

Figure 10-1: Isobars on a weather map indicate air pressure and help predict wind strength and direction (see arrows).

Air pressure is measured by a *barometer* — a good piece of equipment for a larger cruising boat. By paying attention to the changes in pressure, you can get a better idea of what will happen with the wind, especially if you're armed with weather maps, professional forecasts, and other information. Here are a few general rules regarding air pressure and weather:

- ✔ **If pressure is very high or is going up:** The weather is or soon will be nice. High pressure is associated with clear, dry weather.

- ✔ **If pressure is very low or is going down:** Batten down the hatches; you're in for a storm. Low pressure is associated with cloudy, rainy weather.

In the temperate midlatitudes on both sides of the equator, weather usually comes from the west. Even when the local wind is blowing out of the east, the huge weather system (high- or low-pressure area) causing that wind is traveling from west to east, usually around 10 to 15 knots, because the upper atmosphere in these latitudes is moving quite fast from west to east. The *jet stream* (a band of very-fast-moving air high up in the atmosphere) is part of this feature. Therefore, pay special attention to the weather on your west side for an indication of what to expect.

Low pressure and fronts

Really nasty, windy, rainy weather is associated with low-pressure areas. Lows are created in a complex process that involves the meeting of two air masses of different temperatures. Emanating from the center of the typical low on a weather map (and in real life) are often two fronts, a *warm front* followed by a *cold front,* as shown in Figure 10-2. A *front* is a line separating two different air masses (warm and cold, moist and dry) and often is distinguished by a large (more than 20-degree) shift in the wind direction when it passes. Cold fronts typically pack the most punch and are often the site of the most extreme sailing weather. Squalls (smaller-scale storms packing incredibly strong winds delivered down from the upper atmosphere) and even tornadoes and *water spouts* (water-borne tornadoes) can occur just in front of this band where warm and cold air meet.

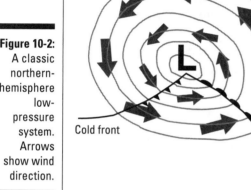

Figure 10-2:
A classic northern-hemisphere low-pressure system. Arrows show wind direction.

Cold front

Warm front

The weather around a typical northern-hemisphere low has three distinct sectors:

- The weather in the area to the north of the warm front is usually described as "dismal" and the entire sky is blanketed by a thick layer of *stratus* clouds (see "Look at the clouds"). If the air cools enough, you get a steady drizzle or rain.

- The weather in the sector between the warm and cold fronts is warmer and more humid. A warm, moist wind comes from the south. When the sun begins to heat the ground, the air near the ground begins to rise, forming cumulus clouds and, if the conditions are right, thunderstorms.

- The western sector behind the cold front is usually cooler and drier. The wind is from the west and northwest and can be quite blustery.

In the northern hemisphere, if you stand facing the wind, the center of the low-pressure system is to your right. In the southern hemisphere, this orientation is the opposite, due to the effect of the Coriolis force.

The small picture

Most sailing is done over the course of a few hours on an area smaller than ten square miles. A sailor going for an afternoon cruise is concerned with a much smaller slice of the weather pie than a crew heading off to set a record sailing around the globe, but both sailors must look for signs of changing weather. The western sky (in the midlatitudes) is often the sailor's most valuable weatherman. Here are some tips to predict a change in weather in the next few minutes to an hour.

These signs indicate a future shift in wind direction or speed:

- ✔ **A change in the sky — more clouds, fewer clouds, or different kinds of clouds.**
- ✔ **Sailboats on the horizon heeling in a new wind.**
- ✔ **Flags or smokestacks on shore indicating a new wind direction.**
- ✔ **A rapid change in temperature.**
- ✔ **A change in the visibility on the horizon.** For example, in California, a clearing haze means that the wind will come from that direction.
- ✔ **A change in the water surface.** Darker water means waves and more wind (see the Beaufort Scale earlier in this chapter).
- ✔ **A changing barometer reading.**

These are the signs of stormy weather approaching:

- ✔ **Dark, cumulonimbus clouds approaching on the horizon.**
- ✔ **Thunder and/or lightning.**
- ✔ **A falling barometer reading.**
- ✔ **A change in wind speed — especially when the wind dies off or blows gently toward the big, dark clouds.**

Look at the clouds

Clouds come in all sizes and shapes, but they can all be categorized in three types:

- ✔ **Cirrus:** The highest clouds, wispy and thin. They signify fair weather — for the next day, at least.
- ✔ **Cumulus:** Puffy clouds like cotton balls. The associated weather depends upon the clouds' color and size. Cumulus clouds mean fair weather when their bases are high in the sky or when they're relatively

thin and bright white at lower altitudes. The taller (thicker) and darker ones with low-altitude bases are the *cumulonimbus* variety, which foretell ominous weather, including sudden thunderstorms.

✔ **Stratus:** Layered clouds, very even-looking from underneath. *Stratus* comes from the Latin word for "spread, stretch out, or cover," which is what these clouds do. Their associated weather depends on their color, thickness, and altitude — the lower, thicker, and darker, the more they're associated with rain, wind, and (sometimes) low visibility.

Thunderstorms, or *squalls,* are sudden, sometimes severe storms that are usually localized in size. Although they may precede the passage of a cold front, they can also be caused by a landmass heating up (with hot air rising into cooler air aloft) during a sultry summer day. Winds can build to over 60 knots quickly and come from any direction, and lightning is common. Squalls are relatively unpredictable (unless you have access to weather radar), but dark cumulonimbus clouds and distant thunder are signs that one may be near. We talk more about preparing for squalls in Chapter 12.

Because sound travels about one-fifth of a mile per second, you can tell how far away the thunder and lightning are by counting the seconds between the lightning and the thunder and dividing by five. Five seconds means the lightning is about one mile away. If you're metrically inclined, count the seconds and divide by three to get the distance in kilometers. For example, three seconds means the lightning is one kilometer away.

Ten "golden rules" of sky watching

1. Red sky at night — sailors delight; red sky at morning — sailors take warning.

2. When the sky changes, so will the weather.

3. Mackerel sky — 24 hours dry.

4. Dew on decks — wind from the sea; no dew on decks — wind from the land.

5. Head for home when the wind speed exceeds the temperature.

6. A halo around the moon means rain or snow. The larger the halo, the nearer the precipitation.

7. Rainbow to windward means rain is coming. Rainbow to leeward means rain has ended.

8. The higher the clouds, the finer the weather. (A lowering ceiling foretells rain.)

9. When smoke descends, good weather ends.

10. Seagull, seagull, sit on the sand; it's a sign of rain when you're at hand.

Using Your Knowledge

As we mention in the beginning of this chapter, you can use your understanding of weather and the information provided by forecasts to make your sail safer, faster, and more comfortable. But first, we want to establish some general premises about your sailing:

- **More wind = more speed:** Wind is like boat speed — more is better, but only to a point. Each boat is different, but when sailing on a beam reach or closer angle to the wind, most boats benefit from increased velocity up to about 15 knots. By then, of course, beginning sailors should be at the dock. Going downwind, most boats respond favorably as the wind picks up to 25 knots, but over that, control becomes a concern.

- **Sailing on a reach is fastest:** If you had a particular destination in mind and could make the wind blow from any direction, you would make your course a reach. That way, you could sail on your boat's fastest point of sail and steer a direct course.

- **Sailing straight downwind is often slower:** As we discuss further in Chapter 15, many boats actually sail directly downwind (on a run) more slowly than if they head up and sail on a reach and then jibe over.

- **Sailing upwind is slower:** Because you have to zigzag your way back and forth to reach a destination directly upwind (as we discuss in Chapter 5), you end up sailing extra distance.

- **Waves matter:** Waves slow you down when sailing toward them and can speed you up when sailing with them.

To make your sail safer and more comfortable, use your wind knowledge to avoid going out when it's too windy or stormy. Here are some ways that you can use your weather knowledge to go faster:

- **If you expect a wind shift when sailing downwind, take the tack away from the new wind direction.** Check out Chapter 16 to see how racers use wind shifts to advantage.

- **If you expect a wind shift when sailing upwind, take your first tack toward the new wind first.**

- **In light air, sail for the puffs.** Look for the "dark water" where the ripples are and other signs of more wind.

- **In strong winds sailing upwind, take the tack toward the windward shoreline (or an area that is more protected) first to get out of the waves.**

- ✔ **On a reach, sail a straight line for your destination except:**

  - If the wind is strong and ahead of the beam, steer slightly below (to leeward) of the destination if you expect the wind to shift more behind.

  - If the wind is light and behind the beam, steer slightly above (to windward) of the destination if you expect the wind to shift more ahead.

- ✔ **When sailing upwind, sail on the longer tack first (if there is one).**

In the northern hemisphere, the stronger wind is normally associated with a shift to the right (clockwise). In the southern hemisphere, the stronger wind is associated with a shift to the left.

Understanding Sea Breezes

Temperature differences can also cause changes to the weather on a local scale. *Sea breeze* is the name associated with a family of winds generated on sunny and partly sunny days, when the extra heat of the land causes a cool breeze to blow inland from the water. In certain parts of the world, the sea breeze is so predictable during the summer months that you can almost set your watch by it. Sea breezes are common in nearly every coastal town in the midlatitudes.

Here's how sea breezes work: As the land heats, the air rises (sometimes creating puffy, cumulus clouds), and an area of low pressure is created along the shoreline by midday. Meanwhile, the water remains cooler, and so does the air above the water. Cool air from the water blows (or, really, is sucked) in to the low pressure over the land. If the conditions are favorable (a light offshore wind and a large temperature difference between land and water), the sea breeze can build fairly quickly to 15 knots or more. Figure 10-3 depicts the classic sea breeze.

As the sun drops on the horizon, the heating of the land diminishes, and so does the sea breeze. In the northern hemisphere, watch for the sea breeze to build until 3 o'clock or so and then slowly die away, shifting to the right (clockwise) in response to the ubiquitous Coriolis force.

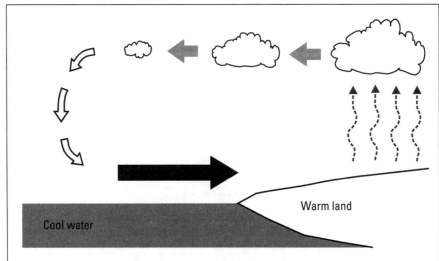

Figure 10-3:
Creating a
sea breeze.

Facing Up to Fog

Nothing can strike fear (or at least a sober thought or two) in the heart of an experienced sailor like being caught in a strange area in dense fog. Sure, a satellite navigation device can tell you where you are within a hundred feet, but only if you have the ability to accurately translate that information onto a nautical chart. When a bank of fog as thick as "pea soup" surrounds you, the visibility can literally drop to less than a boatlength, making safe navigation extremely difficult regardless of your skill and the available navigation aids.

Fog occurs when air contains more moisture than it can hold. When the temperature drops below the *dew point* (the temperature at which the air becomes saturated with water vapor), the excess water vapor becomes visible. Fog comes in several different types, but the same condition occurs in every kind: Moist air gets cooled (usually by water, which is why fog is more likely over cold water) until the air temperature drops below the dew point, and fog appears.

Because fog usually rolls in slowly, you generally have enough time after first spotting it to turn around and hightail it back to the shore before the fog "socks in" completely. For more information about navigating in fog, see Chapter 11.

Going with the Tide and the Current

The *tide* is actually a giant wave that circles the globe roughly twice a day. The gravitational effect of the moon (and, to a lesser extent, the sun) pulls on the Earth's oceans and causes two humps or wave crests — one directly under the moon and the other on the far side of the globe directly opposite its sister — that follow the moon in its 24.8-hour path around the Earth, as shown in Figure 10-4.

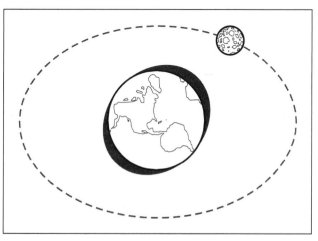

Figure 10-4: The moon and the sun pull on the oceans, creating global waves called tides.

When the moon lines up with the sun, as it does twice every 29½ days (at the full moon and the new moon), those global wave crests get even bigger — and the corresponding *trough* (low part of a wave) gets even lower. In between, at the moon's first and last quarter, the tides are smallest.

The motion of the ocean

If the moon's pull is the same as it orbits the Earth, why is the tidal range 15 feet or more in some parts of the world and only a few inches in others? The mathematical answer can make a university student's head hurt, but, in practical terms, these differences are due to the shape and proximity of land masses, the underwater topography, and the wind.

Fortunately, most regions of the world have tidal predictions readily available in local publications and even on the marine weather radio, so you don't have to do the math to know whether the harbor is deep enough for you to sail through.

As this global wave girdles the planet, it creates water motion called *tidal current* or simply *current*. Current is moving water, and currents that reach 3 knots or more, rivaling the speed of a small sailboat, are not uncommon. That much current definitely gets your attention! In some narrow bodies of water, such as the Bay of Fundy in Canada, the current comes in and out like a big tidal wave at speeds in the teens.

Tidal current coming inbound as the tide is on the rise is called *flood tide;* when the tide is going down, the outbound tidal current is called *ebb tide.* Most areas have tidal information accessible to the mariner in a local almanac or tide book. You can discover tons of information about tides and currents by looking at a nautical chart of an area. Focus on the underwater topography, because the current runs strongest where the water is deepest. Here are some general rules about tides and currents:

- ✔ **Current changes on the beach first.** In a confined area like a bay, the direction of the tidal flow changes with the changing tide near the shores first and in the middle last.

- ✔ **Current is visible by watching the water flow past buoys and other anchored objects.**

- ✔ **Deep water — stronger current; shallow water — less current.**

- ✔ **It takes a knot of current to counteract 10 knots of wind on an anchored ship.** If you see a big ship that's anchored pointing 180 degrees to the 20-knot wind, you know that at least 2 knots of current are flowing against the wind out there.

- ✔ **Strong winds can overcome weak tidal flows.** Strong winds can even create wind-blown current on lakes that have no discernible tide.

- ✔ **When the wind opposes the current flow, waves get steep and choppy.** This makes for a fast but bouncy ride heading upwind.

- ✔ **When the wind is with the current flow, the waves get smoother and more elongated.**

One more type of water current is of interest to sailors — the huge continental boundary currents flowing along coastlines. Two great examples surround North America. On the west side is the cold, south-bound *Alaska current,* and on the eastern Florida coast is the warm, north-bound *Gulf Stream current.* These two currents act like strong rivers within the ocean, with average speeds up to 3 knots. In small, local areas, the speeds can be much higher. They're caused by a combination of the Coriolis force, the prevailing winds, and the orientation of the coastlines.

Chapter 11
Navigation: Holding Your Course

. . . .

In This Chapter

▶ Navigating by using common sense

▶ Using navigational aids

▶ Reading charts

▶ Plotting courses

▶ Determining direction with a compass

▶ Piloting — basic navigation

▶ Exploring electronic navigation

▶ Dabbling in celestial navigation

. . . .

O we can wait no longer,
We too take ship O soul,
Joyous we too launch out on trackless seas,
Fearless for unknown shores.

— Walt Whitman

*N*avigation, as defined in one of Peter's favorite books (the epitome of navigation, *The American Practical Navigator,* by Nathaniel Bowditch, first published in 1802 and revised periodically by the U.S. Navy), is "the process of directing the movement of a craft from one point to another." The history of navigation is rich with fascinating stories of sailors who crossed oceans with limited knowledge of where they were and even less of where they were going. Yet, however crudely, they did successfully direct their crafts from one point to another, and often back again. The lore of navigation spans the globe. For example, ancient Polynesian navigators had a rich oral tradition of sailing directions that enabled them to sail to islands well over the horizon without any instruments.

Fortunately for us, technology and advances in time-keeping, basic sciences, and mathematics enable us to direct our "crafts" from one place to another much more easily and accurately. But despite the satellites in the sky that tell us where we are, the link with this rich history of navigation is not totally severed. Many of the skills that you will find most practical and easy to use are ones developed centuries ago.

From a most basic standpoint, here are some of the primary concerns of a person navigating a sailboat:

✔ **Getting to the destination:** If the sailor has a destination in mind.

✔ **Getting there as fast and safely as possible:** We cover some of the getting-there-fast issues in Chapters 8 and 10, but the navigator has major input into that subject. Safety always comes first, and again the navigator may play a role — not only by avoiding the ignominy of running aground (see Chapter 13), but also by being aware of the proximity of shipping traffic and other dangers that are apparent from reading a nautical chart.

Common-Sense Navigation

Whether you're sailing across the pond or across the ocean, you need to use certain basic skills to help you get there. These skills involve being attuned to the elements and using your senses and your judgment to get where you want to go quickly and safely. This section is most applicable to sailors on a boat with no compass or chart; however, the techniques can be equally valuable on bigger boats with all the navigation goodies.

Judging laylines

When the destination is upwind, so that you have to make at least one tack to get there, you have to be able to judge the *layline* — the line beyond which you can *lay* (sail to the destination on a close-hauled course with no more tacks), as shown in Figure 11-1. Sailing past the layline isn't bad — you simply sail extra distance. In Chapters 10 and 16, we discuss the strategy of which tack to take first when sailing in shifting winds. But after you choose your course (of a series of long tacks or many shorter ones), eventually you have to make that final tack. In order to know where the layline is, you need to know how many degrees your boat tacks through — the difference between your port and starboard close-hauled headings. In moderate air (10 to 14 knots), most boats tack through 90 degrees or a little less.

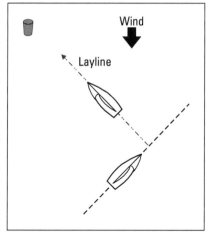

Figure 11-1:
The layline is the close-hauled heading to a destination with no tacks required.

When sailing upwind and your destination appears a little forward of *dead abeam* (perpendicular to the boat's heading), take a tack over and see whether you've reached the layline.

Holding a steady course

If you can see your destination, steering a straight-line course is usually a simple matter. But if current is pushing you sideways or your boat is side-slipping excessively due to too much heel, your "course over the bottom," or *course over ground (COG),* is different than your boat's *heading,* or the course the boat is steering. (For more about currents, see Chapter 10.) If this is the case, you need to alter your heading so that the boat "makes good" the course you want — the straight line to the destination. If land lies behind the destination, you can use it as a *range* (two objects in a line) to stay on track, as shown in Figure 11-2. A visual range enables a sailor to determine whether current or wind is pushing the boat sideways and how much to alter course to counteract that effect.

Avoiding shallow water

If the water is clear and the wind calm, the bottom looks amazingly close through the magnifying glass of the water. But no matter where you are, the visibility goes down when waves kick up. Here are some tips for avoiding potentially dangerous shallow spots:

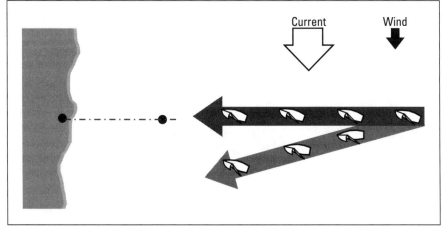

Figure 11-2:
A range helps you steer straight in crosscurrent.

✔ **Follow another boat:** By using another boat (hopefully with similar or deeper draft than your boat) as your guinea pig, you can follow directly behind (at a safe distance so you can turn if it runs aground) and stay in deep water. This technique is especially helpful when entering a strange harbor or following a narrow *channel* (deep water lane).

✔ **Look at the bottom:** In the tropics, sandy bottoms get brighter white as the depth decreases; coral heads become darker.

✔ **Pay attention to the markers and buoys:** Hang on — we discuss these markers that signal deep and shallow water in just a minute.

✔ **Slow down:** If you're in an area where you think that your keel or centerboard may touch bottom, take some pace off. You may not avoid grounding, but at least the contact will be less severe.

✔ **Stay away from the shoreline:** By definition, the bottom comes up at the shoreline, so stay away from the shore unless you're sure (from looking at a chart or past experience) that the water is deep enough.

✔ **Watch for waves:** As every surfer knows, waves break when they reach shallow water. Beware of an area with breakers or with waves that seem to "mound up" bigger than the surrounding waves.

One time I was sailing dinghies off Key West, Florida. We sailed the boat on and off the beach. On windy days, we would sail close to shore and have the crew jump in the water at chest level and hold the boat while the skipper lowered the sails and removed the rudder. One day we were coming in, and the coral heads started looking pretty close. We found a nice sandy spot that looked quite shallow, and I jumped in, only to find myself swimming in 15 feet of water. The moral of the story is that you want to be cautious about running aground, but judging the depth visually can be deceptive.

Buoys: Aids to Navigation

Sailors have used visual aids to navigation since time immemorial. A big willow tree may mark a good fishing spot; a promontory, the entrance to a channel. By definition, an *aid to navigation* is any device (not on board) designed to assist in determining position or a safe course or to warn of dangers. Around the world, you find millions of man-made aids to navigation; the most common are *buoys*. A buoy is any floating (albeit anchored) aid to navigation.

Depending on where you are, buoys are laid out in one of two different systems (or a combination thereof):

- ✔ **Cardinal system:** Buoys of specific shapes and colors are laid out to indicate the compass direction to the hazard. The *cardinal points* of the compass are north, south, east, and west, hence the name. Most European countries use the cardinal system.

- ✔ **Lateral system:** Buoys of specific shapes and colors are laid out along the edges of the channels or areas of safe navigation. The lateral system is used in the U.S. and managed by the U.S. Coast Guard.

Not only do buoyage systems vary somewhat from country to country, but they also vary from region to region in the U.S. Fortunately, most of the country is governed by the *U.S. Aids to Navigation System* (which uses the lateral system), with notable exceptions being the western rivers, intra-coastal waterways, and smaller bodies of water lying totally within a single state. Conveniently, even those areas use most of the key elements of the U.S. system, which are outlined in the next sections. All the important characteristics of a buoy can be ascertained from a nautical chart, as we describe in later sections of this chapter.

Learning your colors

The most important characteristic of a buoy is its color. You may already be familiar with the three "Rs" and the expression "red right returning" (from the sea), which describes the basic rule of the U.S. (lateral) buoyage system: When you're coming inbound, entering a harbor, or moving along a channel toward an area that can be considered more protected, you keep the red buoys on your right side. Conversely, the green buoys are passed on your left side. By convention, the red buoys have even numbers painted on them, and the green ones have odd numbers.

Most experienced boaters use the words *port* and *starboard* while afloat. In their terminology, a red buoy should be "left to starboard" (when returning from the sea), which means passed on your right side. A green buoy should be "left to port." Hey, at least they don't say "right to port"!

The concept of red buoys being on the right side when you're returning from sea implies that a safe passageway, or *channel,* is bounded by buoys. If the "returning" direction isn't obvious, ask yourself which body of water is most protected by land or farthest from a bigger body of water. Along the Gulf, Pacific, and Atlantic coasts of the U.S. away from harbors, the red buoys are used to mark shallow spots close to shore.

Types of buoys

Buoys come in a variety of shapes, which can indicate their meaning, as shown in Figure 11-3.

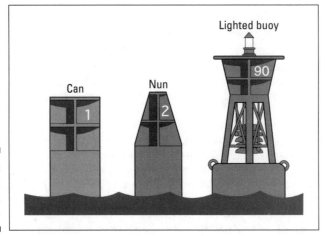

Figure 11-3:
Buoys in the U.S. system.

✔ **Nuns and cans:** The most common buoys (used to mark the edges of the channel as described previously) are the red *nuns* (named for their pointed, conical top) and the green *cans* (named for their shape).

✔ **Lighted buoys:** Lighted buoys are usually taller than nuns or cans, have a floating base and a superstructure supported by an open framework, display a light signal at night, and often emit a sound signal (bell, gong, whistle, or horn) as the buoy rolls in the waves. If they are painted solid red (with a red light at night) or solid green (with a green light), they signal the edges of a channel, just like their unlighted brethren.

✔ **Junction buoys:** Junction buoys can be shaped like a nun, can, or lighted buoy, but they must be horizontally red-and-green striped. These stripes indicate the junction of two channels, with the deeper, or preferred, channel indicated by the color on top. Red on top means that the bigger channel is to port (in other words, pass the red-topped buoy on your starboard side).

✔ **Mid-channel fairway buoys:** If unlighted, these buoys are round balls; otherwise, they are the shape of a lighted buoy and indicate safe water at the center (often the beginning) of a channel. They are vertically striped red and white.

✔ **Danger buoys:** By definition, all buoys mark some sort of danger. An isolated danger (such as a rock or other hazard) in relatively open water may be marked by a lighted buoy with red and black stripes and two black balls at the top. When unlighted, danger buoys can be either nun- or can-shaped and are white with thin orange horizontal stripes at the top and near the water level.

Other government buoys can signal an anchorage, quarantine area, fish nets, dredging operations, or special purpose. Refer to the U.S. Coast Guard's Boating Safety Hot Line (800-368-5647) for any updates to the description of these buoys.

✔ **Daymarks:** Sometimes, in areas protected from waves in relatively shallow waters (like rivers and man-made channels), *daymarks* are used in lieu of buoys. Daymarks are displayed on poles pounded securely into the bottom. As with buoys, color is the most important feature; pass a triangular red marker with a red reflective border on your right side when returning from the "sea"; pass a square green marker with a reflective green border on your left side when returning from the sea.

With all this talk about red right returning, don't forget that when you're leaving a harbor, you pass the red buoys (or daymarks) on your left side!

Lighting up the nighttime sky

At night, certain buoys, daymarks, and other navigational aids such as lighthouses display lights to help the mariner find his way. To prevent confusion, different markers are lit in a variety of ways, utilizing color, pattern, and *period* (a flashing sequence) to identify which buoy or lighthouse is which. Typically, the solid red and green buoys, so important in defining a channel, are lit with corresponding red and green lights. Lighthouses and mid-channel fairway buoys often feature a white light. On a nautical chart (discussed in the next section), the characteristics of each light are indicated by an abbreviation such as "F" for "fixed, unblinking," and "FL Xsec" for "flashing at X-second intervals."

Sometimes, local authorities may anchor their own, unofficial buoys to help mariners avoid hitting bottom in areas that the Coast Guard doesn't service. Usually, these private buoys are red nuns and green cans and use the same "red right returning" system.

All right, I admit it. For all the simplicity of "red right returning," I still get confused on occasion. My hang-up is the word *returning* — are we returning *to* the sea (our primordial birthplace) or *from* the sea (to our relatively new home)? Maybe it's just me who has trouble with this.

You may think that this spot is a logical place to talk about electronic aids to navigation (things like satellites and radio signals), but because these electronic aids require the use and understanding of a chart, we hold off a few more pages. And the great thing about buoys is that after you under-stand the system, buoys help you navigate even if you don't have a chart aboard (although navigating is much easier if you have a chart).

Charts

Charts are maps for mariners, providing a variety of useful, sometimes invaluable information. Anyone can make a chart — even you. But the indisputable authority of charts in the U.S. is the federal government. The National Ocean Service (NOS) publishes about 1,000 charts for U.S. waters, and the Defense Mapping Agency (DMA) issues additional charts of the high seas and other countries' waters. The other major publisher of nautical charts is Great Britain. You can purchase charts at most marine stores.

Charts come in a variety of *scales* (coverage areas). To orient yourself to the scale of a particular chart, refer to the scale of *latitude* (horizontal lines on a chart or globe indicating angular distance — 0 to 90 degrees — north or south of the equator), which bounds the vertical (right and left) edges of every chart, as shown in Figure 11-4.

No matter where you are on the planet, one degree of latitude equals 60 nautical miles. Each degree is divided up into 60 minutes, and each minute is further carved into either 60 seconds or decimal minutes. You can use this catchy phrase to help you glean distances from the edge of your chart: "A minute's a mile the world around."

Be careful: The same isn't true of a minute of *longitude,* which varies in distance depending on how close you are to the equator. Longitude is indicated by the vertical lines on a chart or globe and designates the angular distance (0 to 180 degrees) east or west of the *prime meridian.* The prime meridian is the line of longitude (or *meridian*) that has been arbi-trarily given the value of 0 degrees. The prime meridian passes through Greenwich, England — so guess which country established it!

Latitude and longitude are the navigator's equivalent of streets and avenues in Manhattan (where they run north-south and east-west in a grid). Running at right angles to each other, they provide a universal way of describing

Figure 11-4: The right and left edges of a nautical chart are bounded by a scale indicating latitude.

your position. For example, in my chair right now, I am at 32 degrees 43.28 minutes north latitude and 117 degrees 13.26 minutes west longitude, or 32°43.28'N, 117°13.26'W. Anyone with the right chart can determine where I am from those two numbers.

In addition to latitude and longitude, charts display an enormous amount of information, often coded by a plethora of symbols and abbreviations. Every one of these symbols and abbreviations — from the symbol for a pagoda to water depth — is explained in Chart No. 1, published by the NOS and the DMA. Chart No. 1 is, simply put, an indispensable aid in finding out how to read a chart and a valuable reference for the saltiest seafarer. Chart No. 1 and all the U.S. government's charts can be purchased from most marine stores. If they don't have a particular chart, they can order it.

Here are some of the most valuable pieces of information displayed on a nautical chart.

> ✔ **Buoys and other aids to navigation:** As we mention earlier in this
> chapter, buoys come in a huge variety of different colors, numbers and
> letters, shapes, lights, and sound signals. All those details are communi-
> cated clearly when you understand the code.

For example, "RW 'SD' Mo (A) WHIS" written next to a little black circle surrounded by a solid magenta circle with a split trapezoid peaking out clearly identifies the location of a red and white whistle buoy, with the letters "SD" on top, which displays a white light flashing the Morse Code signal for the letter "A" at night and indicates the middle of the entrance to the channel coming into San Diego Harbor. See why you need Chart No. 1!

✔ **Compass rose:** The compass rose on the chart helps the navigator orient the chart to his compass. The compass rose is so useful that several usually appear on a single chart. A compass rose consists of two concentric circles, each graduated in degrees (0 to 360 degrees) running clockwise from a reference direction (magnetic or true north). The magnetic compass rose is the one navigators usually use, and it is always the smaller, inner one. The true compass rose surrounds it. Farther inside the circle is information about the *variation* (the angular difference between true and magnetic north) as well as how the variation changes over time (slowly).

We have to introduce you to a fact that may shake your belief in Santa Claus. There are two north poles. *True north* sits properly atop the globe (at 90°N and 0°E). *Magnetic north* (which magnetic compasses think is north because of the earth's magnetic field) is a few thousand miles away and wanders around a bit because of the molten iron in the earth's core. Luckily, because navigators use compasses, they only need to concern themselves with magnetic north (unless they are performing the art of celestial navigation where true north is "king"). Unfortunately, some navigators don't feel the same way, so when discussing compass directions you should always indicate which reference system you're using. (270°T indicates true degrees, and 270°M indicates magnetic degrees.)

✔ **Date of printing:** Because important things (such as the position or description of a buoy) change, having a current chart is important. The printing date can be found near the corner of the chart, outside the perimeter of the longitude scale. Old charts make great posters, wallpaper, and gift-wrapping paper!

✔ **Depth of the water:** Given a navigator's aversion to groundings, this is the biggie. Depth at a particular spot is displayed as a number that indicates depth below a fixed *datum* (base value), which is normally *mean low water* (the average level of low tide). This number is usually given in units of feet, *fathoms* (one fathom equals six feet), meters, or some combination thereof. The datum and measurement scale (feet, fathoms, and so on) are indicated somewhere on the chart near the label that identifies the chart by name. The units of depth measurement are so important that they are repeated in magenta ink along the perimeter of the chart. Contour lines joining places of equal depth help provide a picture of the underwater topography.

✔ **Hazards:** Shallow water is a major hazard, and charts often depict shallower water as a different color than the deeper water. Other danger areas, like rocks that are awash at low tide, have their own special symbols. Even military target ranges are clearly noted!

✔ **Land:** Because most of your sailing is near land, you can take advantage of the shore and any major landmarks like radio towers and mountain-tops that are indicated for reference.

Reading a chart

If you haven't figured it out by now, we think that charts are pretty cool because they possess so much information. Here are some tips on working with and reading charts:

✔ **Bring Chart No. 1 along:** Hey, you can't tell the players without a program, can you?

✔ **Fold the chart to size:** Charts are usually much bigger than your chart table or work space, so fold the chart so that you can easily see the area you're interested in. If that area is too big or too small, get the chart that is the next size up or down in scale. Make sure that you can see a compass rose and a portion of the latitude scale (for measuring distance) when the chart is folded.

✔ **Get the right chart:** Before embarking on a trip, go to the local marine store and check the *NOS Nautical Chart Catalogue* for your area. If you're traveling some distance, make sure that you have large scale (close-up) charts of potential harbors you may choose (or be forced to stop at).

✔ **Orient the chart for ease of use:** Some people like to rotate the chart so that the direction they're traveling is straight up. Peter prefers keeping true north up, but that's just his taste.

✔ **Use a pencil:** When writing on your chart (perfectly acceptable), use a pencil so that you can erase your scribbles and reuse the chart.

Establishing a course and range on a chart

With the help of a nautical chart (and a tool or two), you can determine the distance and compass course between any two points on a chart. Our favorite tools for this job are *parallel rulers* (two straight-edged plastic slats connected by two hinges) and *dividers* (an adjustable metal tool with two sharp points, like an adjustable "compass" that's used to draw circles). Here's how you use them to obtain the course and distance between two points:

1. **Pick out the two points.**

   If you like, draw a straight line between them.

2. **Lay one long, outer edge of the parallel ruler on the chart so that it touches both points.**

   Use the edge farthest away from the compass rose.

3. **Find the closest compass rose printed on the chart.**

4. **With two hands, "walk" the parallel ruler to the compass rose, moving one plastic slat at a time and being especially careful that the "other" (nonmoving slat) doesn't move at all.**

   Apply extra force with the hand holding the non-moving slat.

5. **When the first slat reaches the compass rose, set it so that its long, outer edge crosses the plus sign in the center of the compass rose and then read the course in magnetic degrees indicated on the inner, magnetic compass ring.**

   If you think that the nonwalking slat slipped during the walking process, do it again. Make sure that the chart surface is absolutely flat and that the rulers have enough "elbowroom" to walk around.

6. **Measure the distance.**

   Use your dividers to compare the distance between the points to the distance indicated on the latitude scale. Keep in mind that distance is always indicated in nautical miles — it helps to remember that a nautical mile equals 6,076 feet (roughly 6,000), 2,025 yards (roughly 2,000), or 1.852 kilometers.

Compasses

Everyone knows that a compass is a device that feels the pull of the earth's magnetic system and provides a reference direction relative to magnetic north. Sailors use several common types of compasses:

- ✔ **Steering compass:** These are mounted permanently in the boat, usually in a position so that the helmsman can refer to them when steering. They come in two basic varieties:

  - **Binnacle or dome compass:** These are mounted on a horizontal surface such as a pedestal or on deck. They are easier to read and are popular on boats with steering wheels.

  - **Bulkhead compass:** These are mounted on a vertical surface such as the back wall (bulkhead) of a cabin and are used on boats that have no convenient location for a dome compass.

Using a chart on deck

Often times, such as when you're navigating your way along a coastline, you may find having the chart on deck quite helpful. The downside is that the wind may blow the chart overboard (not a good thing), and writing and taking measurements on the chart can be cumbersome, difficult, or nearly impossible. Marine stores often sell a collection of local charts on water-resistant paper bound together in a spiral binder, but keep in mind that nothing but a current official government chart is guaranteed to be up to date and accurate.

In the 1988 America's Cup, I was navigator aboard a 65-foot (20-m) wing-sailed catamaran that was fast and wet. There was no place for a chart table, and there was definitely no quiet "nav area" out of the wind and water. To keep track of the boat's progress on the race course, I used a *plotting board,* a device that sandwiches a folded nautical chart between a clear plastic top and a solid plastic bottom (see the figure). A rotating clear-plastic wheel makes establishing compass courses and plotting lines of positions very easy. Sure, we had the latest GPS receiver (see the later section on GPS) telling us where we were within a few hundred feet. But I had to be prepared just in case a huge fog bank descended on the race course just as the U.S. government switched off the system (unlikely unless we are at war) or our battery ran out. The plotting board worked great, even one time when I had to navigate the boat "blindfolded" (only looking at the plotting board and the compass) in a practice session.

✔ **Hand bearing compass:** Small, portable compasses that are not meant to replace a boat's primarily steering compass. They make taking a *bearing* (measuring the compass course from your boat to an object, discussed later in this chapter) easier than with a bulkhead compass.

✔ **Electronic compass:** Electronic compasses use the principals of magnetism and electricity. They're popular in autopilots, as a back-up steering compass, and even in some hand bearing compasses. Of course, you should never rely solely on an electronic compass — what happens when the battery runs down?

Accounting for deviation

Unfortunately, all compasses don't agree as to the direction of magnetic north. Metal objects (or electrical current) nearby alter the effect of the earth's magnetic field on the compass's internal magnets and cause the compass to *deviate* from magnetic north. To minimize this effect, mount the compass far away from potential problems (like the engine) and never use iron fasteners or fittings nearby.

No matter how careful you are, some deviation (5 degrees plus/minus) is inevitable. So if you plan on using your compass for any sort of serious navigation, get your compass *swung* (calibrated for deviation error). In practice, this involved process is usually reserved for larger boats (30 feet/ 9 m and over) that require compass accuracy to the degree.

Reading a compass

As you may have noticed, the *compass card* (rotating piece on which the numbers are written) is divided into increments. The four biggies are the cardinal points, north (000°), south (180°), east (090°), and west (270°). Sometimes, on larger compasses, the four other points — NE (045°), SE (135°), SW (225°), and NW (315°) — are also indicated by their initials. On a really large compass, the smallest increments (indicated by a hash mark) can be a single degree. Smaller compasses may have a hash mark only for every 5-degree increment. That's why the bigger the compass, the better!

If you're sitting directly behind a dome compass, you can determine your boat's heading by lining up the center *lubber line* — fixed vertical post(s) around the edge of the compass card — with the markings on the compass card. You can read your boat's heading on a bulkhead compass in a similar fashion, but notice that the center lubber line is on the back side of the compass. Both compasses are shown in Figure 11-5.

Figure 11-5:
Reading the
boat's
heading on
a dome
compass
(left) and a
bulkhead
compass
(right).

Steering a compass course

When the navigator sets a course to sail, he announces it to the helmsman, expecting him to follow that heading like a railroad track. Hey, dream on. Holding a compass course is difficult, especially at night in really wavy conditions. First, getting accustomed to the natural movement of the compass card takes a little while. Sometimes, like when sailing close-hauled in shifty winds, holding a compass course is just about impossible. However, at other times (such as in thick fog), holding a steady course is crucial. Here are some tips:

✔ **Pick a spot on the horizon:** Steering while looking down at the compass is difficult. Try to pick a spot on the horizon that seems to line up with the desired compass course, and then rotate your eyes down to the compass only periodically to confirm your heading.

✔ **Steer an average heading:** In big waves, when the compass card is swinging all around, try to bracket the desired heading by steering no more than, say, 5 degrees on either side.

✔ **Pay attention and be honest:** In tricky conditions, pay attention to your average heading and report that to the navigator in periodic increments (say, 30 minutes — more often if the conditions and situation warrant).

Basic Navigation — Piloting

Now we get to the really fun part of navigation, using the skills of *piloting*. Piloting is defined as navigation involving frequent determination of position (or a line of position) relative to geographical points. As you discover at the end of the chapter, an affordable electronic device called a GPS (Global Positioning System) makes navigation so easy that many people never see the need to learn these "old-fashioned" skills of piloting.

Like any electronic device, however, a GPS can go on the blink or fail completely. Even when a GPS is working well, the skills of piloting are sometimes easier and more accurate. We strongly urge you to first master how to navigate the old-fashioned way and then — and only then — turn to the alluring GPS. With that in mind, take a look at this fine art of taking information and then plotting it on a chart to help find your position.

Taking a bearing

Unless you're right on top of a known point such as a government buoy (which is illegal, by the way), you have to determine your position by establishing a series of LOPs, or *lines of position* (lines through some point on which you presume your boat to be located as a result of an observation or measurement). The most common measurement used in piloting is taking a compass bearing on an object of known position, like a buoy or the peak of a mountain. The procedure for taking a bearing changes a bit depending on the type of compass you use. (Bulkhead compasses don't lend themselves to this process because you can't look through them.) However, the basic principles remain the same:

1. **Pick out the object on which you intend to get a bearing.**

   For example, if you're close to the shore, you might pick a mountain. Make sure the object is shown on your nautical chart! Buoys are okay, but they can move slightly. Fixed objects (lighthouses and objects on land) are the best.

2. **Situate your eyes so that an imaginary line from the object to your eyes passes through the center of the compass.**

3. **Read the compass heading on the far side of the compass that is crossed by that imaginary line.**

   Taking a bearing requires a good imagination — and sometimes several readings. The key is to visualize that imaginary line from the object.

4. **With the compass course of the bearing now known, go to your chart and find the object or point that you measured.**

5. **Take the parallel rulers and lay them on the compass rose so that the outer long edge rests on the (magnetic) compass course of your bearing and the center point of the compass rose.**

6. **Carefully "walk" the parallel rulers over to the observed point.**

   Use the same one-step-at-a-time technique described earlier.

7. Draw a line along the edge of the rulers going through the point.

Note this line of position with the time of day. Your actual position is (theoretically) somewhere on this line.

PETER SAYS

Here's a cool (albeit uncommon) and highly accurate way to get a line of position. Whenever you visually line up two points that are on the chart, you can plot them as a line of position. This type of observation is called a *range*. Long Island Sound, where I grew up, has a great range that occurs when two huge smokestacks line up on the Long Island shore. Because we sailed up and down the Sound quite a bit, we drew a line on the chart for this range and always watched for it.

Fixing your position

Where two lines of position taken at the same time cross, you can *fix* your position on the chart, as shown in Figure 11-6. An accurate fix is every navigator's goal, but error can creep in and degrade accuracy in many ways. Here are some tips to help minimize error:

✔ **Take bearings on objects at right angles to each other:** The most accurate fix from two given lines of position (LOPs) is obtained when they're at 90 degrees to each other. When two LOPs cross at a shallow angle, even a small error in one of the bearings can lead to a large error in the fix.

Figure 11-6: Using two LOPs (left), your position fix is where the lines intersect. With three LOPs (right), your position fix is within the triangle.

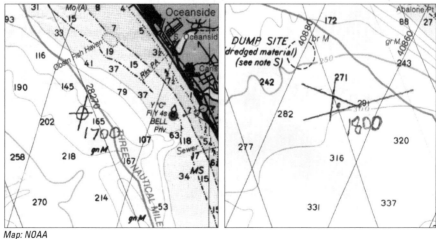

Map: NOAA

✔ **Three is better than two:** By taking bearings on three objects (ideally about 60 degrees from each other), you further minimize the chance of error. Of course, your fix probably ends up looking like a triangle rather than a cross, but you can simply assume that you're in the middle of that triangle, as shown in Figure 11-6.

✔ **Take bearings on nearby objects:** The nearer the object, the less effect an error in bearing has on your fix.

✔ **Take two or three readings for each object:** Multiple readings minimize any error you may make in taking the bearing.

✔ **Use ranges whenever possible:** Ranges are really accurate.

✔ **Cross-check your fix with the depth sounder (if you have one that you know to be accurate):** Don't forget to account for the height of the tide above (or below) mean low water. Comparing the depth measured with the depth on the chart is akin to getting yet another fix.

✔ **Write down the time of the fix adjacent to it.**

Dead reckoning

Dead reckoning, or *DR,* is the process of determining position by advancing a previous position for courses and distances. It's also one of Peter's favorite CDs by the Grateful Dead. By definition, DR is not as accurate as fixing your position with some accurate lines of position; however, many times you don't have an acceptable object (or only one of dubious value) on which to take a bearing. To be able to perform dead reckoning calculations, you must understand the important relationship between speed, time, and distance.

Speed (measured in *knots,* or nautical miles per hour) is simply distance (nautical miles) divided by time (hours). If you are good at basic math, you will have no problem remembering the following relationships:

S = Speed (knots)	D = Distance (nautical miles)	T = Time (hours)
S = D/T	D= S x T	T = D/S

If you know two of the three quantities, you can determine the third. You will use this principle most commonly to calculate distance traveled. If you know your average speed (from your speedometer) and the time you traveled, then you can calculate the distance. Furthermore, if you know the average compass course that you steered, you can advance your position on the chart from your last known (or estimated) position.

Suppose that you have fixed your position on the chart with three bearings taken at noon. You then steer an average heading of 090° at 6.8 knots for 25 minutes. You can calculate the distance traveled as follows.

D = S x T   D = 6.8 knots x (25/60)   D = 2.83 nautical miles

Therefore, you can establish your DR position at 1225 by measuring 2.83 miles along a course of 090°M from the noon fix, using the same techniques of operating the parallel rulers and dividers outlined earlier in this chapter. The updated location is your *dead reckoned position* and should be marked on the chart as such.

The six-minute rule: When determining distance traveled, you must often use a time interval of less than one hour, creating a cumbersome math problem. But because six minutes is one tenth of an hour, you can use this increment of time to ease your calculations. For example, a boat going 6.8 knots travels 0.68 nautical miles (nm) in six minutes, or roughly 1.4 nm in 12 minutes, and so on.

Figuring in current and leeway

When advancing your position with dead reckoning, you may also want to include movement not measured on the speedometer (or log) and compass. Two other types of motion may be taken into account when fine-tuning the DR (in a manner similar to the one described in the preceding section). *Leeway* is the sideslipping motion that occurs when a boat sails a close-hauled course. The impact of leeway varies from boat to boat. Current has a similar "invisible" effect on the boat's motion. For more on currents, see Chapter 10.

Keeping a log

Given the importance of staying on top of your speed (or distance traveled) and heading, you can see why all serious navigators keep logs. A *log* is simply an historical record of various pieces of information. You can design your log to include whatever information you think is important. Common items of entry include

- **Average heading since the last entry:** Whenever the boat changes course (say, after a tack), you should make a new entry.
- **Average speed since the last entry.**
- **Given course:** Course desired by the navigator.
- **Log reading:** Most instrument systems have a *log*, which is simply a distance measuring device, a nautical odometer (as opposed to your written log).
- **Time:** Normally recorded in the 24-hour format (6 a.m. is 0600).
- **Weather information:** Wind speed and direction, cloud cover, barometric pressure, and so on.
- **Other comments:** Like what sails are up, who is driving, when the boat tacked or jibed, what was for dinner, and so on.

When should you keep a log? Obviously, you don't need one when you sail a dinghy in familiar waters (nor do you have a place to store it). If you're crossing the ocean, you definitely should keep a log. In between, use your judgment. Keep a log any time doing so can add to the boat's safety.

Special Piloting Techniques

The key to safe navigation is to make navigating as easy to perform as possible. We began this chapter with the "common sense" section because you sometimes can perform the necessary tasks without fiddling with parallel rulers and dividers.

However, there definitely is a time and place for rigorous dead reckoning and frequent fixing of your position. Navigating at night in a new location with many shoals and hazards is an example. Much of the time, your task requires a level of navigational effort somewhere in between the two extremes. Here are some techniques that you will find helpful.

Danger bearing

Sometimes, navigational aids provide *danger bearings* — a compass bearing to an object or objects that indicates the edge of safe (deep enough) water. Sometimes lighthouses display a different color light (red instead of white) in a sector of its sweep, the edges of which are danger bearings. On one side the boat is safe; on the other could be shallow water. Another type of danger bearing is a range. Often a narrow entrance channel to a harbor is marked by a range of two markers that, when aligned, indicate a safe course, sort of like landing an airplane on an aircraft carrier.

The navigator can also determine a danger bearing from information gained from the nautical chart. For example, if your present course requires you to sail around an island with rocky shoals on one side, you can plot an LOP as a danger bearing tangent to an obvious landmark or navigational aid that you want the boat to stay outside. By monitoring the bearing to this object and comparing it to your danger bearing (measured in the normal manner on the chart), you can avoid the hazard without having to constantly run down to the chart table and plot your position.

Add some "padding" to the danger bearing. For example, if a bearing of 350 degrees to a buoy just skirts a shoal, you should add (or subtract, depending on which side of the line is safe water) 5 degrees or so, especially as you get close to the danger.

Distance off

You can fix your position on a chart with two LOPs obtained from bearings, as described earlier in this chapter, but you can also fix your position if you have one LOP and know your distance, or range, away from that object. You simply find the point at which the LOP crosses the *circle of position* marked by a circle whose radius is the distance you are away from its center. You can obtain a circle of position in many ways. Two of the most helpful are by judging distance and by doubling the relative angle.

Judging distance

Every top navigator likes to think that he or she has the ability to judge distance equal to a pro golfer (or his or her caddie). That skill comes from practice. Any time you're out on the water (or on the shore), you can practice by making a game of judging distance. All you need is a nautical chart (and knowledge of where you are) to be able to check your guesstimate.

I like guessing distance, and I do it all the time. I have stored away in my "mind's eye" a catalogue of what certain distances look like. For example, I know that the distance across Skaneateles Lake (New York) from our dock is two miles, and I know what that distance looks like by heart. So when something is about two miles away, I ask myself whether it's closer or farther than the other side of the lake! My brain has also stored away what six miles looks like from all the time I've spent staring out of jet airplane windows. And of course, 100 yards is ingrained from my early years playing around on a football field. You see, your brain already has a catalogue of what certain distances look like.

Here are some other pointers we've gleaned over the years:

- ✔ **If you can discern individual trees, you're less than a mile away.**
- ✔ **If you can make out house windows, you're less than two miles away.**
- ✔ **If you can't see the true edge of the land and water, you're more than three miles away.**

Doubling the relative angle

You can find plenty of tricky ways to judge distance by using the science and magic of geometry. The easiest one to remember is "doubling the relative angle," but you have to be steering a straight course for it to work. When you pass an object of interest (say, a lighthouse), note the time when it is 45 degrees (relative angle) off your bow. Pay attention to the average speed, and when the lighthouse is dead abeam (90 degrees to the bow), you have "doubled the angle," so note the time again. Through the wonders of geometry, the distance you travel between the two readings equals your distance away from the object at the time of the second reading. Now you can plot a circle of position, take a bearing on that object, and you have a fix.

Navigating in the Fog

By definition, you can't see anything in fog, so the skills of dead reckoning can become crucially important. Here are some good rules to keep in mind when fog descends:

- ✔ **Be aware of the potential for fog (see Chapter 10 on weather).**

- ✔ **If fog starts to roll in (it won't totally blanket you without some warning), immediately fix your position on the chart as accurately as possible.** If you don't have a chart or are simply daysailing, immediately set your course for a safe haven (like home).

- ✔ **Follow the procedures for keeping an accurate dead reckoning.** If you have a depth sounder, use it, especially if you will be passing over some areas with steep transitions in depth that will help accurately provide a fix of position.

- ✔ **Listen for buoys and foghorns.** The nautical chart (and good ol' Chart No. 1) indicates what navigational aids make certain sounds.

- ✔ **Listen for other boats.** Every boat is required to post a "lookout." Keep in mind that sound does weird things in fog, so pinpointing the location of a sound can be difficult.

- ✔ **Make sound signals.** The rules of the road require a sailboat (39 feet/12 m or longer) to make one long horn blast followed by two short blasts every two minutes or less. For the other rules of the road, see Chapter 7.

Remember when we advised you to learn the traditional skills of navigation before using a GPS unit? Well, fog is a good time to disobey us!

Navigating at Night

When night falls, you lose some, but not all, of the visual information important to a navigator. Even in familiar waters, the arrival of night is a good time to break out the nautical chart and increase the level of your navigational efforts.

One of the most important aspects of coastal navigation at night is your ability to identify lighted buoys and lighthouses. As mentioned earlier in this chapter, Chart No. 1 can help you decipher the abbreviations defining the characteristics of the light. You usually need to view two or three cycles of the light sequence to be sure that you have positively identified it. Realize also that the lights on buoys have much shorter range (about two miles; even less in big waves) than lighthouses. You may have an easier time identifying a buoy or lighthouse if you first calculate (on the chart) its expected bearing and then look in that direction.

At night, keeping interior (and deck) lights to a minimum helps the night vision of those on deck (especially the navigator, who may be going back and forth between the chart table below and the cockpit). Many boats have lights with red bulbs for night operation because red light doesn't affect night vision like white lights do. Keep in mind that red lines and symbols on the chart look gray in red light.

Electronic Navigation

We've made it clear that understanding and being proficient at the "traditional" skills of piloting and dead reckoning on a paper chart are absolutely crucial before trusting your boat (and your safety) to a machine. But after you've mastered those traditional skills, electronic navigational aids make the navigator's job a breeze.

Navigating with GPS

The most commonly used electronic navigation system is the GPS, or *Global Positioning System*. The GPS unit is a satellite navigation device, using information from a bevy of U.S. Department of Defense satellites to give your current latitude and longitude with incredible accuracy — within 100 meters (110 yards) or better. Like your TV set, you don't need to know how it works to use it. GPS units have revolutionized the art of navigation.

Several different GPS models are available, so read the instruction manual for specific instructions on how to turn on and properly configure your GPS. When you configure your device, set the GPS to display magnetic degrees (not true degrees), nautical miles (not km or statute miles), your local time (not Greenwich Mean Time), and latitude and longitude. These conventions make navigating by using your own watch and nautical charts easier, because then all the parts are in synch.

The features of different GPS units vary, but one really cool task that most of them can do is save a *waypoint* (the latitude/longitude coordinates of any point you desire) and then display range and bearing to that waypoint. Also, some GPS units can help you plot your position in two other high-tech ways — plugging the GPS into a personal computer and using navigation software, or by using a digitized pad interface with the GPS (a system Peter especially likes because he can still use old-fashioned nautical charts).

One thing you should know is how to plot an indicated position (latitude and longitude) from the GPS onto a chart. Here's the most accurate way:

1. **Write down the indicated latitude and longitude and find them on the appropriate scales bounding your chart.**

   Make a small tick mark with a pencil at each of those points.

2. **Line up the outer edge of the parallel ruler with a nearby latitude or longitude line.**

   Those lines are either at the edge of the chart or somewhere in the middle, marked by a thin black line running horizontally (latitude) or vertically (longitude) across the chart.

3. **Walk the parallel ruler to the tick mark for that value (either longitude or latitude) and draw an LOP.**

4. **Do the same for the other value.**

   Where the LOPs cross is your location!

Other electronic aids

We rely so much on a boat's electronic speedometer and depth sounder that we think of them as "traditional" instruments, but they deserve a little more explanation.

A *speedometer* serves the same function on a boat as on a car — telling you how fast you're going. Most boat speedometers are driven by a tiny paddlewheel fitted under the belly of the hull. A *depth sounder* simply uses sonar waves to tell you how much room is underneath the boat and displays this measurement on a dial or digital readout.

If we had written this book ten years ago, we would have had to discuss *Loran C* (a system of electronic navigation that employs radio waves to determine position) and *RDF* (Radio Direction Finder — another, even less-accurate radio navigation unit), but GPS has supplanted all these systems. You may still find an old Loran C on your boat. It indicates position of latitude and longitude and can work with waypoints just like a GPS, but it doesn't work everywhere and isn't as accurate as a GPS. If you're considering a purchase, get a GPS. RDFs will soon only be good for paperweights in the U.S. because the RDF stations are all being turned off.

Celestial Navigation

From high-tech to really traditional, *celestial navigation* (navigating by celestial bodies like stars, the moon, and the sun) is the coolest form of navigation. Using this system puts you in a league with the greats like Galileo, Copernicus, Magellan, Columbus, and Cook. Well, maybe that's a bit of a stretch, but it is pretty amazing that you can determine where you are in the world (to an accuracy of less than a mile) with a *sextant* (device that accurately measures the angular height of a celestial body over the horizon), a watch, and some books of tables. Oh yes, you need one other thing — a clear or partially clear sky during daylight, dawn, or dusk hours. Nighttime and clouds put a real damper on celestial navigation, because you need to see the celestial object and the horizon.

A general book like this one is too small to do justice to celestial navigation. Fortunately, you can find many good books on the subject. Peter's favorite is *Kindergarten of Celestial Navigation,* by Joseph Sellar.

The basic principal of celestial navigation is easy to grasp. If you can measure the angle between the horizon and a celestial body of known position at a certain time (thank you, Copernicus, et al.), you can generate a circle of position. You are somewhere on that circle of position. Get another reading from a different celestial body or the same one at a different time, and, if you haven't moved, the two circles of position cross at your location (and also on the other side of the planet, which is obviously where you aren't). See an example of celestial navigation in Figure 11-7.

No matter how many GPSs you have on board, never, ever make a major offshore passage (crossing an ocean, out of sight of land) without having a sextant, instruction book, and either the requisite books (tables and almanacs) or a calculator or PC with all that information stored inside.

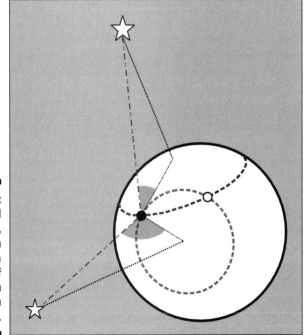

Figure 11-7: By celestial navigation, you can generate a circle of position on which you are located.

Part IV
Sailing Away for a Year and a Day — Special Situations

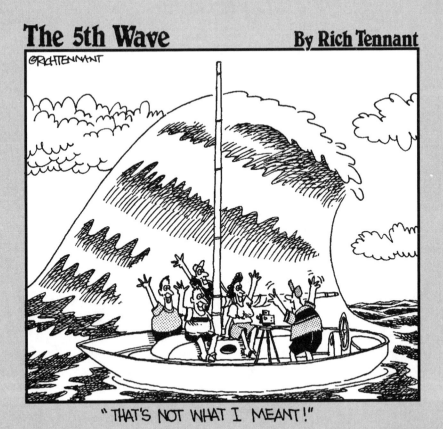

The 5th Wave · By Rich Tennant

"THAT'S NOT WHAT I MEANT!"

In this part . . .

Special situations . . . hmm. That's a nice way of saying, "All the other things about sailing that we think you want to know about." So this section covers what to do in a storm or if your boat breaks down — situations you probably won't experience for a while in your sailing career, if ever. But we do hope that you have a chance to try sailboarding, advanced small-boat techniques, and sailboat racing. These are the three areas of this huge sport that we love the most. So humor us and at least glance at those chapters.

Chapter 12

Blow the Man Down: Heavy Weather Sailing

Hoist up sail while gale doth last,
Tide and wind stay no man's pleasure.

— Robert Southwell

*W*hen the "sheep are in the pasture" (whitecaps all over the water), sailing can be fun or terrifying. It all depends on your boat, you and your crew's level of competence, where you are, and how windy it really is. At some point, conditions are simply too windy for any man or beast. This chapter enables you to raise your wind threshold so that you can enjoy those blustery days and be prepared in the event of a sudden squall. We concentrate on windy but sailable conditions because they are by far the most common. But we also touch on strategy and tactics for true survival conditions, when you should be on shore.

How Windy Is Too Windy?

"Heavy weather" and "heavy air" are sailors' terms for a strong breeze. When do moderate conditions become heavy? Simply put, heavy weather is any wind and wave condition that is so strong and forceful that the sailor is challenged (to some level or another) by its intensity.

JJ's ten reasons why heavy air is fun

1. You get to go fast and blast around with a big grin on your face.

2. That hot shower at the end of the day is the best.

3. You get to wear your cool-looking foul-weather gear.

4. You can surf waves and maybe even *plane* (skim along the water's surface).

5. Pushing your limits and conquering your fears boost your self-confidence.

6. A little spray in the face never hurt anyone.

7. You'll sleep really well that night.

8. When you make it back to shore, you have a new appreciation for the simple things in life — like being on dry land.

9. You will get caught in heavy air sometime, so getting some practice is good.

10. Why ask why? Just do it. (Not to be confused with an excuse to get married at a young age or go bungee jumping.)

As you find out in Chapter 10, sailors measure wind velocity in units called *knots* and can estimate the speed of the wind by looking at the water's surface. We recommend that a beginning sailor head for home when *white-caps* (foamy wave crests) become commonplace, or at about 15 knots. But for an experienced sailor (especially on a high-performance dinghy or catamaran), 15 knots of wind is when sailing gets fun.

We recommend that beginning sailors spend plenty of time refining their skills in light and moderate winds before trying to push the limit of their comfort level in stronger winds. At some point, everyone (no matter what his or her experience level) wants to push his limit. Here are some important considerations when that day comes:

✔ **Don't jump too far too fast.** If your limit has been 17 knots, try 20 or 22 before you jump to 30.

✔ **Go out in familiar waters.** If you're in a "new" area, make sure that the wave conditions aren't excessive and that plenty of deep, open water is around. The last thing you want to worry about is going aground.

✔ **Go on a familiar boat.**

✔ **Have someone with more experience than you on board.** If you're sailing a one-person dinghy, make sure that a potential rescue boat is nearby, with experienced boaters watching you.

✔ **Put on a life jacket.** Follow the preparation and safety procedures outlined later in this chapter and in Chapter 7.

✔ **Use your head.** In sailing, just like in life, knowing your limits is important. This means being able to assess not only the wind and wave conditions, but also the condition of the boat and crew and whether you feel capable.

What Can Go Wrong

We don't want to scare you from sailing in heavy weather; we just want to tell you a few reasons why you shouldn't exceed your limits. Hopefully, a word to the wise. . . .

✔ **The boat may become uncontrollable.** In really heavy conditions, the force of the wind and waves throws the boat around, sometimes steering it wildly out of control. Being out of control isn't fun or safe.

✔ **You may capsize.** You should practice righting your dinghy (as described in Chapter 7) until it's routine. However, things can go wrong, especially when in rough and windy weather. You may not be able to right the boat against the force of the wind. While upside down, the boat may be blown into shallow water, possibly breaking the mast.

✔ **You may lose someone overboard.** The bigger the waves and the more the boat is heeling in the wind, the harder it is to stay on deck. In Chapter 7, we discuss onboard safety, including how to use safety harnesses. In big waves and strong winds, returning and picking up a man overboard is no piece of cake and can be nearly impossible.

✔ **Your mast may break, or you may suffer another major failure.** If your boat is not fully prepared (and sometimes even when it is), things can and will begin to blow apart as Mother Nature's forces increase. We discuss how to deal with potential accidents in Chapter 13 and maintenance in Chapter 19.

Preparing for Heavy Weather

Depending on your boat and the type of sailing you're doing, the steps needed to prepare both you and your boat for heavy weather vary, but some steps are universal.

Preparing in advance

Consider these tips before setting sail on a heavy day and when the wind seems to be picking up while you're out sailing:

✔ **Depower your sails and consider reducing your sail area.**
In Chapter 8, we discuss techniques of depowering your existing sail area. Later in this chapter, we review methods of reducing sail area by *reefing* or even changing sails. Doing these things *before* you're in the raging gale is the key because of the difficulty in even getting around in the boat after the gale hits. At least rig the lines and equipment used to reef the sails, if you have them.

✔ **Make sure everything is shipshape.** When the wind comes up, the boat heels more; if you're on a dinghy, you may even capsize. Tie down or securely stow all loose gear, including batteries, fuel tanks, personal gear, and anything really heavy that could do damage if the boat tips excessively. On a dinghy, make sure that key equipment (like your rudder and centerboard) are tied into the boat. Ensure that all the standing and running rigging is in good condition. Consider replacing that frayed line or swapping in a stronger shackle to replace the one that has a bent pin. Check your sails to ensure that they aren't frayed or torn. (See Chapter 19 for more details on caring for your craft.)

✔ **Make the boat as watertight as possible.** Now is the time to "batten down the hatches." Close any windows or hatches, especially the ones up forward where the first spray comes on board. Bail out the boat — if it's bound to get wet outside, it's nice to start out dry inside.

✔ **Mentally prepare your crew for a blow.** Review safety procedures for capsizing (if you're on a dinghy) and for a man overboard. Do we need to remind you again that these topics are covered in Chapter 7? Review the location of certain equipment, like tools, knife, anchors, pump, life rafts, reef lines, sail ties, and so on, that may come in handy if things turn really nasty.

✔ **Physically prepare your crew for a blow.** In Chapter 3, we go over your options of clothing for various conditions. Bottom line: It's going to get wetter and colder, so put the warm clothes on now; otherwise you risk soaking your all-important interior layers of clothing. After you don the foul-weather gear (or whatever you decide to wear), dole out the life jackets (see Chapter 7) and (on keelboats) safety harnesses.

If you're already at sea

If you're well out to sea, especially on a longer (more than 12 hours) passage, you may not be able to head to shore easily when heavy weather looms. Along with the general steps of preparation outlined in the preceding section, you may want to do the following:

✔ **Feed the crew.** Going into battle against the elements with the fuel tank full is a good idea. Plus, if your boat gets wet down below, a storm may mean the end of the edible food anyway.

✔ **Fix your position.** Consider increasing the level of your navigational energies, too. See Chapter 11 to find out how to fix your position.

Cutting your losses

Have you ever noticed in the old pirate movies that every sailor carried a knife? Well, that knife wasn't just for coaxing the good guy to walk the plank; it's a valuable tool for every sailor to have, especially in an emergency. A very sharp knife, with a blunt point to avoid any accidental perforation of boat or body parts, can cut through a highly loaded halyard or tangled sheet in a second, often saving the mast or the boat in an emergency such as a sudden squall or an accidental jibe or tack.

✔ **Set a watch system.** If you're on a longer passage, you may already have established a rotation of the crew so that everyone can rest. A common rotation divides the crew up into two *watches,* or groups (of equal ability), with each watch being "on" for three or four hours (you decide) and then "off" to get some rest down below in a bunk.

Reducing Your Sail Power

Here's an interesting fact: The force of the wind increases by the square of the velocity, which means that at 14 knots, the wind force on your rigging and sails is double the load on the boat at 10 knots. And that's before you add in the effect of the waves. Sailboats and their component parts can only stand so much load before they begin to break. Anything you do to reduce the forces on the boat in extreme conditions can make a big difference.

Reducing sail area

The first way to reduce the load is to depower your sails. We cover that subject in depth in Chapter 8. The next step would be to reduce the boat's sail area, or *shorten sail.* There are three ways to shorten sail: by dropping a sail, reefing a sail, or changing to a smaller sail. All three methods have their pros and cons, depending on the boat and the conditions.

Dropping a sail

Dropping a sail is a pretty extreme tactic on a catboat (which has only one sail), but this tactic is commonly used on sloops of all sizes. Should you drop the mainsail or the jib? The answer depends upon the boat and the conditions. Here are situations when dropping the jib and sailing with the mainsail alone is appropriate:

✔ **When the jib is very large or when the jib is so lightweight that it is getting blown out.**

✔ **When the boat handles well with the mainsail alone.** On most boats, the jib has less area than the main, so in extreme conditions like squalls, dropping the mainsail may be better because the reduction in sail area (and thus load on the boat) is more dramatic. Dropping the jib may be an interim step as the wind builds.

✔ **When your boat has a roller furler (see Chapter 8).** It's really easy to roll the jib partway, see whether that setting works, and then roll it up all the way if necessary.

Here are situations when dropping the mainsail and sailing with the jib alone is appropriate:

✔ **On dinghies that are rigged in such a manner that dropping the jib causes the standing rigging to loosen dramatically**

✔ **In really extreme conditions, where reefing the main is either not an option or not enough of a reduction of sail area, as indicated by the boat's heel and controllability**

As you lower either sail, keep it under control, bunched up so that it doesn't blow around, until it can either be stuffed down below deck or lashed down on deck securely with ropes so that it can't flog about.

If you must send the crew to the foredeck for a sail change in rough seas, turn the boat onto a very broad reach or run (no accidental jibes, please) to reduce heel. Then everyone on deck can move around on a relatively flat surface. Of course, if your destination is upwind, you will be going away from it at a pretty fast clip.

Turning downwind can also steady the boat's motion to enable a crew member to work up the mast. Once when I was skippering *Courageous,* Ted Turner's famous 12 Meter, in Perth, Australia, our mainsail got stuck at the top of the mast — we couldn't lower it. We had to send a crew member 90 feet up in the air to fix the problem. It was blowing 28 knots, and the waves were steep and choppy. We knew that he couldn't survive pounding along on an upwind course — the length of the mast accentuated the boat's motion too much. So I had to turn downwind to level the boat and smooth out the ride. Still, it took him nearly 25 minutes to solve the problem; by then we were almost on the rocks and four miles farther from home. But at least he lived!

Reefing

Reefing is a system of reducing a sail's exposed area. Reefing a mainsail requires special equipment on the mainsail, mast, and boom. Some jibs can be reefed by rolling the sail up partway on a roller furler. Most dinghies and many small keelboats don't have the special equipment to reef. When reefing is an option, you perform it as an intermediate step (as the conditions became heavier) before dropping a sail.

Reefing the mainsail

Reefing the mainsail entails lowering it partway and attaching it by a "new" tack and clew. The reefing system we discuss here is also called *slab, tie-in,* or *jiffy reefing.* Here are the key components, some of which are shown in Figure 12-1:

- ✔ **Boom lift:** Also called a *topping lift,* this rope holds the boom horizontal when the mainsail is partially lowered.

- ✔ **Reefing line:** This strong line is led through a system of pulleys to the back of the boom and up the mainsail leech to the heavily reinforced *clew cringle* (the aft-most reef point).

- ✔ **Reef points:** The mainsail must have one or more horizontal rows of these reinforced holes built in.

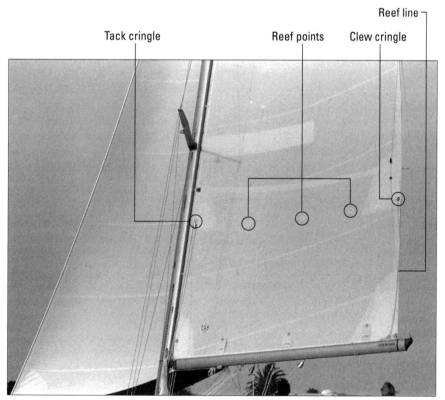

Tack cringle   Reef points   Clew cringle   Reef line

Figure 12-1:
The parts of
a reefing
system.

Some boats also have a *tack horn,* a strong metal hook, horn, or other means of securing the *tack cringle* (the forward-most reef point) near the gooseneck.

Here is the procedure for reefing a mainsail:

1. **Ensure that the reef line is properly rigged.**

   You should have done this step before you set sail. Feeding the reef line through the clew cringle after the mainsail is hoisted can be difficult.

2. **Have the helmsman steer a steady course.**

   Close-hauled or close reaching is preferable because the mainsail drops more easily.

3. **Take the slack out of the boom lift and *cleat* it (tie it off securely).**

   This action keeps the boom from falling into the cockpit and causing all sorts of mayhem. Some boats have fancy, solid boom vangs (see Chapter 8) that keep the boom lifted safely overhead instead.

4. **Ease the mainsheet until the main is fully luffing.**

   The main should luff throughout the reefing procedure to reduce the pressure on the sail so that it can be lowered and reefed easily.

5. **Partially lower the main halyard — slowly.**

   Gather the dropping luff until the person standing at the mast can secure the tack cringle into the tack horns (or alternate arrangement near the gooseneck) to effectively create a "new" tack for the sail.

6. **Rehoist and tension the main halyard.**

   Feed the luff carefully into the mast and tension it very tight; make sure the boom vang is slack.

7. **Tension the reef line and cleat it securely.**

   On a boat over 20 feet (6 m) or so, the reef line needs a winch to get sufficient tension. The reef line should pull the clew cringle down to within an inch or two of the boom.

8. **Trim the mainsheet to fill the sail and ease the boom lift.**

9. **Tie up the middle of the lowered sailcloth.**

   This step is optional, but it aids in your visibility and makes the boat look neater. We recommend using bungee cord to lace up the middle reef points. Then, if the reef line breaks or slips, the sail doesn't shred!

You can see a properly reefed main in Figure 12-2.

Figure 12-2:
A properly
reefed
main.

Some mainsails have more than one set of reef points. Which set you use is determined by how small you want your mainsail to be. The first step down in size is the *first reef;* the next step down is the *second reef.* Very few mainsails have more than two sets of reef points, unless they're designed for real ocean sailing.

Reefing the jib

Occasionally, you may find a jib with reef points, just like a mainsail. The most common (and easiest) way of reefing the jib is with a roller furler, but as the sail rolls up, it loses its designed shape. (In Chapter 8, we discuss the importance of sail shape.) So the only racing boats that would rely on a roller furler for reefing are the shorthanded round-the-world boats, because no one in his right mind wants to go up to the bow and change jibs or wrestle a sail back on board when he is alone in a 60-knot storm in the Southern Ocean.

When should you reef? Well, if you've read this far, you know it depends. You should reef whenever you want to reduce sail area. Reefing is an efficient way to reduce the power in the sails. An old saying is still as valuable today as it is was in the days of the square riggers: "When in doubt . . . reef'er."

Changing down

Another way to reduce sail area is to switch to a smaller sail. This tactic has practically the same effect as reefing, but it can be much more efficient for jibs.

Most dinghies and small keelboats come equipped with only one jib. But as keelboats increase in size (25 feet / 8 m and over), more of them have an extra sailbag or two in the cabin. These bags (and the corners of the sails in them) should be clearly marked so that you know which sail is which. See Chapter 8 for a table of the jib selection for a large racing keelboat.

The process for changing a jib while under way can be as easy or as difficult as you want to make it. Here's the easy way:

1. **Turn the boat downwind onto a very broad reach to make moving around on the foredeck easier for the crew.**

2. **Lower the old, bigger jib and fold it (as described in Chapter 19).**

   Bag it and put it down in the cabin.

3. **Rig the new, smaller jib (as described in Chapter 4).**

4. **Hoist the new jib.**

   Crank the halyard good and tight.

5. **Bring the crew back into the safety of the cockpit and then turn onto your desired course, trimming the sheet accordingly.**

For most sailors, sail changes are few and far between. A corollary of the "when in doubt, reef'er" policy is to err on the side of putting up too small a jib initially — especially in a building breeze.

When reducing sail, it's okay — and considered good seamanship — to reduce too much sail. Even if the boat *could* be sailed in the present conditions with a double-reefed main and a small jib, deciding to lower the mainsail and sail in to shore at half-speed under jib alone because of your comfort level is perfectly all right.

Using an engine

One way to handle your boat in heavy weather is to use the engine so that you can take more sail area (and load) off the boat. You may even drop all sails and just use the engine alone. Usually, you should consider using an engine only when you're headed on an upwind course. Otherwise, sailing is probably faster and easier on the boat and crew. If you have a reliable engine that is easy to use, here are some things to consider before you use the engine in heavy weather:

✔ **Can the engine power the boat?** Some engines don't have enough horsepower to get you upwind against a strong wind.

✔ **Consider motorsailing.** When your destination is to windward, the best tactic may be to keep up a reefed mainsail or small jib and use the motor at the same time. *Motorsailing* like this still provides some power from the sail. Plus, if your engine fails or runs out of gas, the last thing you want to do is try to hoist the sails while wallowing about.

✔ **Don't let the boat heel too far.** If you motorsail, the heeling force of the wind may cause the boat to heel so much that the cooling-water intake comes out of the water, which causes the engine to overheat. Other systems on the engine may not like excessive heel either.

✔ **Keep all your lines out of the water.** Nothing ruins your day faster than having a jib sheet or halyard tail get wrapped up in a propeller.

Picking the Best Course

Being smart pays off in heavy weather, and you can do a great deal to make your sailing easier, safer, and more fun when the wind picks up. As important as anything else is picking the best course to sail. Select a path that minimizes all the difficult things about heavy weather so that you can enjoy the ride.

Getting out of the waves

Often the big problem with heavy weather is not so much the wind but the waves. We have sailed in the Gulf Stream in waves that are so big and steep that the crew calls sailing upwind "condo-jumping," because it feels like the boat is jumping off a condominium with the passing of every wave. Because wave size (and shape) is a function of wind velocity, *fetch* (the distance of open water the wave has to grow), current, and water depth, you can sometimes plot a course that minimizes condo-jumping. Here's how:

✔ **Avoid shallow water.** If you encounter big waves, you may run aground even where the chart indicates the water is deep enough. Plus, sailing in big waves in shallow water makes for a very bumpy ride.

✔ **Don't select a destination that is upwind.** Hey, that's pretty simple, but it's easier said than done.

✔ **If the wind is going to build and you can predict its direction accurately, do your upwind work now and fly downwind later!**

✔ **Plot a course that makes use of the natural breakwater created by land.** For example, if you have a choice of sailing along the windward or leeward side of the island, go to leeward.

If you must sail upwind in big waves, try to pick a route that minimizes the bumps in the road. Sailing in big waves can be fun — like off-roading, except that the road is moving. If the waves are so big that you can feel them pushing your boat backward, turn toward the wave — perpendicular to the crest just as it reaches your bow. This action minimizes the surface area that the waves can push upon, similar to a surfer paddling out through the breakers. The key when using this technique is keeping your speed — hence steerageway — up. Bear off and regain speed as soon as your boat is on top of the wave.

Avoiding a lee shore

A *lee shore* is a shoreline to leeward of a boat, onto which the wind is blowing. If the shoreline is an island, the lee shore is the windward shore of the island. A very important rule of heavy-weather sailing is to avoid getting close to a lee shore. As the wind builds, you always want an escape route of open water to leeward. Then, in a worst-case scenario, you can simply drop your sails and drift until the storm abates. A lee shore forces you to sail close-hauled, the most demanding point of sail, to get away from its dangerous shallow waters.

Sailing off the wind

Sailing *off the wind,* on a course lower than a beam reach, can be the ultimate fun in heavy air. But as the breeze and waves increase, you must be aware of some common pitfalls.

Rounding up

Broaching or *rounding up* can occur on any type of boat on any point of sail, but it's most aggravating when you're sailing off the wind. Rounding up occurs when a massive amount of weather helm (described in Chapter 8) from all the forces acting on the boat causes the boat to "round up" toward the wind fast. In a round up, you feel as though the rudder is gone because you have no steering control. Actually, the rudder has just stalled. A round up is preceded by a telltale sign — increasing weather helm. Here are some ways to avoid this embarrassing fate when sailing on a reach:

- **Ease the boom vang:** This tip is especially important when the boat is heeling so much that the boom is close to the water.

- **Move the crew weight back:** This action keeps more of the rudder in the water. Make sure the crew is hiking, too.

- **Play the mainsheet aggressively:** In big wind and waves, you must play the mainsail to keep the boat "on its feet." The helmsman should ask the trimmer (sometimes one and the same on a dinghy) for a quick ease if he starts feeling weather helm building.

✔ **"Pump" the rudder:** By rapidly jerking the helm from "straight" to "bearing away sharply" and then back to "straight," you may avoid stalling and help the rudder stay gripped to the water.

✔ **Reduce heel:** See Chapters 8 and 15 for ideas.

✔ **Take down your spinnaker:** Spinnakers are fast and fun, but not when your boat is floating full of water after swamping during a broach.

A broach is inevitable if the conditions are severe enough. If you do find your boat heeled over on its side and pointing into the wind, put the helm to center, ease all the sails, and then try, with what little forward motion you have left, to coax the boat back away from the wind again by jerking the rudder hard to bear off.

Rounding down

The *round down* or *death roll* is probably the most spectacular crash imaginable. It occurs most commonly on dinghies, resulting in a capsize, although keelboats in really heavy air are not totally immune. The round down starts with the boat sailing on a very broad reach, run, or by the lee (see Chapter 5 for a description of the points of sail). Due to the forces of the wind and/or the waves, the boat rolls over, heeling dramatically to windward while it turns "down," away from the wind direction. Rounding down often results in a dangerous accidental jibe; aboard a dinghy, it's a sure way to capsize.

Here are some valuable preventative measures to help you avoid the death roll when sailing on a broad reach or run:

✔ **Don't let the mainsail out too far and keep the boom vang on tight:** On this point of sail, you want to minimize mainsail twist (see Chapter 8 for tips on shaping the sails).

✔ **Don't sail too low:** Turn the boat toward the wind until you're clearly on a broad reach, the higher the better — to a point, because you risk a broach and may be steering way off course.

✔ **Drop your spinnaker:** Spinnakers are fast and fun, but not when your boat is floating upside down. You may want to reduce sail area by dropping the jib and even reefing the mainsail.

✔ **Keep the crew weight in the middle of the boat:** Don't hike out to windward. If you're on a keelboat, send the crew to leeward.

If you do capsize in a dinghy, then we hope that you have read all about getting out of this position in Chapter 7. On a keelboat, you end up on your side, like in a broach.

You don't have to jibe, ever; you can always turn the other direction by tacking and then bear off again. In heavy air, try to minimize any jibes — planned or not!

Accidental jibes

Accidental jibes are bad. When the boom comes crashing to the other side, woe to the person whose head is in the way. In Chapter 8, we discuss techniques for jibing (intentionally) in strong winds. Not only does an unintended jibe risk the safety of any crew in the path of the boom or the mainsheet, but it also can put tremendous (maybe even excessive forces) on the mast and boom. You can avoid accidental jibes by vigilant steering and by never letting the boat get near a dead run. Because waves can easily throw the boat off course by 10 or even 20 degrees, in heavy air you need some "money in the bank."

Heaving-to and Running before It

If you're ever in really heavy weather — like when it's blowing the dogs off their leashes — you may need to use an extreme technique for survival. *Heaving-to* is a technique for extreme conditions that also works (on boats with jibs) any time you want to "park" your boat, even in light air. It involves *backing* your jib (filling it backwards with wind) while filling your main partially on a close-hauled or close-reaching course. If it isn't too windy, the boat stays balanced, moving forward and to leeward very slowly. You can get into the heaved-to position by sailing along close-hauled and tacking over while keeping the jib cleated. Then adjust the mainsail until the boat "feels" comfortable. Heaving-to is a great way to take a break.

Look at the jib while you heave-to, and if it seems to be impaled on the windward *spreader* (the strut that holds the shrouds away from the mast), ease the sheet some, or you'll have to cancel your lunch break.

Running before it is a heavy-weather tactic for when it's too windy to sail in any direction, upwind or downwind, without getting into trouble. This technique entails slowing the boat down until it has minimal headway (just enough to keep steerage), which, in really strong winds, means taking all your sails down and even dragging ropes or any sort of object that slows the boat down enough to be safe.

Chapter 13

Taking on Water and Other Mishaps

Give me a spirit that on this life's rough sea
Loves t' have his sails filled with a lusty wind,
Even till his sail-yards tremble, his masts crack,
And his rapt ship run on her side so low
That she drinks water, and her keel plows air.

— George Chapman

Ah yes, the chapter on what to do when everything goes wrong. Is it a coincidence that this is Chapter 13? Most sailors have their own great disaster stories — the time they were aground until the next high tide, or how the mast broke and bits of aluminum rained down on the deck, missing them by inches. The best sailors have fewer exciting stories because they are prepared for most situations and can fix any minor problem before it turns major.

When things go wrong, you're under stress. Because you can't walk away and ignore the problem, you have to deal with it. Keeping your cool under pressure is very valuable when you have to make important decisions that affect the safety of your boat and your crew.

PETER SAYS

Planning ahead

Having a clearly defined game plan for the crew to follow, with one person who is ultimately in charge, really helps in emergencies. A great example was during the 1987 America's Cup races in windy Perth, Australia.

During one practice race a jib blew out, and most of the crew (myself included) rushed up to the pitching bow to help drag it down and set a new one. The waves were throwing the boat all around, and it was definitely "one hand for yourself and one for the boat" conditions. Despite the talent and years of experience on the boat, we bungled the recovery so badly that Dennis Conner finally turned downwind to give us a break, giving up the practice race.

On the way in, we discussed the problem. Everyone knew that we had to get the tattered sail down, but some of the crew stuffed pieces down one hatch and some down another, creating a hopeless mess. We agreed that in any subsequent situations like that, we would let Scott Vogel, our bowman, decide the plan for solving the problem.

Ultimately, that meeting won us a race, maybe even the America's Cup, because another jib exploded in the Challenger Finals while we were racing against *New Zealand*. Not only did we get the pieces of the old sail down, but we got the new sail up so fast that we retained the lead!

Hopefully, none of these calamities will ever strike any of your sailing trips, but just in case your lucky day was yesterday, read through this chapter so that you can be the one who stays calm, knows just what to do, and saves the day.

Running Aground

Running aground is a very common mishap. When any part of your boat touches the shore or the bottom, you've run aground. Most cases of running aground involve your keel or centerboard, although we have seen boats run aground with their masts — when they capsize in shallow water and stick the tip of the mast in the mud. A grounding can be (hopefully) a gentle kiss or an ordeal in which you're really stuck with the tide dropping, or even worse. Most experienced sailors have run aground at some point — usually in their home waters on a warm, sunny afternoon when they weren't paying attention.

Prevent those groundings

The following tips can prevent the majority of groundings:

- **Brush up on your navigational skills.** Be familiar with the nautical chart of your sailing area and, if you're in unfamiliar waters or have shallow, tricky home waters, be able to determine *(fix)* your position on a chart and perform piloting skills (see Chapter 11).

- **Know how to raise your centerboard and rudder.** On a dinghy, you can often pull up the foils and slide over shallow waters. Just make sure that you're headed to deeper water!

- **Know how to "read" the bottom.** Chapter 11 covers how the color of the water (bottom) and shape of the waves can help you spot shallows.

- **Know the depth of the water under your boat.** A good depth sounder is helpful for larger keelboats with battery power.

- **Know the exact depth *(draft)* of your boat.**

- **Know the shape of your keel.** Some keelboats get deeper when all the passengers are in the stern or when the boat is under power. If you do run aground, knowing your keel shape is crucial for making the right assessment of how to get free, as we discuss in a minute.

- **Understand the local tides.** See Chapter 10 on tides. Have a local tide book (available at marine stores), which predicts the estimated range of tides, on board. Use this information with a grain of salt. You can cross-check the predicted current direction with the wakes on buoys.

If you must sail over a shallow area to get home, sail slowly (at half speed or less). Doing so makes it easier for you to get free if you do get stuck.

When you do go aground

First, we look at the ways to free your boat from a nice soft bottom. Then, in the "Hull Damage" section, we tell you what you should do in the rare event that you hit rocks and sustain serious damage.

- **If you hit softly, slow down and immediately turn the boat to deeper water.** Hopefully, you can sail free.

- **Send someone below to check for damage.** Look in the *bilge,* where the keel attaches inside the hull, for water leaking into the boat.

- **If you have a centerboard (lucky you), immediately pull it up partway.**

✔ **Heel the boat.** Heeling works for all sailboats, except for those with a twin or winged keel, because it reduces the boat's draft. When you hit, immediately move all the crew weight to leeward.

✔ **Consider using the engine, but only in combination with some of these other remedies.** First, check that the rudder is not stuck — you can break it by moving the boat. Depending on the situation, you may want to try forward or reverse gear. Watch the temperature gauge — silt can clog the water intake and cause overheating.

✔ **Take the sails down if they're driving you farther onto the shallow area.**

✔ **Try to make the boat less deep.** Heeling works. Moving all the crew to the bow may also help.

Obviously, the preceding procedures should be done as quickly as possible. If you're still not afloat after trying these tricks, try one of these more involved actions:

✔ **Really heel the boat.** Drop and secure the mainsail, then release the mainsheet and push the main (supported at the outboard end by a halyard or other secure line) all the way out to the side the boat is heeling toward, and then have some crew climb up on it and slide as far outboard as they can. Falling into the water is easy to do while performing this trick, so this act is only for the acrobatically inclined. Have the crew don life jackets first, and leave at least one person on board.

If you have a dinghy, you can try suspending it (filled with water if necessary) from the end of the boom to increase heel, as shown in Figure 13-1. You can also overtrim the sails (if you're on a reaching heading) to generate heel from the wind.

Figure 13-1:
Use any means necessary (including flooding a dinghy) to heel your boat.

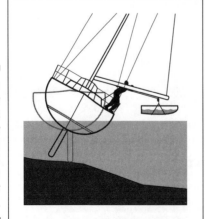

When a boat is heeled further than normal, check for leaking fuel or other potential problems.

✔ **Lighten the ship.** Offload extra crew and heavy gear into a dinghy to reduce draft.

✔ **Use the anchor to pull you off.** This system, called *kedging* or *setting a kedge,* requires sending a rowing dinghy (or other boat) out with an anchor to set. Put the anchor and sufficient anchor line in the boat and head toward deep water, making sure that the end of the anchor line is tied to the sailboat. When the anchor is set (and the farther away, the better chance the anchor will hold), start pulling yourself free. Use the winch if you have one. Meanwhile, keep heeling, powering with the engine or sails, and trying other measures.

✔ **Wait until high tide.** Even if you get stuck at high tide, you will eventually float free. Having an anchor set hopefully keeps you from getting pushed further aground as the tide comes in. Try to heel the boat toward shallow water so that the incoming tide doesn't swamp your boat. If you're really "high and dry," take heart — most boats are built to withstand lying on their sides. Try to cushion the hull if possible.

✔ **As a last resort, you can accept a tow.** Towing can be dangerous and can lead to damage to both boats. If your boat is hard aground, pulling it off can cause extensive keel and rudder damage. Or the tow line can snap and hurt someone as it recoils. Hiring a professional towing service can be expensive (not as expensive as salvaging a sunken ship, however). In case of a true emergency, you should contact the Coast Guard (or other international safety organization) on VHF Channel 16. (For more on using the radio, see Chapter 7.) The Coast Guard may refer you to a towing company.

Biscayne Bay Blues

When I was part of a crew delivering a racing boat back to New England from Florida, we went hard aground at night as we were leaving Miami for the long sail north. Fortunately, the keel was stuck in nice, soft sand, and we were in the protected waters of Biscayne Bay. So after trying all the easy tricks, we gave up until morning and went to sleep with the boat on a 30-degree heel.

At dawn, we put up the spinnaker (to heel the boat more), put out an anchor, and ultimately flagged down a passing boat to add some towing power. When the tide rose, we finally clawed our way off and were on our way. Because going aground is kind of embarrassing, we agreed to keep the episode to ourselves. That was, until a friend mailed me a copy of the front page of the *Miami Herald* with our beautiful spinnaker photogenically framing a boat that was clearly very hard aground!

Towing Tips

At some point in your sailing career, you probably will be forced to accept a tow from a powerboat. But any time you put your boat's fate in the hands of another boater (which is the case in a tow), you take a risk. Even in smooth water and ideal conditions, things can go wrong. We have already warned you about a few of the dangers of towing. Here are more tips to make your towing experiences as carefree as possible:

- **Don't take a tow unless you need one.**

- **Use a good rope.** An anchor line is an ideal tow line because it's long, strong, and stretchy, all good things for towing. (For more about line, see Chapter 19.)

- **Attach your tow line securely.** If the loads are moderate (you aren't in heavy weather and you're not aground), tie your tow line to a secure object. The mast is usually best. Tie it as low as possible around the mast, just above the cabin top or deck. If you're concerned about stress, you can spread the load on the tow line to several places, such as the mast and two cockpit winches, as shown in Figure 13-2. Make sure that the rope isn't chafing anywhere.

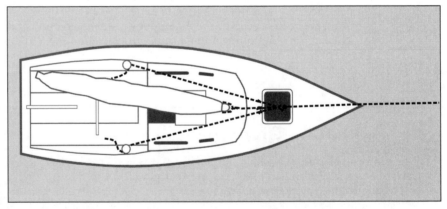

Figure 13-2:
Spreading the load of the tow line to the mast and two cockpit winches.

- **Use good knots.** A bowline is always acceptable, and two (or three) round turns and two half hitches are really good. See Appendix B for how to tie knots.

- **Make sure the boat and crew are ready before speeding up.**

- **Make sure you can get free in a hurry.** If the captain of the powerboat is a yahoo, you want to be able to free your boat quickly. A sharp knife works (on the line, that is, not on the yahoo!). You may be able to untie the round turns and half hitches in a hurry even when they're under load, but a bowline isn't going to budge.

Abandoning ship means abandoning your claim

Don't give away your boat! The law of the sea says that if someone finds an abandoned boat drifting along and tows it home ("salvages" it), it's his! So don't abandon ship. If you must leave your boat, leave a note saying that you intend to return. Even if you're aboard and in need of help, you don't want to risk any outrageous salvage claim, so clearly establish the terms of the helper's aid *before* you get too far along in the rescue process. Also, it looks better in the eyes of the law if you pass your rescuer a line (indicating a voluntary acceptance of aid) rather than having your rescuer pass a line to you.

✔ **Stay away from the tow line.** The line can break and whip back.

✔ **Don't tow too fast.** Arrange a comfortable speed with the tow boat ahead of time and fine-tune that speed with hand signals if necessary.

✔ **Slow down in waves.** Big waves can add tremendous load, so watch for ones that can surprise you, such as the wake of a ship. If practical, the tow boat should slow down and turn toward these temporary waves to minimize their effect on your boat.

✔ **Adjust the length of the rope to go downhill.** When you get to a comfortable towing speed, you may want to extend the tow rope to its maximum length to make it easier to steer your boat and to let the stretchy tow rope cushion your ride. Fine-tune the rope's length so your bow is pointed downhill, riding on the towing boat's wake. This little trick really eases the load on the tow line — always a good thing.

Jury-Rigging

A body of knowledge called *jury-rigging* (the fine art of replacing broken gear with a temporary fix) covers many possible emergencies. A list of all the possible jury-rig solutions is beyond the scope of this book, but we can provide a list of the equipment and tools that are common to many different solutions — plus some examples of how these items can be used. Creativity is the key to effective jury-rigging. Keep in mind that you can't stuff as much equipment into a small dinghy as you can in a big keelboat.

✔ **Duct tape:** Duct tape can fix just about anything, including a boo-boo on your finger when you run out of bandages.

✔ **Knife:** A sailor's best friend. Use a knife to cut a heavily loaded sheet or halyard that is hopelessly tangled.

✔ **Rope:** Sailors can do amazing things with rope. Besides an anchor line, you should have at least one other rope that is long and strong enough to serve as a sheet, halyard, or dock line. A 15- to 30-foot (5- to 9-m) length of ultra-strong, small-diameter rope ($^3/_{16}$ inch or 4 mm) can be nearly as valuable as duct tape in an emergency. Braided rope with Kevlar, Spectra, or some other low-stretch core is best for this. *Sail ties* or *webbing* (strong, ribbonlike straps available at sail lofts) can also fit through some tiny holes and provide great lashing material.

✔ **Spare parts:** The list depends on your boat. However, no matter how big the boat, bring a few shackles (matching the size of common ones on the boat) and some clevis pins or machine screws with nuts. A couple of medium or large pulleys *(blocks)* are also great *ditty bag* (bag in which good jury-rigging things go) stuffers.

✔ **Sticky-back:** This stuff is also called *insignia cloth.* A wide (3 feet or 1 m) roll of this Dacron sail-repair material with adhesive backing can repair holes in boats and in sails.

✔ **Tools:** A dinghy may have only a screwdriver and vice grips (the multi-purpose Leatherman tool is a great option), while an ocean-circling keelboat may carry several tool boxes. Bottle-openers (hey, jury-rigging is thirsty work), hammers, adjustable wrenches, wire cutters, and hacksaws often get pulled out of the box first in an emergency. Don't forget a few good sailmaker's hand-sewing needles, Dacron thread, and a *palm* (leather device that fits over your palm, enabling you to push a needle through many layers of sailcloth — sort of a super thimble).

So what do you do with all these good things? Use your imagination, because that's what jury-rigging is all about.

Sail Problems

Without functional sails, you can't do much sailing. Sails can blow out and rip — sometimes from misuse, sometimes from simple wear and tear. If your sail does blow out or get torn, take it down right away, before any further damage can occur. Depending on the size of the rip, you may be able to fix it up, sometimes as good as new. Your best friend in this procedure is that roll of sticky-back cloth you brought aboard after reading this book. Here are the steps to a repair job on a sail:

1. **Make sure the area you're operating on is clean, dry, and salt-free.**

   You may have to rinse the sail in freshwater before it will dry completely.

2. **Lay the repair area on as flat a surface as possible.**

3. **Try to position the torn edges into their original positions.**

   Getting the edges into position may take several hands.

4. **Calculate the size of the sticky-back bandage (make sure you overlap the edges sufficiently) and cut it.**

5. **Apply the sticky-back.**

   Start at one edge of the tear and work slowly to the other, trying to keep the sail as smooth and as close to its pretear position as possible.

6. **Press the applied tape firmly to the repaired area.**

   Use a solid object and press hard on the repair, sandwiching it to the table or work surface. Really work the sticky-back onto the repair, especially any stitched seams that are covered up. For most sails, this repair is enough. But if the repair is in a high-load area, like the leech of a jib or mainsail, consider stitching the tear through the sticky-back.

Fouling the Prop

Sailors sometimes "cheat" by using their boats' engines. A mishap known as "fouling the prop" proves that power and sailing don't mix all the time. Getting a rope tangled up in the propeller is a drag; when it happens on a boat with an inboard engine, the engine stalls and the propeller gets stuck, unable to turn. Next thing you know, someone (probably you) has to jump in the water (probably cold) and untangle the prop. Usually the culprit is a halyard or sheet (or dock line or tow line) from your boat.

The prevention is simple. Keep your lines out of the water and always look around the boat before turning on the engine.

Unfortunately, people aren't as vigilant as they should be, so here's how to deal with a fouled prop on a boat with an inboard engine. (If you have an outboard, what are you waiting for? Pull it up and unwrap the rope!)

1. **Turn off the engine immediately (it may have already stalled out).**

2. **Find the transgressing rope and gently pull it.**

   Pull harder and pray, because if the rope doesn't release, you're swimming.

3. **Consider whether you really need the engine.**

   If you don't really need the engine, or if the conditions are too rough and dangerous to go in the water, then you just have to sail or drift. Keep in mind that in big waves, the boat is going up and down fast, so swimming underneath it, near the propeller blade, is no fun. If you delay the swim until later, tighten the fouled rope and tie it off on deck.

4. **You can try, as a last resort, putting the engine in reverse (dead slow) just for an instant and then pulling hard on the line.**

   We have never found this trick to work, but you never know.

5. **If the conditions are safe, or after you return to shelter, you can jump in.**

   A mask, snorkel, and fins are nice. If the boat is drifting (no sailing, please), make sure that it's dragging a line that you can grab.

6. **Using the wrapped rope as a guide, swim down to the prop (engine's off, right?) and try to untie the knot down there.**

7. **If untying the knot is impossible, get your knife so that you can chop that stupid rope into tiny little pieces.**

   Hey, be careful with that thing!

Once every blue moon, the same fate befalls a rudder on a keelboat. You know when that happens because the steering system seems to be stuck. The problem is that a rope is wedged between the top of the rudder and the hull. Usually, you can get out of this situation with a good tug on the infringing line from the right direction. If not, turn the helm hard one way and try again (you may have to drop the sails in strong winds). That usually works. If not, did you bring your swimsuit?

Breaking the Mast

Breaking a mast is a real drag. Not only does a broken mast mean that you (or your insurance company) are out a good chunk of change, but it can be dangerous, especially in strong winds and big seas (common conditions when the mast breaks). Clearly, the best cure is an ounce of prevention. We cover the basics of spar care and maintenance in Chapter 19, but even with the best care, seemingly perfect fittings can fail for no apparent reason. When this happens, the next thing you know — bang — a gravity storm. Another cause for a *dismasting* is a violent capsize and subsequent *turtling* (a capsized position when the mast points straight down) in shallow water. To avoid breaking the mast, keep out of shallow water when sailing dinghies in strong winds.

Every dismasting is a little different. Masts can break at a fitting or at some other weak point. The broken mast may fall in the water, or it may dangle from the remaining stump. On a dinghy, you may be able to pick up and secure the broken pieces with one hand, whereas even lifting the standing rigging is a task for more than one person on a 40-foot (12-m) keelboat. Therefore, there is no one "right way" to deal with a broken mast. You must use your common sense and creativity to solve the unique problem it creates. That said, here are some general rules to keep in mind:

✔ **Save the crew and the boat first.** If the process of retrieving and securing the broken pieces of the mast is endangering the safety of the crew or the boat, cut it away, as fast as you can.

✔ **Don't run the engine while rigging and stuff are in the water.** See the "Fouling the Prop" section earlier if you don't believe us.

✔ **Be conscious of the loads.** Consider the direction of forces on things. As you clean up the broken gear, you're like a lumberjack cutting a tree; cutting one thing may have a domino effect on other things.

✔ **Get the boat downwind of the mess.** If the mast falls into the water, try to maneuver the boat so that the mast is upwind. That way, the waves don't drive the hull onto the mast. Fortunately, Mother Nature should be on your side, because the mast and sails want to drag upwind like a sea anchor.

✔ **Recover all the wreckage, if you can.** If you're way out to sea, you may find that those pieces of mast, sails, and rigging come in handy in jury-rigging a new sail so you can get home.

If you must jettison the broken pieces for safety, being able to do so quickly is nice. Sharp hacksaw blades (several) and heavy-duty wire cutters are invaluable tools. Often, the easiest way of freeing the rigging is by removing the clevis pins at one end. See Chapter 19 about shackles with clevis pins.

The race isn't over until . . .

In a recent Transpac Race (2,200 miles — 3,540 km — from Los Angeles to Honolulu), the 70-foot (21-m) *Cheval* was 25 miles (40 km) from the finish (and in first place with a nice lead) when the unthinkable occurred: The mast broke during a jibe.

As the disheartened crew rushed to clean up the mess before the boat blew onto the rocks, the owner climbed on deck after doing some calculations at the chart table. "Hey guys," he said, "we can still win this race — all we have to do is average 6 knots the rest of the way!" Rekindled with enthusiasm, the crew cut away the broken pieces and began jury-rigging

halyards to the 15-foot (5-m) mast stump sticking out of the deck. Soon they had a small sail hoisted and were doing 5 knots — hardly the 20 knots or better the boat was capable of doing in the conditions, but movement, at least.

After some more macramé and creative use of spinnaker poles and booms, the crew had managed to set another, bigger sail — sideways. More "canvas" was added as the boat began surfing the swells in the Molokai Channel. *Cheval* did win that race, and this story is a great example of how human creativity (and probably a fair amount of duct tape) can solve most any problem.

Hull Damage

Serious hull damage can be a major problem. It can happen when you run aground, especially in rocks or coral, or if you run into a solid object floating just under the water's surface. Fortunately, this misfortune taken to its extreme is rare, but minor or medium-size leaks caused by a keel jarred loose in a grounding or a collision are more common. Here are some ways to stave the flow and save your boat:

- ✔ **Plug it with any available material.** Clothing or cushions can work well, and so can a life raft or a rubber dinghy. You can use a paddle or convenient brace to secure the plug, as shown in Figure 13-3. A sail can be used as an external bandage, and we're sure you aren't surprised to hear that we have used duct tape to plug holes.

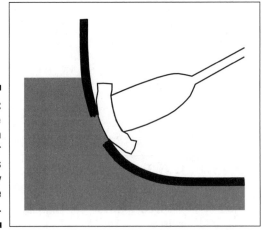

Figures 13-3: Plug a hole with whatever materials are handy and brace the plug.

- ✔ **Use heeling to your advantage.** This situation is one time when more heel can be good. If the hole is near the waterline along the side of the boat, you may be able to sail the boat on a particular point of sail (using the reverse of all the tips to limit heel discussed in Chapter 8) so that the hole comes partially or completely out of the water. This direction may not get you to safety, but at least this tactic gives you time to repair the damage.

- ✔ **Get out the pumps.** If leaking water is a problem, everybody should be bailing. Buckets work great.

- ✔ **Get to safety as soon as possible.** This may mean sailing to a different port than the one from which you started. In an extreme case in which the boat is truly sinking, you may have to intentionally ground the boat (or beach your dinghy). If you must use this tactic, pick a spot that is as sheltered (especially from waves) as possible and has a nice, soft sand or mud bottom.

✔ **Review the distress signal information in Chapter 7.** The most basic is the arm wave — if you're in trouble, it comes naturally.

Abandoning Ship

Between the two of us, we have been on boats that have run aground, blown out sails, been towed to safety, fouled a prop, been holed, been dismasted, and sunk (just a dinghy — Peter got it back up), but neither of us has ever had to abandon ship into a life raft. Hopefully, you will be able to say the same thing after thousands of miles have passed under your keel. But, remembering the Boy Scouts' line, it doesn't hurt to be prepared.

You can't abandon ship into a life raft if you don't have one. They are big and bulky, but carrying one when sailing significant distances out of sight of land is wise. Obviously, we're talking about keelboats; no one should sail a dinghy out of sight of land.

An old adage about this subject says, "Don't abandon ship into a life raft until you have to step up to get into the raft."

This saying highlights an important fact. The situation has to be pretty darn desperate before you exchange your big sailboat for a glorified air mattress with K rations. Don't take this the wrong way — we believe in life rafts; the modern ones are marvelous pieces of technology. But still, things have to be pretty bad before you're safer in a life raft than aboard your boat.

A modern life raft is packed into a hard plastic case and is very heavy to lift. Therefore, you want to be sure that the raft is up on deck in a very accessible spot (and tied down securely) if abandoning ship is in the cards. Peter did inflate and get inside a life raft once, for a TV show, and he remembers a few things about that experience worth relating:

✔ A cartoon-style description of how to deploy and inflate the life raft is drawn on its case.

✔ Tie the life raft's bow line (which is apparent outside the case) securely to the boat before throwing the raft into the water and inflating.

✔ The K rations taste kind of like vanilla wafer cookies — and the water comes in cans.

For a great true story about this subject, check out Steve Callahan's best seller, *Adrift.*

Fighting Fire

Fire is one of the most serious dangers a sailor can face. Fire can occur by any number of means, but most start in the *galley* (kitchen), around the engine, or in the electrical system. Needless to say, you should put out fires immediately.

In Chapter 7, we discuss the federal requirements for fire extinguishers aboard boats. Having the boat's fire extinguisher(s) easily accessible and checked once a year is very important.

Depending on the type of fire, your best strategy and equipment for extinguishing the fire varies. Table 13-1 covers the action to take for the most common types of fires on board.

Table 13-1	Putting Out a Fire
Problem	*Action to Take*
Gasoline, diesel, or grease fires	Use a Type B fire extinguisher — *not* water.
Engine fires	Turn off the engine and use a Type B fire extinguisher. Be careful not to "blast" the fire to other areas.
(LPG) Propane — liquid gas fires	Turn off the fuel supply at the tank (not just the stove) and then let the fire burn out. Prevent the fire from spreading by dousing surrounding area with water.
Alcohol, wood, and textile fires	Flood with water.
Electrical fires	Use a Type C fire extinguisher designed for electrical fire or flood with water.

Chapter 14
Sailing Sailboards

. . . .

In This Chapter

▶ Picking the right location and conditions

▶ Choosing the right equipment

▶ Rigging the sailboard

▶ Getting familiar with the board and the sail

▶ Getting out on the water

▶ Maneuvering with the wind

. . . .

At the bottom, so, and bent them, gently curving
So that they looked like the wings of birds, most surely.

— Ovid, translated by Rolfe Humphries

*O*ne of the great things about sailing is that after you master the basics on one boat, you can transfer those skills to other boats with relative ease. In this chapter, we introduce you to our favorite kind of sailboats — sailboards.

If you've spent any time trying to sailboard, you may think that these boats are the exception to the "If you can sail one boat, you can sail any boat" rule. Not really. Sailboards are a little more difficult to learn to sail than other boats because they require more balance and coordination, but we show you exercises that you can do to get comfortable standing on the board. And take it from us — sailboarding is definitely worth the effort.

An offshoot of surfing, sailboarding developed in the U.S. in the late 1960s and now is popular all around the world. Sailboarding (also called *windsurfing,* but that's really a trademark of a brand of boards and sails) requires just what the name says — a board and a sail. Plus, you can sailboard just about anywhere. We've even tried it in a swimming pool!

Windswimming, Anyone?

Just as with any other type of sailing, we recommend finding a certified instructor to show you the basics. Most sailboard schools have special equipment, such as "simulator" boards that let you get the feel on shore before heading out and getting wet. And you're definitely going to get wet. This phase of your sailboarding career isn't called *windswimming* for nothing!

A sailboarding vacation may be the best way for you to start. Great vacation packages are available in sailboarding hot spots around the world — *hot* being the operative word. We recommend that you take a good look at these possibilities, because the warmer the water, the easier it is to enjoy and get through the windswimming phase.

If you're hooked up to the Internet, check out windsurfing online at `http://www.worldzine.com/windsurfing`.

The sailing skills that you've developed — being attuned to and feeling the wind direction — are just as important with sailboards. The safety rules that we review in Chapter 7 — make sure that you've checked your equipment, that you have sufficiently warm clothing and a life jacket, and that you aren't heading out in conditions that are too windy or rough — still apply. A qualified instructor can make sure that your learning experience is as safe (and fun) as possible.

If you want to take up high-wind sailboarding, we again recommend taking instruction from a qualified instructor. A number of schools and resorts can give you great instruction and expose you to the myriad equipment options you face when you want to get into this end of the sport. Careful, though — sailboarding is very addictive!

Parts is parts

The parts of a sailboard are similar to the parts of any sailboat, as shown in Figure 14-1. Your arms become the mainsheet; your body becomes the standing rigging. The biggest difference is that a sailboard doesn't have a rudder — you steer a sailboard with the sail and your body weight.

Most sailboard parts are exactly the same as those we described on a generic sailboat in Chapter 1. However, here's a rundown on a sailboard's distinctive parts and features:

- ✔ **Boom (or wishboom):** Wishbone-shaped tubes.
- ✔ **Camber inducers:** Fittings in the sail's luff into which the battens sit. Their shape creates a three-dimensional, winglike shape for the sail. Used primarily on high-performance (not beginner) sails.

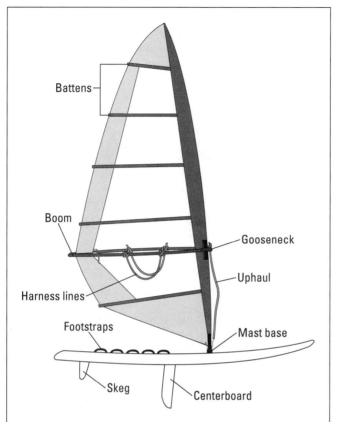

Battens

Boom

Gooseneck

Uphaul

Harness lines

Footstraps

Mast base

Figure 14-1:
The parts of
a sailboard.

Skeg

Centerboard

✓ **Footstraps:** Straps to secure your feet; normally used in high-speed and wave sailing; not found on all boards.

✓ **Gooseneck:** Fitting (often a clamp) attaching the boom to the mast.

✓ **Harness:** A harness you wear with a hook that can connect temporarily to the harness lines, thereby taking the load off your arms.

✓ **Harness lines:** Rope loops on either side of the boom that you hook your harness into; not found on all boards.

✓ **Mast base:** Fitting at the bottom of the mast that connects to the universal joint.

✓ **Mast sleeve:** The sailcloth tube along the luff of the sail into which you insert the mast when getting ready to sail.

✓ **Skeg:** A fixed fin providing directional stability under the back of the board.

✓ **Towing eye:** A loop near the front of the board for attaching a tow line.

> ✔ **Universal joint:** Fitting connecting the rig to the board. It enables you to rotate the rig in any direction.
>
> ✔ **Uphaul line:** Line attached to the gooseneck to help pull the rig out of the water.

The ideal setup

The ideal conditions for beginning sailboarders are flat (no waves), warm water and a steady, light-to-moderate breeze parallel to the shore. Because beginners start out with sailing on a reach (for a review of the points of sail, see Chapter 5), this orientation makes going out and coming in easy. If the breeze is blowing offshore (away from the land), you have to sail close-hauled back to shore, a difficult point of sail for a beginner. When the breeze is blowing onshore, trying to sail away is difficult and frustrating. Sailboarding in too much wind is nearly impossible for beginners.

Fortunately, I began sailboarding in Florida, where the water is nice and warm. I started sailboarding right at the beginning of the windsurfer craze, so no one was really an expert yet. We sailed out of a marina with lots of boats and very tight confines — not the ideal place to begin. We would sit for hours, watching our friends struggling through the shifting winds and falling every few seconds — to the glee of the crowd on the dock. Today, you can avoid much of that embarrassment, thanks to the much-improved teaching techniques that have evolved over the years.

Bigger is better — at least at the beginning

Start on the biggest, floatiest board you can find — it provides the most stable platform. Make sure that the deck has sufficient roughness to prevent you from slipping off. If not, try wearing rubber slippers (available at marine stores) to increase your traction.

After you master the basics, you'll probably be tempted to try out different boards, including the much-less-buoyant high-wind boards that are so popular around the world. You'll be amazed at the difference in maneuverability and performance between the different boards.

One reason why you may want to take your first few lessons at a school is that its boards are ideal for beginners, and you may want to delay your first purchase until you can handle a slightly more advanced board.

Your instructor probably recommends a "training sail" that is smaller than the sails you will graduate to. A smaller sail is easier to pull out of the water (you're going to get plenty of practice at pulling up your sail), and it lets you get the feel of how to balance without being overpowering and pulling you into the water.

Rigging the Board

The great thing about sailboards is that they're easy to rig. The more high-performance sails, with their long battens and camber inducers, can be a bit trickier to rig, but a beginner's sail should have few (if any) battens. Rigging your sailboard (especially the sail) is similar in many ways to rigging any sailboat (see Chapter 4). Like some dinghies, you don't have a halyard to hoist; the sail's luff sleeve simply slides down onto the mast. The trickiest part can be securing the boom to the mast so that it's at a comfortable height (roughly chest height), so have your instructor help out.

Making a Not-So-Dry Run

Have we mentioned that you're going to get wet and look a little foolish when you first begin sailboarding? You can minimize your embarrassment (a little) by practicing some basics first.

Getting used to the board

After you assemble the right equipment, leave the sail on shore for a while and familiarize yourself with the board. Here are some drills you can do to get comfortable on your board:

- ✔ **Practice lying on your stomach and paddling the board.** Try paddling in a circle.

- ✔ **Stand up and work on your balance.** Keeping your knees bent and your hands out to the side — just like a tightrope walker — helps.

- ✔ **Move your feet out to each side of the board and practice rocking the board from side to side.**

- ✔ **Walk toward the front of the board, practice turning around, walk toward the stern, and turn again.** You can't do this drill on a small, high-wind board — it's too small and unstable.

When you feel comfortable on the board, put it back on the beach near your starting point and get the sail.

Getting used to the sail

Balance is the first tricky part about sailboarding. The second tricky part is that a sailboard doesn't have a rudder. You steer the boat with the sail and your weight.

Even if your instructor doesn't have access to a simulator, you can still get a feel for the dynamics of handling the sail as follows:

1. **Stand the sail up on shore, bracing the mast base with your foot.**

2. **Stand to windward of the sail and hold onto the mast at or near the gooseneck.**

   The sail luffs like a flag with the wind.

   Note: With full-length battens, the sail doesn't flap the way a normal sail does, but we recommend avoiding sails with full-length battens when you're starting out because they're so much harder to pull out of the water.

3. **Face directly downwind, with your back to the wind and the sail pointing downwind away from you.**

   Get comfortable in this luffing or "safety" position, as shown in Figure 14-2, because you'll be in this position quite a bit at first.

Figure 14-2:
Standing on the shore with the sail in a luffing position.

4. **Try tilting the sail to your left and then to your right.**

   When you're on the water, you turn the board by tilting the sail in this manner.

Getting Your Feet (And the Rest of You) Wet

After you attach your mast and sail and have gotten used to the feel of the board and the sail, you're ready to climb aboard.

Here are the steps to getting the rig (the sail, mast, and boom) out of the water:

1. **Put the board in deep enough water that the centerboard can be down all the way.**

2. **Put the sail downwind of the board so that the mast and board form a T.**

3. **Kneel on the board at the mast base and grab the uphaul line.**

4. **Stand up and start pulling the sail out of the water with the uphaul.**

   Use your full body weight. Bend your knees — don't strain your back.

5. **When the sail is all the way out of the water, hold the mast in the luffing position, like you practiced on land.**

   Your feet straddle the mast.

6. **Holding the mast with your back hand (the hand that will be farthest back when you get under way), cross your forward hand over and grab the boom about a foot behind the mast.**

7. **Bend this arm and bring the rig across your body, as shown in Figure 14-3.**

   The sail is still luffing.

8. **Take slow baby steps around to the side of the board as you grab the boom with your back hand about 3 feet behind where your forward hand is. Keep both hands on the boom.**

   Your back arm is the mainsheet. Your front arm is like the *shrouds* (wires supporting the mast). If you pull in your back arm and keep your front arm steady, you trim in the sail and start to move forward.

9. **Pull in your back arm so that you're facing the middle of the sail — perfectly positioned to balance the force of the wind.**

   You're sailing on a reach!

Figure 14-3:
The steps to getting going.

Lean your body away from the rig as much as you need to keep your balance. You can control the trim of the sail by the position of your arms. To trim in, pull in your back hand. To ease out, either push out your back hand or pull in your front hand. To stop, just return to the luffing or "safety" position by first releasing your back hand from the boom and then bringing it forward to hold onto the mast or uphaul line.

Of course, by now you're great at the other method for stopping — falling in.

If you fall, make sure that you always swim back to the board right away, or else it may drift off. Use the board as your swim platform to take a break.

Whether you're in the Caribbean on a learn-to-sailboard vacation, taking lessons at a local lake, or at your friend's beach house on the shore, keep these points in mind as you practice your sailboarding skills:

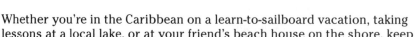

✔ When you fall in, try to fall backward on your butt instead of jumping feet first. Otherwise, if the water is shallow, you could twist your ankle.

✔ As you come back to the surface after a fall, put your hands up above your head so that you don't hit your head on the sail or board.

✔ If you find that you're constantly sliding off the board, the board's original nonskid surface may be worn off. We've also seen boards that have suntan lotion all over them and are as slippery as a seal. If you're having a problem, ask the school or rental shop for a different board. Some people swear by those special rubber booties.

Steering the Board

After you master getting moving, you'll quickly want to know how to turn. Many beginners get the first part right, but then they keep going and going because they don't know how to turn around and get back, or they're so fearful of attempting a tack that they get too far from shore. (If this scenario happens to you, you'll be happy that the resort or the instructor has a motorboat!)

Practice the leaning techniques you tried on land. With the rig in the safety position, lean it to the right, and the board swivels left — and vice versa (see Figure 14-4). Keep practicing until you can turn the board 360 degrees. As the board turns, take baby steps around the mast base to keep your back facing the wind direction.

When you pull in the sail and are moving forward, you can also steer by leaning the rig forward or backward while keeping the sail sheeted in with your back hand, as shown in Figure 14-5. The key is to stay in balance and tilt the rig without changing the angle of the sail to the wind too much.

As you experiment with turning, you quickly discover that sailing upwind and reaching are very similar, but sailing on a run is a real challenge. Therefore, the first maneuver a sailboarder tries is a tack rather than a jibe.

Figure 14-4: With the rig in the safety position, lean it to one side to make the board turn the other direction.

Wind

Look, Mom! No rudder!

To understand how a sailboard can maneuver without a rudder, consider a simplified picture of the forces involved. First, the sail: As we explain in Chapter 8, when properly trimmed to the correct angle to the wind flow, a sail generates lift just like a wing does. The *center of effort* of the sail is the spot where all the forces on the sail balance out — roughly halfway up and one-third of the way back from the front of a sail.

On the hull is a similar balance point called the *center of lateral resistance.* Simply put, this is the pivot point of the board in a turn.

When a sailboard is *in the groove* (sailing in a straight line), all the forces are in balance, including the center of effort and center of lateral resistance. But tip the rig back some while keeping it trimmed into the wind, and the balance is disturbed. The sail's center of effort is now behind the board's pivot point, and the boat turns up toward the wind. Conversely, by tipping the mast top forward, the center of effort is in front of the board's pivot point, and the board turns down, away from the wind.

What does this all mean? Simple: To turn the boat toward the wind, tip the sail back so that the sail's center of effort is behind the board's pivot point. To turn the boat away from the wind, tip the sail forward (see Figure 14-5).

Figure 14-5:
To turn the sailboard toward the wind, tip the sail back (center); to turn the sailboard away from the wind, tip the sail forward (right).

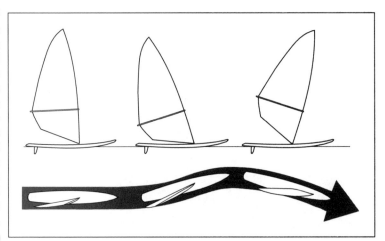

Tacking

To *tack* means to maneuver through the no-sail zone so that the wind is blowing on the opposite side of the boat. Here are the steps to tacking on a sailboard:

1. **Tilt the rig aft (toward the back) to turn the board toward the wind.**

2. **When the board is almost pointed directly toward the wind in the dreaded no-sail zone, step your forward foot around the front of the mast so that you end up straddling the mast with your back to the wind.**

3. **Now, with the sail luffing, lean the rig sideways — as described in "Steering the Board" — to get the board pointed on a reaching course on the new tack.**

   The wind is now coming over the new side of the board.

4. **As the board bears away, cross your new forward hand over to grab the boom — as described in the "Getting Your Feet (And the Rest of You) Wet" section — and pull the sheet in with your back hand.**

   Take baby steps around to just behind the mast on the new windward side and off you go!

Going straight on a reach or close-hauled is relatively easy to master because all the forces are pretty balanced, and you can make fine adjustments with your arms. Balancing only becomes a challenge when the board slows down (such as in a maneuver) and when sailing downwind. Just like in so many other sports, the best advice is *bend your knees!*

Sailing downwind

When you go downwind, all that nice stability and control goes out the window. With the wind straight behind, you must stand facing the front of the board, counteracting the forward pull of the sail. Now, any movement to the right or left really rocks the board, and it's only a matter of time before you go swimming.

To begin downwind sailing, follow these steps:

1. **Get in the safety position with the sail luffing and rotate the board around by leaning the sail until the bow is pointed downwind.**

   Hang out like this for a while. Now you can get the feel of the stability problem you encounter when the sail is trimmed in.

2. **Turn the board back to windward and get going on a reach (as usual) and then turn the boat down (away from the wind), constantly moving your feet and rotating your body to counteract the sail's force.**

   As the wind comes from more dead behind, the force on the sail may feel more powerful.

3. **To counteract the force on the sail, bring both hands closer to you or take a step or two back — thereby tipping the top of the sail backward — until you feel like you can control the sail.**

   If you get hit with a huge puff, you can always release your back hand (the hand closest to the *clew,* or back corner, of the sail) and luff the sail to keep from being pulled forward into the water.

Bend your knees to maintain your balance.

Jibing

Now that you're sailing downwind, you may want to try a jibe. A *jibe* is a maneuver where you change tacks by turning away from the wind. Jibing on a short, high-performance sailboard can be downright thrilling — like carving a turn on a slalom water ski or on a snowboard. But on a big *longboard* (trainer sailboard), tacking around and then bearing off is much easier than jibing because the big board is tough to turn.

The easiest way to jibe is simply to unload the sail and revert to the safety position, holding onto the mast near the gooseneck, and then tilt the rig to turn the boat until it's pointed on a comfortable reaching course. Then get going again in the standard fashion.

A cool, exhibition-style jibe maneuver is possible on a longboard. Here's how to pull off one of these maneuvers:

1. **As you sail downwind, step aft to sink the transom.**

2. **Rotate the sail (keeping it full of wind) so that the board turns on to the new jibe.**

3. **Quickly release your back (closest to the clew) hand and pull in your front hand.**

4. **As the clew of the sail goes winging away from you, cross your old back hand over and grab the boom about a foot back on the new windward side.**

   The momentum of the clew rotating around enables you to grab the boom with your new back hand.

5. **Pull the boom in and go!**

   All the while you're doing this maneuver, you're keeping your balance precariously on the board. If you don't fall in the water, then you'll be ecstatic!

Sailing straight downwind in anything but light air is a pain on a longboard. So if I need to get to a downwind destination, I make a series of reaches across the wind, tacking (not jibing) each time I want to zigzag back the other way. If it's windy, this approach is a really fun way of getting downwind, because your board creates its own wind and flies across the water.

Keeping in balance

Anticipating wind shifts helps you keep the sails trimmed properly — which means you stay drier, too:

- As a puff of wind hits, lean your weight out more and be ready to let out your back hand and pull in your front hand to ease the sail slightly so that you stay balanced and don't get pulled over.

- If you anticipate the end of the puff, you can bring your weight to the center as the wind dies away.

- If you aren't paying attention to the wind, you may still be able to avoid falling backward into the water by quickly bending your knees and getting your torso over the top of the board as the wind dies away.

If you've ever been skiing, you know how easily you can pick out the beginning skiers coming down the hill. The same applies with sailboarding — just look for the guy with his butt sticking way out. If you want to look cool, tilt your hips forward and bend your knees!

Getting Back to Shore in Case of Problems

If you have a problem, such as a dying wind or broken equipment, you can always paddle the board and the rig back to shore. The ability to rescue yourself is crucial to sailboarding safety.

While you're sailing, make sure to keep an eye on your distance away from shore. Don't sail too far from shore for any reason.

If you must paddle a short distance, try laying the rig over the stern of the board so that it's partially out of the water, lie or kneel on the board, and start using those arms. The problem with this technique is that the sail is like a big brake dragging in the water. If it's windy or if you have a long distance to go, derigging the sail helps. Release the outhaul, roll up the sail along the mast, fold the boom up against the mast, and start paddling, as shown in Figure 14-6.

Figure 14-6:
Self-rescue
on a
sailboard.

If you need to signal for help, kneel or stand on the board and wave your arms. In an emergency, always stay with your board — it's your primary source of flotation. Staying out of the water on the board keeps you much warmer. If you have tried to paddle back to shore but the extra windage and drag of your rig components make forward motion difficult, you can always sacrifice the rig to Poseidon to save the board — and yourself.

Peter's ten favorite sailboarding spots

1. Perth, Western Australia

2. British Virgin Islands

3. San Francisco Bay, California

4. Columbia River Gorge, Oregon

5. North Shore, Oahu and Maui, Hawaii

6. Canary Islands

7. Seal Beach, California

8. Jalama Beach, California

9. Anywhere the water is warm and the wind is over 18 knots.

10. Anywhere the water is not too cold and the wind is over 18 knots.

Europe also has a number of hot sailboarding spots; I just haven't had a chance to check them out yet!

Chapter 15

Advanced Small-Boat Techniques

. . . .

. . . .

A wet sheet and a flowing sea,
A wind that follows fast,
And fills the white and rustling sail,
And bends the gallant mast.

— Allan Cunningham

*I*n Chapters 4, 5, and 6, we cover the basics of sailing a dinghy — an agile, tippy boat. Dinghies can capsize (some more easily than others), but because of their responsiveness, no boat is better for practicing and refining your sailing skills. In fact, many of the topics discussed in this chapter apply equally well to a keelboat.

When the wind comes up, above 12 knots or so, the fun really begins. In this chapter, we focus on how to get the most speed and enjoyment in those windy conditions, and we discuss a few tips that work no matter what the wind is doing.

Before we look at the advanced techniques, review the basic skills you need to sail a dinghy:

✔ **Be able to swim:** And know enough to wear a life jacket anyway.

✔ **Move your weight quickly:** By definition, a dinghy doesn't have a *keel* (a fixed, weighted fin that replaces a centerboard) to reduce tipping. Your and your crew's weight plays an important role in keeping a dinghy upright, so you need to be able to react quickly when the wind changes.

✔ **Recover from a capsize:** Capsizing can be fun, so review small-boat safety in Chapter 7.

✔ **Steer and hold (and adjust) the mainsheet at the same time:** At the helm of a one- or two-person dinghy, you need both hands to make it go.

After reviewing a few of the basics and getting your gear safely tied into the boat (ready for a capsize), you're ready to find out how to go fast.

Going Upwind in a Breeze: Flat Is Fast

In Chapter 8, we cover why sailing flat (or at least limiting heel to a minimum) can make you go faster when sailing upwind in a breeze. The best small-boat sailors can anticipate the changes in wind speed by reading the wind as it comes across the water. They keep their boats almost perfectly flat (not heeled over by the wind) when sailing *close-hauled* (toward the wind). Here's how: When a *puff* (an extra bit of breeze) hits, the crew takes one or more of these three actions to keep the boat from heeling:

✔ **Hike out:** Lean their weight over the side more.

✔ **Ease the mainsail:** Let out the sail slightly to bleed some power from it. When the puff is over, *trim* the sail back in.

✔ **Pinch:** Steer the boat a little bit closer to the wind so that the front of the sail begins to *luff* (flutter).

Hiking Out

When sailing upwind in a good blow, the harder you hike, the faster you go. Saying "hike hard" is easy, but doing it is tough — hiking is physically exhausting. If your butt is on the rail, you aren't hiking very hard. If your thighs are the last part of you touching the rail, as shown in Figure 15-1, you're really maximizing the leverage of your body.

Here are some tips to help you hike your hardest:

✔ **Make sure that the *tiller extension (hiking stick)* is long enough.** This steering stick or handle connects to the end of the tiller so that you can hike out.

✔ **Make sure that your *mainsheet* (the rope used to control the trim of the mainsail) is as easy to hold as possible.** Consider adding a ratchet block (see Chapter 6) and/or a cleat (one that's easy to uncleat in a puff!).

Figure 15-1:
To sail fast
in strong
wind, you
must hike
out.

✔ **Shift your position from time to time.** Try crossing your ankles one way, then the other. Try *straight-leg* style hiking for a while and then switch to the more comfortable (but less efficient) *droop* hiking technique in which your knees are bent.

✔ **Try adjusting the length/tension of your hiking strap for comfort.**

Take a good look at the straps and how they're secured in the boat. Inspect for chafe and loose fittings. Nothing is more surprising (or wetter) than having your hiking strap fail.

Trapezing for Speed

Imagine that you're sailing in windy conditions and are hiking as hard as you can. A really tall person of equivalent weight would be able to keep his boat flatter because he has more leverage. Because flatter is faster, off he goes. But what if you could hike out so far that you were standing on the side of your boat? Then you could pass that guy like you were shot out of a cannon.

That is what a *trapeze* lets you do — stand on the side of your boat to maximize the effect of your body weight. Trapezing is like "super-hiking."

Whoever invented the trapeze must have a) really hated to hike out, or b) been a really smart person. A trapeze system includes a support wire *(trapeze wire)*, which runs from near the top of the mast to a ring just above deck level, and a *trapeze harness* that you wear with a hook at belly-button level in front that enables you to "hook in" to the trapeze wire, as shown in Figure 15-2.

Many dinghies and catamarans are designed to have one or more crew members ride on a trapeze. Trapezing requires athletic ability, balance, and sailing skills (to anticipate those wind shifts and to keep from being dragged in the water or flung around the bow by a wave).

JJ SAYS

The trapeze artist in Figure 15-2 is my Olympic teammate, Pamela Healy. You're probably wondering how Pam can tack while on a trapeze. As the boat begins the turn, she swings in to the boat and unhooks, supporting her weight by holding on to a small handle on the trapeze wire. Then, with her other hand, she uncleats the jib sheet as the boat turns through the no-sail zone. When the boat is on the new tack, she leaps out over the water on the new side, holding onto the handle of the new trap wire (yes, there are two wires — one on each side). In her other hand, she trims in the new jib sheet. Finally, she hooks in, and off we go. An excellent dinghy crew like Pam can go from tack to tack in less than two seconds.

Figure 15-2:
Pam Healy
(JJ's
Olympic
teammate)
on a
trapeze.

Positioning for Proper Fore-and-Aft Trim

So far in this chapter, we have been talking about techniques for sailing upwind in a strong wind. Now we want to talk about something that's important in all wind conditions, sailing upwind or downwind — fore-and-aft weight position of the crew. Sitting in the wrong position *athwartships* (across the boat) on a dinghy is pretty obvious, because it heels one way or the other. Fore-and-aft weight position errors don't give you an instant indication that something is out of whack, but they're very important if you're looking to maximize speed.

Here is a good general rule: Make sure that the boat is sitting *on its lines* — that is, level in the water as the designer intended, with neither the bow nor the stern sitting abnormally low or high in the water.

Keeping the boat on its lines usually means sitting somewhere near the boat's *center of buoyancy* (the central point of all the buoyancy forces on the boat). If you could push your boat down with a huge finger, the center of buoyancy would be the point where downward pressure results in both ends of the boat sinking evenly (that is, the boat stays on its lines as it sinks). Generally, if you sit near the fore-and-aft position of the centerboard or keel, you're very close to the right spot.

Here are some basic guidelines to fine-tune your weight position for proper fore-and-aft trim:

- ✔ **Stay out of the "ends" of the boat.** Have you ever seen a dinghy being sailed with the crew sitting all the way in the stern, making the boat pop a wheelie? Nothing is a surer tip-off to the inexperience of the crew.

- ✔ **If you have more than one person on board, sit close together.**

- ✔ **In light air, shift your weight forward one or two bodywidths.** This action sinks the bow, reducing hull drag when the boat is going slowly.

- ✔ **When hiking out or trapezing while sailing upwind, position yourself at the widest point of the boat for maximum leverage.**

- ✔ **In strong winds when reaching or running or if the waves come over the bow, move back one or two bodywidths.** This action keeps the bow out of the water and floats the boat more on the back end, which has a flatter shape, resulting in less drag for high-speed sailing.

Steering without the Rudder

Every time you turn your rudder to steer, you slow down the boat slightly. You see, the rudder is like a huge sea-brake. Imagine the water flow past the rudder when it's straight. Now turn the rudder hard over, and all that flow becomes disturbed and very turbulent. The net result is that the boat turns, but it also slows down.

However, you can steer the boat without the rudder to avoid losing speed by using two techniques. These methods can also help you get back to shore in case your rudder breaks.

- ✔ **Using your weight:** By heeling the boat one way or the other, you change the balance of the boat and make it turn. When you (and your crew) heel the boat to *windward* (toward the wind), the boat turns to *leeward* (away from the wind), and vice versa (see Figure 15-3).

- ✔ **Using the sails:** You can also change the balance of a sloop by filling one sail and luffing the other. When you trim the jib and let out the main, the boat turns to leeward. Overtrimming the main and luffing the jib causes the boat to turn to windward.

Note: The technique of moving your weight to steer doesn't work as well on a heavy keelboat because your weight is too light to substantially change the heel of the boat.

Figure 15-3:
Using your weight to turn the boat avoids the braking effect of the rudder.

Rockin' and Rollin' the Boat

You've heard the expression, *don't rock the boat,* right? Well, in most dinghies, if you want to go fast in a straight line, then lose the word *don't.* *Rocking* (repeatedly rolling) the boat is akin to a bird flapping its wings — especially in light air as the sail flaps through the air. Techniques for flapping your boat's "wings" (both above and below the water) are called *kinetics.* These include rocking, *pumping* (repeatedly trimming and easing) the sails, roll tacking, and roll jibing. Kinetics are fun because they enable you to get more physical with the boat. Plus, in windy and wavy conditions, these techniques can give you that extra burst of speed that enables the boat to start *planing* (skimming along the surface of the water) and surfing waves.

Rockin' and rollin' your boat is so fast that doing so is prohibited in the racing rules. However, intentional rocking is legal during tacking and jibing maneuvers. Experienced dinghy racers have turned this loophole into an art form, rolling the boat during tacks and jibes so effectively that the boat actually accelerates.

Roll tack

Here are the steps to a successful *roll tack,* as shown in Figure 15-4:

1. **Begin the tack by leaning in slightly, adding about 10 degrees of leeward heel.**

2. **Start turning the rudder just like in any tack.**

3. **When the boat is nearly pointed directly at the wind, hike the boat hard to windward (windward on the original tack) to begin the roll and trim the mainsheet in tight at the same time.**

   Keep turning!

4. **When your butt is about to get wet, quickly change sides to the new windward side.**

   Normally, you change sides when the turn of the tack is about 75 percent complete (that is, you're almost on the new close-hauled course).

5. **Ease the mainsheet about 1 foot and trim the jib on the new side.**

6. **As the boat turns onto the new close-hauled course, the skipper and crew hike (in unison) the boat flat on the new side, trimming the mainsheet back in the amount that you eased it in Step 5.**

   The boat squirts forward on the new tack!

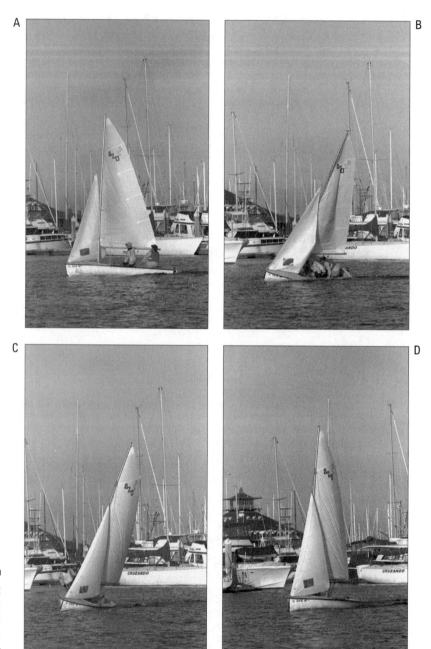

Figure 15-4:
Sequence
of a roll
tack.

Be careful — too much roll and over you go in a capsize.

In light air, the skipper's weight alone may be enough to flatten the boat on the new tack. In that case, the crew just moves to the centerline of the boat or whatever position brings the boat level.

Roll tacking takes a great deal of practice and coordination between skipper and crew, because you get the biggest roll when the whole crew moves their bodies together. Timing is crucial. Starting the roll too early or not hiking hard enough results in a lame excuse for a roll tack that may even slow the boat down.

Roll jibe

Roll jibing is very similar to roll tacking and requires just as much practice. Here are the steps to a successful roll jibe:

1. **Heel the boat to windward by hiking out.**

2. **Begin your smooth turn downwind with the rudder.**

3. **Grab the mainsheet and fling the mainsail quickly across.**

   Alternatively, the crew can grab the *boom vang* (sail control rigged between the boom and the mast) to fling the main onto the new jibe.

4. **Just before your butt drags in the water, quickly switch sides and gently but forcefully flatten the boat by hiking out with your weight.**

5. **At the same time as you switch sides, give the mainsheet a quick pull in to help acceleration.**

6. **Return the boat to its optimum downwind course and let the mainsheet back out.**

If you've been reading carefully, roll tacking and roll jibing may seem somewhat contrary to what you read in the "Steering without the Rudder" section regarding using your weight to steer the boat. But think about it: The initial change in heel for both the tack and the jibe helps start the turn so that you use less rudder motion. The second, more forceful roll contradicts the steering principles, but gives you an incredible boost, as if you flap the "wings" (sails and underwater foils) of your boat!

As the wind comes up, all this rocking and rolling may be a quick ticket to a capsize — so be careful. These techniques work best in light to medium wind.

You've gotta rock it

You can actually rock your sailboat back and forth to generate a good head of steam when absolutely no wind is blowing, as shown in Figure 15-5. On a light dinghy, rocking works better than paddling. Rocking is even possible when sailing a one-person boat.

Figure 15-5:
No wind?
No problem;
rock your
boat home.

Here's how to rock your boat to generate your own wind:

1. **Put the centerboard/daggerboard all the way down.**

2. **Set the sails to a loose close-hauled trim.**

3. **Have the skipper hold the tiller straight or, if single-handing, let the tiller go where it pleases.**

4. **Violently rock the boat one way.**

5. **Right before the boat begins to capsize (which is always a risk if you aren't careful), violently rock the boat back the other way.**

   Having the primary "rocker" stand up and hold the mast helps.

6. **Continue until you reach your destination.**

Planing and Surfing the Waves

Nothing compares with the thrill of sailing a small dinghy on a high-speed reach, with water spraying off the bow like a fire hose. You may be going only 10 or even 20 knots, but the sensation of speed is greater than going four times that fast in a car — really!

Most heavy keelboats are stuck within the waves that they create as they cruise through the water. But, given enough power from the wind, light dinghies can jump over these self-induced waves and skim over the water, similar to a speedboat or a surfer. This skimming action, called *planing,* occurs on reaches and runs and is shown in Figure 15-6.

If you have enough wind, planing doesn't require any special action on the part of the crew — the boat just lifts off and starts flying across the water. As soon as you begin to plane, you know it — because of the huge smile that spreads across your face as you realize that you're going faster than you had thought possible.

A close cousin to planing is surfing. Technically speaking, planing occurs any time the boat breaks free of its own bow and stern wave and rips along, regardless of the texture of the water's surface; surfing only happens when a wave *crest* (top) grabs the boat and gets it speeding along, sliding "downhill" on the face of the wave.

Figure 15-6:
JJ and Pam
planing at
high speed
in big
waves —
this is fun!

When we talk about surfing the waves, we're not talking about going in close to the shore break. You have a mast overhead, a mast that would get crumpled if you capsize in the surf close to shore — not to mention what would happen to you and your boat.

The great thing about surfing waves is that you can surf ocean swells, powerboat wakes — anything with a slope to it. Because waves usually run the same direction as the wind, your best chance to catch them is when sailing on a very broad reach or a run.

Any surfer can tell you that to catch a wave, you need to be going close to the wave's speed. On a sailboat, you need to use those kinetic techniques (such as rocking and pumping) to accelerate your boat when the wave starts to pick up your transom.

1. **Get the boat pointed on a broad reach with the sails perfectly trimmed.**

   If the boat has a spinnaker, use it for extra horsepower. See Chapter 8 for how to use a spinnaker.

2. **If you have a centerboard or daggerboard, pull it up partway.**

   This action reduces the drag underwater.

3. **When you feel the wave start to pick up the transom, consider turning the boat slightly (5 to 20 degrees) more to windward (and trimming the sail in accordingly) to accelerate.**

   When your boat is pointed downhill on the wave and is starting to accelerate, give a good pump to the mainsheet by pulling it in 3 feet or so very fast and then immediately releasing it. If you're reaching with a spinnaker, you can pump it, too.

   Another good kinetic technique to try here is *ooching* — having one or more crew rapidly lurch forward and then stop suddenly.

   If you pumped and/or ooched successfully (and if you have enough wind), you feel the boat scoot forward and start to shoot down the face of the wave, like in that picture of JJ and Pam in Figure 15-6.

4. **Quickly slide your weight back in the boat to raise the bow out of the water and enable the boat to sit on the flatter (more surfboard-shaped) back half of the hull.**

   Now you're surfing, and you can steer the boat straight down the face of the wave. You need to trim your sails because your apparent wind moves forward the more you accelerate.

   Don't get greedy! Don't stay surfing one wave so long that your bow plows into the back of the wave ahead of you, flooding the cockpit with water.

5. **As you get near the bottom of the wave (the** *trough***) and the bow starts to point uphill, turn to windward about 10 to 20 degrees to try to stay riding on the downhill portion of the wave or at least build speed so that wave passes under you.**

6. **When you feel the boat slow down, slide forward to your normal position again.**

Catamaran Sailing

If you know how to sail a keelboat or dinghy, then you can sail a catamaran, because a catamaran is simply a sailboat with two hulls instead of one. Figure 15-7 shows a basic cat. Sure, some multihulls are big, heavy cruisers, but we're talking about the kind you launch off a beach, around 20 feet (6 m) or smaller. Note that a cat has some features you don't find on other sailboats, including a crossbar to hold its unique twin hulls in place; the trampoline — rope mesh or fabric surface between the two hulls; full-length battens in the mainsail; and a rotating mast.

Because the principles of sailing a catamaran are the same as any boat, this section focuses on some areas where you run into significant differences.

Making your own wind

The big difference between cats and dinghies is their speed. Cats are faster on almost every point of sail, in every wind condition. The reason for the speed is twofold: The narrow hulls cause very little drag, and the "wide wheelbase" enables the crew to sit very far away from the sails, providing great mechanical advantage to keep the boat from heeling. The added width is sort of like having a super-trapeze — in fact, many cats have trapezes, too!

The quickness of a catamaran highlights a phenomenon that we allude to in the planing and surfing sections earlier in this chapter — the apparent wind shifts forward and increases as the boat accelerates. (For a basic overview of apparent wind, see Chapter 8.) Because of the apparent wind effect, catamarans feel like they're going close-hauled, requiring you to trim the sails tight, when they're actually sailing at a wider angle to the wind. They just keep going faster and faster, making their own wind as you bear away.

Flying a hull

A catamaran doesn't heel over — it flies. That's certainly the feeling you get the first time the windward hull (which you're sitting on) lifts up out of the water. *Flying a hull* is akin to heeling on a monohull and is caused by the

Figure 15-7:
A
catamaran.

excess wind force. For maximum speed, you want to have the windward hull just kissing the waves. That state minimizes the drag of the craft going through the water but keeps the sails and foils (centerboard and rudder) at nearly an optimum angle to their respective fluids.

Flying the hull isn't fast, and if you go too far, you invite a capsize, but seeing the windward hull 5 feet out of the water certainly looks spectacular. You can get the hull back down closer to the water the same way you reduce heel in a dinghy:

- ✔ **Hike out harder (or use your trapeze).**

- ✔ **Ease the mainsheet a few inches to bleed power from your biggest sail.**

- ✔ **Turn the boat toward the wind to bleed power from the sails by pinching.**

Pinching works fine in most conditions. But if conditions are windy, you can fly a hull when sailing very close to a dead-downwind course. In this case, turning the boat toward the wind adds power into the sails, and the boat heels even more. The correct reaction, then, is to bear away more to slow the boat down. The only way to know which way (toward or away from the wind) will depower you best is by experience — and paying attention to your heading relative to the true wind direction.

Fully battened sails

Almost all catamarans have a fully battened mainsail — that is, the battens in the sail go all the way from *leech* to *luff* (back edge to front edge). This extra support from the long battens enables the sailmaker to build more area onto a given mast and boom combination. Fully battened sails aren't unique to catamarans; some monohulls, such as the America's Cup-class boats, have them, too.

Watching the leading edge of the sail for the small "bubble" that indicates slight undertrim can be difficult on these sails because they don't luff as dramatically as a "soft" sail. Make sure that your mainsail is equipped with *telltales*. See Chapter 8 for how to use telltales.

Reaching downwind

Although catamarans, like any other boat, can sail directly downwind (with the wind dead astern), you do have another way to get there, one that is often much faster. This method is commonly called *tacking downwind* — a misnomer really, because tacking downwind entails reaching one way and then jibing and reaching the other way. Although the distance sailed is longer than steering the shortest route, the extra speed generated by reaching up and making some of that magic, apparent wind (see Chapter 8), is usually well worth the trouble. Of course, such a strategy requires that you take a zigzag route so familiar in sailing any boat toward an upwind destination and then jibe once or more, as shown in Figure 15-8.

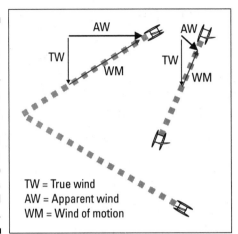

Figure 15-8:
Catamarans perform best by reaching up and making some extra wind and then jibing later to reach a downwind destination.

TW = True wind
AW = Apparent wind
WM = Wind of motion

Special tacking tips

Not all catamarans were created equal, and some can be a real chore to tack. If you find yourself on one of those cats that has trouble tacking, take a look at these tips:

- ✔ **Make sure that you're going as fast as possible on a close-hauled course before starting your tack.**
- ✔ **Pick a smooth spot in the waves to begin the turn.**
- ✔ **Turn the boat in a fairly sharp arc.**

If the boat has a jib, keep it cleated on the old tack and let it *backwind* (fill backward) as the boat turns through the wind. At the same time, release the mainsheet so that it's free to run. This "backing" jib and eased mainsail combination helps spin the boat down onto the new close-hauled course.

If the boat doesn't have a jib, completing the tack can be difficult. Often, the boat loses too much momentum and ends up stopping as it comes on a course pointed directly at the wind direction. Congratulations — you're now in irons. Review Chapter 5 on getting out of irons. Next time, try jibing instead.

Recovering from a capsize

When catamarans capsize, you can be in for some real excitement. If you aren't careful, you can get catapulted from the high side and land on the sail or the mast. See Chapter 7 for the basics on righting a capsized boat, but this section has tips just for cats.

The key is to avoid falling off the boat, if at all possible. Hold on to a *shroud* (wire that supports the mast) or some part of the trampoline or hull, but try to stay on board. If you do fall, try to land feet first (presuming that you have shoes or booties on) with your knees bent. That way, if you fall on a hard object, you're more likely to come through unscathed.

The next step is preventing the boat from *turning turtle* (flipping over all the way so that the mast is pointed straight down), because recovering from a turtle is much harder than recovering from a regular capsize, when the mast stays horizontal on the water. If you're clever enough to still be high and dry on the upper hull, get off: Your weight on the upper hull isn't helping the situation and may, in fact, be adding more pressure to sink the mast. Fortunately, most production cats have sealed mast sections that inhibit the boat turning turtle. Some cats even have a float attached to the top of the mast.

All cats should be rigged with a *righting line.* This inventive piece of equipment is a fairly thick (mainsheet-size) piece of rope rigged for easy access in the event of a flip. Leaning your weight (and your crew's) out on the extended righting line (as shown in Figure 15-9) can hopefully provide the necessary leverage to overcome the wind and muscle the boat upright.

Try to get the boat to rotate around so that the bow is pointed into (or close to) the wind direction. You may be able to rotate the boat simply by standing on the "lower" bow, adding drag so that the stern blows downwind more. If that strategy doesn't work, you can try swimming the bow upwind — a

Figure 15-9: Using a righting line to add leverage and right a capsized catamaran.

tiring task! Popping the battens in the mainsail so that they're convex (looking down on the boat) can also help you right the boat, because as the sail begins to come out of the water, the wing shape of the mainsail helps lift the mast farther out of the water.

Watch out for falling hulls! When the boat begins to come upright, the cat reaches the critical point of balance where the upper hull is going to fall down fast. Stay clear of the hull and the *dolphin striker* (the support strut mounted to the front cross beam below the mast). Have the crew grab the lower hull or front cross beam near the lower hull to prevent the boat from continuing to roll over and capsize the other way, to keep them clear of falling objects, and so that they're ready to climb on the boat and get sailing again.

If you capsize on a boat that doesn't have a righting line, you may be able to create a makeshift one by tying a rope (the jib sheet may work well) to the mast or "upper" trampoline support bar. The mainsheet is also a possible righting line, but first make sure that it's long and rigged in such a way that the sails can still be fully eased as the boat is righted. Otherwise, the sails may fill with air as the mast comes up, and the boat flips back over again.

A not-so-grand exit

Back in 1988, we defended the America's Cup in a high-tech, 65-foot (20-m), wing-sailed catamaran. Because many of us, including our skipper, Dennis Conner, had limited experience on cats, our *Stars & Stripes* team purchased two 40-foot (12-m), Formula 40 cats as trainers. We then "turbocharged" the boats by adding 10 feet (3 m) more mast (and sail area) and shortening the "wheelbase" by chopping the crossbars down by a few feet. These turbo-40s were really fun to sail, even in San Diego's light winds, but they were also very tippy!

The annual springtime Opening Day at San Diego Yacht Club is a festive affair. Hundreds of members and guests come for the ceremonies and celebration. At the beginning of the

ceremony, Dennis and crew were recognized on stage, and then we excused ourselves to go out and train. The crowd cheered as the turbo-40 left the dock in about 3 knots of wind. The boat made it another 100 yards (91 m), and then a whopping 4-knot puff struck the towering sails. The crew was a bit distracted, and *splash* — the San Diego Yacht Club's great hope to defend the America's Cup capsized right next to the club.

Needless to say, a 40-foot cat is too big for the crew to right, and we took the better part of three hours to get the boat back up, while the celebration continued on shore. We did, however, win the America's Cup, and we never capsized our racing cats.

Chapter 16

The Basics of Sailboat Racing

> *O Captain! my Captain! our fearful trip is done,*
> *The ship has weathered every rack, the prize we sought is won,*
> *The port is near, the bells I hear, the people all exulting.*
>
> — Walt Whitman

As you read this chapter, one fact becomes obvious, so we may as well state it up front — we love sailboat racing. It is our passion, so this chapter is very biased. But hey, at least we're warning you.

We have competed at all levels, and sailboat racing has enriched our lives in many ways. Through our racing, we have traveled and made friends around the world. JJ, with teammate Pamela Healy, represented the U.S. in the 1992 Olympics, winning the Bronze Medal in the Women's 470 (a two-person dinghy with spinnaker and trapeze) and achieving every athlete's dream of standing on the medal podium. Peter was navigator for the Dennis Conner-skippered *Stars & Stripes* boats that won the America's Cup in 1987 in Perth, Australia, and again in 1988 in San Diego, California. The victory tour included a trip to the White House and a New York City ticker-tape parade! JJ has been racing sailboats since she was 8, Peter from age 13. If it weren't for sailboat racing, we wouldn't have met and had the opportunity to write this book. (Of course, editing each other's writing has been an interesting challenge. We've needed *Marriage Counseling For Dummies* occasionally.)

Whether you plan on embarking on a racing career or just want to know what those boats are doing when you see racing on the water or on television, this chapter introduces you to the incredibly diverse sport of sailboat racing.

Getting into Sailboat Racing

Sailboat racing comes in many forms, from casual weekend racing to grand prix professional racing with television coverage and even prize money. No doubt sailors have been racing against that boat nearby since man first put to sea. In the 1800s, the sport of *yachting* — formalized sailboat racing — began to develop. By the turn of the century, England and the U.S. almost went to war over an alleged incident (the British crew claimed that the Yanks had cheated) in the most famous sailboat race, the America's Cup. Sailboat racing has been part of every modern Olympics. It's a fantastic sport for many different reasons; here are a few of them.

Racing is for everyone

Racing sailboats is for people of all sizes and all ages. Although certain crew positions on certain boats are very physically demanding (such as the grinders in the America's Cup), the most important characteristics of a good racer are mental — concentration, quick reactions, analytical skills, and a desire to learn. Even physically challenged individuals can participate.

Men and women can compete equally in sailing at all levels. In 1995, JJ had the incredible opportunity to be a part of an all-women's America's Cup team, America[3]. It was the first time at the top level of a professional sport that women competed head-to-head against men. But in any given local race, you can find women and men racing against each other.

Racing teaches sportsmanship

Sailboat racing encourages fair play because the sport is self-policing, relying on a set of right-of-way rules (see the section "The Rules of the Game"). A few competitions have on-the-water referees, but most sailboat races rely on the competitors' sense of sportsmanship to obey the rules.

Racers are at one with the environment

Sailboat racing has all the intensity of NASCAR racing without the noise, the burning rubber, and the burning fossil fuel. You're out in the middle of nature just like an off-road racer, yet you're not tearing up the tundra. After your boat goes past, the only thing left is your wake.

To win a sailboat race, you must let all your senses work for you, from feeling the wind on your skin to reading the water for clues to the wind shifts. When racing, you have to sail the boat as fast as possible while looking around and planning which way to go.

Sailboat racing in cold weather

Some people are so keen on sailboat racing that they continue to race all year around — even in frigid climates. This sport is called *frostbiting* — for good reason. Personally, I think that any time you have to break the ice out of a boat to go sailing, the trip should be very short, followed by something hot to drink in front of a blazing fireplace.

In college, I raced in a dinghy regatta on Lake Michigan in late November. My crew and I used rock salt (the stuff they throw on roads to melt the ice) to keep the deck from turning into a skating rink and the ropes from freezing solid — now that's frostbiting!

Iceboats are incredibly fast sailboats that skate across the ice on runners similar to ice skates. These boats can fly at incredible speeds — over 100 miles per hour (161 kilometers per hour). If you get a chance to go iceboating, don't forget your helmet.

Racers are always learning something new

Imagine a football game that takes place on the water, where the waves and wind constantly change the playing field — that's sailboat racing. It's like a three-dimensional chess game in which the board and the competitors are always moving. Match racing, the one-on-one racing format used in the America's Cup, has been compared to aerial dogfighting. In any type of racing, you discover so much about the weather, the current, the hydro- and aerodynamics of the sails and boat, tactics, how you perform under pressure — the list goes on and on.

Racing takes place in nice places

Sailboat racing has literally taken each of us around the globe. We have been to some of the nicest places in the world, such as Perth, Australia, and Saint-Tropez, France. And, unlike most of the other visitors who are shorebound, we get to go sailing. Now that's what we call a great sport!

How Sailboat Racing Works

As you know, boats come in thousands and thousands of different types, and you can race any type. On top of that, races take place all over the globe, from Cape Horn to the fjords of Norway. You can race model boats on ponds and ice boats on frozen lakes. Some races are around *buoys* (anchored, floating turning marks), and other races go offshore from point to point.

Races can be as short as ten minutes, or they may last for months. You can race *one-design* (in which all the boats are identical) or under a *handicap* system (in which boats of different types race together with the faster boats owing time to the slower boats). The majority of sailboat racing is done in fleets (hence the term *fleet racing,* in which many boats compete together).

Taking into account all that variety, here's the big picture of what you need to know to race in a common type of sailboat race — a fleet race around a course defined by buoys.

Entering the race

Most races are run by local sailing or yacht clubs. A document called the *Notice of Race* explains the basic details of the *regatta* (series of races scored together as a whole): when the racing starts, what type of boats can enter, if you need to pay an entry fee, when you can register, who is organizing the event, and so on.

After you register, you receive a copy of the *Sailing Instructions.* The SIs cover important details like a schedule of races, a chart of the race area, and the type of race courses. Figure 16-1 shows you a windward-leeward course typical for an around-the-buoys race. The *starting line* is an imaginary line between an anchored, race-committee boat and a buoy. The finish line is similarly identified.

After you enter a race, you need to prepare your boat and crew to maximize your chances of performing well.

Preparing the boat

One of the most important aspects of racing is boat speed. If your boat is slow, you can still win a race by using clever tactics and maneuvering better than the competition, but winning is much easier with a fast boat. Boat speed comes through preparation — refining your equipment so that it's fast and easy to sail. Having the right mast and sails for the wind conditions is incredibly important. Making sure that your boat can handle the stress of heavy winds and big waves can help you avoid the agony of a breakdown. Even the little things, like polishing your boat's bottom, can make the difference between winning and losing.

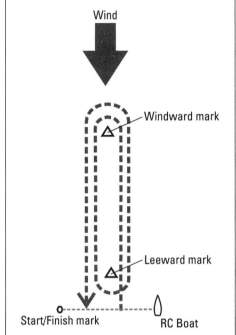

Wind

Windward mark

Leeward mark

Start/Finish mark   RC Boat

Figure 16-1:
A common
windward-
leeward
course,
including
the start/
finish line.

Preparing the crew

Some boats are sailed single-handed; others race with a large crew. No matter how many people are on board, the abilities, motivation, and teamwork of the crew are critical to success. A blown maneuver like a spinnaker takedown at a mark rounding can cost dearly, but a good crew can make an average helmsman look like a superstar. The crew constantly feeds the skipper information about wind shifts, wave conditions, and boat-on-boat positioning so that the driver can steer as quickly as possible without looking around too much. The more competitive the racing, the more important it is that the entire crew work smoothly as a team.

Before the start

For the hour or so before the first start, crews develop a strategy by carefully monitoring the changes in the wind direction and velocity and watching for variations in current. Based upon their observations, the team may decide to favor one side of the course because it has more wind. They also may use the time to practice maneuvers.

Getting a good start

The start is often the most important part of the race. A good start can propel you into an untouchable position — or at least give you a better shot at a top finish. A series of sound and visual signals from the race committee boat counts the time down to the start.

The goal is to be just behind the starting line at full speed, just as the countdown clicks to zero and the starting gun is fired. Sounds easy, but as many as a hundred or more boats are all trying to do the very same thing! Other prestart considerations include which end of the line is "favored" with respect to the wind conditions and your competitors. Basically, the five minutes or so before the starting gun is a massive free-for-all in which boats randomly zig and zag around until *boom!* At the gun, the mayhem magically becomes a spectacular water ballet, with boats all lined up and headed for the first mark. Figure 16-2 shows a perfect big fleet start.

Against the wind — the first leg

The first turning mark is commonly positioned directly upwind of the starting line. As you discover in Chapter 5, no sailboat can sail that close to the wind, so on this leg, the fleet works its way to the top mark tack by tack. Of course, a boat can reach the mark by tacking only once, but often, because of wind shifts and other competitors, boats must make more tacks. Strategic considerations include wind shifts — even a small 5-degree clockwise wind shift affects the positions in the race. Boats that head to the right side of the race course (by first sailing on port tack) benefit greatly from such a shift, as shown in Figure 16-3. But if the wind goes counterclockwise, those same boats lose out — which is why you try to figure out what the wind will do before you start.

While racing upwind, you're also concerned with keeping clear wind in your sails, avoiding the exhaust coming off a competitor's sails. The boats ahead often try to "cover" their competition and force them farther back. Throughout all these various tactics and strategy, the crew tries to keep the boat at maximum speed, adjusting the sails to stay in perfect tune with the changing wind conditions.

Around the mark

On the open course, the boats spread out across a mile or more, and then they all converge at the mark. Mark roundings provide an opportunity for the crews to strut their stuff as sails are set and dropped (when turning the first mark to go downwind, many boats set the colorful spinnaker), and the

Figure 16-2:
A perfect
fleet race
start.

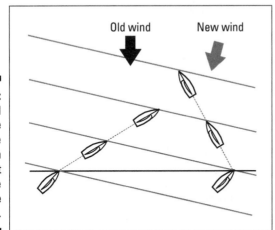

Figure 16-3:
If the wind
shifts to the
right, the
boats on
the right
side of the
course
gain.

boats turn the corner. A well-practiced crew can gain valuable boatlengths. Luckily, universal sailing rules cover which boat has the right-of-way, or crowded mark roundings would be complete chaos.

With the wind — the downwind leg

Many race courses are set up with two buoys: a *top* (windward) and a *bottom* (leeward) mark near the starting line. On the second, downwind leg, the boats continue to focus on boat speed (see Figure 16-4) while keeping an open eye on the puffs of wind and the position of the competition. The boats in the back now have the opportunity to attack by using their wind shadows to slow down the leaders. Downwind speed is increased by setting big spinnakers. As noted in Chapter 8, the spinnaker is tricky to set, take down, and maneuver *(jibe),* so the spotlight is on the crew to handle the boat perfectly on this leg.

Figure 16-4:
On the downwind leg, the crews try to get every ounce of speed out of their spinnakers.

The finish gun

Like the starting line, the finish is an imaginary line between two objects, usually a buoy on one end and a flag on the committee boat on the other. No sound is sweeter than the blast of the gun as you cross the line in first place, but you don't need to win every race to win a regatta. You just need to be in the top group consistently.

The Rules of the Game

In order to play a game with other people, you have to agree on the rules. The *Racing Rules of Sailing* are written by the governing body for the sport, the *International Sailing Federation* (ISAF). Every four years, the ISAF updates the rules. In 1997, the ISAF dramatically altered the rules in an effort to simplify them.

If you want to race, get a copy of these universal racing rules from your national authority (see Appendix C) or at your local marine store. To give you an idea of how the rules work, we outline the seven most basic rules in sailboat racing in the following list:

- ✔ **Avoid collisions with other boats and any buoys or turning marks.** This is not bumper boats.

- ✔ **You must start properly.** The starting line is meant to be crossed after the starting gun. If you cross before the gun, you have to go back and restart.

- ✔ **Starboard tack has right-of-way over port tack.** This rule and the next two are in force under the rules of the road (nonracing) and the Racing Rules (racing only). See Figure 16-5.

- ✔ **The leeward boat has the right-of-way over the windward boat.** This rule applies when two boats are on the same tack; if they're on opposite tacks, then the preceding rule applies. See Figure 16-5.

- ✔ **The overtaking boat must keep clear.** Makes sense, doesn't it? The boat that's passing must stay out of the way of the boat being passed.

- ✔ **When rounding marks, the inside boat is king!** If two or more boats approach a turning mark or some sort of obstruction while overlapped, the boat on the inside of the turn has right-of-way.

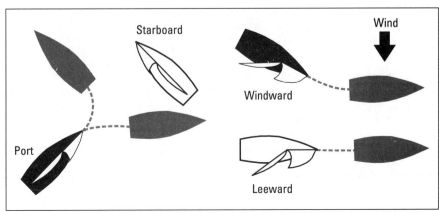

Figure 16-5: Racing rules: starboard/ port, windward/ leeward.

✔ **You can make amends — sometimes.** The penalties in sailing vary depending on the Sailing Instructions. Some regattas allow you to exonerate a foul (where you break a rule) by immediately sailing two complete circles or by accepting a percentage penalty to your finish score. However, in many races, if you foul another boat, don't take a penalty, and are found guilty in a post-race hearing, you're disqualified from the race — ouch!

How to Win — or at Least Get Started

Here is our advice for mastering the basics of sailboat racing:

✔ **Become a student of the sport.** A number of outstanding books on sailboat racing have been written, including *Expert Dinghy and Keelboat Racing,* by maybe the best sailboat racer ever, Paul Elvström, winner of four Olympic Gold Medals; the *Sail To Win* series (from Fernhurst Books in the United Kingdom); and *Winning in One Designs,* by Dave Perry. You can also find great magazines on sailboat racing such as *Sailing World, Sail, Seahorse* (U.K.), and *Yachting.*

PETER SAYS

Biker Bob's wild ride

A few years ago, a friend of mine was racing on windy San Francisco Bay. After the first practice day, the crew agreed that they needed more weight on the rail to keep the boat from heeling over in the strong winds. That night at a local watering hole, they met the biggest guy they had ever seen, "Biker Bob." Bob was dressed in leather from head to toe and had his motorcycle parked on the street outside. Bob was keen to go racing, and the deal was done.

The next morning, the yachting types were horrified to see a motorcycle pull into the yacht club parking lot, and they stared with amazement as Bob walked down to the boat in his big boots. As the fleet sailed off the starting line, one boat was rocketing away, much faster than the rest of the fleet. It was my friend's boat. Thanks to Bob's extra weight hiking out on the rail, the boat was flying — until it reached the first mark and the crew had to make maneuvers. You see, Bob had a little trouble moving quickly around the boat in his boots.

The story ends without the blast of the victory gun. Bob's mobility problem grew worse and worse, until the crew had to send him down below deck so that he wouldn't fall overboard. During the distraction, the rest of the fleet sailed past. One can only hope that Bob continued racing so that he could improve, but somehow I think that was his last time in a race.

✔ **Enroll in a racing seminar.** Check with your local sail loft for information. Here are our favorite racing seminars in the U.S.:

- **Kolius Racing School:** John Kolius is one of the top sailors in the world and an exceptional sailing coach. 800-276-SAIL.

- **North U:** Run by North Sails, it has seminars that cover speed and tactics. 410-269-5662.

- **Performance Racing Seminars:** Run by Bill Gladstone and a host of instructors (including both of us). 800-347-2457.

If you live outside of the U.S., your national authority (see Appendix C) or a sail loft may be able to recommend courses in racing.

✔ **Find the right boat.** Most racing venues feature active fleets of boats. Some popular fleets even have casual races on weekday evenings. Many dinghies (like the Snipe or Lido 14, Lightning, 470, and Tasar) are great for husband-wife racing teams. Make the effort to race different types of boats and to learn all the different jobs on board.

✔ **Know the rules.** Tactics are dependent on using the rules to your advantage. For example, as you get close to a mark, the boats converge. So, being on starboard tack (which has right-of-way) on the approach gives you a tactical advantage.

✔ **Practice makes perfect.** In order to succeed on the race course, you must do many things well. You must sail fast, work well with your team, handle your boat and your sails smoothly, and be perceptive to the strategy and tactics of the race. The best racers spend much more time practicing than racing.

✔ **Sign on as crew.** You can't improve your sailing skills unless you get out there and do it. Many local sailing magazines (find them at your local marine store) publish lists of interested crew. Put your name on the list. Join the local racing fleet, and go to its dinners — most people like to race with friends rather than strangers. And go to the marina where the boats are docked and introduce yourself to the racers. Sometimes, a boat needs a last-minute replacement, or if it's windy, they may want to bring more crew to keep the boat from heeling too much.

Sailboat Racing around the World

Many places are great for racing, and most sailors rarely leave their home waters. But many top international sailors spend most of the year living out of a duffel bag. Here's a look at the world's most prestigious and competitive sailboat races.

The Olympics

Most sailors consider the Olympics to be the premier sailing competition. The Sydney 2000 Olympics will feature ten separate sailing events in different classes of boats, the largest of which is the Soling, a 26-foot, three-person keelboat. The other nine events are men's and women's sailboard (Mistral One-Design), women's single-handed (Europe Dinghy), men's single-handed (Finn Dinghy), open single-handed (Laser), men's and women's double-handed (470), open double-handed (49er), and open Catamaran (Tornado).

The 2000 Olympics in Sydney promises to be an outstanding venue for sailing (officially called *yachting* by the International Olympic Committee). Certain portions of the competition will take place directly off the Sydney Opera House as well as all over the beautiful Sydney Harbor and nearby sailing hot spots like Pittwater.

Olympic sailing competition is the purest test of sailing skill because all the boats are strictly one-design. Teams often try for many years before earning an Olympic berth (there's only one per country per class of boat). JJ and Pam Healy trained in the 470 class for seven years before achieving their dream of being on the U.S. Olympic Team.

The America's Cup

The America's Cup is the oldest international sporting event in the world, and today it's the biggest event in sailing (measured by media and general public interest). The event started in 1851 when a group of clever Yankees sailed their quick schooner *America* over to England looking for some suckers to race (and wager). They were unsuccessful in drumming up a challenge for money, so they entered a race around the Isle of Wight in southern England, and the rest is history. *America* beat 14 British boats around the course (although there was some controversy over whether the Yankees had cut a mark of the course) and took home a sterling silver ewer, which was renamed the America's Cup, after the boat that won it.

For 132 years, the trophy was in the possession of the New York Yacht Club — the longest winning streak in the history of sports. But in 1983, a team of Aussies with a very fast boat with a winged keel carried the Cup back home. A U.S. crew (including Peter as navigator) representing the San Diego Yacht Club went to Perth, Australia, and won the Cup back in 1987 and then defended it in San Diego in 1988. The Cup was successfully defended in 1992 by the *America³* team, but San Diego finally lost it in 1995 to Team New Zealand. The next Cup match race will be conducted in February 2000 in Auckland, New Zealand.

Over the years, the America's Cup has drawn its share of characters. Around the turn of the century, Sir Thomas Lipton tried, unsuccessfully, five times to win the coveted trophy. He did, however, win America's tea business in the process. Other notable players over the decades include Sir Thomas Sopwith (of Sopwith Camel biplane fame), Cornelius Vanderbilt (yes, one of those Vanderbilts), Baron Bic (you probably have one of his pens), and Ted Turner (you probably get a few of his channels on cable). In recent years, one man has become synonymous with the America's Cup — Dennis Conner. "DC," shown in Figure 16-6, has won the Cup four times, lost it twice, and has been at the forefront of the increased professionalism in the competition.

Figure 16-6:
Dennis
Conner
holding the
coveted
America's
Cup.

In recent years, the Cup has usually been conducted every three or four years, and for most of the last century and a half, the fastest boat has usually won. As in any sailboat race, boat speed is ultra-important in the America's Cup, and teams spend millions of dollars on their design efforts.

If you have to ask how much vying for the Cup costs, you can't afford it. In winning the Cup in 1992, Bill Koch's *America³* team spent a record $64 million over three years. Most of that money went into the design and construction of an armada of boats, masts, sails, and other equipment. Although new rules limiting team expenditures were implemented after Koch's victory, a winning Cup effort still has a budget with eight figures to the left of the decimal point.

If you're hooked up to the Internet, check out the America's Cup online at http://www.americas-cup.co.nz/.

Which race is more important in the world of sailing, the America's Cup or the Olympics? Certainly the Cup garners more public attention, but if you took a poll of racers, the Olympics would probably come out on top. Maybe this is because individual sailing skill is a bigger part of an Olympic Gold Medal. But for a top professional racer, the America's Cup does have something going for it — it's a real job.

Major international races

This section is a quick guide to the major races around the world. We list the most well-known distance races, as well as the other major fleet, match, and team races.

- ✔ **Admiral's Cup:** An historic event held every two years in Cowes, England, this six-race series features both day-racing around the buoys and long-distance races, including the famous 600-mile (965 km) Fastnet Race to Ireland and back. Countries enter international teams of three boats each, many with professional, America's Cup-level crews. They race 36- to 50-foot (11- to 15-m) ocean-racing sloops under a handicap system. The Admiral's Cup is concurrent with one of the oldest regattas, Cowes Week, an annual event that draws hundreds of smaller, amateur boats.

- ✔ **Around Alone:** Similar to the Whitbread Round the World Race, but in this race, the 60-foot (18-m) sailboats are sailed single-handed. The race, which takes place every three to four years, used to be called the BOC.

- ✔ **Australian skiffs:** These popular dinghies are affectionately known as the "eyedeen-foot skiffs" in their home waters of Australia. Professional crews sail these exciting, high-speed dinghies around short, buoy race courses for prize money. Recently, the circuit has been making stops overseas as well and has changed from a three-person to a

---

Match racing

When just two boats are on the starting line, the race is called *match racing*. The premier match racing event is the America's Cup. Match racing has its own set of rules, which are slightly different from the regular racing rules, that create very close, aggressive competition in which collisions are certainly not rare.

Match racing also has on-the-water judging, with umpires doling out "instant justice" on the water.

Match racing is tremendously exciting to participate in. And, unlike watching other sailing competitions (which has been compared to watching paint dry), match racing can be thrilling to watch (and we think that team racing — discussed in the next section — can be even more exciting). Before the start, the boats vie for control, circling each other and trying to wipe each other off on spectator boats in an elaborate game of cat and mouse.

two-person boat (the Olympic 49er, shown in Figure 16-7). Aside from wave-sailing on sailboards, no spectacle is more exciting in the sport of sailboat racing.

✔ **European multihull circuit:** The European multihull circuit is comprised of a variety of offshore (across oceans) races aboard huge, 60-foot-(18-m) plus catamarans and trimarans. Professional crews race these incredibly high-tech and high-speed (20-30 knots!) craft, often with two-person crews. Big prize money and big sponsors!

✔ **Grand prix handicap racing:** Fully crewed monohulls from 36 feet to 80 feet (11 m to 24 m) race in a variety of grand prix-level events (both day-race and ocean-race format) around the world. Some crews are professional. Popular events are in Sardinia, Kiel, Palma, Hawaii, San Francisco, Newport, Bermuda, Sydney, and Key West.

✔ **One-design racing:** Maybe the most competitive sailing in the world is in the incredibly diverse world of one-design dinghy, keelboat, catamaran, and sailboard racing. Races are hosted literally around the globe, and many of the more popular classes (both Olympic and non-Olympic) have exceptionally well-organized regional, national, and international circuits. One-design racing is the backbone of the sport of sailboat racing, and virtually all the world's top sailors have spent most of their sailing lives in these competitions.

✔ **Team racing:** Team racing is extremely exciting. Usually sailed in two-person dinghies, team racing's most common format has six boats racing, three boats per team. Tactics and boat handling are crucial to

Figure 16-7:
The
Olympic
49er.

this exciting sport, as competitors try to hold back their opponents to enable their teammates to catch up.

✔ **Vendee Globe:** A nonstop around-the-world race for single-handed sailors — it takes a really special person to want to enter the Vendee Globe! Can you imagine being in a high-tech, 60-foot (18-m) sloop, racing as fast as you can around the globe for over 100 days? Needless to say, doing so is very dangerous.

✔ **Volvo Ocean Race:** Formerly known as the Whitbread Round the World Race, this every-four-years contest pits 60-foot (18-m) sloops with full crews (approximately 12 people) on a race around the world. The race is divided into legs, with several-weeks-long stopovers in various ports. The longest and most grueling legs are in the Southern (Antarctic) Ocean, blasting downwind at full speed dodging icebergs! That part of the race makes for some great television coverage.

The next race will run from September 2001 to May 2002. The last race — and the last to be called the Whitbread — started in September 1997 in Southampton, England, and ended there eight months later after stopovers in South Africa; Australia; New Zealand; Brazil; Florida and Maryland in the United States; and France. Stopover cities for the next race were not announced at the time of this writing. You can get the latest race news, realtime coverage of the race, and participate in a virtual race on the Internet at `http://www.whitbread.org`.

✔ **World Match Racing Circuit:** This series of nearly 20 pro-level match racing regattas is the training ground for America's Cup and Olympic hopefuls. Events take place on four continents, and most have prize money and television coverage. They consist of short, 20-minute races packed into weeklong events.

If you're hooked up to the Internet, check out Semaphore World Sailing at `http://www.semaphore.co.uk/sailing/` for a comprehensive guide to worldwide, leading-edge racing. *Sailing World* magazine has a weekly Grand Prix newsletter online (`http://www.sailingworld.com`). Another good source is the International Sailing Federation Web site at `http://www.sailing.org/`.

Sailing on TV

No matter what kind of sailboat racing you're a fan of, you can now see more racing on television than ever before. Thanks to the interest (and technology) generated by the America's Cup, sailboat racing is getting increased exposure on the tube. Grand prix-level match racing also enjoys television coverage, but the races are usually taped and edited down to a 30-minute or hourlong program. Occasionally, you may see special programs featuring other races, including the Whitbread Round the World Race and other grand prix-level competitions, as the sport keeps growing in popularity. *Sailing World* magazine has a guide to sailing on television at the magazine's Web site at `http://www.sailingworld.com`.

Part V
Special Considerations

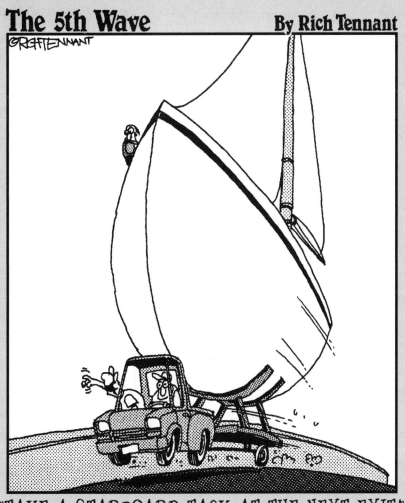

The 5th Wave — By Rich Tennant

"TAKE A STARBOARD TACK AT THE NEXT EXIT!"

In this part . . .

Remember the Owl and Pussycat who went to sea in a beautiful pea green boat? They sailed away for a year and a day, to the land where the bong tree grows. Haven't you always wanted to see what a bong tree looks like? No? Well, then, have you always wanted to sail away? Yes? The skills that you've acquired by reading this book and practicing on the water have you ready to embark on an adventure. In this part, you can daydream in earnest as we introduce you to the world of cruising. Find out about chartering (renting) a boat in beautiful vacation destinations around the world. And if you have kids, we show you tips for making sure that they enjoy the sailing trip, too. Finally, we assume that you enjoy sailing enough to care for your craft.

Chapter 17

Chartering: Changes in Latitude

• •

• •

> *O we can wait no longer,*
> *We too take ship O soul,*
> *Joyous we too launch out on trackless seas,*
> *Fearless for unknown shores.*
>
> — Walt Whitman

*I*magine spending a week's vacation with your closest friends and family in some of the most beautiful spots in the world. Thanks to sailboat charter companies, you can take short vacation cruises in sailing paradises around the world. You can sail in remote areas and spend a week without ever seeing another soul, or you can cruise to hot spots in the Mediterranean and spend your nights surrounded by the Cote d'Azur chic in a local nightclub.

In this chapter, we look at your options for chartering a boat and sailing away. We also help you prepare for the business side of the charter. You need to be able to sail to bareboat charter, and we review the skills you should possess. And to top it off, we look at the top cruising spots around the world. So what are you waiting for? You don't even have to own a boat!

Chartering

Thanks to the recent growth of excellent charter companies around the world, chartering a boat doesn't require as much preplanning as you may expect. Hey, you can go today — just pick up the phone! The larger charter companies help you arrange everything from air travel to provisioning. You can even schedule a "cruise and learn" vacation to brush up on your sailing skills during the whole trip or just the first part of your trip, and afterward you can take the boat for a bareboat run.

The most common way to book your trip is directly with the charter company, but charter brokers can do the deal on your behalf. You can research the various charter companies by scanning the advertising sections in the back of some sailing magazines.

If you're hooked up to the Internet, `http://www.charternet.com` has more than 25,000 charter-related listings.

A great magazine for charter aficionados is *Cruising World.* It has monthly features on different cruising locales, as well as an annual readers' survey of the best charter companies. Just to let you know how popular cruising vacations are, over 90 percent of the respondents to *Cruising World*'s annual surveys felt that the cost was worth the experience and that their sailing vacation went smoothly. We think that the other 10 percent probably never left the islands!

Bareboat cruising

The most common way to charter is a *bareboat charter,* in which your group rents a *bare* boat from a charter company, without any skipper or paid crew on board.

Planning the trip

Here is the information you need to plan a successful bareboat charter vacation:

- ✔ **About the boat:** One great thing about chartering is that it enables you to try sailing different boats. If a specific boat is important, make sure to get a commitment in writing from your charter company. Keep in mind that a newer boat is probably less likely to have broken equipment, although the top charter companies have fantastic maintenance programs. Ask about the turnaround time between charters; the boat should be at the charter base for at least a day for routine maintenance. Ask about the contingency plan if the boat you request isn't available or isn't ready when you arrive. If you're sailing with a large group, make sure that you get a plan of the boat's sleeping arrangements. (Pick the biggest bunk with a private head!)

- ✔ **The deposit and charter contract:** When you book a charter, expect to pay a deposit (usually 50 percent of the total) several months in advance and receive a charter contract. This contract should include a refund schedule. The average price of a weeklong bareboat charter is about $2,000. Prices vary with the season, type of boat, and location. You can also purchase travel insurance to cover you if you cancel; your charter company should have rates. You may also be asked to prove your sailing ability; often a resume is helpful.

- ✔ **Liability coverage:** Each charter company has its own policy for damage and loss. The typical policy is either a large, refundable deposit ($500 to $2,000) or a small, nonrefundable premium ($20 to $40 per day).

- ✔ **On-site support and repair service:** Make sure that you know how to contact the charter company through VHF or SSB radio (see Chapter 7) and that you know its policy if you need assistance. Cellular phones are becoming more common in popular charter regions. Some charter companies have small support bases throughout the cruising area.

- ✔ **Provisioning the boat:** The charter company can organize partial or full provisioning, saving you a day of shopping in unfamiliar markets. When you get aboard, stow the food yourself so that you know where to find it. Unless cooking in a sailboat-size galley is your idea of a great vacation, we advise you to keep your menus as simple as possible and plan on eating out a bit as part of your vacation budget.

- ✔ **What's included:** You need a rowing dinghy to get to shore; it should be standard equipment. The charter company can organize snorkeling and other watersports gear. We usually bring our own masks and snorkels and rent the fins. Make sure to put any specific gear requests in writing and get a confirmed response.

Having a hibachi grill mounted on the stern pulpit is the best way to cook the fish you're going to catch!

- ✔ **What to bring:** In general, pack much less than you think you need. The charter company can advise you on expected weather conditions. Space is at a premium, especially if you're chartering with several people. See Chapter 3 for tips on clothing needs afloat. And if you're going to subject lily-white skin to the tropic sun, you will want to be able to cover up no matter how warm the weather.

Checking out your craft

Here's what to expect when you arrive at the front door of the charter company, ready to go cruising:

- ✔ **Boat inspection:** Make sure that all the required equipment is on board. Check all lines for signs of wear and make sure that all the winches and blocks are functioning properly. Go over all the equipment with the charter company representative.

- ✔ **Boat orientation:** When you arrive, the charter company representative should give you a thorough orientation to the boat. Make sure that you understand how the onboard systems work, such as the sails, safety equipment, sun shades, ventilation system, windlass system for anchoring, storage, galley facilities, navigation gear and radios, marine heads and showers, and, of course, use of the rowing dinghy.

✔ **Orientation to the cruising area:** Always take the time to sit down with a company representative to look over the nautical chart of the area. You want to be briefed on the local attractions and any hazards. Be sure to ask for help in planning your ideal itinerary as well as backup plans in case of adverse weather.

✔ **Prove your ability:** An old joke in the charter industry goes like this:

Q: What qualifications do you need to be able to bareboat charter?
A: A check that doesn't bounce.

We hope that the charter company has you prove your ability. Certainly, certification to a recognized standard such as the American Sailing Association or US Sailing Bareboat Charter Standard is helpful. If, after a checkout, the charter company doesn't think that you possess the ability to handle the boat, it has the right to refuse your business or give you the opportunity to pay for a captain to come along.

Cruising with a skipper

If you need to be pampered on your vacation, chartering a fully crewed yacht is for you. You can help with the sailing as much or as little as you like. Delicious meals appear at the proper times, and you can just relax and enjoy the sights. Of course, your next bank statement will reflect this first-class treatment. We have seen some truly *awesome* boats, 80 feet (24 m) in length and longer, in the islands on fully crewed charters. They can even rig up the sailboard for you!

One in-between option is to have a partially crewed trip in which you "cruise and learn" the first half of the trip, and then, if the charter company feels that you're qualified, you can go the rest of the way bareboat.

Chartering Skills

What skills do you need to operate a charter boat safely for a week? You should have at least one full sailing season of experience skippering a similar-size boat in similar conditions. Fortunately, most charter destinations are in fairly protected waters. (Who wants to vacation in the middle of the ocean?) Many popular bareboat charter destinations don't require any night sailing, but that, too, is a consideration. Still, if you've mastered sailing on your lake aboard a two-person dinghy but have never been aboard a keelboat, you need to take some lessons and build more experience.

The general description of the American Sailing Association's Bareboat Chartering Standard, to which students can become certified, is instructive:

> An Advanced Cruising Standard for individuals with *cruising experience.* The individual can act as skipper or crew of a 30- to 50-foot boat sailing by day in coastal waters. The Standard includes knowledge of boat systems and maintenance procedures.

Not everyone on the crew needs to be an expert sailor, but at least two should be competent. Here's a list of ten pieces of knowledge and skills that you should possess and be able to demonstrate:

- ✔ **Experience as a skipper on a live-aboard cruise of at least 48 hours.**
- ✔ **Ability to anchor safely, using the equipment provided.**
- ✔ **Ability to interpret the weather forecast.**
- ✔ **Ability to perform coastal piloting by using a nautical chart.**
- ✔ **Understanding of basic safety procedures for the type of boat you are aboard — including man-overboard rescue routines.**
- ✔ **Ability to handle the boat under power in confined areas.**
- ✔ **Understanding of onboard systems, including navigation equipment, engine, marine head, and galley facilities.**
- ✔ **Understanding of etiquette when anchoring in a crowded harbor.**
- ✔ **Ability to instruct and advise nonsailors and less-expert sailors on the operation of the boat and basic safety considerations.**
- ✔ **Ability to sail.** Just tell them you've read *Sailing For Dummies!*

Dinghies — Your Ticket to Shore

Throughout this book, we use the word *dinghy* to describe any sailboat with a centerboard. So far in this chapter, we have referred to a *rowing dinghy* when discussing the small boat that you bring on cruises to get to the beach or dock when your big sailboat is anchored. But enough is enough. Really, we call these boats *dinghies,* too; they just aren't rigged with sails (although some can be). In fact, some have an outboard for power. So for the rest of this chapter on chartering, when we say dinghy, we mean a rowing dinghy. Okay?

A good dinghy is small and light enough to be easily towed behind the boat (or even hauled aboard for longer passages). It should be big enough to carry at least two or three people at one time and seaworthy enough so that you don't need the balance of Baryshnikov to be able to stay right-side-up in the thing. Because your dinghy is often your ticket to freedom on a cruise, you want to make sure that it stays around. Here are some tips to make life afloat with a dinghy more enjoyable:

- ✔ **Bring a paddle:** Your dinghy may be powered by an outboard engine. But make sure that you have some alternate means of propulsion — just in case!

- ✔ **Stop that banging:** Dinghies have a habit of banging against the hull as the wind shifts in the anchorage at 3 a.m. If you tie it alongside with a fender or two, consider padding the hull so that you can sleep through the night.

- ✔ **Tie it securely:** Whether you're towing your dinghy behind the boat or leaving it high and dry on an idyllic beach while you do some exploring, make sure that it's tied up well. Inspect the dinghy's bow line for chafe; if it looks shaky, tie on a new one. On a beach, always secure the dinghy above the highest possible level that the tide and waves can reach.

- ✔ **Tow it safely:** If you decide to pull your dinghy behind you from place to place, then take everything out of the boat (oars, fuel tank, engine, swim fins, and so on) before you get under way. Check with the charter company for its recommendations of dinghy storage. The same principles of safe towing that we cover in Chapter 13 apply. Also, when backing or maneuvering in close quarters, bring the dinghy close alongside so that you don't run over the tow rope.

- ✔ **Watch out for surf:** Don't try landing your dinghy on a beach with breakers the size of the Banzai Pipeline; find a quiet place to make the landing. If you must beach your dinghy in waves, try to time it so that a wave washes you far up the beach, and then quickly climb out and grab the bow line so that it doesn't drift back. Always land bow first and depart bow out. Avoid standing in the water between the dinghy and the beach, because a wave can throw the boat right at you.

Popular Cruising Grounds

This list covers ten of the nicest places we know to go cruising. All of these areas have great charter companies, but you can always sail your own boat there.

- ✔ **Australia's Whitsunday Passage:** Located in the Coral Sea between Queensland and the Great Barrier Reef, the Whitsunday Passage features great diving and a steady southeast trade wind, especially May through August.

- ✔ **Bahamas:** Especially the Abacos (the Family Islands), Eleuthera, and the Exumas, the Bahamas are popular and easily accessible from the U.S. They have plenty of shallow waters, so be attentive to the visual clues of depth and the reading on your depth sounder as well as being

Extreme chartering

Ever dream of rounding Cape Horn or sailing to Antarctica? You can on a crewed charter with expert sailors! A few outfits specialize in expedition-style charters. Peter cruised the Beagle Channel and the region around Cape Horn aboard Skip Novak's 55-foot (17-m) sloop *Pelagic*. You can contact Skip at `http://meridianlink.co.uk/pelagic/home.html` on the Internet, by phone at 44-01703454-120 in the United Kingdom, or at 101671,762 on CompuServe.

a vigilant pilot, as described in Chapter 11. Many safe anchorages in close proximity to each other provide for variety and carefree planning when you're afloat. "We can go mañana, mon."

✔ **Caribbean Islands:** Without doubt, the Caribbean is the number-one charter destination in the world. Especially popular are the U.S. and British Virgin Islands. Great year-round weather (although you may want to avoid hurricane season). These islands are especially good for novice charterers because of the predictable winds, deep waters, numerous protected sailing areas, easy navigation, and plenty of beautiful and safe anchorages.

✔ **Florida Keys:** Easy access from the mainland U.S. to the Sunshine State. The Florida Keys feature warm, shoal waters.

✔ **Great Lakes:** Get out of the nearby big cities, and you would swear that you were in the middle of nowhere when you're on the Great Lakes. Did you know that the water of northern Lake Huron is crystal clear?

✔ **Greek Isles:** Mild, Mediterranean climate — except for winter months. Cruising areas of the Greek Isles can be quite crowded in the peak summer months.

✔ **Maine:** Maine has beautiful cruising grounds, but they're not for beginners. Prime sailing months are July to early September, but the weather is fickle. Secluded anchorages are plentiful. Difficulties for cruising include large tidal ranges, strong currents, possibility of fog, and the rocky coastline.

✔ **New Zealand's Bay of Islands:** Mild enough to sail year-round. Summer is the peak season for the Bay of Islands — February and March.

✔ **Pacific Northwest:** Uncrowded, scenic anchorages are the highlight in the Pacific Northwest. The protected waters of Puget Sound are great cruising grounds, but they have strong currents, big tidal ranges, and cold water.

✔ **South Pacific:** Tahiti, Tonga, and Fiji have big charter fleets. Watch out for cyclones in the South Pacific in the summer months.

Plus, here are a few more (fitting the world in a list of ten is hard):

- **California:** We love the Channel Islands of California — a pristine cruising ground just offshore from Los Angeles.

- **Chesapeake Bay:** We love the softshell crabs of Chesapeake Bay. Just make sure that you have a shallow-draft boat to get to all the neat little harbors on the Eastern Shore.

- **Holland:** Sail the canals of Holland on barges.

- **Mexico:** The waters of the Gulf of California inside Baja, Mexico, can be magical.

- **Scandinavia:** Can you say "fjords"? You will after sailing these waters.

- **Thailand:** An "up and coming" charter destination.

- **Turkey:** We've heard that sailing on the Mediterranean and Black seas off Turkey is beautiful.

The *high season* is the time of the year when a destination is most popular. Weatherwise, high season is the best time to go to a particular place, but be aware that some areas get pretty crowded during this peak season — plus it's more expensive. Table 17-1 outlines the high seasons of ten of the most popular charter destinations.

Table 17-1	Charter Destinations' High Seasons
Location	*High Season*
Bahamas	December to May
Florida	December to April
Caribbean	December to April
Mexico	November to May
South Pacific (Tahiti, Tonga, Fiji, New Caledonia)	April/May and October/November
Australia	December to May
New Zealand	December to April
California	May to November
Greece and Turkey	May to October
New England	June to October

Chapter 18

Cruising with Children

O, well for the fisherman's boy,
That he shouts with his sister at play!
O, well for the sailor lad,
That he sings in his boat on the bay!

— Alfred Lord Tennyson

*H*ere's an important fact: You get to sail more frequently if your family also enjoys the sport. And sailing with your family brings other benefits. Sailing for the day can bring your family closer as you work together to keep the boat moving. On a weeklong cruise, your kids may even discover that some of the "necessities" at home — such as the TV, VCR, and video games — are really luxuries that they can live without.

In this chapter, we look at how to enjoy a sailing trip with your children. We focus mainly on making the most of an extended sailing trip on a bigger sailboat, but we also include information on planning a day trip and on sailing with children on smaller boats.

JJ SAYS

Bonding on the bounding main

I began sailing at a very young age on my parents' 30-foot sailboat. Each summer, we went cruising for a month to the Channel Islands off the coast of Southern California with a dog, at least three kids (often friends came, too), and tons of gear. We had great adventures sailing, snorkeling, swimming, rowing around coves, hiking, collecting shells, reading, and playing on the boat.

My dad worked long hours when I was small, so our monthlong cruise was a wonderful chance for us to see him in action. Dad caught, cleaned, and cooked fish and abalone. Mom had a chance to relax and read books while we were off with Dad, something she could rarely do at home with three children.

Preparing Your Family Crew

A big reason why our daughter, Marly, feels comfortable on a boat is that all the adults feel comfortable having her on board. That comfort level is important. Children are very sensitive to their parents' emotions and can pick up on their fears. If you're afraid to have children on the boat, they're afraid to be there. If you're nervous, try to assess *why* you're concerned and then take concrete steps to conquer those fears.

Teach your children to swim

SAFETY

Probably every parent's biggest fear on a boat is a child drowning. We can't say it often enough: One of the most important things to do before taking your family sailing is to *make sure that everyone can swim*. At this stage, your children's ability to swim and be comfortable in the water is far more important than their knowledge of the finer points of sailing. Plus, when children are confident of their swimming abilities, they seem to learn to sail much more easily because they're more relaxed and more likely to have fun.

When picking a school, make sure that the instructors are trained in the techniques they're teaching *and* know basic safety procedures. In the United States, look for swimming instructors who have first aid, cardiopulmonary resuscitation (CPR), and Water Safety Instructor (WSI) certifications, which are available from the American Red Cross.

If you sail on the ocean, keep in mind that your children won't enjoy swimming in saltwater as much as swimming in a pool at first. Saltwater tastes "funny," stings the eyes, and often isn't as warm as a pool; the waves are hard to handle.

Of course, nonswimmers can enjoy sailing, too. In fact, four-time America's Cup winner Dennis Conner can't swim. Nonswimmers (and small children) should always wear a life jacket. Check out the section "Life jackets and safety harnesses," later in this chapter, and Chapter 7 for more information.

Other preparation considerations

Another important way to prepare your children to go sailing is to teach them about boating safety before you go on the water. Review with your kids the safety information in Chapter 7, especially the information about where the safe areas are on deck.

Having your children learn to sail is obviously an excellent way to prepare them for a family trip. Most children learn to sail very quickly on small dinghies at camp, sailing schools, or with an older friend or relative who sails. See Chapter 2 for where your children can learn to sail.

Picking the Boat

While your crew is getting shipshape, you can think about what kind of boat to ship them out on. The most important factor is the *experience level of the parent.*

We do *not* recommend that novice sailors ever take children sailing on most boats. Novice sailors should try to go sailing with people who have *more* experience than they do. For intermediate sailors, the most important thing is to pick a boat that they feel comfortable in — so that the children feel comfortable and enjoy the experience.

Which boat to use

Beginning sailors, young and old, usually feel more comfortable on a keelboat than aboard a dinghy. A *keelboat* — discussed in greater detail in Chapter 1 — has a heavy, ballasted keel fin under the boat that provides stability and prevents capsizing. *Dinghies* are usually smaller (under 20 feet or 6 m) and have a lightweight, retractable *centerboard* fin instead of a heavy lead keel, and therefore are less stable and can flip over.

Because of their size, keelboats are the only practical choice for extended family trips. Here are some other reasons why keelboats are the best choice even for shorter sails:

When is a child old enough to sail?

A child is never too young to enjoy a sailing trip as long as you, your boat, and your crew are prepared. We've been taking our daughter, Marly, sailing since before she was born. Every summer, we go to Catalina Island — 20 miles off Los Angeles — on my parents' sailboat. Games and books can keep her occupied while we're under way, but her favorite time is while we're at anchor.

As a toddler, Marly saw boats as fun jungle gyms, and she spent hours turning the winches to hear the sounds of the gears. Feeding bits of bread to the fish (and smart seagulls) kept her entertained as well. Now, at age three, she loves fishing with her dad and spends a great deal of time imagining grand adventures — such as catching pretend fish and feeding them to her ever-hungry stuffed animals. (Her favorite is a shark.)

✔ Keelboats often have cabins down below that are handy for nap time, storing snacks, and spreading out toys.

✔ Most keelboats have a deep cockpit, where kids can play safely and see the sights without the risk of falling overboard. A boat over 25 feet (8 m) long probably has lifelines that provide extra security for the very little ones.

✔ Although dinghies offer the thrill of being close to the water, they have less room, and often each crew member has a specific job. That makes caring for the comfort, entertainment, and safety of a small child difficult, no matter how good a sailor you are.

If you're adamant about sailing with your kids, but you've only completed a basic sailing course and have little other experience, then your best boat choice is a small keelboat (under 25 feet) — but *only* daysailing in light and moderate winds in protected waters.

Table 18-1 offers some general guidelines for the *minimum* age of children on various types of boats, given the experience of the sailor.

Note: The table assumes light to moderate wind and sea conditions in protected waters. For the purposes of the table, a *novice* sailor has the equivalent of one basic sailing course and little practical experience; an *intermediate* sailor has completed basic sailing training and has six months to two years of practical experience; and *advanced* sailors have three or more years of experience in a variety of wind conditions. An "x" indicates that we don't recommend that novice sailors take children of any age on these boats.

Table 18-1   Suggested Minimum Age of Child on Different Boats

Type of Boat	Novice	Skill Level of Adult Intermediate	Advanced
Dinghy under 13 ft (4 m)	x	10 years old	5 years old
Dinghy over 13 ft (4 m)	x	6 years old	3 years old
Keelboat 18-25 ft (6-8 m)	10 years*	6 years old	Newborn
Keelboat over 25 ft (6-8 m)	x	6 years old	Newborn

* For novice sailors, we recommend sailing with children on a small keelboat only if the children are good swimmers and are comfortable in new situations.

If you choose a dinghy

In our experience, the scariest parts about dinghy sailing for small children are the sudden changes in *heel* — the tipping motion — and the fear of capsizing. But if you're taking the kids out in a dinghy, here are some tips to make the day a success:

- ✔ Warm day, warm water, warm clothes — make sure that the kids will be warm enough, even if they get wet.

- ✔ Before you leave the dock or beach, talk about heeling. Put them in the boat and show them how to move their weight to counteract heel.

- ✔ Run through what to do if the boat capsizes (see Chapter 7). Go on the water and do a controlled capsize (where you pull the boat over) so that they can see how easy it is to get the boat upright.

- ✔ Be prepared to move your weight around often to minimize heeling while sailing.

- ✔ Hold on tight to the little ones so that they feel secure.

- ✔ If possible, let your children sit in the center of the boat in a secure spot where they can hold on.

- ✔ Be confident so that your children feel confident, too.

- ✔ Make sure that you and your children are wearing life jackets.

Picking the Right Trip

Although keeping children happy on long-distance trips is quite possible, short sails interspersed with longer periods at anchor or dockside at your destinations are best, unless you don't mind being asked "When are we going to get there?" a million times.

✔ **Distance:** Keep the first few trips short. Begin with afternoon daysails, then try an overnight trip, and slowly work toward your big goal.

✔ **Climate:** If you must head out in cooler climes, make sure that everyone has enough clothing to stay warm and dry. For some advice on what to wear, see Chapter 3.

Childproofing Your Boat

Sailing safety begins before you get under way. Before your family steps onto a cruising sailboat, keep these safety precautions in mind:

✔ **Weave netting onto the lifelines.** Netting, as shown in Figure 18-1, provides a barrier between your child (and toys and pets) and the water. Even with netting, never leave your child unsupervised on deck.

✔ **Don't allow leaning over or through the lifelines — netting or not.**

✔ **Rule out running (especially while under way).**

✔ **Ensure that any lifeline gates have clasps that little fingers can't undo.**

✔ **Look at where a child would land if he or she fell down the hatch.** Are there any sharp corners in the cabin that should be padded?

✔ **Put an awning over the cockpit while at anchor.** Sunburn can ruin a child's enjoyment of sailing. Awnings provide a shady, cool resting spot.

Figure 18-1:
Weave
netting onto
the lifelines
of your
boat.

Practicing Safety on the Water

So, after you childproof the boat for your children, your job's over, right? You know better than that. A parent's job is never over, and that's especially true while sailing.

Life jackets and safety harnesses

Do you let your small child go for a car ride without getting in a car seat? Probably not. The same consistency will help you get your child to always wear a life jacket on the water. See Chapter 7 for information regarding life jackets. When purchasing a child's life jacket, look for the following specifics:

- ✔ A bright color for visibility. Reflective tape is great, too. You want to be able to spot the child quickly if he falls in the water.

- ✔ A strap between the legs to keep the jacket from slipping off.

- ✔ The Personal Floatation Device should not be so bulky that the child can't put both hands together in front (or else he won't be able to hold on properly).

If you're still nervous about your child being near the water even in a life jacket, test it in the pool first.

Many families who live aboard a sailboat use safety harnesses instead of life jackets while at sea. A safety harness provides the ultimate security from falling overboard and allows a child freedom to move around without the bulk of the life jacket. A safety harness should fit a child snugly without falling off the shoulders and, for small children, should have a strap between the legs. The tether can be attached in front or in back and should be clipped onto a solid fitting in the center of the boat, as shown in Figure 18-2. Make sure that the tether is short enough that the child can't reach the water. (See Chapter 7 for more on harnesses.)

Keeping tabs on the kids

Watching your child play around a boat is like watching your child play near a busy street — real danger lurks close by, and parents must know where their children are at every moment.

When Marly is on a boat, knowing that she can swim reassures us because we know that she won't panic if she falls in. But we still *never* leave her alone on deck for even a second.

Figure 18-2:
A safety
harness is
safe only if
the tether is
properly
clipped on.

Here are some safety rules and guidelines to get you started when cruising with kids:

- ✔ Children can only be on deck with an adult, and children have to tell the adult when they are going back down below.

- ✔ While sailing, children can't go on deck without an adult's permission nor without their safety harness and/or life jacket.

- ✔ Know all the ways that children can get on deck — they may surprise you by opening and climbing through the front hatch by themselves.

- ✔ Know when you are "on watch." We always hand off the caretaker's responsibility verbally.

- ✔ Be just as careful when you're at the dock.

Earning the right to go on their own

As a child, getting to go off in the rowboat by yourself or with your friends is a big step. As a parent, watching your older child head off in the rowboat for the first time is as nerve-wracking as letting your child ride his bike to a friend's house a few blocks away for the first time (even though the peace and tranquillity after they're gone is well worth it). The key is to teach the kids about safety and set some guidelines.

Your older children need to master several skills before heading off on their own:

> ✔ **They must know how to handle the equipment.** They must know how to operate and get a boat onto and off a beach safely, and how to tie secure knots if docking the boat.

> ✔ **They must be prepared for emergencies.** Practice a man-overboard drill, what to do if the boat swamps, and how to propel the boat if they lose one oar. Review the appropriate safety information covered in Chapter 7.

> ✔ **They have to prove that they will act responsibly.** Responsible behavior includes continuing to wear their life jackets even when they're out of sight and being careful with the equipment.

> ✔ **They have to know about wind direction, tides, currents, and rocks in the area.** Rowing upwind or upcurrent can be exhausting or impossible. Before they go, review Chapter 11 on navigation and look at a chart of the area with your children.

Having a second rowing dinghy, kayak, or some other means of transportation while they're gone is pretty nice for you and can be crucial for safety (in other words, a rescue) if they don't come back. If you don't have another boat, make sure that you have a plan to borrow one if things go wrong.

Essentially, you must make sure that your children feel comfortable and safe in the boat. Then you can trust them while they're off having fun — because, as the Water Rat says in *The Wind in the Willows,* "There is nothing . . . half so much worth doing as simply messing about in boats."

Letting Children Help on the Boat

Even if your children have never had a sailing lesson, they can learn a great deal from a day on the water, especially if you let them help with certain jobs.

Children can do almost anything on a boat with adult supervision, but certain jobs, including the following, can always be in the kids' domain:

> ✔ **Making all the lines shipshape.** Both of us spent hours as kids carefully coiling all the ropes.

> ✔ **Putting up the flag in the morning and taking it down at night (see Figure 18-3).**

> ✔ **Relaying commands when anchoring or mooring.**

> ✔ **Scrubbing the decks.** Or else they can walk the plank!

> ✔ **Stowing fenders and and dock lines.**

> ✔ **Tying knots.**

JJ SAYS

School stuff afloat

Letting older children help study the chart, plot the course, and dead-reckon (all navigational skills covered in Chapter 11) can be a great way to put your child's math and geometry skills to work while improving map-reading skills. Celestial navigation is also a mind-bender, but even if you don't own a sextant, being out on the water is a great time to explore the joys of astronomy. On a boat you are surrounded by nature, both above and below the water; bring some books along to make identifying your wild companions easier.

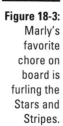

Figure 18-3: Marly's favorite chore on board is furling the Stars and Stripes.

TIP

Of course, the job your children want most of all is steering. Unlike handing over the keys to the family wagon, steering a sailboat is a safe way for kids to satisfy the "Dad, let me drive" urge. It's also a great chance to give them an introductory sailing lesson.

Enjoying a Longer Trip

This section has tips for what gear and books to bring to keep older kids happy on a longer trip — and how to sail with a baby without filling an entire bunk with baby paraphernalia. Obviously, you have the best idea of what to bring to keep your kids happy, but here are some suggestions.

Rock-a-bye, baby

At anchor, letting a baby sleep on the floor, up forward so that no one steps on him, is easier than worrying about him falling (or climbing) out of a bunk. Figure out a safe place to leave a wakeful baby in case all hands are needed on deck.

For sleeping under way, make sure that the bunks have *leecloths* — a piece of fabric that creates a soft "wall" on the "downhill" side of the bunk, or a *bunkboard* — a removable wood slat that serves as a wall to the bunk — so that a sleeping body doesn't roll out when the boat tips.

First and foremost — food. Nothing makes sailors grumpier than running out of food, even on an afternoon sail. With all the new experiences that your children have while sailing, they find it comforting to eat their favorite foods at mealtime. And although getting back to nature and fishing for your meals is great, assume in your packing that the fish won't be biting.

Sailing with baby

On a longer sailing trip with a baby, using disposable diapers probably makes sense, because cleaning cloth diapers can run through your water supply very quickly. Disposables take up a great deal of space, though, and you need to pack plenty of plastic bags to keep those used diapers sealed well until you can throw them into a trash can on shore.

You can leave the portable crib at home — it takes up too much space, and the cockpit (with a canvas awning to protect baby from the sun) works great as a playpen.

Keeping it clean

One of the great things about sailing is the way you're in tune with nature. Over the years, we have watched certain bodies of water get cleaner, while others seem to have more junk floating in them every day. Because our children will inherit this Earth, we should set a good example both ashore and afloat.

Keep our waters clean. If you live in the U.S., check the Coast Guard's regulations on dumping, rules which are quite strict if you sail close to the shore. Always *pack out* your garbage when sailing. Our friend Cam Lewis (who set a record sailing around the world in 79 days nonstop on a catamaran!) made his crew keep and store all their garbage in plastic bags. Avoid chemical and fuel spills. And teach your children at an early age how important clean water is to us all!

We use a bucket as a portable bathtub for babies while on board, and a *sunshower* (a black plastic bag filled with freshwater that is warmed by the sun) works well for keeping older kids clean (and adults, too). A sunshower is shown in Figure 18-4.

Figure 18-4:
A sun-shower is the closest thing to a hot shower on a sailboat.

Tips for pregnant moms-to-be

So you think a pregnancy rules out sailing? Not so. In fact, I sailed in the U.S., Japan, and Spain while pregnant. A quick tip for pregnant sailors: Your center of gravity is higher than usual — so be extra careful when you step into a tippy dinghy (especially if you're as big as I was and can't see your feet).

Also, even if you haven't had any morning sickness or don't usually get seasick, the motion on a sailboat may make you feel queasy during pregnancy. Of course, pregnant women can't take seasickness medicine. I tried the acupressure wrist bands, and they seemed to help me. I also kept a supply of saltines, apples, and ginger ale handy and always tried to keep a little food in my stomach. For more tips on combating seasickness, see Appendix A.

Packing the right gear

Even if you're like JJ and the thought of baiting a hook with a piece of squid makes you gag, the kids may want to spend all day fishing. The following are suggestions for gear to keep the kids entertained when you're at anchor:

- ✔ **Extra buckets for holding "beach finds" such as hermit crabs**
- ✔ **Fishing poles and gear**
- ✔ **Snorkels, masks, and fins, as well as "viewfinders," which are great for watching the creatures on the bottom from a rowboat**

Watch out for games and toys with small parts that can get lost on deck — some games may have to remain below. Designate a certain area (an out-of-the-way space like an aft cabin) to store toys, games, and invaluable collections of shells and rocks.

We've mentioned how useful buckets are as baby washtubs and hermit crab houses, besides their regular function for *swabbing* (cleaning) the decks. But be careful when trying to fill a bucket by dunking it over the side while under way: The force of the water can pull the bucket out of your hand — or pull a child overboard.

Books to bring

Children on a boat read more than they do at home (especially if you ditch the portable video games). And they may surprise you by reading thicker and older books than you expect. So in addition to the romances and mysteries that you tote on board, make sure to pack books for your kids, too. Many good books are available for younger kids about sailing and sealife. At age three, Marly has already memorized *The Owl and the Pussycat,* by Edward Lear. Here are some other books we hope she enjoys (because we have) when she gets a bit older:

- ✔ *Dove,* Robin Lee Graham
- ✔ *Maiden Voyage,* Tania Aebi
- ✔ *The Kon Tiki Expedition,* Thor Heyerdahl
- ✔ *Around the World in Eighty Days,* Jules Verne
- ✔ *Around the World in Seventy-Nine Days,* Cam Lewis and Michael Levitt
- ✔ *Jonathan Livingston Seagull,* Richard Bach
- ✔ *Treasure Island,* Robert Louis Stevenson

> ✔ *Island of the Blue Dolphins,* Scott O'Dell
>
> ✔ *The Voyage of the Dawn Treader,* C.S. Lewis

And don't forget to pack the encyclopedia-type books with information about the stars, weather, local birds, fish, rocks, and shells!

Spinnaker flying — nature's roller coaster ride

When you and your family are seasoned sailors, a fun way to spend the afternoon while anchored is to position the boat so that the kids can go *spinnaker flying,* as shown in the figure. You need moderate winds and warm water, and then follow these steps:

1. Anchor the boat in the wrong direction — with the stern into the wind. (See Chapter 9 on anchoring.)

2. Secure a bosun's chair as a seat to slide along a line attached to both lower corners of the spinnaker. Hook the top of the spinnaker to the halyard.

3. Tie an extra-long safety retrieving line from one clew (lower corner of the sail) to the bow of your boat.

4. Have your friends on deck hoist the spinnaker, but keep it from filling by having someone pull on the retrieving line hard to keep the sail luffing close to the water.

5. Jump in the water with a friend.

6. Climb into the chair and slide it along to the center point of the rope between the two corners.

7. Release the retrieving line and have a friend in the water help spread the corners of the sail so that the wind catches it, and off you go!

On a puffy day, spinnaker flying can make for a wild ride!

Chapter 19

Caring for Your Craft

. . . .

In This Chapter

▶ Maintaining your boat and sails

▶ Choosing the right gear

▶ Using the engine

▶ Storing your boat

. . . .

> *It is time to be old,*
> *To take in sail.*

— Ralph Waldo Emerson

*I*n this chapter, we talk about the skills and techniques involved in outfitting and caring for your boat and its parts. Thirty years ago, this subject was a much bigger part of boat ownership, but as builders have shifted from wood to fiberglass, maintenance has become much easier. For those who prefer to leave the grunt work to others, you can choose from a virtual plethora of boatyard and marine maintenance professionals. Plus, you can rent boats from charter companies and sailing clubs and avoid any maintenance work. (See Chapter 17 on chartering and Chapter 2 on finding sailing clubs.)

Doing basic maintenance on our own boat is fun, and we hope that this chapter makes you feel the same way. When it comes to the major repairs, however, we usually turn to the pros, not because we can't do the job, but because that kind of project takes forever and never seems to come out as nice when we do it ourselves.

Keeping Things Shipshape

In the grand old days of Admiral Horatio Nelson's British Navy, the crew of a square rigger would *holystone,* or scrub, the decks every day at dawn in all but the most extreme conditions. Unused sails had to be furled with a military precision rivaling the beds of today's U.S. Marines. This tradition of keeping your boat looking good, with everything in its proper place and stored absolutely correctly, is still with us today. Part of the tradition is simply good seamanship and part is pride of ownership. Your boat and your sails are a reflection on you — and you don't walk around town with seagull poop on your head, do you?

Regular inspection of your boat for wear and tear helps avoid problems on the water. Many parts of the boat show signs of rust or stress cracks prior to breaking. The key is knowing where to look to find signs of a worn-out part — and remembering to look. In this chapter, we start by looking at the areas requiring the most regular maintenance (the lines, rigging, and sails) and then cover the mast, hull, and engine (if you have one).

Running Rigging

Running rigging, as we cover in Chapter 1, is all the control lines and gear used to adjust the sails and includes the sheets and halyards. Because running rigging gets a real workout every time you sail, you need to keep it in top condition — you can't sail a sailboat with a broken mainsheet. So we talk first about something every boat has plenty of — rope.

A few lines about line

In Chapter 5, we define line as "rope with a purpose." Because all the millions of ropes on a sailboat have some use, they're all called lines, although Peter still uses the word *rope* sometimes — very uncouth. When selecting a line, consider the following characteristics in determining what is appropriate for the task at hand.

- ✔ **Strength:** All lines used as running rigging should be made of some sort of synthetic material because of its superior performance. Lately, most of the rope we use on racing boats has a space-age Vectran, Spectra, or Kevlar core — very light and incredibly strong.

  Different lines have different strength needs, depending upon what they're used for. A jib sheet must be stronger than a mainsail cunningham. An anchor or tow line should be strong but very stretchy. Your man-overboard retrieval line should float, as we discuss in Chapter 7. A dock line should be strong and very resistant to chafe. Some storage applications may call for incredibly stretchy rope called *bungee cord* or *shock cord*.

- ✔ **Diameter:** A line increases in strength with its diameter. Some high-tech fibers are stronger than the same diameter of wire. Comfort is most important in a line that you hold onto constantly — that's why you want a relatively thick, fuzzy mainsheet. If a line must pass through several pulleys and is usually kept cleated (like a block-and-tackle backstay adjuster), you should opt for smaller line for less friction (and smaller, less expensive blocks).

- ✔ **Color:** If every rope on the boat is white, life gets pretty confusing (not to mention boring).

- ✔ **Cost:** Check out the rope department in your local marine store (most hardware stores don't stock good sailing rope), and you see why so many boats have white polyester line — all those fancy colors and high-tech materials are EXPENSIVE!

- ✔ **Feel:** A rope that is softer and smoother is easier to hold — but more expensive (and you may wear gloves anyway).

Laid rope versus braided rope

Rope that has three visible, primary strands twisted in a spiral is called *laid* rope. Laid rope, which is usually less expensive, is common in dock lines and tow lines. However, for the running rigging in your boat, *braided* rope is much nicer. As the name implies, braided rope looks like the tiny fibers have been braided together. Braided rope often has an inner core (where those space-age fibers are used) that carries most of the load. Laid and braided rope are shown in Figure 19-1.

Figure 19-1:
Laid line (left) and braided line (with core, on right) with their component parts exposed.

Using splices

In Appendix B, we show how to put a loop in a line by tying a bowline knot. Another, much more permanent way to make a rope loop is an *eye splice*. Eye splices are neater, less bulky than knots, and are commonly found at the working end of a halyard (where the rope attaches to a shackle) and at the end of an anchor line. They're time-consuming for a beginner to create, but a professional rigger can whip one up in under five minutes (but will probably charge for an hour!). If the splice will have a major load (like an anchor line), you must insert a *thimble* (metal or plastic teardrop-shaped fitting) into the loop to distribute the load and prevent chafe. Figure 19-2 shows an eye splice at the end of a braided line halyard attached to a snap shackle (on the left) and an eye splice at the end of a laid line anchor rope with a thimble inserted to prevent chafe (on the right).

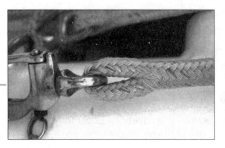

Figure 19-2:
Two examples of eye splices.

Your local marine store should have a book about knots and splices. (You will discover that there are more types of both than you could ever learn!)

Going to the bitter end

No matter what kind of rope you use, the very end of it can be a problem area if it starts to fray — because the usable part of the line gets shorter and shorter. The easiest solution for most ropes is simply to melt the end with a butane lighter, some matches, or a special *hot knife* (commonly found in the rope department of a marine store). With braided rope, sometimes the inner core won't burn. So pull out and cut off a few inches of the inner core. Then slide the cover over and melt that part of the cover. If burning doesn't work, you can always tie an overhand knot in the end (a temporary fix), wrap tape around it, or *whip* it, as shown in Figure 19-3.

Whipping, the old-fashioned way to secure a splice or the end of a rope, requires the use of a special sailmaker's needle and strong synthetic thread. Wrap the thread tightly around the rope to hold it together, and then stitch the thread securely through the rope so that it doesn't unravel during use. Burning the rope's end "outside" the whipping is still a good idea.

Caring for your line

You should securely coil and store any line not in use. (We discuss how to coil a line in Chapter 6.) If you sail in saltwater, flush the wet lines with fresh-water after sailing. Hang wet line where it can dry and try to store it (when-ever practical) out of the incredibly damaging rays of the sun. Check your ropes periodically for wear, especially where they commonly load up on a

Whipping

Figure 19-3:
A whipping
used at the
end of a
rope to
keep it from
unraveling.

pulley or other corner. To extend the life of your ropes, consider switching
your halyards and sheets end for end occasionally — sort of the yachting
equivalent of rotating your tires.

Sailing gear

Now we focus on the fittings that help your lines do their work — the winches,
blocks, shackles, and cleats. As mentioned previously, a key part of caring
for this gear is visual maintenance — looking for hairline cracks in metal
parts, signs of corrosion, or other indications that things aren't quite right.

Blocks

Your boat has many of these pulleys; they're probably hanging from the
boom, bolted to the deck, and built into your mast (see Chapter 6). Blocks
come in all different sizes and shapes and must be matched to the task at
hand, or they may cause problems. Here are the key considerations:

- ✔ **Strength:** The manufacturer provides information on the working load.
  Usually (but not always), the bigger the block, the stronger. The size of
  the metal strap or shackle used to attach the block to the boat indicates the block's strength. A block that is too weak starts to deform.
  Often, a sticky *sheave* (the moving wheel-shaped part that the rope
  turns over) is the first sign of problems.

- ✔ **Proper use:** Some blocks are designed specifically for wire; they often
  have metal sheaves. If you put wire on a rope block, the sheave can
  crack or wear a groove in it. Also, don't use too thick a rope in a block.
  Err on using too small a rope diameter, and you have less friction.

The great thing about most sailing blocks is that they're very low maintenance. Rinse any block with freshwater after a day of sailing in saltwater, and all blocks appreciate being stored out of those ultraviolet rays. Some blocks require occasional lubrication; however, check with the manufacturer's directions first, as the lubricant may gum up the works. Often, the way the block is attached to the boat — by its shackle — is the weak link.

Shackles

Shackles are everywhere on your boat, just like blocks. There are twist shackles, snap shackles, brummel hooks, and captive pin shackles, to name a few. Here are the considerations when picking out, installing, and maintaining shackles:

- **Strength:** The shackle's manufacturer specifies the safe working load; however, you can get a good idea of its strength by looking at the diameter of the metal.

- **Accessibility:** A *snap shackle* is the easiest type of shackle to open, but it can be large and expensive. The *D-shaped shackle* is by far the most common, but it's more difficult to open in a hurry.

- **Security:** Shackles, especially the ones that are attached to the corners of the sails, can really get flapped about when the sails are luffing. Wrapping duct tape around a snap shackle keeps it from opening accidentally. D-shaped shackles are often secured by a screw pin; tighten it securely with a wrench. As with any nut and bolt, be careful not to cross-thread these shackles.

  Other D-shaped shackles have a *clevis pin* with a *cotter pin* or *ring ding* securing it, as shown in Figure 19-4. Ring dings are easier to put on and take off, but they must be taped so that they don't catch something and open up. Cotter pins should not be too long and should be spread open, with the ends bent out just enough to facilitate removing the pins in an emergency, and taped, because their points are very sharp.

Winches

In Chapters 4 and 6, we discuss winches and the techniques for using them. Because of their many moving parts, they need more attention than pulleys. The manufacturer's literature or the folks at the local marine store can help you pick out a winch (although most boats already have plenty) and maintenance supplies. In the following list, we provide the keys to maintaining your winches.

- **Clean your winch:** Take the winch totally apart at least once a year (doing so is sort of like playing with an erector set — just don't forget where each piece goes!) and clean all the internal metal parts. A big bucket with an inch or so of gasoline or paint thinner in it and a toothbrush make a great washtub and scrubber. Lay out a huge drop cloth and have plenty of rags for this very messy job.

Ring dings   Cotter pins

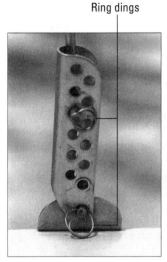

Figure 19-4:
Clevis pins
secured by
ring dings
(left) and by
cotter pins
(right).

✔ **Keep your winch salt-free:** Flush it with freshwater after use and make sure that all the drain holes around its base are open so that any rainwater can escape.

✔ **Lubricate your winch:** Check for any special instructions from the manufacturer. After taking the drum off and setting it aside, inspect and lubricate all the moving parts and bearing surfaces. Pay special attention to the *pawls,* which allow the winch to spin one way and not the other, shown in Figure 19-5. The pawls should swing easily with the touch of a finger, with the spring providing sufficient power to return it to the "open" position. If they don't move freely after cleaning and a lube, replace both spring and pawl. Inspect and lubricate your winches at least twice a year (and more if you use the boat frequently).

Pawl

Figure 19-5:
Checking
the pawls
inside a
winch.

Don't forget — regular visual inspection is important. Pay attention to how well the winch works, and be especially concerned about any jerking under load or weird noises. Also, when you have the winch apart for lubrication, take a close look at all the internal parts for wear or signs of fatigue.

Inspecting the Mast

As you know by now, a mast is supported by wires called, as a group, the *standing rigging*. In Chapter 13, we discuss the potential hazardous consequences of one of a sailor's biggest nightmares — a dismasting.

To inspect your mast, start by making sure that it is straight (or *in column*) by looking up the mast at its base. On a keelboat with shrouds, you can adjust the *turnbuckles* (devices used to maintain correct tension) to get the mast straight. If your mast is crooked, ask a local rigger to help.

Depending on your use of the boat, you may have to inspect your mast twice a year, every month, or even more often — especially after sailing in heavy weather, when things get stressed to the maximum. On a dinghy or small boat, you can take the mast down to inspect it. For a larger boat, you have to send someone up the mast.

To hoist someone up the mast, you need a *bosun's chair* — a harness-type device that provides a "seat" and can be attached to the halyard. You may need to use a winch if the person going up is heavy. Never trust your safety to a halyard shackle; always tie the halyard rope with a bowline to the bosun's chair. The person going aloft should be ready for a wild ride if you're under way, especially if there are waves, because the motion of the ocean is accentuated at the top of the mast. Always ensure that any tools or hard objects (which can put a major dent in the deck if they fall) are secure when going aloft. For that same reason, never stand beneath anyone who is working up in the rig.

Whenever possible when going aloft, use a second halyard as a backup. You don't want to find out about a worn halyard when you're up the mast!

Examine the following areas for signs of stress or damage:

- **Mast section:** Dents and cracks are bad — so are missing rivets.

- **Sheaves:** Every halyard has a sheave that you need to examine and possibly even lubricate.

- **Spreaders:** Try moving the spreaders by shaking them at the end. Movement is bad, unless they're clearly designed to move laterally (fore and aft at the tip). Look for fatigue at the inside end and check the attachment to the shrouds.

✔ **Standing rigging:** The ends of the standing rigging, where they're terminated into some sort of loop or fitting for attachment, are the first places to look. Check carefully, because a broken stay is a sure way to lose a mast. As with all metal fittings, look for cracks, signs of deformation, and corrosion.

✔ **Tangs:** *Tangs* are the attachment points for the standing rigging.

✔ **Turnbuckles:** Some turnbuckles — which are adjustment devices used primarily to tighten rods — are on deck; some may be aloft. These should be lubricated when they're tuned under load.

✔ **Water pockets:** Anywhere that water can sit is a prime location for corrosion. Look under taped fittings and anywhere else water may hang out.

Maintaining Your Sails

Sails are your boat's engine, so keep them well oiled and in tune.

Folding sails

After use, a sail should be put away in a manner that is easy on both the sail and you. Some racers roll their sails after a day on the water. Rolling may be easier on the sailcloth, but doing so is a cumbersome task. An easier way is folding the sail.

You can easily roll sails that are fully battened, like most catamaran mainsails, because the battens provide support, like a venetian blind. Rolling these sails is preferable to taking out all the battens and then folding the sail.

You can fold sails from bottom to top with creases horizontal to the foot, like an accordion. Mainsails on keelboats can be flaked in this manner right on top of the boom for easy storage, as shown in Figure 19-6.

All sails can be folded in the following manner:

1. **Pick your spot and stretch the sail out to its full size (if possible).**

   Find a spot that is at least as long and wide as a single fold on which to fold the sail. Grass lawns make great sail folding surfaces; parking lots are bad because they're rough and dirty.

Figure 19-6:
A mainsail flaked on the boom and secured with ropes or sail ties.

2. **Remove the battens.**

   Except for the very short, permanently installed battens found in the leeches of some jibs, remove all the battens so that you can fold the sail into a smaller bundle.

3. **Stretch the foot out and, with one person at the tack and one at the clew, begin folding the sail like an accordion, starting at the bottom, as shown in Figure 19-7.**

   Pull against each other just enough to define the crease of the next fold.

Figure 19-7:
Folding a sail — start at the bottom and work up.

4. Work to the top.

Each fold should be approximately the same width — about 1 foot (30 cm) wide for a dinghy sail and 3 feet (1 m) or more for a 50-foot (15-m) keelboat sail.

5. Roll it up and bag it.

When you reach the head of the sail, begin rolling or folding the sail lengthwise into a shape that fits in the sail bag.

Storing sails

Here are some tips to consider when you're putting sails away after a day on the water:

✔ **Keep all the pieces together.** If battens or other fittings come with the sail, store them with the sail in its bag.

✔ **Keep them out of the sun.** The sun's ultraviolet light degrades sailcloth and the stitching that holds the seams together. Therefore, you should cover the sails or store them away from the sun's rays while you aren't using them.

✔ **Minimize the creases.** If you don't have to roll them up into a tiny bundle, don't. Try not to crease any plastic windows.

✔ **Store them dry.** If you're going to sail again tomorrow, you don't have to dry your wet sails, but if you plan to store your sails for longer than a few days, make sure that they're dry. A lawn or the deck of your boat can be a good spot for spreading the sails out to dry. If you're storing them for the winter, take the extra effort to rinse the salt off, too.

Caring for your sails

Most sails suffer their worst damage when you're under way. Here are some ways to keep your sails looking good and holding together longer:

✔ **Don't let them flap too much.** Luffing degrades sails faster than the sun. In the America's Cup, crews actually keep track of the number of times a sail is tacked because it flaps when it tacks, shortening the sail's competitive life. Never leave your sails luffing at anchor or at the dock.

✔ **Don't sail without battens.** Without their support, the sail becomes overloaded in the region around the missing batten.

✔ **Don't use them in too much wind.** Some sails, especially spinnakers, are made out of lightweight cloth that can blow out in moderate wind.

> ✔ **Inspect the seams, batten pockets, and corners for wear and tear.** Sails usually blow out in these places. If they look questionable, take them to a sailmaker, drag out your needle and thread, or slap on some of that sticky-back tape we discuss in Chapter 13.
>
> ✔ **Protect them from chafe.** Common chafe locations occur where the sails hit the spreader and the lifelines during tacks. A layer of sticky-back applied over the at-risk location provides sufficient protection.

When your sails do get a rip or a hole, have a sailmaker fix it. However, you can always refer to Chapter 13 if you're in a "do it yourself" frame of mind.

Caring for the Hull

As you hose off your boat after sailing, take a good look at some of the high-load areas where serious structural problems may be apparent. Keep your eye open for cracks or signs of water leakage that indicate weak areas. Sometimes, supposedly "stainless steel" fasteners attached to the hull begin to show signs of rust. If possible, apply a light amount of force and "shake" any attached fittings to see whether they're still secure. Here are some parts of the hull and deck above the water line that come under high loads and should be inspected after each sail:

> ✔ *Chain plates* **(metal fittings on the side of boats to which the shrouds are attached)**
>
> ✔ **Jib tracks**
>
> ✔ **Main traveler and mainsheet**
>
> ✔ **Mast step and *partners* (the point where the mast leaves the deck)**
>
> ✔ **Attachment point of other fittings**

Under Your Boat

If your sailboat is a dinghy, you may be able to flip it upside down on shore easily to look at and work on the underside of the hull. Keelboats are most easily inspected on a trailer or other support on dry land — or you can always don a mask and snorkel. The same principles and guidelines apply under the waterline as those above the waterline. Pay attention to the following high-load areas:

> ✔ **The attachment point of your foils (keel/centerboard and rudder):** Look for small, horizontal cracks that can develop where the lead keel meets the hull or keel stub, or rust stains around the keel bolts. Ask a professional to look at any problem areas.

✔ **The steering system:** Check the rudder and its attachment points for signs of wear and tear. If you have a wheel, check the *quadrant* (bracket around the rudder post that connects to the steering cables) and steering cables.

✔ **The propeller shaft and its support structure (if you have an inboard engine)**

Most dinghies and keelboats that are *drysailed* (stored out of the water when not sailing) are happy with their original gel coat bottom. If your boat lives in the water, it probably already has *anti-fouling bottom paint* on it. This stuff inhibits the growth of barnacles and slimy grass. If you're considering a new coat of anti-fouling bottom paint, check with a local boatyard to find out about any restrictions in your waters. Certain types of these toxic paints are restricted, especially in clean freshwater lakes.

When selecting a bottom paint, consider the manufacturer's information. Certain types of paints work better for different situations. We like to refer to *Practical Sailor* (203-661-6111), the *"Consumer Reports"* of the sailing world, when considering things like this.

Engine

Hey, isn't this a book about sailing? Yes, but most larger (over 25 feet or 8 m) keelboats have a noisemaker that can come in handy when docking in tight situations, in emergencies, and when, heaven forbid, the wind dies.

Using the engine

Because we haven't yet discussed the operation of engines, now is as good a time as any. First, read your owner's manual; it's the best source of operation information. Here are some general operating rules for all types of engines:

✔ **Don't count on reverse:** We discuss operating a boat under power in docking situations in Chapter 6. Just remember, the reverse gear's effect, if you're moving forward at any significant speed, is laughable, so don't count on a blast of reverse to be able to stop the boat.

✔ **Look for water:** Most inboard engines have water-coolant and exhaust exit holes or pipes visible from on deck. These are often in the transom. When you start the engine, confirm that water is coming out (usually a slow, pulsing flow) of the exhaust — this means the cooling system is working properly.

✔ **Slow down to shift:** Hey, this isn't a rental car. Idle the throttle down to a bare minimum before shifting gears.

✔ **Ventilate first:** Explosive fumes from all sorts of sources can collect in the bilge of your boat. Make sure that the area around the engine (which can get hot and often has sparks involved) is ventilated before starting. If the boat has a *blower,* a fan in the engine compartment, run it for a minute or more. Make sure that the cabin of the boat has been open for a while, and check below for any funny smells before starting the engine.

✔ **Watch the temperature:** A high temperature tells you that you have a cooling system problem (often a plastic bag sucked into the intake). Avoid operating your engine at maximum throttle — doing so may cause overheating. Watch the RPM meter if you have one, and keep the RPMs at or below the engine's safe operating speed. If your manual doesn't tell you this speed, check with a professional for advice.

Caring for the engine

Like with your car, you probably want to leave the major (and maybe even the minor) stuff to a professional. Maintaining the engine in your boat is very, very important. The saltwater environment, often less-than-pristine fuel sources, and operation at various angles of heel can wreak havoc on the best power plant. Here are some important points to remember:

✔ **Change your oil.** Do it regularly; it's the lifeblood of any engine. Check the oil level regularly.

✔ **Check your filters.** Along with having an adequate fuel filter, you should have a water separator/sedimenter in the fuel line — check and clean it regularly.

✔ **Rinse out that salt.** Saltwater corrodes metal. You can flush the cooling systems of most outboard engines with freshwater by using a special set of ears that attach to a hose. Rinse off all the external parts of the engine with freshwater.

✔ **Take along spares.** If you plan on making a longer trip, make sure that you have some common spare parts and know how to install them. Ask your engine mechanic for a good list and instructions.

Leaving Your Boat

When the sailing is over and it's time to go home, you want to make sure that your boat is happy and safe while you're away.

Short-term

If you will be back to the boat in the next few days, or even within the month, here are some tips to make sure that your boat is ready to go again when you decide to take it out for another spin:

- **Minimize water collection:** Dinghies can be stored upside down if you take down the mast. If you leave the mast up, try to angle the boat so that rainwater drains out quickly. Many boats have drain plugs on the stern for this purpose. Most cockpits of keelboats drain automatically, but make sure that all hatches and openings are well sealed. A cover over the boom tied to the rails can also help keep the rain out.

- **No dents, please:** Be careful when storing your dinghy on land. If stored with the mast up, make sure that the hull is supported in several locations, not a single point where the hull can depress and weaken. If stored upside down, consider where the deck is strongest — often at the very bow, near the chain plates, and at the transom.

- **Protect it from the sun:** Store as much stuff (rope, blocks, sails) as practical out of those rays.

- **Protect your gear from the wind:** You know to tie down the hull, but consider other things that can loosen up and blow on a windy day (such as any sail, including a roller-furled jib and halyards, which can cause a real racket).

- **Secure the hull:** If your boat is stored on land, make sure that it's tied down securely. If your boat lives afloat, check the dock or mooring lines. In Chapters 6 and 9, we cover the best way to secure the boat to a dock.

Long-term

If you're going to leave your boat for longer than a month, consider further efforts to keep the boat happy:

- **Cover it:** Whenever possible, cover your equipment to protect it from rain, sun, and dirt.

- **Engine:** Ask your mechanic what, if anything, should be done, including winterizing to avoid ice forming in the block. Disconnect the battery terminals.

- **Fluids:** Drain water and gasoline tanks and top off diesel tanks.

- **Haul out:** Most large keelboats are hauled out at a boatyard, cleaned (especially below the waterline), derigged, and covered with protective tarps for the winter. Make sure that the boat is supported and secured adequately.

- ✔ **Lubricate:** Consider lubricating all your moving fittings, including parts of the mast, to protect them from inactivity.

- ✔ **Mildew:** If you live in a wet area and plan to store your boat under plastic tarps, it's going to be like a mildew factory under there. Take home for storage anything that can be damaged.

- ✔ **Sails:** If rolling your sails is ever worth the time and effort, this is it — if you have the space to store them. You may want your sailmaker to check out your sails in the loft.

Part VI
The Part of Tens

The 5th Wave   By Rich Tennant

FEW MOMENTS IN SAILING COMPARE IN MAJESTY TO THE SHRINERS' SUNSET REGATTA.

In this part . . .

So you want to buy a boat? A great Walt Disney video shows Goofy walking to work every day past a boat store. One day, while he's daydreaming about boating, he walks in and buys a boat, no questions asked. He's in a trance as he hooks the boat and trailer to his car and drives to the lake. Luckily, the cartoon ends happily (they always do), and we want to make sure that any boat purchase you make ends happily, too. It's easy to start looking at boats and fall into a trance as you daydream about sailing away. In this part, we cover all the right questions to ask the salesperson (and yourself) to get a boat that fits your needs. And we list ten sailing schools in great destinations so that you can learn to sail on your next vacation — now that's worth daydreaming about!

Chapter 20

Ten Questions to Ask When Buying a Boat

· ·

There was a great difference in boats, of course. For a long time I was on a boat that was so slow we used to forget what year it was we left port in. But of course this was at rare intervals.

— Mark Twain, *Life on the Mississippi*

*E*very year, boat shows are held around the world to woo potential buyers. The boats are clean and shiny, and the brochures are glossy and inviting. Some of the best boat shows are in the cold winter months when everyone loves to dream of summer fun on the water. Now that you're hooked on sailing, you've probably been daydreaming of having your own boat.

Buying a boat when you're new to sailing can be intimidating. This chapter can help you gather the information to make that big decision. In many ways, buying a boat is a bigger decision than buying a house. Hey, if your house burns down, you can always sleep in your boat. (Your family may not agree with the last sentence.) Prices for a new 12-foot (4–m) dinghy begin around $2,000, while prices for a 25-foot (8–m) keelboat begin in the neighborhood of $13,000.

If you're hooked up to the Internet, check out *Sail* magazine's sailboat buyer's guide (http://207.149.72.198) or the Starboard Tack Sailboat Trader (http://starboardtack.com).

What Will You Use the Boat For?

Are you planning to go for daysails or on extended cruising trips? Do you want to start racing? Do you need to entertain the boss or other friends? Are you into athletic exercise, or are you more of a couch potato-type sailor?

Where Will You Use the Boat?

Will you sail in protected waters or out on the open ocean? What are the heaviest wind and seas you expect during your sailing? Different boats work better for different locations. In Southern California, for example, a cruising ground is the Channel Islands, and Catalina Island, the most popular destination, is 20 miles (32 km) out from Los Angeles. Because sailing to Catalina Island requires an open-ocean crossing, you need a bigger, better-equipped boat to sail there than if you plan to stay inside the confines of the Long Beach breakwater.

Another question to ask is, "How deep is the water?" Some manufacturers sell two models of popular cruising boats — a "shoal-draft" model, which is popular in shallow areas, and a standard, full-draft model.

When I taught sailing one summer in Nantucket, I had a chance to go daysailing on my time off on a Beetle Cat. With its centerboard and shallow draft, the Beetle Cat was perfect for the sandbars around Nantucket. One of my favorite trips was to sail down the harbor, go clamming for the afternoon, and then come back and eat a feast.

Where Will You Keep the Boat?

Is a place available to launch your boat, so that you can keep it on a trailer or car-top it and store it at home? Do you have access to in-water storage at a marina or yacht club? Ask around to find out whether slips are available in your area before buying.

Who Do You Want to Bring Along?

Some dinghies, and even some small keelboats, can be sailed comfortably single-handed. Other boats can be handled by one or two people but can easily carry other, nonexpert guests. Some high-performance dinghies and keelboats require expert crew and may not have room for extra guests.

Lining up a number of expert sailors for each and every daysail can become a hassle. Make a list of your potential crew members and make sure that you won't need each and every one of them before you can leave the dock. (This may surprise you, but some of your crew may have other commitments from time to time.)

How Much Can You Afford to Spend?

Ah, yes, every so often you read in the tabloids about some real-estate mogul having to auction off his mega-yacht when a couple of deals go south. When you're calculating how much you can afford, don't forget to put together a realistic yearly operating budget, including money for some new gear from time to time. For a dinghy, that rope you need to replace may be just a few dollars, but the same part on a keelboat can set you back $50 or more. Call marinas to find out their slip fees, and call the local boatyard to get a quote for a yearly haul out and maintenance. As a rough guide, the bigger and more active the boat, the more it costs to run.

Is "high maintenance" your style? If so, you may consider a classic wooden boat or a race boat that needs new sails for every big regatta. The upkeep on an old wooden schooner is like the maintenance on the Golden Gate Bridge — by the time you finish painting it, it's ready to be painted again. But many modern fiberglass boats require very little yearly maintenance. See Chapter 19 for a guide to the maintenance needs of a typical boat.

Where Should You Buy a Boat?

Most new boats are sold by dealers, similar to cars, but some manufacturers sell their products directly to consumers. Used dinghies and small keelboats are usually sold privately. Look on bulletin boards of marinas and in the classified section of the local boating newspaper. Boat brokers typically get involved only in the sale of larger used keelboats. They get their fee from the seller, and they can help in all aspects of the purchase, including financing, kind of like a real estate broker.

Are You Getting a Good Value?

Buying a boat with good resale value may be important, especially when you're buying your first boat. One consideration is the taste in your local market. For example, a classic wooden boat has much more value in Maine than in the Caribbean. Try to think ahead: As you gain experience, your taste in boats may change, so a rash purchase today may not suit you tomorrow. New boats are like new cars — they can lose a great deal of their value as soon as you drive them off the lot. Make sure that you're provided with a complete inventory of what comes with the boat so that you know whether that cool depth sounder will still be there when you have the pink slip.

Is the Boat Seaworthy?

The best way to find out whether a used boat is seaworthy is to pay to have a survey, which includes a haul out for inspection, done on the boat. A marine surveyor can give you a comprehensive report on the boat's seaworthiness. Usually, a marine survey is more applicable to the sale of a keelboat. With a dinghy, you may have to rely on your skills of observation. Also, ask the seller for the maintenance history on the boat. A "sea trial" on a windy day (the nautical equivalent of a test drive) can also help you assess the boat's seaworthiness.

What Equipment Should You Get?

Read this book to get a feel for the equipment you want to have on your boat. As usual, the local conditions and your sailing plans affect what you need. Check out other boats at the local marina or ask local sailors for gear recommendations. For example, in San Diego, where the wind rarely exceeds 12 knots, you may never use a small, heavy-air jib, but if you're sailing in San Francisco Bay, it will be the sail you use all the time.

What Kind of Boat Is That?

Admit it — you look at other cars on the highway to find one that you like. The same is true with boats. One day, you may see the perfect boat go sailing past, but how will you know what it is? Many boats have an insignia on their mainsail that indicates its type. Sometimes the insignia is a class logo, and other times it's a manufacturer's logo. Some use stylized artwork (like the Laser or Thistle) that you have to know to recognize, while some logos are obvious even to the uninitiated (505, Melges 24).

Chapter 21

Ten Sailing Schools in Paradise

• •

Whenever I find myself growing grim about the mouth; whenever it is a damp, drizzly November in my soul . . . then, I account it high time to get to sea as soon as I can. . . .

— Herman Melville, *Moby-Dick*

*H*ave you ever found yourself dreaming of packing it all in and setting sail over the horizon . . . or of simply having your own boat to sail near home on a warm, breezy afternoon? What are you waiting for? Permission to come aboard and enjoy the enchanting and wonderfully varied sport of sailing is hereby granted — and the first step is easier and more fun than you may think!

Keep our recommendation in Chapter 2 in mind: Take a course from a school that features certified instructors. Certification is your only real guarantee of quality instruction. In the United States, look for schools that offer American Sailing Association (ASA) or US Sailing (USSA) certification. If you plan to take instruction in other countries, check out the list of international organizations in Appendix C.

How much does learning to sail cost? The courses listed here vary from a couple hundred dollars to more than a thousand. Generally, you get what you pay for: the more the course costs, the more extensive the instruction, and sometimes the package price includes lodging. Some courses may offer lodging and travel arrangements separate from the package price. Call for more information.

Whichever school you choose, make your reservations early. The best sailing schools, just like the best hotels, tend to fill up early, especially during their areas' peak season.

As we discuss in Chapter 2, you have many options for beginning to sail — hopefully one in your own community. But in case you want to combine a vacation with a first-class introduction to sailing, here are ten of our favorite sailing schools, all located in great places to visit.

Harbor Sailboats

San Diego, California, 800-854-6625

The former home of the America's Cup, San Diego is a great year-round sailing destination. Harbor Sailboats, which has one of the highest-rated instructor staffs in the country, offers top-level instruction and ASA certification.

Harbor Sailboats has two basic sailing courses aboard Capri 22s (small keelboats) in San Diego's beautiful harbor. The two-day basic keelboat course runs from 9 a.m. to 5 p.m. This course is popular because you can take sailing lessons and still have time to enjoy San Diego's many sights, including its world-famous zoo. Or you can spend your time daysailing one of the facility's boats after you graduate from the course.

A five-day live-aboard program includes lodging aboard a 34-foot (10-m) cruising keelboat. The first two days feature instruction in the Capri 22, followed by a day for you to do some soloing. Then you get two days of instruction in your 34-foot floating home.

Florida Yacht Charters

Miami and Key West, Florida; and the Bahamas, 800-537-0050

Florida Yacht Charters offers two introductory courses — a weeklong live-aboard course and a weekend program. The weekend program begins Friday afternoon in the classroom and then takes you out on Miami's beautiful, protected Biscayne Bay for all-day sailing sessions Saturday and Sunday. That way, your evenings are free to enjoy Miami's nightlife — but we're sure that you'll want to get ahead in your textbook instead!

On the weeklong vacation-and-learn-to-sail course, you set sail with your class of four plus an instructor from Miami on Saturday, heading for Key West down the magical cruising grounds of the Florida Keys. On the way is the world-renowned diving mecca of John Pennekamp (underwater) State Park, where you can enjoy snorkeling in the 80-degree F (27-degree C) Gulf Stream water.

The shorter course is taught in new Hunter 336s and 376s (33- and 37-foot cruising sailboats), and the weeklong course offers Hunter 376s and the 430 (a 43-foot model). All the boats are fully provisioned and outfitted with the latest goodies, including air-conditioning. Each course features ASA certification. It also has boats and instructors available in Key West and Marsh Harbour, the Bahamas, adjacent to the world-class Great Abaco Beach Resort, where the little ones can stay and play on the beach.

The Penny Whiting Sailing School

Auckland, New Zealand, 64-9-376-1322

What better place to begin to sail than in the "City of Sails" in the country that loves sailing and its sailors — Auckland, New Zealand. Penny Whiting is a celebrity in Auckland, coming from a famous yachting family (New Zealanders say *yachting* instead of *sailing*). Her Penny Whiting Sailing School is the place to discover sailing in Auckland. Plus, you can probably get her to autograph a copy of her book *(The Penny Whiting Sailing Book)* and show you some sights around this beautiful harbor aboard her 50-foot (15-m) sailboat, *Endless Summer*. Don't forget to check out the America's Cup trophy at the Royal New Zealand Yacht Squadron. If you happen to be in town during the spring and summer months (which are the opposite from the Northern Hemisphere, in case you forget), you can probably see some teams training for the big race in February 2000!

Steve and Doris Colgate's Offshore Sailing School

Florida; Tortola, British Virgin Islands; Chicago; New York; New Jersey; and New England, 800-221-4326

Steve Colgate is the big name in sailing instruction. An Olympic sailor, he started the Offshore Sailing School 33 years ago, one of the first schools in the business. Since then, the school has expanded to a number of locations, including Captiva Island on Florida's Gulf Coast. Steve's expertise is pervasive throughout the program: He designed the text and curriculum, hand-picked the instructors, and even helped design the sailboat, a Colgate 26. This brand-new craft is the first keelboat designed specifically for sailing instruction. You can see a photo of a Colgate 26 in Chapter 2.

Two basic introductory packages are available, including a three-day course featuring two hours of classroom and five hours of sailing every day. You get to solo on the final day. Or, if you like, you can stretch out those lessons over the course of a week, giving you and your family an opportunity to enjoy the local surroundings in one of the school's eight locations. Upon graduation, you receive Offshore Sailing School certification, and US Sailing certification is optional.

Bitter End Yacht Club

Virgin Gorda, British Virgin Islands, 800-872-2392

If there is a sailor's paradise on Earth, it can be found at the Bitter End Yacht Club on Virgin Gorda. A first-class island resort awaits you, with facilities that are uniquely focused on sailing. From Mistral sailboards and Laser dinghies to J-24s and Freedom 30s, the Bitter End and the in-house Nick Trotter Sailing School offer the newcomer or the old salt plenty of opportunity for instruction at all levels. For a change of pace, you can also enjoy world-class diving or idyllic conditions to just sit under a palm tree and read a book. The Bitter End is a legendary stopping point for Caribbean cruisers and charterers, thanks to its beautiful anchorage and world-class restaurant and bar. Hey, we're believers — we get there at least once a year. Nothing like discovering sailing in paradise!

Mission Bay Aquatic Center

San Diego, California, 619-488-1036

We like San Diego so much that we have another place to recommend. The Mission Bay Aquatic Center is an amazing facility. Located in the smooth, protected waters of Mission Bay, the facility is internationally renowned for its breadth of watersport activities. It has rowing shells and surfboards (although you have to go across the street to the ocean beach to find any waves), but the reason we like it is the sailboats. The Aquatic Center has sailboards, small dinghies, catamarans, and small keelboats, and it offers instruction in whatever flavor you're interested in. Mission Bay is a great place to begin to windsurf, with smooth water and steady wind, and the instructors are top-rate. If you're planning a vacation to San Diego, make sure you call ahead of time to schedule your class and begin registration.

International Sailing School

Punta Gorda, Florida, 800-824-5040

Located in the middle of Florida's Gulf Coast, the International Sailing School offers three different learn-to-sail programs, all featuring ASA's Basic Sailing Keelboat certification. The two- and three-day courses are all-day affairs, with your evenings free. A five-day program lets you choose morning or afternoon instruction, giving you time to explore the beautiful nearby beaches and islands (Sanibel and Captiva). Disney World is only 2 1/2 hours away (or less, if you drive like JJ). Instruction is aboard a 22-foot (7-m) Catalina sloop, sailing in the protected waters of Charlotte Harbor, which teems with nature. Dolphins and manatees share your water, and you may even catch a glimpse of a bald eagle.

Marina Sailing

Southern California — Long Beach, Newport Beach, Oxnard, Marina del Rey, Redondo Beach, and San Diego, 800-262-7245

Marina Sailing has been a leading sailing club in Southern California since 1962, offering instruction, rentals, charters, and social activities. Its introductory "Complete Sailing Course" is designed for the local or regular traveler to the Southern California area. You receive 14 hours of on-the-water instruction in seven separate sailing sessions, plus three hours in the classroom. ASA certification is included. Upon conclusion, you're qualified to join the club and begin building your experience in its large fleet of boats (including powerboats) at any one of its six locations. For a person or family vacationing in the area, Marina Sailing will also design a custom course to suit your schedule.

International Sailing Center

Key Largo, Florida, 305-451-3287

This school is unique, located at Rick's Place Motel along Blackwater Sound on lush Key Largo, only about an hour's drive from Miami. The big chief is Rick White, a legend in the sport of multihull sailing, and his teaching fleet includes catamarans. His motel specializes in vacations, but it's small — only five units, all of which have complete kitchens — so make your reservations early. Otherwise, it may already be full of experienced cat sailors hanging out with Rick; his wife, Mary (a world champion cat sailor and leading educator); and his son, David (also a multihull specialist).

A typical learn-to-sail course is taught in the school's 20-foot (6-m) Flying Scot dinghy, but if you want catamarans, you can switch over to a boat of the two-hulled variety after the first day of instruction. Cats ranging from the new 13-foot (4-m) Hobie Wave to the Hobie 18 are available. Both ASA and US Sailing certification are available.

Cort Larned Windsurfing

Maui 808-877-4816
Oregon 541-386-5787
San Francisco 415-925-0543

If you're going to windsurf, you may as well get instruction from the best. Cort Larned is a two-time world champion boardsailor and the instructional editor for *Windsurfing Magazine*. His sailing schools are located in the meccas of boardsailing, and they cater to all levels of sailors, including the beginner. You take lessons from expert instructors on Hi Fly's Trainer, a big, floaty board designed specifically for the entry-level sailboarder. Classes can be scheduled to suit your schedule, giving you time to enjoy the local environs or practice more.

Appendix A
First Aid Afloat

··

Out of this nettle, danger, we pluck this flower, safety.

— William Shakespeare

This appendix is meant to give you an idea of what are the most common afflictions aboard a boat and the basic remedies for those ills. Obviously, anything can happen when you're out to sea, so you may be called upon to help with a wide variety of medical situations, from sunburn to childbirth. This appendix gives you some presailing advice and then covers the most common illnesses on board a boat, including hypothermia, seasickness, and sunburn.

Preparing Beforehand

We say this elsewhere in the book, but it bears saying again: Make sure that you and everyone you're planning to take sailing knows how to swim. See Chapter 18 for tips on how to choose a swim school for your children.

We also strongly recommend that you know CPR (cardiopulmonary resuscitation), regardless of whether you plan to go sailing. Being on the water increases the amount of time that emergency personnel need to get to you, and CPR is the best way to keep someone alive while rescue personnel are on their way. CPR is beyond the scope of this book to teach, but your local Red Cross can teach you the technique in only a few hours.

Be sure to ask your CPR instructor to show you how to use the technique with the drowning-victim recovery position.

In addition, smart sailors should strongly consider taking along a first aid manual and a first aid kit.

Pick a first aid manual

Even if you're not planning an extended cruise, investing in a good first aid manual for your boat makes sense. Ask your doctor and check your local bookstore or marine store for a good first aid manual. Here are some manuals that we recommend:

- *Red Cross First Aid Manual*
- *Advanced First Aid Afloat,* by Peter Eastman, M.D.
- *The Essentials of First Aid,* by St. John's Ambulance, England
- *The Waterlover's Guide to Marine Medicine,* by Dr. Paul Gill
- *Emergencies at Sea,* from *Chapman's Nautical Guides,* by Sid Stapleton
- *First Aid at Sea,* by Douglas Justins and Colin Berry (from US Sailing)
- *Sailing and Yachting First Aid* by Drs. Bergan and Guzzetta (from US Sailing)

Pack a first aid kit

On any trip, even a short one, take along plenty of food and water, a good first aid book (see the list of recommended books in the preceding section), and a well-stocked first aid kit if your boat has sufficient storage space. Ice is important to bring, and we also recommend those fancy products that become cold compresses when you squeeze or shake them.

Stow a first aid kit in a dry, watertight compartment with a list of contents on the box for easy reference. Those contents should include the items listed in Table A-1.

Table A-1	What You Should Pack in a First Aid Kit
Sterile, nonadhesive dressings*	Gauze packs*
Several types and sizes of bandages (adhesive and elastic)*	Rolled cotton*
Hydrogel dressing and/or moleskin (for open blisters and burns)	Skin closure strips
Antiseptic solution (for cleaning wounds)	Antibiotic ointment (to reduce infection of cuts and burns and to promote healing)
Bulb irrigating syringe (for cleaning wounds)	Scissors (for cutting dressings)
Safety pins	Disposable syringe and needle

Reflective blanket	Thermometer
Splinter tweezers	Seasickness pills (oral as well as suppositories or injectables)
Suppositories to stop vomiting	Pain relievers
Antacid tablets/liquid	Antidiarrheal medicine
Laxatives	Allergy tablets
Eye wash/drops	Calamine lotion (to dry rashes)
Hydrocortisone 1% cream	Sunscreen
Splints	Foot cream/powder
Aloe vera	Insect sting kit
Instant cold packs	Hot water bottle(s)
Flashlight	

*Keep these in separate watertight containers

Before you sail, familiarize yourself with these items and review your first aid manual for how to use them to deal with burns, cuts, bleeding, and head injuries.

One other thing: If anyone on board requires medication for an ongoing condition, make sure that medicine is on board. You never know when the fickle wind may turn a three-hour sail into a late-night adventure, so be prepared!

Recovering from Hypothermia

We talk about the danger of losing body heat in Chapter 7. The loss of body heat is called *hypothermia* or *exposure*. Your body temperature cools down 25 times faster in cold water than in the same temperature of air, so hypothermia is most common in people who have fallen overboard, but it can also affect people on deck when they're sailing in cold weather, especially at night. The symptoms of hypothermia start with loss of circulation to the extremities — fingers and toes. As your head gets cold, your mental and physical responses slow down, and you may have difficulty speaking and be disoriented. Shivering is the body's attempt to warm up, and hypothermia is more dangerous when shivering stops. At its most advanced stage, hypothermia can result in loss of consciousness, heart failure, and death. As we point out in Chapter 7, the Coast Guard has a 50/50/50 rule about hypothermia: If a person has been in 50-degree (10 degree C) water for 50 minutes, he has a 50 percent chance of survival.

Hypothermia victims must be warmed *gradually,* and you need to warm their core area (around the heart) first:

1. **Remove the victim's wet clothing.**

2. **Place the victim in a sleeping bag with warm blankets.**

3. **Use warm compresses on the center part of the victim's chest to warm his core temperature or have a crew member (or two) climb in the sleeping bag to warm the victim with body heat.**

   This method of warming up the victim may sound kinky, but it can be a lifesaver.

4. **Use CPR if the victim is unconscious without a pulse.**

5. **When the victim regains consciousness, give him warm (not hot) drinks and high-energy food.**

   Avoid giving the victim caffeine or alcohol.

Staving Off Seasickness

Some old salts swear that they never feel the least bit queasy, but having that feeling come on can ruin an otherwise great day afloat. Here's a list of several actions you can take to minimize your chances of feeling nauseous:

- ✔ **Avoid alcohol (or a hangover).**
- ✔ **Avoid rich, greasy foods.**
- ✔ **Focus on the horizon.** Distractions such as steering the boat or helping with a job on deck can help you feel better, too.
- ✔ **Keep some solid food in your stomach at all times.** Crackers or bread make good choices.
- ✔ **Sip small amounts of fizzy drinks such as ginger ale or clear soft drinks.** Some people swear by this rule.
- ✔ **Stay on deck.** Stay in the fresh air, away from exhaust fumes (if your boat has an engine).

Several medicines can help combat seasickness, but most must be taken before the symptoms start. Of course, like just about any other medication, you shouldn't take any of these medicines if you're pregnant without consulting with your doctor. Even if you aren't pregnant, your doctor may be able to recommend a good remedy. Over-the-counter seasickness pills, such as Dramamine, must be taken an hour before sailing and can cause drowsiness and a dry mouth. A patch that administers Scopolamine, the prescription motion-sickness drug used by the astronauts, was pulled off the market in the U.S. but may be available again soon. You can even buy a drink called *Sailor Sparkling Fruit Drink* that tastes like ginger ale and works to soothe your stomach.

Keep an eye on anyone who is feeling seasick. Seasickness can make you weak, disoriented, and extremely sleepy — a danger when on deck. Help the seasick person to a comfortable spot in the fresh air. If he or she is just feeling a little queasy, try letting him steer as a distraction. If you aren't feeling well, don't be ashamed; almost all sailors feel queasy at some point.

If you throw up, try to do so off the leeward side of the boat, downwind of everyone (including yourself).

For those of you fixing lunch for a group of sailors, a meal on the water isn't the time to get fancy with spicy or greasy recipes. Stick with basic foods like sandwiches, with easy-to-digest meats such as turkey, and throw in plenty of crackers, apples, cookies, and easy-to-eat (and digest) foods. On a rough day on the water, your crew will thank you for following this tip.

Steering Clear of Sunburn

The effects of being out in the sun all day, combined with the sun's rays reflected off the water, make sailors prime candidates for sunburn. These tips can help you avoid having a painful sunburn at the end of the day:

- ✔ **Put sunscreen on *before* you leave the dock.**
- ✔ **Reapply sunscreen several times during the day — especially in wet conditions.**
- ✔ **Always use a sunscreen with an SPF (Sun Protection Factor) of at least 15.** We try to always carry a stick of sunscreen in our pockets so that we can frequently reapply sunscreen to our noses, lips, and ears.
- ✔ **Always wear a hat and sunglasses.**
- ✔ **If you're fair-skinned or are sailing in a tropical locale, wear a long-sleeved, lightweight cotton shirt (one with a collar to help protect your neck) and long pants.** Guarding your skin this way makes your trip much more enjoyable. You'll be amazed at how tan you get even when you're covered up all day.

With so many people we know being lifelong sailors, we have a number of friends who have battled skin cancer, and it's not a pleasant fight. So please be careful out in the sun. If you do have severe sunburn, using aloe vera products helps soothe the skin. Drink plenty of cool fluids and try to wear loose-fitting cotton clothes to help your skin heal.

Defeating Dehydration

Dehydration and heat exhaustion are two of the most dangerous illnesses for sailors because the body rejects the cure, which is to get cool and drink plenty of fluids. With severe dehydration, your body rejects any fluid intake by throwing up, making you further dehydrated. Severe dehydration can result in staying in a hospital hooked up to an IV to rehydrate. So try to drink as much fluid as you can while you're on the water.

In very hot conditions, you can get dehydrated even when you feel like you've been consuming fluids all day. One way to tell whether you're getting dehydrated is by how much you have to urinate. If you haven't had to use the *head* (marine toilet) all day, you need to drink a lot more water.

When you have to go, you have to go. But some people we know get nervous about using the head. How to use the head is a question worth asking the boat captain in advance because heads can be confusing, and getting a demonstration before you use the head is better than using it and then discovering that you can't flush it (gross!). If the boat doesn't have a head, you can either hang over the side or use a bucket. The key to using the bucket is — don't spill (really gross)!

Appendix B
Tying the Knot(s)

· ·

No one but an acrobat or a sailor could have got up to that bell-rope from the bracket, and no one but a sailor could have made the knots with which the cord was fastened to the chair.

— Sir Arthur Conan Doyle

*Y*es, you can tie the knot on a boat, but we're not talking about marriage. This appendix reviews the basic knots on a sailboat. On most boats, you can find a bowline, a figure-eight knot, a square knot, and maybe a couple of half hitches somewhere. With a five-foot length of rope, you can practice these knots at home and master them quickly. (If you need to secure a line around a horn or t-cleat, see Chapter 4.)

Overhand Knot

An *overhand knot* is the basic knot that you use to begin tying your shoes and, as you see in the following sections, is the first step of many sailing knots. If your mother only lets you wear shoes with Velcro straps and you can't make an overhand knot, see Figure B-1 on how to begin tying your shoes. (You may want to buy *Getting Dressed For Dummies* as soon as it comes out.)

Figure B-1:
The basic overhand knot.

Figure-Eight Knot

The *figure-eight knot* is a lightweight, but it's fun to tie and can save you a great deal of aggravation. While you're sitting in the boat, let your eyes follow the sheets or halyards from start to finish. The "finish" is probably at some sort of cleat. On smaller boats, all these *running rigging* lines should have figure-eight knots, as shown in Figure B-2, at the very end to prevent the line from getting pulled out of its rigged path (that is, through pulleys and so on). Trust us — when a line "sucks" out of its normal path, it's a hassle, especially if the rope is a halyard!

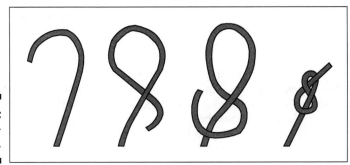

Figure B-2:
The figure-eight knot.

Note that with the additional loads on bigger boat lines, you don't want to tie knots in the ends of spinnaker sheets because you may need to let the line run through the block in an emergency.

The reason to use a figure-eight knot instead of a simple overhand knot is that the figure-eight is easier to untie after it has been under load (a characteristic of most good sailing knots); an overhand knot can get very tight. Plus, the figure-eight is a bulkier knot and is thus less likely to slip through a cleat or block.

To tie a figure-eight knot, follow these steps:

1. **Make a loop in the end of the line.**

2. **Pass the end of the line under, back over, and through the loop, so that it looks like a figure eight.**

Bowline Knot

The *bowline* (pronounced *bow-lynn,* so it rhymes with *rollin'*) is a beautiful knot, and it can be called the essential sailing knot — quick to tie, easy to untie, and a practical knot all around the boat. It forms a loop (of any size you want) at the end of a line and is commonly used to tie jib sheets onto the sail. On many dinghies, you use a bowline knot to attach the halyard to the sail.

The easiest way to remember how to tie a bowline is the kid's way — by imagining a bunny rabbit coming out of his hole, as shown in Figure B-3.

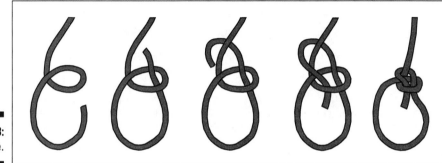

Figure B-3:
A bowline.

Follow these steps for tying and untying a bowline:

1. **Make the rabbit hole as shown.**

2. **The rabbit comes up through the hole, around the back of the tree.**

3. **The rabbit goes back down the hole.**

4. **Pull the three ends to tighten.**

To untie a bowline, bend back the part formed when the rabbit goes "around the back of the tree," and the knot loosens up nicely.

Square Knot

The *square knot* is a knot that you may have practiced in Scouts. It's just two overhand knots with the first tied right over left, and the second tied left over right (or vice versa), as shown in Figure B-4. (A *granny knot* is when you tie both overhand knots the same way.)

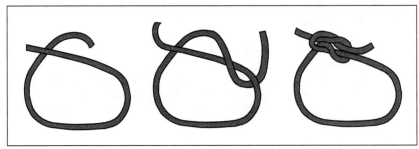

Figure B-4:
The square
knot.

Tie a square knot like this:

1. Tie an overhand knot (the first knot you tie when tying your shoes).

2. On the second overhand knot, tie it the opposite way.

If you put the left piece over the right on the first knot, put the right piece over the left for the second knot.

You've tied it right if the ends of the lines are parallel to the *standing* (working) part of the lines — so that it looks like two symmetrical loops. Use a square knot to tie two lengths of the same type of line together.

Reef Knot

The *reef knot* is sort of a temporary version of the square knot. It's very useful for low-load, cosmetic tasks, such as tying sail ties around a furled sail on the boom. The reef knot is simply the bow knot you use when tying your shoes.

Two Half Hitches

Two half hitches is also called the *double half hitch*. It's really two overhand knots tied around the standing part of a line. This quickie knot has many temporary uses, including tying a tow line around your mast in a dinghy to get a quick tow. Tying two half hitches is a quick way to temporarily cleat off a line on a winch or other fixed object. If the rope is going to be under load, add the extra friction of a wrap or two around the object before tying the hitches (hence the term *round turn and two half hitches*). That way, you can untie it easily later, even if the rope has been stressed to its limit. Tying a round turn and two half hitches is shown in Figure B-5.

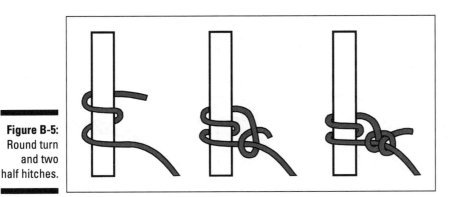

Figure B-5:
Round turn
and two
half hitches.

Here are the steps to tying a round turn and two half hitches:

1. **Make two turns around the mast or object so that you can comfortably hold the line in your hand.**

2. **Tie two half hitches (two overhand knots) around the standing part of the line.**

The round turn and two half hitches is, in my opinion, the most underrated of knots. It's the most practical knot there is; it's just so darn useful, all over the boat. And the thing I like best is how easy this knot is to tie, even under pressure situations when you need to make that rope fast *now!*

Clove Hitch

The *clove hitch,* a close cousin to two half hitches, must be tied *around* something, such as a lifeline or piling. It's a quick knot for tying on fenders, tying a dock line to a piling, and anything used temporarily. With the first loop, you can hold the line in place, and then you can tie the second loop to be secure. Unlike a round turn with two half hitches, the clove hitch can get very difficult to undo under pressure. See the step-by-step details of tying a clove hitch in Figure B-6.

Follow these steps to tie a clove hitch:

1. **Make a loop around the pole or object.**

2. **Make a second loop by crossing over the first loop.**

3. **Put the tail under the second loop.**

4. **Pull both ends to tighten.**

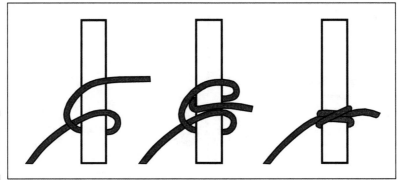

Fisherman's Bend

The *fisherman's bend* isn't a common knot because other knots, such as the bowline and the round turn with two half hitches, can also do its job. This knot is less likely than a bowline to loosen but is more difficult to untie, making it a good knot to use when you want to leave the knot in place for a long time. The fisherman's bend is often used to attach an anchor to its line, so it's sometimes called an *anchor bend.* Check out the how-to in Figure B-7.

Here are the steps to tying this knot:

1. **Make two loops around the shackle or anchor chain.**

2. **Pass the end of the line through both loops and tighten.**

3. **Add another hitch for safety.**

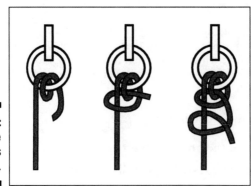

Figure B-7:
The
fisherman's
bend.

Rolling Hitch

This is an all-around great knot, one that can really impress your fans because you can use it to get out of trouble. The *rolling hitch* is used for tying one line to another. It grips so tight that you can use it to take the load off the end of the other line in an emergency (such as a winch override; see Chapter 6). If you look closely at Figure B-8, you'll see that a rolling hitch is a clove hitch with another twist or two.

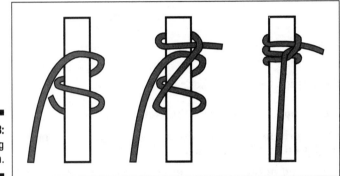

Figure B-8: The rolling hitch.

Tie a rolling hitch like this:

1. **Make two loops around the rope or other item to be attached.**

2. **Put the tail over the two loops and then make a third loop.**

3. **Put the tail under the third loop and tighten.**

Always wrap the first two loops of a rolling hitch on the side closer to your intended pulling direction. For example, if you're tying a line to a halyard coming out of the mast, wrap around the bottom first, because you intend to pull down. The third loop (the "hitch" that turns it into a real knot) wraps above the first two.

Trucker's Hitch

We used to show the kids at different sailing clinics a great old Warren Miller video that shows a 15-foot dinghy flying off a car and sliding down a ditch. Somehow, the music and Warren Miller's dry humor make the scene hilarious, but having *your* boat fly off *your* car isn't funny. Tying your boat on the car or trailer well is a rare art, but the *trucker's hitch* (a combination purchase system and knot all wrapped up in one) makes the task much easier. For the how-to, see Figure B-9.

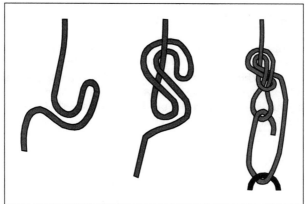

Figure B-9:
The
trucker's
hitch.

Follow these steps to tie a trucker's hitch:

1. **Make a loop a few feet from the end of the line.**

2. **Tie an overhand knot with the loop and tighten, keeping the loop big enough to pass a line through.**

3. **Pass the end of the line around your roof rack or trailer bar.**

4. **Put the line up through the trucker's hitch loop and pull.**

   You've made a quick 2:1 purchase. You can tie off the line with two half hitches.

Whenever I packed up my Olympic dinghy for a drive up the coast or out to Florida, Peter went around the boat and retied every line before I left. His favorite knot for cinching a boat onto a roof rack (or onto a trailer) is the trucker's hitch.

Knowing how to tie these knots (especially the bowline and the round turn with two half hitches) and using them properly can save you a great deal of time and make your life afloat safer. Master them, and you're well on your way to becoming an "able seaman."

Appendix C

Sailing Associations around the World

- -

Mothlike in mists, scintillant in the minute brilliance of cloudless days, with broad bellying sails.

They glide to the wind tossing green water from their sharp prows while over them the crew crawls.

— William Carlos Williams

*A*s we mention in Chapter 2, most countries have an organization that can help you find a local sailing school. Some of these organizations are listed below. Contact the International Sailing Federation if your country isn't on this list or to get the most recent update.

International Sailing Federation
Ariadne House, Town Quay, Southampton, Hampshire, SO14 2AQ,
United Kingdom.
Phone 44-1703-635111
E-mail: 100574.3126@compuserve.com

Country	Organization	Contact Information
Algeria	Federation Algerienne de Voile	CFS BP 88, El Biar, Algers, Algeria, 213-2-121854
Australia	Australia Yachting Federation	Locked Bag 806, Post Office Molisons Point NSW, Australia 2061, 61-2-99224333
Austria	Vereinigung Osterreichischer Yachtsport Windsurfschulen (VOYMS)	Zochbauerstrasse 4/54 A1160 Wien, Austria, 43-229827095
Barbados	Barbados Yachting Youth Training Association	P.O. Box 40, Bridgetown, Barbados, 1-246-436-9037

(continued)

(continued)

Country	Organization	Contact Information
Belgium	Federation Royale Belge du Yachting Halve	Maanstraat 2C, 8620 Nieuwpoort, Belgium, 32-58-230282
	Vlaamse Trainersschool Sportkaderopleiding, BLOSO	Kolonienstraat 31, B-1000, Brussels, Belgium, 32-2-5103551
Bermuda	Bermuda Yachting Association	P.O. Box HM 1418, 12 Reid St., Walker Arcade, HM FX Hamilton, Bermuda, 1-295-7935
Brazil	Federacao Brasiliera de Vela e Motor	R. Alcindo Guanabara 15/8 Andar, Conjunto 802 20031, Rio de Janeiro, Brazil, 55-21-2203738
Canada	Canadian Yachting Association	1600 James Naismith Drive, Gloucester, Ontario, K1B 5N4, Canada, 1-613-7485687
Chile	Federacion Chilena de Navegacion a Vela Vicuna	Mackenna 40 Casilla 2239, Santiago, Chile, 56-2-222-8564
China	Chinese Yachting Association	9 Tiyuguan Rd., Beijing, 100763 China, 86-107122438
Denmark	Danish Sailing Association	Idraettens Hus, DK 2605 Broendby, Denmark, 45-43262626
Estonia	Kalev Yacht Club	Pirita tee 17, EE0019 Tallinn, Estonia, 372-2-239127
	Sailing School Regati	pst. 1-6K EE0019 Tallinn, Estonia, 372-2-237241
Finland	Finnish Yachting Association	Radiokatu 20, SF-00240, Helsinki, Finland, 358-9-34812461
France	Federation Francaise de Voile	55 Avenue Kleber, 75784 Paris Cedex 16, France, 33-1-44058100

Country	Organization	Contact Information
Germany	Deutscher Segler-Verband Abt. Führerscheine, Segelschulen und Ausbildung	Gründgensstrasse 18, D-22309 Hamburg, Germany, 49-40-6320090
Hong Kong	Hong Kong Yachting Association	1009 Sports House, 1 Stadium Path, So Kon Po, Causeway Bay, Hong Kong, 852-2504-8159
India	Yachting Association of India	c/o Chief of Naval Staff, Room No. 326 'C' Wing, Sena Bhavan, DHQ PO, New Delhi, 110011, India, 91-11-3012183
Ireland	Irish Sailing Association	3 Park Road, Dun Laoghaire, Co Dublin, Ireland, 353-1-2800239
Israel	Israel Yachting Association	P.O. Box 4575, 4 Marmorek St., Tel Aviv 64254, Israel, 972-36856262
Italy	Centro Nautico Levante	P. Campanella 10 10146 Torino, Italy, 011- 7723529
Japan	Japan Yachting Association	Dr. Kishi Memorial Hall, 1-1-1 Jinnan, Shibuya-ku, Tokyo, 150 Japan, 81-334812357
Mexico	Federacion Mexicana de Vela	Cordoba 42, Piso 11, Col. Roma Norte del Cuauhtemoc, 06700 Mexico, D.F., 52-55334664
Monaco	Yacht Club de Monaco	16 Quai Antoine Ier, MC 98000, Monaco, 377-93-106300
Netherlands	Koninklijk Nederlands Watersport Verbond	Postbus 87, 3980 CB Bunnik, Runnenburg, 12,3981 A2 Bunnik, The Netherlands, 31-306566550

(continued)

(continued)

Country	Organization	Contact Information
	Commissie Watersport Opleidingen (CWO)	Postbus 87, 3980 CB Bunnik, Netherlands, 31-30656566
New Zealand	The New Zealand Yachting Federation	P.O. Box 90-900, AMSC, Auckland, New Zealand, 64-9-3032360
Norway	Norwegian Sailing Federation	Hauger Skolevei 1, 1351 Rud Oslo, Norway, 47-67-568575
Poland	Polski Zwiazek Zeglarski	Chocimska 14, 00791 Warsaw, Poland, 48-22-495731
Portugal	Federacao Portuguesa de Vela	Doca de Belem, 1300 Lisboa, Portugal, 351-13647324
Singapore	Singapore Yachting Association	495, Tampines Ave. 5, Tampines Sports Hall, Singapore 529649, 65-7833379
Sweden	Svenska Seglarforbundet	Box 14232. 104 40 Stockholm, Sweden, 46-84590990
Switzerland	Schweizerischer Segel Verband SSV/USY	Haus des Sportes, Laubeggstr. 70, 3000 Bern 32, Switzerland, 41-31-359-7266
United Kingdom	Royal Yachting Association	RYA House, Romsey Road, Eastleigh, Hampshire SO50 9YA England 44-1703627400
United States	US Sailing Association	P.O. Box 1260, 15 Maritime Drive, Portsmouth, RI 02871-6015, USA, 1-401-683-0800
	American Sailing Association	13922 Marquesas Way, Marina del Rey, CA 90292, 1-310-822-7171
Uruguay	Yacht Club Uruguayo	Casilla de Correo 527, Montevideo, Uruguay, 598-2-701433
	Yacht Club Punta del Este	598-42-40219

Glossary

abeam: At right angles to the boat.

aft: Toward the stern; opposite of forward.

apparent wind: The wind felt on board your boat. A combination of the wind from your forward motion and the true wind blowing onto the boat.

athwartships: Across the boat.

back: To trim a sail to windward so that it fills with wind backward.

backstay: The support wire between the top of the mast and the back of the boat.

battens: Slats inserted into pockets along a sail's leech to help maintain its shape.

beam: The width of the boat at any point; also the side of the boat.

beam reach: Reaching on a heading perpendicular to the wind direction.

bear away: To turn away from the wind (or to turn to leeward).

bearing: The angle to an object measured in compass or relative degrees.

block: A pulley through which ropes run.

bolt rope: A rope (often covered with fabric) sewn to the luff or foot of a sail.

boom: The horizontal pole that supports the bottom edge of the mainsail.

boom vang: The control line system, running from the boom to the base of the mast, that controls mainsail twist when reaching and running.

bow: The front of the boat.

broach: A sudden, unplanned turning of a boat toward the wind that occurs in strong winds.

broad reach: Reaching at a wide or broad angle to the wind (greater than 90 degrees).

buoy: A floating (albeit anchored) object that can be a navigation aid or a mooring.

by the lee: Sailing downwind with the wind coming over the same side of the boat as the boom is trimmed, which can cause an accidental jibe.

capsize: To flip the boat over so that the top of the mast is in the water.

centerboard: The retractable, unballasted center fin on a dinghy that keeps the boat from sideslipping (moving sideways).

chafe: Abrasion; wear.

chain plate: Attachment point of the standing rigging on the hull.

charter: To rent (as in chartering a boat).

chop: Short, steep waves.

cleat: A fitting that is used to tie off or secure a line under load so that the line doesn't slip.

clevis pin: A metal pin that secures a shackle or other fitting on a boat.

clew: The aft, bottom corner of a sail.

close-hauled: The closest course to the wind that you can effectively sail. Also called sailing *upwind, on the wind,* or *beating.*

close reach: A reach at any heading between 90 degrees to the wind and close-hauled.

cockpit: The area where the crew sits to operate the boat.

cunningham: The control line system near the tack of a sail used to adjust luff tension.

current: Horizontal movement of water caused by tidal change, gravity, or wind.

daggerboard: A centerboard-type fin that is raised and lowered vertically through a slot in the hull.

daymarks: Warning markers displayed on poles used in lieu of buoys, typically in shallower water.

dead reckoning: Plotting your position based on the course and distance from a previously known position.

death roll: A capsize to windward; generally occurs while sailing downwind.

deck: The top of the hull.

depth sounder: An instrument that measures depth of water below the boat.

deviation: The angular difference between the real magnetic heading and the one indicated by a compass; compass error.

dew point: The temperature at which the air becomes saturated with water vapor.

dinghy: (1) A sailboat with a centerboard (or daggerboard or leeboard); (2) a small rowboat.

dividers: An adjustable metal tool with two sharp points used in navigation.

downwind: (1) A run, but can mean any point of sail when the wind is aft of the beam (broad reach). (2) The direction that the wind is blowing toward.

draft: (1) The distance from the water's surface to the deepest point on the boat. (2) The amount and position of fullness in a sail.

ease: To let out (a rope or sail).

ebb: A tidal current flowing out to sea.

fender: Rubber cushion placed between a boat and a dock for protecting the hull.

fetch: (1) The distance of open water that waves have to grow. (2) To sail a course that will clear a buoy without tacking; to lay.

flood: Tidal current coming inbound from the sea; a rising tide.

foils: The keel (or centerboard), rudder, and the sails.

foot: (1) The bottom edge of a sail. (2) To sail slightly lower than close-hauled in order to go faster.

forestay: The support wire that runs from the mast down to the bow.

freeboard: The distance between the deck of the boat and the water; the height of the topsides.

furl: To roll or fold a sail and secure it.

gaff: The shorter boom at the top of a four-sided mainsail.

galley: A boat's kitchen.

genoa: A large jib that overlaps the mast.

gooseneck: The fitting that attaches the boom to the mast.

GPS (Global Positioning System): A navigation system that uses satellites to plot location.

grommet: A small plastic or metal ring pressed or sewn into a sail, creating a hole.

guy: The spinnaker sheet (control rope) on the windward side that attaches through a fitting on the spinnaker pole to the tack. Also called the afterguy.

halyard: The rope running up the mast, used to pull the sails up.

hanks: Snaps or clips at intervals along the luff of a jib, used to attach it to the forestay.

head: (1) The top corner of any sail. (2) The bathroom/toilet aboard a boat.

head up: To turn the boat toward the wind (to windward).

header: A wind shift that causes the boat to turn away from the old wind direction.

headsail: Any sail that sets up forward, in front of the mainsail.

headstay: See **forestay.**

heavy air: Strong winds.

heel: When the boat leans or tips to one side.

helm: (1) The wheel or tiller — the steering device. (2) A technical word for the balance of forces on the rudder. (3) The position of the helmsman on the boat.

helmsman: The driver or skipper of the boat.

hike: To lean over the side, usually to counteract the heeling forces.

hiking stick: See **tiller extension.**

hoist: To pull up the sails.

horn cleat: A common cleat shaped like a T; also called a *t-cleat.*

hull: The body of the boat.

in irons: When a boat has stopped moving and is stuck pointing directly into the wind.

jack lines: Ropes, webbing, or cables that run along the deck on either side of the cabin the length of the boat, specifically for use with safety harnesses.

jammer: A mechanical fitting with a lever arm that cleats a rope.

jib: The most common headsail.

jibe: To change tacks by turning away from the wind.

jury-rigging: Temporarily fixing broken equipment.

kedge: To use an anchor to get a grounded boat back to deep water.

keel: A fixed, ballasted center fin that keeps the boat from sideslipping and provides stability to prevent capsizing or tipping over.

keelboat: A sailboat with a keel.

knot: (1) Nautical mile (6,076 feet) per hour. (2) A rope trick.

layline: The line beyond which you can *lay* (make) the destination on a close-hauled course with no more tacks.

lee shore: A shoreline to leeward of a boat onto which the wind is blowing.

leeboard: A retractable fin like a centerboard but attached to the side of the boat.

leech: The back edge of a sail.

leeward: Downwind; away from the wind.

lifeline: A wire supported by low poles called *stanchions* that encircles the deck to keep crew from falling overboard.

lift: A wind shift that enables the boat to sail closer to the old wind direction.

line: A rope used on a sailboat with a specified purpose.

log: (1) A nautical record of a ship's voyage. (2) A device that measures distance traveled.

longitude: The vertical lines on a chart or globe designating the angular distance (0 to 180 degrees) east or west of the prime meridian.

LOP (line of position): A line through some point on which you presume your boat to be located as a result of an observation or measurement.

lubber line: Fixed vertical post(s) around the edge of the compass.

luff: (1) The front edge of a sail from the head to the tack. (2) The flapping motion of sailcloth when a sail is undertrimmed (or not trimmed at all).

mainsail: The aft-most sail on a boat with one mast, normally attached to the mast along its front edge.

mainsheet: The adjustment rope that pulls the boom (hence the mainsail) in and out.

mast: The vertical pole that supports the sails.

mooring: A permanently anchored buoy to which a boat can be tied.

nautical mile: 6,076 feet, 1.15 times longer than a statute (regular) mile; equal to one minute (1/60th of a degree) of latitude.

no-sail zone: Zone where a sailboat can't sail; about 90 degrees wide, with the center point being directly toward the true wind direction.

off the wind: Sailing on a broad reach or run.

outboard: (1) Out to the side of the boat. (2) A removable engine.

outhaul: The control line system used for adjusting the tension of the foot of the mainsail.

parallel rulers: A navigation tool with two straight-edged plastic slats connected by two hinges; used to measure and draw compass courses.

PFD (personal flotation device): A life jacket or other buoyancy device.

piloting: Navigation involving frequent determination of position.

pinch: Steering slightly closer to the wind than a close-hauled course.

plane: To skim along the water's surface.

pole lift: See **topping lift.**

port: (1) Left. (2) A small round window on a boat, also called a "porthole." (3) A commercial harbor.

port tack: Sailing with the wind coming over the left side of the boat.

puff: An increase in wind velocity.

purchase system: Block-and-tackle system that gives a mechanical advantage.

quadrant: Bracket around the rudder post that connects to the steering wheel cables.

Quick-Stop method: A man-overboard rescue technique in which you instantly stop the boat as close to the victim as possible.

ratchet block: A block that turns freely when you pull the line but doesn't turn at all in the other direction.

reaching: Any heading between close-hauled and running.

reef points: Horizontal line of reinforced holes built into the sail to facilitate reefing.

reefing: A system of reducing the exposed sail area of a given sail.

regatta: A series of races scored as a whole.

relative bearing: A bearing measured in degrees relative to a boat's heading.

rig: (1) The mast and standing rigging. (2) A term for preparing the boat (or sail or fitting) for use.

righting moment: Leverage provided by crew weight or ballast that inhibits heeling.

roller furling system: System of sail storage and reefing where the sail wraps up on a narrow spool; most commonly used for headsails.

rope clutch: See **jammer.**

rudder: The underwater fin that steers a boat; controlled by a tiller or wheel on deck.

running: The course you're steering when the wind is behind you.

running lights: A boat's navigation lights.

running rigging: The ropes and pulleys used to raise, lower, and adjust the sails.

sail: Fabric that catches the wind and enables you to sail the boat.

shackle: A metal fitting often used to attach a sail to a rope.

sheave: The moving "wheel" part of a block or pulley.

sheet: The primary line that adjusts the sail's trim. Usually referred to with the sail it adjusts, as in, "Pull in the mainsheet."

shoal: A shallow area.

shock cord: Elastic rope; also called *bungee cord.*

shrouds: The support wires that run from the mast down to the edge of the deck on the left and right sides of the mast.

slip: A dockside parking space for a boat.

snap shackle: Fast-opening fitting that attaches the corner of a spinnaker to a control rope.

spinnaker: A big, colorful, parachute-like specialty sail used when sailing downwind.

spring lines: Additional dock lines that are tied from the middle of the boat at opposing angles to the dock lines to prevent the boat from surging forward or backward.

standing rigging: All the wires that support the mast, including forestay, shrouds, and backstay.

starboard: Right.

starboard tack: Sailing with the wind coming over the boat's right side.

stern: The back end of the boat.

swamp: To fill up with water.

tack: (1) The front, bottom corner of a sail. (2) The boat's heading in relation to the wind (that is, on *starboard* or *port tack*). (3) To change tacks by turning toward the wind, entering the no-sail zone from one side and exiting on the other.

telltales: Strands of yarn or cassette tape that are attached to the sail or standing rigging to help judge the wind angle and whether the sails are trimmed properly.

tiller: The lever arm that controls the position of the rudder.

tiller extension: A device attached to the end of the tiller that enables a person to sit farther outboard while steering.

topping lift: Halyardlike control rope running from the mast; used to lift the outboard tip of the spinnaker pole.

topsides: The outer sides of the hull.

transom: The outer side of the stern.

trapeze: A system for adding righting moment by standing on the side of a boat wearing a harness with a hook, which is attached to a wire running down from the mast.

traveler: A sail-control system that can move the mainsheet attachment point on the boat from side to side.

trim: (1) To pull in a rope or a sail. (2) The set of the sails. (3) The bow-up or bow-down position of the boat when not moving.

trough: The low part of a wave.

true wind: The actual wind (as opposed to the *apparent wind*) that would be measured by a boat at anchor (that is, not moving).

turtle: A capsize position where the mast is sticking straight down.

variation: The angular difference between true and magnetic north.

waypoint: The latitude/longitude coordinates of any point you desire.

whitecap: Foamy crest on the top of waves.

winch: A revolving geared drum turned by a handle that provides mechanical advantage and increases the sailor's ability to pull on a rope under load.

windward: Toward the wind; the side the wind blows upon.

wing the jib: When sailing on a run, to trim the jib on the opposite side as the mainsail.

Index

IDG BOOKS WORLDWIDE BOOK REGISTRATION

Register This Book and Win!

We want to hear from you!

Visit **http://my2cents.dummies.com** to register this book and tell us how you liked it!

- ✔ Get entered in our monthly prize giveaway.

- ✔ Give us feedback about this book — tell us what you like best, what you like least, or maybe what you'd like to ask the author and us to change!

- ✔ Let us know any other *...For Dummies*® topics that interest you.

Your feedback helps us determine what books to publish, tells us what coverage to add as we revise our books, and lets us know whether we're meeting your needs as a *...For Dummies* reader. You're our most valuable resource, and what you have to say is important to us!

Not on the Web yet? It's easy to get started with *Dummies 101*®: *The Internet For Windows*® *95* or *The Internet For Dummies*®, 5th Edition, at local retailers everywhere.

Or let us know what you think by sending us a letter at the following address:

...For Dummies Book Registration
Dummies Press
7260 Shadeland Station, Suite 100
Indianapolis, IN 46256-3945
Fax 317-596-5498

BUSINESS AND GENERAL REFERENCE BOOK SERIES FROM IDG

COMPUTER BOOK SERIES FROM IDG